THE BEST
AMERICAN
MAGAZINE
WRITING

2021

THE BEST AMERICAN MAGAZINE WRITING 2021

Edited by
Sid Holt for the
American Society
of Magazine
Editors

Columbia University Press   New York

Columbia University Press
Publishers Since 1893
New York   Chichester, West Sussex
cup.columbia.edu
Copyright © 2021 the American Society of Magazine Editors
All rights reserved

Library of Congress Cataloging-in-Publication Data
ISSN 1541-0978
ISBN 978-0-231-19803-5 (pbk.)

Columbia University Press books are printed on permanent and durable
acid-free paper.
This book is printed on paper with recycled content.
Printed in the United States of America

Cover design: Julia Kushnirsky

Contents

Clara Jeffery

Introduction

With the benefit of hindsight, which an annual compilation of some of the best magazine writing in America necessarily provides, the historic trash fire that was 2020 seems inevitable, a black hole whose event horizon predated the year itself but propelled us with ever-gathering speed toward a national singularity.

It's right there in many of the titles: "The Plague Year," "The Collaborators," "The Trayvon Generation," "The Patriot Slave," "Witness and Respair."

Our country faced three interlocking crises: a pandemic, a racial reckoning, an accelerating slide toward authoritarianism. We survived (though not all of us, not by a long shot), battered and depressed, staggering across the annual tape of January 1, only to face an insurrection against democracy that is not yet over, yet another battle in a war for fair representation that may not be won. This was, in other words, a year, more than perhaps any in several generations, where the reporting, the analysis, the perspective of long-form magazine writing helped us make sense of a world gone mad. Or at least crystallized why we felt insane. And why we were furious.

This anthology is not organized chronologically. Yet in rereading many of these pieces I felt compelled to try to remember: *What was happening when this article came out, when it was on press, and when it was written?*

In a year in which Twitter and cable news dispensed nonstop hits of chaos, magazines provided context, the big picture. Playing to that strength, this anthology begins with Lawrence Wright's masterful distillation of our plague year, a series of chronological postcards from the edge of the pandemic, emblematic incidents we might have otherwise forgotten alongside newly reported accounts that together tell the story of our response to COVID, shambolic and corrupt, heroic and heartbreaking. The *New Yorker* piece ends with Wright and his wife at the ballot box in Texas: "Across America, people waited in long lines to vote—despite the disease, despite attempts to discredit or invalidate their vote, despite postal delays, despite Russian or Iranian meddling, despite warnings from the White House that the president would not go quietly if he lost. They voted as if their country depended on it."

A few months earlier, Barton Gellman published "The Election That Could Break America" in *The Atlantic*. In it, he laid out the case that we were headed for a constitutional crisis: "If Trump sheds all restraint, and if his Republican allies play the parts he assigns them, he could obstruct the emergence of a legally unambiguous victory for Biden in the Electoral College and then in Congress. He could prevent the formation of consensus about whether there is any outcome at all." Many of Gellman's predictions, including the attempt to hijack the January 6 election certification and the malignant mischief of rogue state legislatures, came to pass. This piece was much discussed, of course, and he wasn't the only journalist sounding the klaxons, but rereading it now, it's hard not to feel the curse of Cassandra.

Halfway through the year, the murder of George Floyd unleashed a racial reckoning, and this anthology is replete with, yet provides only a small sampling of, writing by Black Americans that gives voice to every manner and method of systemic repression and amplifies demands for change. Jesmyn Ward's

Vanity Fair essay conjoins her promise to remember the husband she lost to COVID to Black America's demands for acknowledgement and equality:

> When my Beloved died, a doctor told me: *The last sense to go is hearing. When someone is dying, they lose sight and smell and taste and touch. They even forget who they are. But in the end, they hear you.*
> I hear you.
> I hear you.
> You say:
> *I love you.*
> We love you.
> *We ain't going nowhere.*
> I hear you say:
> *We here.*

Published three weeks after George Floyd was murdered, Mitchell S. Jackson's "Twelve Minutes and a Life" retells how Ahmaud Arbery was stalked and murdered, even as it reifies everything—from his love of family to his love of McChicken sandwiches and cheese—about him. For the readers of *Runner's World*, the piece laid bare how the sport that's a joy, an obsession, a safe harbor to white runners, is a deadly obstacle course through bigotry for Black Americans: "That Maud's jogging made him the target of hegemonic white forces is a certain failure of America. Check the books—slave passes, vagrancy laws, Harvard's Skip Gates arrested outside his own crib—Blacks ain't never owned the same freedom of movement as whites." This piece, which Jackson must have begun and probably completed long before Floyd's murder, may have taken on more resonance to readers because it came out during a national uprising, but is also a clarion call not to reduce the causes of protest to one incident, not to reduce a murdered man to a symbol:

Ahmaud Marquez Arbery was more than a viral video. He was more than a hashtag or a name on a list of tragic victims. He was more than an article or an essay or posthumous profile. He was more than a headline or an op-ed or a news package or the news cycle. He was more than a retweet or shared post. He, doubtless, was more than our likes or emoji tears or hearts or praying hands. He was more than an RIP T-shirt or placard. He was more than an autopsy or a transcript or a police report or a live-streamed hearing. He, for damn sure, was more than the latest reason for your liberal white friend's ephemeral outrage. He was more than a rally or a march. He was more than a symbol, more than a movement, more than a cause. He. Was. *Loved*.

Of course, magazines must—individually and certainly collectively—provide contrast to big, weighty, public-affairs journalism. In this collection we have some juicy profiles of New York buildings—with all the requisite architectural trivia, co-op board dramas, and oversharing and humble-bragging of the residents. As we were all binge-watching Netflix's Michael Jordan bio series, *The Last Dance*, ESPN provided us a view of MJ that he did not executive produce, one in which author Wright Thompson notes that his colorful suits, which "took on an air of sophistication in the glare of Jordan's fame," are perhaps better understood as reflecting a country boy dressing up for Sunday service at an AME church. Susan Choi's short story for *Harper's*, "The Whale Mother." takes the despair of divorce and glazes it ever so delicately with the surreal.

I remember grasping hold of Sam Anderson's *New York Times Magazine* profile of Weird Al Yankovic, which came out amid the first lockdown, much as a person lost in the desert might stagger toward an oasis. It was a balm, a salvation, and I did not care if the joy that it gave me might shimmer away in the heat of current events once I was done reading. It was relief, and God knows in 2020, we needed relief.

And that's what magazines do: They challenge, they juxtapose, they synthesize, they inspire, they sound a call to action. And they provide beauty and comfort and succor and, yes, some blessed diversion, when you need them most. The title of Jesmyn Ward's essay, "Witness and Respair," distilled 2020. "Witness," to see, to testify. "Respair," not a word in common usage, means the return of hope after a period of despair. And we can only hope for that.

Sid Holt

Acknowledgments

Pandemic, political conflict, racial crisis—the twenty-two articles collected in this year's edition of *Best American Magazine Writing* are a record of the concerns that Americans shared during a year that most will always remember but would happily forget. More than a record, however, they are the stories that helped us then—and will help us later—understand where we have been and where we are going. Here, too, are the diversions that magazines also provide, whether profiles of the gifted (and sometimes bizarre) or once-in-a-lifetime glances behind closed doors.

Each of the stories in *BAMW 2021* was published in 2020, many of them first online, then in print, and each was either nominated for a National Magazine Award or received an Ellie, the copper statuette modeled on Alexander Calder's 1942 stabile *Elephant Walking* that is given to each winner. Founded in 1966 (the honorees that year included *Life* and *Look* as well as the *New Yorker* for Truman Capote's "In Cold Blood"), the awards were originally limited to print magazines but now honor magazine storytelling published in any form, including videos and podcasts. The awards are sponsored by the American Society of Magazine Editors in association with the Columbia University Graduate School of Journalism and are administered by ASME.

But it's not all about winning fancy trophies. National Magazine Awards entry fees and ticket sales provide support for the Osborn Elliott Scholarship at the Columbia University Graduate School of Journalism. Named in honor of the former editor in chief of *Newsweek*, who also served as president of the American Society of Magazine Editors and dean of the Columbia University Graduate School of Journalism, the Osborn Elliott Scholarship is awarded to students who intend to pursue careers in magazine journalism.

This year's National Magazine Awards were presented in twenty-three categories, ranging from Design and Photography to Feature Writing and Public Interest. There were, of course, dozens of finalists and winners, only a few of which can be included in *Best American Magazine Writing* but all of which will reward the interest of any reader. A complete list of finalists and winners is posted at https://asme.media.

Despite the pandemic, the editors of more than 230 magazines and websites submitted nearly 1,200 entries in the National Magazine Awards this year. Three hundred writers, editors, art directors, and photo editors participated in the judging of the awards, which took place virtually in April. The presentation of the awards was then livestreamed in June. A video of the presentation is posted at https://youtube.com/asme1963.

Sixty media organizations received nominations for National Magazine Awards in 2021, led by the *New Yorker* with fourteen. The *New Yorker* also won six awards. The other top finalists were *The Atlantic* with eight nominations, the *New York Times Magazine* with six, and *ProPublica* and *Texas Monthly*, both with five. Aside from the *New Yorker*, two organizations brought home multiple awards this year: *ProPublica* won five, and *Stranger's Guide* won two.

I say it every year, but it nonetheless remains true that hundreds of magazine journalists make the National Magazine Awards possible. There are the editors in chief who choose to enter the awards; the staff members who organize the submissions; and of course the judges, who read, watch, or listen to dozens of stories, videos, and podcasts before they even meet with their fellow judges to pick the finalists and winners.

The ASME board of directors is responsible for overseeing the administration, judging, and presentation of the National Magazine Awards. The members of the 2020–21 board—all of whom are journalism educators or the editors in chief of well-known publications—are listed, along with the judges, at https://ASME .media. The president of ASME, Jonathan Dorn, deserves special recognition for the success of the 2021 awards. I also want to thank Clara Jeffery, the incoming president of ASME, for writing the introduction to this year's edition of *BAMW*.

As director of operations at ASME, Nina Fortuna is largely responsible for the day-to-day management of the National Magazine Awards. Every member of ASME, every entrant in the National Magazine Awards, every Maltese named Penny Lane is eternally in her debt. Deserving of thanks as well are Overland Entertainment's Leane Romeo, Michael Scarna and Michael Lockmeyer, the longtime producers of the National Magazines Awards show who this year also managed the virtual judging of the awards.

On behalf of ASME, I want to thank Steve Coll, the Pulitzer Prize–winning reporter who now serves as the dean and Henry R. Luce Professor of Journalism at the Columbia Journalism School, and Abi Wright, the executive director of professional prizes at Columbia, for their continuing support of the National Magazine Awards.

Thanks are also due to David McCormick for his representation of ASME's interests as the society's literary agent and especially to the editors of *Best American Magazine Writing* at Columbia University Press, Philip Leventhal and Michael Haskell, whose enthusiasm for the BAMW series only seems to grow with each passing year.

But most deserving of our gratitude are the writers who not only graciously consented to the publication of their work in the 2021 edition of *Best American Magazine Writing* but who, during an extraordinary year—a year in which many labored in isolation—provided inspiration to both colleagues and readers.

THE BEST
AMERICAN
MAGAZINE
WRITING

2021

New Yorker

WINNER—REPORTING

The judges who chose Lawrence Wright's "The Plague Year" as the recipient of the 2021 National Magazine Award for Reporting described the story as "the definitive account of the nation's catastrophic response to COVID-19" and praised the "exclusive interviews, exhaustive reporting and authoritative analysis" that lay behind it.

A staff writer at the New Yorker since 1992, Wright previously won the National Magazine Award for Reporting in 1994 for "Remembering Satan," which explored what the magazine described as "the national obsession with cults and 'recovered memory'" and in 2012 for "The Apostate," his account of the defection of the screenwriter and director Paul Haggis from the Church of Scientology. Wright's book The Looming Tower: Al-Qaeda and the Road to 9/11 won the Pulitzer Prize for General Nonfiction in 2007. His book The Plague Year: America in the Time of Covid was published in June 2021.

Lawrence Wright

The Plague Year

1. "An Evolving Situation"

There are three moments in the yearlong catastrophe of the
COVID-19 pandemic when events might have turned out differently. The first occurred on January 3, 2020, when Robert Redfield, the director of the Centers for Disease Control and Prevention, spoke with George Fu Gao, the head of the Chinese Center
for Disease Control and Prevention, which was modeled on the
American institution. Redfield had just received a report about
an unexplained respiratory virus emerging in the city of Wuhan.

The field of public health had long been haunted by the prospect of a widespread respiratory-illness outbreak like the 1918
influenza pandemic, so Redfield was concerned. Gao, when
pressed, assured him that there was no evidence of human-to-
human transmission. At the time, the theory was that each case
had arisen from animals in a "wet" market where exotic game was
sold. When Redfield learned that, among twenty-seven reported
cases, there were several family clusters, he observed that it was
unlikely that each person had been infected, simultaneously, by
a caged civet cat or a raccoon dog. He offered to send a CDC team
to Wuhan to investigate, but Gao said that he wasn't authorized
to accept such assistance. Redfield made a formal request to the
Chinese government and assembled two dozen specialists, but no

invitation arrived. A few days later, in another conversation with Redfield, Gao started to cry and said, "I think we're too late."

Perhaps Gao had just been made aware that the virus had been circulating in China at least since November. Certainly, Redfield didn't know that the virus was already present in California, Oregon, and Washington and would be spreading in Massachusetts, Wisconsin, Iowa, Connecticut, Michigan, and Rhode Island within the next two weeks—well before America's first official case was detected.

Redfield is convinced that, had CDC specialists visited China in early January, they would have learned exactly what the world was facing. The new pathogen was a coronavirus, and as such it was thought to be only modestly contagious, like its cousin the SARS virus. This assumption was wrong. The virus in Wuhan turned out to be far more infectious, and it spread largely by asymptomatic transmission. "That whole idea that you were going to diagnose cases based on symptoms, isolate them, and contact-trace around them was not going to work," Redfield told me recently. "You're going to be missing 50 percent of the cases. We didn't appreciate that until late February." The first mistake had been made, and the second was soon to happen.

●   ●   ●

Matthew Pottinger was getting nervous. He is one of the few survivors of Donald Trump's White House, perhaps because he is hard to categorize. Fluent in Mandarin, he spent seven years in China, reporting for Reuters and the *Wall Street Journal*. He left journalism at the age of thirty-two and joined the marines, a decision that confounded everyone who knew him. In Afghanistan, he cowrote an influential paper with Lieutenant General Michael Flynn on improving military intelligence. When Trump named Flynn his national-security adviser, Flynn chose Pottinger as the Asia director. Scandal removed Flynn from his job almost overnight, but Pottinger stayed, serving five subsequent national-security chiefs. In September 2019, Trump appointed him deputy national-security adviser. In a very noisy administration, he had quietly become one of the most influential people shaping American foreign policy.

At the *Journal*, Pottinger had covered the 2003 SARS outbreak. The Chinese hid the news, and, when rumors arose, authorities minimized the severity of the disease, though the fatality rate was approximately 10 percent. Authorities at the World Health Organization were eventually allowed to visit Beijing hospitals, but infected patients were reportedly loaded into ambulances or checked into hotels until the inspectors left the country. By then, SARS was spreading to Hong Kong, Hanoi, Singapore, Taiwan, Manila, Ulaanbaatar, Toronto, and San Francisco. It ultimately reached some thirty countries. Because of heroic efforts on the part of public-health officials—and because SARS spread slowly—it was contained eight months after it emerged.

The National Security Council addresses global developments and offers the president options for responding. Last winter, Pottinger was struck by the disparity between official accounts of the novel coronavirus in China, which scarcely mentioned the disease, and Chinese social media, which was aflame with rumors and anecdotes. Someone posted a photograph of a sign outside a Wuhan hospital saying that the ER was closed because staff were infected. Another report said that crematoriums were overwhelmed.

On January 14, the NSC convened an interagency meeting to discuss the virus. Early that morning, the WHO—relying on China's assurances—tweeted that there was no evidence of human-to-human transmission. The NSC recommended that screeners take the temperatures of any passengers arriving from Wuhan.

The next day, President Trump signed the first phase of a U.S.-China trade deal, declaring, "Together, we are righting the wrongs of the past and delivering a future of economic justice and security for American workers, farmers, and families." He called China's president, Xi Jinping, "a very, very good friend."

On January 20, the first case was identified in the United States. On a Voice of America broadcast, Dr. Anthony Fauci, the head of the National Institute of Allergy and Infectious Diseases, said, "This is a thirty-five-year-old young man who works here in the United States, who visited Wuhan." Trump, who was at the World Economic Forum, in Davos, Switzerland, dismissed the threat, saying, "It's one person coming in from China. It's going to be just fine."

·   ·   ·

On January 23, 2020, all the members of the U.S. Senate gathered for the second day of opening arguments in President Trump's impeachment trial. It was an empty exercise with a foreordained result. Mitch McConnell, the majority leader, had already said that he would steamroll Democratic attempts to introduce witnesses or new evidence. "We have the votes," he decreed.

The trial posed difficulties for the four Democratic senators still running for president. As soon as the proceedings recessed, on Friday evenings, the candidates raced off to campaign for the weekend. One of them, Amy Klobuchar, of Minnesota, recalled, "I was doing planetariums in small towns at midnight." Then it was back to Washington, to listen to an argument that one side would clearly win. In the midst of this deadened theater, McConnell announced, "In the morning, there will be a coronavirus briefing for all members at ten-thirty." This was the first mention of COVID in Congress.

The briefing took place on January 24, in the hearing room of the Health, Education, Labor, and Pensions Committee, which Lamar Alexander, Republican of Tennessee, chaired. Patty Murray is the ranking Democratic member. A former preschool teacher, she has been a senator for twenty-seven years. Her father managed a five-and-dime until he developed multiple sclerosis and was unable to work. Murray was fifteen. The family went on welfare. She knows how illness can upend people economically and how government can help.

A few days earlier, she had heard about the first confirmed COVID case in the United States—the man had traveled from Wuhan to Washington, her state. Murray contacted local public-health officials, who seemed to be doing everything right: the man was hospitalized, and health officials were tracing a few possible contacts. Suddenly, they were tracking dozens of people. Murray said to herself, "Wow, this is kinda scary. And this is in my back yard."

But in the outbreak's early days, when decisiveness mattered most, few other politicians were paying attention. It had been a century since the previous great pandemic, which found its way from the trenches of the First World War to tropical jungles and Eskimo villages. Back then, scientists scarcely knew what a virus was. In the twenty-first century, infectious disease seemed like a nuisance, not like a mortal threat. This lack of concern was reflected in the diminished budgets given to institutions that once had led the world in countering disease and keeping Americans healthy. Hospitals closed; stockpiles of emergency equipment weren't replenished. The specter of an unknown virus arising in China gave certain public-health officials nightmares, but it wasn't on the agenda of most American policy makers.

About twenty senators showed up to hear Anthony Fauci and Robert Redfield speak at an hour-long briefing. The health authorities were reassuring. Redfield said, "We are prepared for this."

•　　　•　　　•

That day, Pottinger convened forty-two people, including NSC staffers and Cabinet-level officials, for a meeting. China had just announced a lockdown of Wuhan, a city of eleven million, which could mean only that sustained human-to-human transmission was occurring. Indeed, Pottinger's staff reported that another city, Huanggang, was also locked down. The previous day, the State Department had heightened its travel advisory for passengers to the Wuhan region, and the meeting's attendees debated how to implement another precaution: sending all passengers coming from Wuhan to five U.S. airports, where they could be given a health screening before entry.

The next day, Pottinger attended a Chinese New Year party on Capitol Hill. Old diplomatic hands, émigrés, and Chinese dissidents relayed stories about the outbreak from friends and family members. People were frightened. It sounded like SARS all over again.

Pottinger went home and dug up files from his reporting days, looking for phone numbers of former sources, including Chinese doctors. He then called his brother, Paul, an infectious-disease doctor in Seattle. Paul had been reading about the new virus on Listservs but had assumed that, like SARS, it would be "a flash in the pan."

If flights from China were halted, Matt asked, could America have more time to prepare?

Paul was hesitant. Like most public-health practitioners, he held that travel bans often have unintended consequences. They stigmatize countries contending with contagion. Doctors and medical equipment must be able to move around. And by the time restrictions are put in place, the disease has usually infiltrated the border anyway, making the whole exercise pointless. But Matt spoke with resolve. Little was known about the virus *except* for the fact that it was spreading like wildfire, embers flying from city to city.

Paul told Matt to do whatever he could to slow the virus's advance, giving the United States a chance to establish testing and contact-tracing protocols, which could keep the outbreak under control. Otherwise, the year ahead might be calamitous.

No one realized how widely the disease had already seeded itself. Fauci told a radio interviewer that COVID wasn't something Americans needed to "be worried or frightened by," but he added that it was "an evolving situation."

2. The Trickster

In October 2019, the first Global Health Security Index appeared, a sober report of a world largely unprepared to deal with a pandemic. "Unfortunately, political will for accelerating health security is caught in a perpetual cycle of panic and neglect," the authors observed. "No country is fully prepared." Yet one country stood above all others in terms of readiness: the United States.

During the transition to the Trump administration, the Obama White House handed off a sixty-nine-page document called the "Playbook for Early Response to High-Consequence Emerging Infectious Disease Threats and Biological Incidents." A meticulous guide for combating a "pathogen of pandemic potential," it contains a directory of government resources to consult the moment things start going haywire.

Among the most dangerous pathogens are the respiratory viruses, including orthopoxviruses (such as smallpox), novel influenzas, and coronaviruses. With domestic outbreaks, the playbook specifies that, "while States hold significant power and responsibility related to public-health response outside of a declared Public Health Emergency, the American public will look to the U.S. Government for action." The playbook outlines the conditions under which various federal agencies should become involved. Questions about the severity and the contagiousness of a disease should be directed to the Department of Health and Human Services, the Federal Emergency Management Agency, and the Environmental Protection Agency. How robust is contact tracing? Is clinical care in the region scalable if cases explode? There are many such questions, with decisions proposed and agencies assigned. Appendices describe such entities as the Pentagon's Military Aeromedical Evacuation team, which can be assembled to transport patients. Health and Human Services can call upon a Disaster Mortuary Operational Response Team, which includes medical examiners, pathologists, and dental assistants.

The Trump administration jettisoned the Obama playbook. In 2019, HHS conducted Crimson Contagion, a simulation examining the government's ability to contain a pandemic. Among the participants were the Pentagon, the NSC, hospitals, local and regional health-care departments, the American Red Cross, and twelve state governments. The scenario envisioned an international group of tourists visiting China who become infected with a novel influenza and spread it worldwide. There's no vaccine; antiviral drugs are ineffective.

The Crimson Contagion exercise inspired little confidence that the government was prepared to handle such a crisis. Federal agencies couldn't tell who was in charge; states grew frustrated in their attempts to secure enough resources. During the simulation, some cities defied a CDC recommendation to close schools. Government policies, the report concluded, were inadequate and "often in conflict." The Public Health Emergency Fund and the Strategic National Stockpile were dangerously depleted; N95 masks and other medical essentials were in short supply, and domestic manufacturing capacity was insufficient. Congress was briefed on the findings but they were never made public. By the time COVID arrived, no meaningful changes had been made to address these shortcomings.

· · ·

"I just love infectious diseases," John Brooks, the chief medical officer of the COVID response team at the CDC, admitted to me. "I know diseases are terrible—they kill people. But something about them just grabs me."

Each generation has its own struggle with disease. In 1939, Brooks's mother, Joan Bertrand Brooks, developed polio. Her legs were covered with surgical scars, and her right leg was noticeably shorter than her left. "She spoke about that experience often— how she was teased, stigmatized, or blatantly discriminated against," Brooks recalled.

For Brooks, who is gay, the disease of his generation was HIV/ AIDS. He grew up near the Dupont Circle neighborhood of Washington, DC, which had a large gay population, and watched men he knew disappear: "Guys would get thin and develop lesions and then be gone. It was scary." Science offered no solution, and that was on Brooks's mind when he decided to become a doctor. The day he was accepted at Harvard Medical School, he and his mother went to lunch to celebrate. "Afterward, we dropped into a ten-dollar palm reader, who said she saw me marrying a tall Swedish woman and owning a jet with which I flew around the world with our three children," he told me. "We had a good laugh. I should have asked for a refund."

In 2015, Brooks became the chief medical officer of the HIV/ AIDS division at the CDC Every HIV researcher has been humbled by the various manifestations of this disease. "At every turn, there was something different," Brooks said. "All these opportunistic infections show up. What in the world is this all about? Very cool." The experience of studying HIV helped prepare him for the myriad tricks that COVID would present.

• • •

The CDC was founded in 1946, as the Communicable Disease Center. Atlanta was chosen as its home because the city was in the heart of what was called "the malaria zone." Five years later, America was declared malaria-free. The CDC's mission expanded to attack other diseases: typhus, polio, rabies. In 1981, the organization, by then renamed the Centers for Disease Control, reported the first known cases of AIDS, in Los Angeles. Until this year, the CDC maintained a reputation as the gold standard for public health, operating above politics and proving repeatedly the value of enlightened government and the necessity of science for the furthering of civilization. During the twentieth century, the life span of Americans increased by thirty years, largely because of advances in public health, especially vaccination.

The CDC campus now resembles a midsize college, with more buildings under construction, including a high-containment facility for the world's most dangerous diseases. Lab animals— mice, ferrets, monkeys—inhabit cages inside Biosafety Level 4 chambers. Humans move around them like deep-sea divers in inflated suits, tethered to an overhead airflow system.

The Emergency Operations Center is a large, bright room, with serried rows of wooden desks facing a wall of video screens. The place exudes a mixture of urgency and professional calm. On one side of the room, operators triage incoming phone calls. In 2014, during the Ebola crisis, Brooks received a call from Clay Jenkins, a county judge in Dallas. A Liberian citizen visiting the city, Thomas Eric Duncan, had contracted the disease. Jenkins wanted advice about how to safely approach Duncan's fiancée and her family members. On a monitor, Brooks could see the fiancée's apartment complex, shot from above by cameras on helicopters. Brooks told Jenkins that he could safely enter the apartment as long as the family had no symptoms: it would be an important public gesture for him to choose compassion over fear. Brooks watched footage of Jenkins escorting the family out of the complex. (Thomas Duncan eventually died; two nurses who had cared for him were infected but survived.)

Brooks was working on the COVID response team with Greg Armstrong, a fellow epidemiologist. Armstrong oversaw the Advanced Molecular Detection program, which is part of the CDC's center for emerging and zoonotic infectious diseases. (Zoonotic diseases come from animals, as coronaviruses typically do.) Humanity's encroachment into formerly wild regions, coupled with climate change, which has forced animals out of traditional habitats, has engendered many new diseases in humans, including Ebola and Zika. At first, SARS-CoV-2—as the new virus was being called—presented itself as a less mortal coronavirus, like the common cold, spreading rapidly and sometimes asymptomatically. In fact, SARS-CoV-2 was more like polio. Most polio infections are asymptomatic or very mild—fever and headaches. But some are deadly. The polio cases that doctors actually see are about one in every two hundred infections. Stealth transmission is why polio has been so hard to eradicate.

Armstrong was in Salt Lake City, conducting a training session, when he noticed an article on the website of the *New England Journal of Medicine*: "Early Transmission Dynamics in Wuhan, China, of Novel Coronavirus-Infected Pneumonia." The article was one of the first to describe the virus's spread among humans, a development that didn't surprise Armstrong: "Anybody with any epidemiology experience could tell you it was human-to-human transmission." Then he noticed table 1, "Characteristics of Patients," which noted the original source of their infection. Of the Chinese known to have contracted the virus before January 1, 26 percent had no exposure either to the Wuhan wet market or to people with apparent respiratory symptoms. In subsequent weeks, the number of people with no obvious source of infection surpassed 70 percent. Armstrong realized that, unlike with SARS or MERS—other coronavirus diseases—many infections of SARS-CoV-2 were probably asymptomatic or mild. Contact tracing, isolation, and quarantine would likely not be enough. These details were buried in table 1.

Other reports began to emerge about possible asymptomatic spread. Although SARS-CoV-2 was genetically related to the SARS and MERS viruses, it was apparently unlike them in two key ways: people could be contagious before developing symptoms, and some infected people would never manifest illness. In late February, University of Texas scientists, led by Lauren Ancel Meyers, reported that it could have a "negative serial interval," meaning that some infected people showed symptoms *before* the person who had given it to them.

The CDC's early guidance documents didn't mention that possibility because the evidence of asymptomatic spread was deemed insufficient. "In the beginning, for every mathematical analysis that indicated a shorter serial interval than incubation period, others reported no difference," Brooks said. "When the science changed, we changed. And our recommendations changed, too." But, by that time, the CDC had been muzzled by the Trump administration.

. . .

"There are three things this virus is doing that blow me away," Brooks told me. "The first is that it directly infects the endothelial cells that line our blood vessels. I'm not aware of any other human respiratory viruses that do this. This causes a lot of havoc." Endothelial cells normally help protect the body from infection. When SARS-CoV-2 invades them, their powerful chemical contents get dumped into the bloodstream, resulting in inflammation elsewhere in the body. The rupture of individual endothelial cells coarsens the lining in the blood vessels, creating breaks and rough spots that cause turbulent blood flow.

The second surprise was hypercoagulability—patients had a pronounced tendency to develop blood clots. This reminded Brooks of Michael Crichton's 1969 novel, *The Andromeda Strain*, in which a pathogen causes instant clotting, striking down victims in midstride. "This is different," Brooks said. "You're getting these things called pulmonary embolisms, which are nasty. A clot forms—it travels to the lung, damaging the tissues, blocking blood flow, and creating pressures that can lead to heart problems." More puzzling was evidence that clots sometimes formed in the lungs, leading to acute respiratory distress. Brooks referred to an early report documenting autopsies of victims. Nearly all had pulmonary thromboses; until the autopsy, nobody had suspected that the clots were even present, let alone the probable cause of death.

"The last one is this hyperimmune response," Brooks said. Most infectious diseases kill people by triggering an excessive immune-system response; COVID, like pneumonia, can unleash white blood cells that flood the lungs with fluid, putting the patient at risk of drowning. But COVID is unusual in the variety of ways that it causes the body to malfunction. Some patients require kidney dialysis or suffer liver damage. The disease can affect the brain and other parts of the nervous system, causing delirium, strokes, and lasting nerve damage. COVID could also do strange things to the heart. Hospitals began admitting patients with symptoms of heart attack—chest pains, trouble breathing— and preparing emergency coronary catheterizations. "But their coronary vessels are clean," Brooks said. "There's no blockage." Instead, an immune reaction had inflamed the heart muscle, a condition called myocarditis. "There's not a lot you can do but hope they get through it." A German study of a hundred recovered COVID patients with the average age of forty-nine found that twenty-two had lasting cardiac problems, including scarring of the heart muscle.

Even after Brooks thought that COVID had no more tricks to play, another aftereffect confounded him: "You get over the illness, you're feeling better, and it comes back to bite you again." In adults, it might just be a rash. But some children develop a multiorgan inflammatory syndrome. Brooks said, "They have conjunctivitis, their eyes get real red, they have abdominal pain, and then they can go on to experience cardiovascular collapse."

3. Spike

When I was around six, I woke up one morning and couldn't get out of bed: I was paralyzed from the waist down. It was during the polio era, in the early fifties, before there was a cure. I remember the alarm in my mother's eyes. Our family doctor made a house call. He sat on the edge of the bed and took my temperature and pulse; there was little else he could do. The terror of polio haunted children and parents everywhere.

I was lucky. After a day or so, I could move my legs again. I was never certain what had caused my brief paralysis, but the memory was searing. Soon after the polio vaccine, invented by Jonas Salk, became available, in 1955, I was inoculated, along with millions of other children.

So I had a personal interest when I entered Building 40 of the main campus of the National Institutes of Health, in Bethesda, Maryland, which houses the National Institute of Allergy and Infectious Diseases. Dr. Barney S. Graham, the deputy director of the Vaccine Research Center and the chief of the Viral Pathogenesis Laboratory and Translational Science Core, works on the second floor. He studies how viruses cause disease, and he designs vaccines.

The first thing you notice about Graham is that there's a lot of him: he's six feet five, with a gray goatee and a laconic manner. Graham's boss at NIAID, Anthony Fauci, told me, "He understands vaccinology better than anybody I know."

Bookshelves in Graham's office hold colorful 3D printouts of viruses that he has worked with, including Ebola, Zika, and influenza. While I was researching *The End of October*, a novel that I published earlier this year, about a deadly pandemic, Graham helped me design a fictional virus and then concocted a vaccine for it. As we collaborated, I came to understand that researchers like Graham are essentially puzzle solvers. This past year, he solved one of the most consequential puzzles in modern science. He is the chief architect of the first COVID vaccines authorized for emergency use. Manufactured by Moderna and Pfizer, they differ only in their delivery systems.

On Graham's wall is a map of Kansas, where he grew up. His father was a dentist and his mother was a teacher. For part of his childhood, they lived on a hog farm. Barney and his brother did much of the farming. Working with the animals, he learned a lot about veterinary medicine. At Rice University, he majored in biology. He earned a medical degree at the University of Kansas, where he met his wife, Cynthia Turner-Graham, a psychiatrist. In 1978, on an infectious-disease rotation in medical school, he spent time at the NIH., where he first encountered Fauci. "Cynthia noticed when I came back how excited I was," Graham recalled. "People were willing to battle each other's ideas. She thought I would end up here."

First, he and Cynthia had to complete residencies. They wanted to be in the same town, a problem many professional couples face, but additionally complicated in their case because Cynthia is Black. She suggested Nashville: he could apply to Vanderbilt School of Medicine and she to Meharry Medical College, a historically Black institution. Tennessee had only recently repealed a ban on interracial marriage.

Driving back to Kansas from Maryland on Christmas Eve, Graham stopped in at Vanderbilt. To his surprise, the director of the residency program, Thomas Brittingham, was in his office and willing to meet with him immediately. When the interview was over, Graham told Brittingham, "I know this is the South. I'm going to marry a Black woman, and if that makes a difference I can't come here." Brittingham said, "Close the door." He welcomed Graham on the spot. Cynthia was accepted at Meharry, and so they moved to Nashville.

By 1982, Graham had become the chief resident at Nashville General Hospital. That year, he saw a patient suffering from five simultaneous infections, including cryptococcal meningitis and herpes simplex. It was a mystery: most infections are solitary events. The medical staff was terrified. Graham realized that he was treating Tennessee's first AIDS patient. "We kept him alive for three weeks," he said.

Millions of lives would be changed, and so many ended, by this remorseless, elusive disease. Immunology, then a fledgling field, was transformed by the battle. "It took us a couple years just to figure out that HIV was a virus," Graham said. He started running vaccine trials. "It was not till the mid-nineties that we had decent treatments. There were some really hard years. Almost everyone died."

In 2000, the NIH. recruited Graham to create a vaccine-evaluation clinic. He insisted on keeping a research lab. With space for two dozen scientists, his lab focuses on vaccines for three categories of respiratory viruses: influenza, coronaviruses, and a highly contagious virus called respiratory syncytial virus (RSV), which ended up playing a key role in the development of a COVID vaccine.

RSV causes wheezing pneumonia in children and sends more kids under five years old to the hospital than any other disease. One of the last childhood infectious diseases without a vaccine, RSV also kills about as many of the elderly as seasonal influenza. It's wildly infectious. In order to stop its spread in a hospital pediatric ward, staff must wear gloves, masks, and goggles; if any of these items is omitted, RSV will surge. Like COVID, it is dispersed through particle droplets and contaminated surfaces. In the 1960s, a clinical trial of a potential RSV vaccine made children sicker and led to two deaths—a syndrome called vaccine-enhanced disease. Graham spent much of two decades trying to solve the riddle of what causes RSV, but the technology he needed was still being developed.

In 2008, he had a stroke of luck. Jason McLellan, a postdoc studying HIV, had been squeezed out of a structural-biology lab upstairs. HIV has proved invulnerable to a vaccine solution, despite extraordinary technological advances and elegant new theories for designing one. "I thought, Let's try things out on a more tractable virus," McLellan recalled. "Barney thought RSV would be perfect for a structure-based vaccine."

A vaccine trains the immune system to recognize a virus in order to counter it. Using imaging technology, structural biologists can intuit the contours of a virus and its proteins, then reproduce those structures to make more effective vaccines. McLellan said of his field, "From the structure, we can determine function—it's similar to how seeing a car, with four wheels and doors, implies something about its function to transport people."

The surface of an RSV particle features a protein, designated F. On the top of the protein, a spot called an epitope serves as a landing pad for antibodies, allowing the virus to be neutralized. But something extraordinary happens when the virus invades a cell. The F protein swells like an erection, burying the epitope and effectively hiding it from antibodies. Somehow, McLellan had to keep the F protein from getting an erection.

Until recently, one of the main imaging tools used by vaccinologists, the cryogenic electron microscope, wasn't powerful enough to visualize viral proteins, which are incredibly tiny. "The whole field was referred to as blobology," McLellan said. As a work-around, he developed expertise in X-ray crystallography. With this method, a virus, or even just a protein on a virus, is crystallized, then hit with an X-ray beam that creates a scatter pattern, like a shotgun blast; the structure of the crystallized object can be determined from the distribution of electrons. McLellan showed me an "atomistic interpretation" of the F protein on the RSV virus—the visualization looked like a pile of Cheetos. It required a leap of imagination, but inside that murky world Graham and McLellan and their team manipulated the F protein, essentially by cloning it and inserting mutations that kept it strapped down. McLellan said, "There's a lot of art to it."

In 2013, Graham and McLellan published "Structure-Based Design of a Fusion Glycoprotein Vaccine for Respiratory Syncytial Virus" in *Science*, demonstrating how they had stabilized the F protein in order to use it as an antigen—the part of a vaccine that sparks an immune response. Antibodies could now attack the F protein, vanquishing the virus. Graham and McLellan calculated that their vaccine could be given to a pregnant woman and provide enough antibodies to her baby to last for its first six months—the critical period. The paper opened a new front in the war against infectious disease. In a subsequent paper in *Science*, the team declared that it had established "clinical proof of concept for structure-based vaccine design," portending "an era of precision vaccinology." The RSV vaccine is now in phase 3 human trials.

•　　　•　　　•

In 2012, the MERS coronavirus emerged in Saudi Arabia. It was extremely dangerous to work with: a third of infected people died. Ominously, it was the second novel coronavirus in ten years. Coronaviruses have been infecting humans for as long as eight centuries, but before SARS and MERS they caused only the common cold. It's possible that, in the distant past, cold viruses were as deadly as COVID and that humans developed resistance over time.

Like RSV, coronaviruses have a protein that elongates when invading a cell. "It looks like a spike, so we just call it Spike," Graham said. Spike was large, flexible, and encased in sugars, which made it difficult to crystallize, so X-ray crystallography wasn't an option. Fortunately, around 2013, what McLellan calls a "resolution revolution" in cryogenic electron microscopy allowed scientists to visualize microbes down to one ten-billionth of a meter. Finally, vaccinologists could truly see what they were doing.

Using these high-powered lenses, Graham and McLellan modified the MERS spike protein, creating a vaccine. It worked well in mice. They were on the way to making a version for humans, but, after MERS had killed hundreds of people, it petered out as an immediate threat to humans—and the research funding petered out, too. Graham was dismayed, realizing that such a reaction was shortsighted, but he knew that his energies hadn't been wasted. About two dozen virus families are known to infect humans, and the weapon that Graham's lab had developed to conquer RSV and MERS might be transferrable to many of them.

What was the best way to deliver a modified protein? Graham knew that Moderna, a biotech startup in Cambridge, Massachusetts, had encoded a modified protein on strips of genetic material known as messenger RNA. The company had never brought a vaccine to market, concentrating instead on providing treatments for rare disorders that aren't profitable enough to interest Big Pharma. But Moderna's messenger-RNA platform was potent.

In mice, Graham had proved the effectiveness of a structure-based vaccine for MERS and also for Nipah, a particularly fatal virus. In 2017, Graham arranged a demonstration project for pandemic preparedness, with MERS and Nipah serving as prototypes for a human vaccine using Moderna's messenger-RNA platform. Almost three years later, as he was preparing to begin human trials for the Nipah vaccine, he heard the news from Wuhan.

Graham called McLellan, who happened to be in Park City, Utah, getting snowboard boots heat-molded to his feet. McLellan had become a star in structural biology and was recruited to the University of Texas at Austin, where he had access to cryogenic electron microscopes. It took someone who knew Graham well to detect the urgency in his voice. He suspected that China's cases of atypical pneumonia were caused by a new coronavirus, and he was trying to obtain the genomic sequence. It was a chance to test their concept in a real-world situation. Would McLellan and his team like to get "back in the saddle" and help him create a vaccine?

"Of course," McLellan said.

"We got the sequences Friday night, the tenth of January," Graham told me. They had been posted online by the Chinese. "We woke up on the eleventh and started designing proteins."

Nine days later, the coronavirus officially arrived in America.

·   ·   ·

Within a day after Graham and McLellan downloaded the sequence for SARS-CoV-2, they had designed the modified proteins. The key accelerating factor was that they already knew how to alter the spike proteins of other coronaviruses. On January 13, they turned their scheme over to Moderna for manufacturing. Six weeks later, Moderna began shipping vials of vaccine for clinical trials. The development process was "an all-time record," Graham told me. Typically, it takes years, if not decades, to go from formulating a vaccine to making a product ready to be tested: the process privileges safety and cost over speed.

Graham had to make several crucial decisions while designing the vaccine, including where to start encoding the spike-protein sequence on the messenger RNA. Making bad choices could render the vaccine less effective—or worthless. He solicited advice from colleagues. Everyone said that the final decisions were up to him—nobody had more experience in designing vaccines. He made his choices. Then, after Moderna had already begun the manufacturing process, the company sent back some preliminary data that made him fear he'd botched the job.

Graham panicked. Given his usual composure, Cynthia, his wife, was alarmed. "It was a crisis of confidence that I just never see in him," she said. So much depended on the prompt development of a safe and effective vaccine. Graham's lab was off to a fast start. If his vaccine worked, millions of lives might be spared. If it failed or was delayed, it would be Graham's fault.

After the vaccine was tested in animals, it became clear that Graham's design choices had been sound. The first human trial began on March 16. A week later, Moderna began scaling up production to a million doses per month.

4. "It's More Like 1918"

Since 2016, Dr. Rick Bright has run the Biomedical Advanced Research and Development Authority. A division of HHS, the authority is responsible for medical countermeasures in the event of bioterrorism or a pandemic. According to a whistle-blower complaint, on January 22 Bright received an e-mail from Mike Bowen, an executive at the Texas-based firm Prestige Ameritech, the country's largest maker of surgical masks. Bowen wrote that he had four "like new" N95 manufacturing lines, which weren't in use. He added, "Reactivating these machines would be very difficult and very expensive but could be achieved in a dire situation and with government help." In another message, Bowen wrote, "We are the last major domestic mask company. . . . My phones are ringing now, so I don't 'need' government business. I'm just letting you know that I can help you preserve our infrastructure if things ever get really bad. I'm a patriot first, businessman second."

Bright had already been worried about the likely shortage of personal protective equipment in the Strategic National Stockpile. He also felt that not enough was being done to develop diagnostics for the virus from Wuhan. On January 23, at an HHS leadership meeting with Secretary Alex Azar, he warned that the "virus might already be here—we just don't have the tests to know." Many Trump administration officials seemed determined to ignore scientists who shared bad news.

On January 25, Bowen wrote Bright again, saying that his company was getting "lots of requests from China and Hong Kong" for masks—a stunning piece of intelligence. About half the masks used in the United States come from China; if that supply stopped, Bowen said, American hospitals would run out. Bright continued pushing for immediate action on masks, but he found HHS to be unresponsive. On January 27, Bowen wrote, "I think we're in deep shit. The world."

.   .   .

The same day, at the White House, Matt Pottinger convened an interagency meeting of Cabinet officers and deputies. Attendees fell into four camps. There was the public-health establishment—Redfield, Fauci, Azar—data-driven people who, at the moment, had no data. Another group—the acting White House chief of staff, Mick Mulvaney, along with officials from the Office of Management and Budget and the Transportation Department—was preoccupied with the economic damage that would result if drastic steps were taken. A State Department faction was concerned mainly with logistical issues, such as extracting Americans from Wuhan. Finally, there was Pottinger, who saw the virus not just as a medical and economic challenge but also as a national-security threat. He wanted dramatic action now.

For three weeks, the United States had been trying unsuccessfully to send medical experts to China. The public-health contingent didn't want to make decisions about quarantines or travel bans without definitive intelligence, but the Chinese wouldn't supply it. When Pottinger presented a proposal to curtail travel from China, the economic advisers derided it as overkill. Travel bans upended trade—a serious consideration with China, which, in addition to PPE, manufactured much of the vital medicine that the United States relied on. Predictably, the public-health representatives were resistant, too: travel bans slowed down emergency assistance, and viruses found ways to propagate no matter what. Moreover, at least fourteen thousand passengers from China were arriving in the United States every day: there was no way to quarantine them all. These arguments would join other public-health verities that were eventually overturned by the pandemic. Countries that imposed travel bans with strict quarantines, such as Vietnam and New Zealand, kept the contagion at a manageable level.

The State Department's evacuation of Americans, particularly diplomatic staff in Wuhan, outraged the Chinese; Tedros Adhanom Ghebreyesus, the director-general of the WHO, said that the United States was overreacting. In part to placate the Chinese, the 747s that were sent to collect Americans were filled with eighteen tons of PPE, including masks, gowns, and gauze. It was a decision that many came to regret—especially when inferior substitutes were later sold back to the United States at colossal markups.

The morning after the meeting, Pottinger spoke to a doctor in China who was treating patients. People were getting infected and there was no way to know how and where it happened—a stage of contagion called community spread.

Pottinger asked, "Is this going to be as bad as SARS?"

"Don't think 2003—it's more like 1918," the doctor said. That flu lasted two years, and killed between forty and a hundred million people.

•   •   •

On January 28, the national-security adviser, Robert O'Brien, brought Pottinger into the Oval Office, where the president was getting his daily intelligence briefing. According to contemporaneous notes from someone present at this meeting, the briefer mentioned the virus but didn't present it as the top threat. O'Brien warned the president, "This will be the biggest national-security threat you will face." Trump asked if the outbreak posed as big a danger as SARS, and the briefer responded that it wasn't clear yet.

Pottinger leaped to his feet and recounted what he'd heard from his sources—most shockingly, that more than half the disease's spread was attributed to asymptomatic carriers. Yet, every day, thousands of people were flying from China to the United States.

"Should we shut down travel?" Trump asked.

"Yes," Pottinger advised.

Pottinger left the Oval Office and walked to the Situation Room, where a newly formed Coronavirus Task Force was meeting. People were annoyed with him. "It would be unusual for an asymptomatic person to drive the epidemic in a respiratory disorder," Fauci said. That certainly had been true of SARS. He still wanted U.S. scientists to report from China, in order to get more data. Redfield, of the CDC, considered it too early for disruptive actions. He said that there were only a handful of cases outside China and that in the United States the pathogen wasn't moving that fast. The public-health contingent was united. "Let the data guide us," they advised.

Pottinger pointed out that the Chinese continued to block such efforts: "We're not getting data that's dependable!"

The economic advisers, meanwhile, were frantic—a travel ban would kill the airline industry and shut down the global supply chain. Larry Kudlow, the president's chief economic adviser, had been questioning the seriousness of the situation. He couldn't square the apocalyptic forecasts with the stock market. "Is all the money dumb?" he wondered. "Everyone's asleep at the switch? I just have a hard time believing that." (Kudlow doesn't recall making this statement.)

Pottinger, sensing that he'd need backup, had brought along Peter Navarro, an abrasive economic adviser who had been part of the trade negotiations with China. Many White House officials considered Navarro to be a crackpot, but he was known to be one of the president's favorites because he advocated tariff wars and other nationalist measures. Navarro warned the group, "We have got to seal the borders now. This is a black-swan event, and you're rolling the dice with your gradualist approach."

Within minutes, Navarro was at odds with everyone in the room. He pointed out that the new virus was spreading faster than the seasonal flu or SARS. The possible economic costs and loss of life were staggering. Azar argued that a travel ban would be an overreaction. No progress was made in that meeting, but Navarro was so strident that Mulvaney barred him from future sessions.

Then data surfaced that shifted the argument. In mid-January, a Chicago woman returned from a trip to China. Within a week, she was hospitalized with COVID. On January 30, her husband, who hadn't been to China, tested positive. Fauci, Redfield, and others in the public-health contingent changed their minds: human-to-human transmission was clearly happening in America.

Trump was told the news. The timing couldn't have been worse for him. The bitter trade war he had initiated with China had reached a tentative pause. Since then, he had been praising Xi Jinping's handling of the contagion, despite evidence of a cover-up. A travel ban would reopen wounds. Nevertheless, Trump agreed to announce one the next day.

It was a bold gesture, but incomplete. The administration blocked non-Americans coming from China, but U.S. citizens, residents, and their family members were free to enter. A two-week quarantine was imposed on travelers coming from the Wuhan region, but, unlike Taiwan, Australia, Hong Kong, and New Zealand, which rigidly enforced quarantines, the United States did little to enforce its rules, and the leaks soon became apparent.

5. Flattening the Curve

In 1989, Dr. Howard Markel was in graduate school at Johns Hopkins, specializing in both pediatrics and the history of medicine. He had just lost his wife to cancer, a month after their first anniversary. Markel began volunteering at a local AIDS clinic. He found that helping men his own age who were facing their mortality or their partner's was immensely consoling—"the most spiritually uplifting work I did in my entire clinical career."

Markel's patients often asked him, "Doc, do you think I'll be quarantined because I have HIV?" He'd reply that it wasn't appropriate for the disease. But, realizing that these men feared being shut away, like victims of leprosy, he began studying "the uses and misuses of quarantine." His first book was about two epidemics in New York City in 1892, one of typhus and one of cholera, in which Jewish immigrants were blamed for the outbreak and many were sent to quarantine islands.

In the early 2000s, Markel studied "escape" communities that had essentially closed their doors during the 1918 flu pandemic—among them Gunnison, Colorado, and a school for the blind in Pittsburgh. All had survived the contagion virtually unscathed. In 2006, Markel continued his work on the 1918 flu with Martin Cetron, who now directs the Division of Global Migration and Quarantine at the CDC. For an initiative undertaken by the George W. Bush administration, Cetron and Markel were asked to help identify the best way to manage the early waves of a pandemic that had no vaccine or treatments. They considered school closures, public-gathering bans, business shutdowns—traditional tools of public health. Markel assembled a dozen researchers— "the Manhattan Project for historians," he jokes—who combed through more than a hundred archives.

In 1918, Americans faced the same confounding choices as today. Twenty-five cities closed their schools once; fourteen did so twice; and Kansas City, three times. More than half the cities were "double-humped"—suffering two waves of the flu. "They raised the bar too early because the natives got restless," Markel, who is now a professor at the University of Michigan, told me. "They each acted as their own control group. When the measures were on, the cases went down. When the measures were off, the cases went up." After Philadelphia permitted a Liberty Loans parade, there was a huge uptick in cases. St. Louis, by contrast, canceled all parades, and local officials broadcast a unified message. The city's health commissioner published an op-ed alerting citizens to the threat, immediately closing entertainment venues and banning public gatherings. St. Louis's death rate was half of Philadelphia's. By quickly imposing several non-pharmaceutical interventions, a city could dramatically lower the peak of infection—on a graph, it would look more like a rainbow than like a skyscraper. Markel compared each intervention to a slice of Swiss cheese; one layer by itself was too riddled with holes to be effective, but multiple layers made a profound difference. "Early, layered, and long" was the formula.

JAMA published the study in 2007. The authors declared, "We found no example of a city that had a second peak of influenza while the first set of nonpharmaceutical interventions were still in effect." In the century since 1918, technology has transformed so much, but the tools for curbing a novel pandemic haven't changed. Masks, social distancing, and frequent hand washing remain the only reliable ways to limit contagion until treatments or vaccines emerge.

One night, Markel and Cetron were in Atlanta, talking over their study, and they ordered Thai food. When their dinner arrived, Markel opened his Styrofoam container: instead of a fluffy mound of noodles, he gazed on a level, gelatinous mass. "Look," Markel said. "They've flattened the curve, just like we're trying to do." A slogan was born.

6. The Lost February

By January 20, ten days after the Chinese posted the genetic sequence of SARS-CoV-2, the CDC had created a diagnostic test for it. Secretary Azar reportedly boasted to Trump that it was "the fastest we've ever created a test" and promised to have more than a million tests ready within weeks. (Azar denies this.) But the FDA couldn't authorize it until February 4. And then everything really went to pieces.

The testing fiasco marked the second failed opportunity America had to control the contagion. The CDC decided to manufacture test kits and distribute them to public-health labs, under the Food and Drug Administration's Emergency Use Authorization provision. According to Redfield, the CDC published the blueprint for its test and encouraged the labs to ask the FDA for permission to create their own tests. But Scott Becker, the CEO of the Association of Public Health Laboratories, told me that the labs weren't made aware of any change in protocol. They kept waiting for the CDC to supply tests, as it had done previously.

At a Coronavirus Task Force meeting, Redfield announced that the CDC would send a limited number of test kits to five "sentinel cities." Pottinger was stunned: why not send them everywhere? He learned that the CDC makes tests but not at scale. For that, you have to go to a company like Roche or Abbott—molecular-testing powerhouses that have the experience and the capacity to manufacture millions of tests a month. The CDC, Pottinger realized, was "like a microbrewery—they're not Anheuser-Busch."

At the time, Azar, a former top executive at the pharmaceutical firm Eli Lilly, led the Coronavirus Task Force. He agreed with Pottinger that test kits needed to be broadly distributed, yet nothing changed. Everyone on the task force understood the magnitude of the crisis; they attended meetings every weekday, with conference calls on weekends. North Korea and Iran didn't receive such concentrated attention. Yet the administration was simply not accomplishing tasks crucial to limiting the pandemic. There was a telling disparity between what Azar said in private or in the task-force meetings and what he told the president. He was hammering Redfield and the CDC on testing delays while assuring Trump that the crisis was under control.

· · ·

A bottleneck of constraints imposed by the CDC meant that testing was initially limited to symptomatic patients who had come from China or had been in close contact with an infected person. Even health-care workers who'd developed COVID-like symptoms while treating patients had trouble getting tests because the CDC's capacity was so limited.

Pottinger kept in frequent touch with his brother, Paul, the infectious-disease doctor in Seattle.

"You getting enough test kits?" Matt asked him.

"We use none of the CDC kits," Paul responded. "They have been way too slow in coming." They also hadn't been approved for screening asymptomatic patients. Seattle doctors had instead devised a "homemade" diagnostic platform, but their testing capacity was "way less than demand." Paul was frantically setting up triage procedures—guessing which cases were COVID and trying to sequester those patients, in order to prevent them from infecting everyone at the hospital.

But there was an even bigger problem.

Microbiologists are acutely aware of the danger of contamination. Viral DNA can linger for hours or days on surfaces, adulterating testing materials. CDC scientists wipe down their instruments every day. Chin-Yih Ou, a Taiwanese microbiologist who retired from the CDC in 2014, told me that while he was creating a test for HIV in infants he refused to let janitors into his lab, mopping the floor himself. In some labs, the last person to leave at night turns on ultraviolet lamps, to kill DNA that might be on the floor or a lab bench. A new pathogen is like an improvised bomb: one wrong decision can be fatal.

The development of the CDC's test kits was overseen by Stephen Lindstrom, a microbiologist from Saskatchewan, who was known for his ability to function under pressure. CDC scientists began working sixteen-hour days. The CDC's Biotechnology Core Facility is in charge of producing the components used to detect such pathogens as flu, HIV, and SARS. To save time, Lindstrom asked the Core Facility to produce both the components and a template of a coronavirus fragment, which would be used to generate the positive control for the CDC test. But just as the kits were being boxed up to be mailed, a last-minute quality-control procedure found a problem that could cause the tests to fail 33 percent of the time. A decision was made—perhaps by Lindstrom, perhaps by his superiors—to send the kits anyway. According to *ProPublica*, Lindstrom told colleagues, "This is either going to make me or break me." (The CDC did not make Lindstrom available for comment.)

Almost immediately, public-health labs realized that something was wrong with the kits. The labs are required to do a negative control on the test—for instance, using sterile water—and the tests kept showing false positives.

The CDC test kit had three sets of primers and probes, which are tiny bits of nucleic acid that find a segment of RNA in the virus and replicate it until it gets to a detectable level. Two were aimed at SARS-CoV-2 and a third would detect any coronavirus, in case the virus mutated. The third component failed. Public-health labs figured this out quickly. On their behalf, Scott Becker communicated with the CDC on February 9, seeking permission to use the test without the third component. "I got radio silence," he told me. Later, he learned that an internal CDC review showed that it hadn't passed the quality-control check before the test kit was sent out. "That was a gut punch," Becker said.

·   ·   ·

In 2009, Matt Pottinger was in Kabul, in his final deployment as a marine. While walking through a tunnel connected to the U.S. embassy, he passed a young woman and then suddenly wheeled around. Her name was Yen Duong. She was working with the Afghan government on improving its HIV testing. "It was, like, seven o'clock at night," Yen remembers. "He came up to me and asked if I knew where so-and-so's office was. I was thinking that I'm pretty sure so-and-so's office is closed right now. It was just a ploy to talk." Matt and Yen married in 2014.

They have lived very different American lives. He grew up in Massachusetts. His parents divorced when he was young, and he lived mostly with his mother and stepfather. His father, J. Stanley Pottinger, was a lawyer in the Nixon administration. Matt had an ear for languages, and majored in Mandarin and Japanese at the University of Massachusetts, Amherst, and that is how he found his way to China as a reporter.

Yen was six months old when her family left Vietnam, in 1979, in a boat that her father had secretly built in his sugar factory. At sea, the Duong family—sixty-eight in all—were shot at. A storm nearly capsized the vessel. Pirates robbed them. Finally, the family reached a refugee camp in Indonesia. Six months later, the Duongs were sponsored by four American churches on Long Island and ended up living in the Hamptons. Yen's mother cleaned houses and took in sewing and then found a job in a bakery. Her father painted houses and worked in construction. Eventually, they saved enough money to send Yen to boarding school.

Yen, drawn to science, fell in love with studying viruses. She got a doctorate in pharmacology at the University of California, Davis. In 2007, she became a virologist at the CDC, where she developed the global-standard test to measure HIV incidence. None of this would have happened if the family had stayed in Vietnam, if the boat had sunk in the storm, if the pirates had murdered them, or if they hadn't been taken in by Americans who wanted to help them achieve the opportunities that freedom allowed.

·　　·　　·

Yen Pottinger, who is now a senior laboratory adviser at Columbia University, told her husband what she thought had gone awry with the test kits. Once the Chinese had posted online the genetic sequence for the virus, Yen explained to Matt, primers would have been easy to design. "It's a pretty standard task," she told him. But SARS-CoV-2 is an RNA virus, which is "sticky"— tending to cling to any surface. Contamination was the only plausible explanation for the test kit's failure. Perhaps a trace amount of the virus template had found its way into the primers and probes. "Contamination has felled many a great scientist," she said, which is why a pristine lab environment is essential.

On February 10, the FDA learned that ten labs working with CDC test kits were reporting failures. The CDC assured the FDA that it could quickly fix the problem with the third component. The Trump administration—in particular, Azar—insisted on continuing with the CDC test kits. Although FDA rules generally require that any procedure granted an Emergency Use Authorization be used exactly as designed, the agency could have allowed public-health labs to use the CDC test kits without the third component, as they were pleading for. The test kits largely worked, even without it, but the FDA says that it didn't have the data from the CDC to justify that simple solution. The CDC wanted to stick with its original design. Moreover, university scientists, hospital researchers, and commercial labs were eager to develop their own tests, but they were hampered by the bureaucratic challenge of obtaining an Emergency Use Authorization.

On February 12, the CDC estimated that it would take a week to remanufacture the third component. Six days later, Redfield informed Azar that doing so might take until mid-March. By February 21, only seven labs in the country could verify that the test worked. Redfield admitted that he had no idea when new test kits might be ready.

·   ·   ·

On Saturday, February 22, the FDA sent Dr. Timothy Stenzel, the director of the Office of In Vitro Diagnostics and Radiological Health, to the CDC to investigate what had gone wrong with the test. When he arrived, there was no one there to receive him, and he was turned away. The next day, he was allowed in the building but forbidden to enter any labs. It was still the weekend. Stenzel made some calls. After he was finally permitted to visit the labs where the test kits were manufactured, he spotted a problem: in one lab, researchers were analyzing patient samples in the same room where testing ingredients were assembled. The tests are so sensitive that even a person walking into the room without changing her lab coat might carry viral material on her clothing that would confound the test. According to the *Wall Street Journal*, an FDA official described the CDC lab as "filthy." It was the lowest point in the history of a proud institution.

According to an internal FDA account, CDC staff "indicated to Dr. Stenzel that Dr. Stephen Lindstrom—who oversaw a different lab in the manufacturing process—directed them to allow positive and negative control materials to occupy the same physical space of the lab, even though this is a violation of their written protocols." The clear remedy was to hand over part of the test's manufacture to two outside contractors. Within a week, tens of thousands of tests were available. But America never made up for the lost February.

I recently asked Redfield, a round-faced man with a white Amish-style beard, how the contamination had occurred and if anyone had been held accountable for the corrupted kits. He replied, vaguely, "One of the newer individuals hadn't followed protocol." It also could have been a design flaw that mangled results. Both mistakes might have happened, he conceded. "I wasn't happy when we did our own internal review," he said, and acknowledged that the CDC shouldn't have mass-produced the test kits: "We're not a manufacturing facility." He insisted, "At no moment in time was a COVID test not available to public-health labs. You just had to send it to CDC." But the CDC couldn't process tens of thousands of tests.

The CDC wasn't entirely responsible for the delay. The FDA might have authorized a version of the test kit without the problematic third component and loosened the reins on tests developed by other labs. Not until February 26 did the FDA permit public-health labs to use the CDC test kit without the third component. Only on February 29 could other labs proceed with their own tests.

Secretary Azar held the FDA responsible for the absence of alternative tests. A senior administration official told me, "Instead of being more flexible, the FDA became more regulatory. The FDA effectively outlawed every other COVID test in America." Stephen Hahn, the FDA's commissioner, says, "That's just not correct," and notes that more than three hundred tests are currently authorized. But there was only one other test by the end of February. Whether the delay was caused mainly by the CDC or the FDA, Azar oversaw both agencies.

Without the test kits, contact tracing was stymied; without contact tracing, there was no obstacle in the contagion's path. America never once had enough reliable tests distributed across the nation, with results available within two days. By contrast, South Korea, thanks to universal public insurance and lessons learned from a 2015 outbreak of MERS, provided free, rapid testing and invested heavily in contact tracing, which was instrumental in shutting down chains of infection. The country has recorded some fifty thousand cases of COVID. The United States now reports more than four times that number per day.

7. "This Is Coming to You"

"One day, it's like a miracle, it will disappear," the president told the American people on February 27. At the time, there were only fifteen known cases of COVID in the United States, and nearly all involved travelers or people close to them.

As Trump made his promise, 175 employees of the biotech firm Biogen were heading home from a conference held at a Marriott in Boston. The attendees, many of whom had traveled from other states or foreign countries, had gathered for two days in banquet rooms, shared crowded elevators, and worked out in the gym. Soon, many fell ill.

Researchers affiliated with Massachusetts General Hospital and the Broad Institute of MIT and Harvard believe that SARS-CoV-2 was probably introduced to the conference by a single individual. About a hundred people associated with the conference eventually tested positive. The viral strain that they contracted had unusual mutations, allowing researchers to track its spread. In a recent study published in *Science,* the researchers reported that the Biogen outbreak may have been responsible for three hundred thousand cases in the United States alone.

During the study's initial stages, in February and March, the researchers were discomfited by the implications of their data. "The rapidity and degree of spread suggested it wasn't a series of one-to-one-to-one transmissions," Dr. Jacob Lemieux, a lead author, told me. Rather, it was "one-to-*many* transmission events." That raised the question of airborne transmission. "At the time, the idea was heretical," Lemieux said. "We were afraid to consider it because it implied a whole different approach to infection control"—one in which masks played a central role, especially indoors. But the WHO had repeatedly proclaimed that large respiratory droplets—as from a sneeze or a cough—drove the spread. This wasn't based on data about the new virus, Lemieux said: "It was received wisdom based on how previous respiratory viruses had behaved. The global public-health infrastructure has egg on its face. There's a component of human nature that, until you get burned, you don't know how hot the fire is."

•   •   •

Vaccines were in development around the world, but Pottinger was hearing that they wouldn't be available for eighteen months at the earliest. Even that would be a record. A vaccine must be subjected to three trials of increasing size, to determine safety, effectiveness, and proper dosage. Pharmaceutical companies then invest in production, ramping up from thousands of doses to millions.

Pottinger and Navarro, the China-trade adviser, advocated for a way to radically shorten the time frame: companies would be paid to manufacture vaccine candidates that were still in trials and might never be used. If any ended up being successful, Americans could be inoculated in less than a year.

At the end of February, Navarro wrote a memo proposing a 3-billion-dollar supplemental budget appropriation to cover the cost of an accelerated vaccine process, PPE for frontline workers, and effective therapeutics. Azar recognized the need for a major budget supplement, but after he met with Mulvaney, Trump's acting chief of staff, he declared that eight hundred million dollars was enough for now.

Pottinger was apoplectic. The administration was in denial. There were now more cases outside China than within. Italy and Iran were exploding. And yet Mulvaney and the Office of Management and Budget insisted on viewing the contagion as a kind of nasty influenza that could only be endured. At home, Pottinger fumed to Yen that eight hundred million dollars was half the sum needed just to support vaccine development through phase 3 trials.

"Call Debi," Yen suggested.

Debi was Deborah Birx, the U.S. global AIDS coordinator. In the mideighties, as an army doctor, Birx studied immunology and AIDS at Fauci's clinic. They walked the hallways together, watching their patients die. Birx then moved to Walter Reed Army Medical Center, where she worked on an HIV/AIDS vaccine. At Walter Reed, Birx worked with Redfield. From 2005 to 2014, she led the CDC's Division of Global HIV/AIDS (making her Yen Pottinger's boss). Birx was known to be effective and data-driven but also autocratic. Yen described her as "super dedicated," adding, "She has stamina and she's demanding, and that pisses people off." That's exactly the person Pottinger was looking for.

Birx was in Johannesburg when Pottinger called and asked her to join the Coronavirus Task Force, as its coordinator. She was ambivalent. When she had started her job at the CDC, some African countries had HIV-infection rates as high as 40 percent. Through the steady application of public-health measures and the committed collaboration of African governments, the virus's spread had been vastly reduced. What if she turned her attention and the numbers skyrocketed? Then again, COVID would likely run rampant through the same immune-compromised population she was devoted to protecting. She went to Washington.

.　　.　　.

As March approached, Secretary Azar had to defend his supplemental budget request before a Senate appropriations subcommittee. Earlier, the senators had been briefed that a grave coronavirus outbreak in the United States was likely. Patty Murray, the Democrat from Washington State, was on the committee. "You've had a month now to prepare," she said. "Is our country ready?"

"Our country is preparing every day," Azar responded.

"You sent over a supplemental that wasn't clear to me at all," Murray said. She listed actions that Azar had said were necessary. None were listed in the budget on the table. "Did you stockpile *any* of these critical supplies that we are told we need—masks, protective suits, ventilators, anything?"

"We do have in the Strategic National Stockpile ventilators, we have masks, we have—"

"Enough?"

"Of course not, or we wouldn't be asking for a supplemental," Azar said.

"I didn't see any numbers in your request," Murray said.

Azar said that the details were being worked out. Murray persisted: "I'm very concerned about this administration's attitude. We're not stockpiling those things right now that we know we might possibly need." She concluded, "We are way behind the eight ball."

.　　.　　.

On February 27, the CDC began allowing tests for people who hadn't been to China or in close contact with someone known to be infected. The next day, doctors in Washington State tested two people from a nursing home, in the Seattle suburb of Kirkland, that was overrun with pneumonia. Both tested positive. America's blindfold was finally coming off.

Trump, however, continued offering false assurances. "We're testing everybody that we need to test," he proclaimed. "We're finding very little problem."

On February 29, Washington's governor, Jay Inslee, reported that someone in his state had died of COVID. It was the first official death from the disease in the United States, although it was later established that two Californians had died from it weeks earlier. Many others may have as well.

Inslee declared a state of emergency. One of Senator Murray's relatives had been in the Kirkland facility a few years earlier. "I knew how many people came in and out of it, visitors and staff," she told me. She said to herself, "Wow, this contagious virus, it can't have just stayed in a nursing home." Soon, friends of Murray's got sick. She urged them to get tested, but they said, "I've asked my doctor, I've asked the public-health people in the county, I've called the state health people—*nobody* has these tests." Her state was in turmoil. In Senate hearings and briefings, though, she sensed a lack of coordination and urgency.

The Democratic caucus went on a retreat in Baltimore. Murray received a text from her daughter, whose children attended school near the nursing home. "They closed the schools," her daughter said. She added, "Kids are sick, teachers are sick. This is really frightening."

Murray told her colleagues, "My daughter's school closed. This is coming to you."

8. "Just Stay Calm"

While this was happening, I was in Houston, in rehearsals for a play I'd written about the 1978 Camp David summit. Oskar Eustis, of New York's Public Theatre, was directing. I have a memory of the preview performances that later came back to me, charged with significance. The actors were performing in the round, and slanted lighting illuminated their faces against the shadowy figures of audience members across the way. When one actor expostulated, bursts of saliva flew from his mouth. Some droplets arced and tumbled, but evanescent particles lingered, forming a dim cloud. At the time, I found this dramatic, adding to the forcefulness of the character. Later, I thought, This is what a superspreader looks like.

I have no idea how Eustis got sick. But when he abruptly flew back to New York and missed opening night, on February 20, I knew that something was wrong. Texas was thought to be outside the danger zone that month, but retrospective modeling suggested that the virus likely had been infecting at least ten people a day since the middle of the month. The same was true for New York, California, Washington, Illinois, and Florida. By the end of February, there was probable local transmission in thirty-eight states.

The virus continued hitchhiking with passengers coming from other hot spots. Between December and March, there were 3,200 direct flights from China to the United States, many of them landing in New York. More consequentially, 60 percent of flights from Italy to the United States landed in the New York area. Some of these passengers carried a more contagious mutation of SARS-CoV-2. On March 10, Italy entered lockdown, and the next day the WHO finally declared a pandemic. By that time, there were more than 100,000 cases in 114 countries.

"Just stay calm," Trump remarked. "It will go away."

Weeks had passed from the point when containment was possible. On February 25, Nancy Messonnier, a senior director at the CDC, warned, "We will see community spread in this country. It's not so much a question of if this will happen anymore but rather more a question of exactly when." Without vaccines or treatments, communities needed to rely on such measures as school closures, social distancing, teleworking, and delaying elective surgeries. People should expect missed work and loss of income. Parents needed a child-care plan. "I understand this whole situation may seem overwhelming," she said. "But these are things that people need to start thinking about now."

A steep drop in the stock market followed Messonnier's blunt assessment. The president, who had encouraged Americans to judge his performance by market indicators, was enraged. The next time Messonnier spoke in public, she was quick to praise Trump, saying that the country had acted "incredibly quickly."

. . .

Amy Klobuchar dropped out of the presidential race on March 2 and flew to Dallas to endorse Joe Biden. The stage was filled with supporters. As the crowd cried, "Let's go, Joe!" she embraced Biden. But as she did so she said to herself, "Joe Biden shouldn't get COVID." She warned his advisers to begin taking greater precautions.

On the first Friday in March, she attended a Biden rally in Detroit. That night, employees in the Wayne County sheriff's office gathered for an annual party at Bert's, a soul-food and jazz venue. Most of the officers were Black; some had retired. At the time, there were no known cases of COVID in Michigan. Three weeks later, seven of the attendees had COVID, and dozens more in the sheriff's office were ill. By the end of March, three law-enforcement officials had died.

At the rally, Klobuchar noticed that people had become more careful. "I put on gloves," she said. "We didn't know about masks at the time."

Democratic rallies soon came to a halt.

. . .

Bellevue Hospital, on First Avenue in Manhattan, is "the grande dame of America's public hospitals," the historian David Oshinsky told me. Since it opened, as an almshouse, in the eighteenth century, nobody has been turned away, whether the patient can afford treatment or not. Bellevue has endured epidemics of cholera and yellow fever, diseases that sent untold thousands to their graves in the potters' fields that are now Washington Square and Bryant Park. In the 1980s, Bellevue treated more AIDS patients than any other American hospital.

In 1983, Nate Link began an internship at Bellevue, and almost immediately pricked himself, by accident, with a contaminated needle. He thought it was a death sentence, but he escaped infection. The work was both harrowing and thrilling. "I felt like I was in the epicenter of the universe," he told me. He is now Bellevue's chief medical officer.

During the 2014 Ebola outbreak in Africa, Link and his colleagues knew that, if Ebola spread to New York, the patients would end up at Bellevue. The hospital built an Ebola unit and a dedicated laboratory, training hundreds of staff and storing additional personal protective equipment. The instant they finished their preparations, a patient appeared. He survived. Bellevue then sent emissaries across the country to help hospitals prepare special facilities, develop protocols, and train their staffs for novel infections. Had it not been for the foresight of Link and his colleagues, America would be far less prepared for the COVID onslaught.

Once the coronavirus emerged, Bellevue's special-pathogens team began preparing a protocol. "We thought we'd get one or two cases, just like Ebola," Link recalled. But by early March the hospital was admitting a stream of patients with fever and unexplained respiratory problems. They were labeled PUI: patients under investigation. Tests weren't available. "We had this sense that there was this invisible force out there," Link recalled. He believes that the city already had tens of thousands of cases, but, "without testing, there was just no way to know—it was a sneak attack." When the city reported its first positive case, on March 1, only thirty-two tests had been conducted. Asymptomatic carriers and people with mild symptoms slipped through the nets. The testing guidelines almost seemed designed to undercount the spread.

• • •

On March 10, Eustis, the theater director, walked half a mile from his home, in Brooklyn, to an emergency clinic on Amity Street. His muscles ached. Twice he had to stop and catch his breath, sitting for a while on a fire hydrant. He was too exhausted to be afraid.

His vital signs showed dangerously low potassium levels, and his heart kept skipping beats. An ambulance ferried him to a Brooklyn hospital. An antibody test eventually showed that he had the coronavirus. Despite his condition, there was no room for Eustis. He was placed on a gurney with an IV potassium drip and left in a corridor overnight. He soiled himself, but nobody came to change him. He was given no food for thirty-six hours. The COVID surge had begun.

On March 11, Dr. Barron Lerner was at his office in Bellevue. The hospital had begun implementing triage at the front desk for patients with respiratory problems. That morning, at a staff conference, doctors were told, "If you're talking to a patient you think might have COVID, you excuse yourself from the room. You say, 'OK, I need to leave now. A nurse is going to come in and give you a mask.'"

Lerner met with a regular patient, an Asian immigrant who didn't speak English. Bellevue maintains a staff of a hundred translators, and one of them connected to a dual telephone system. "About ten days ago, she had a fever," the translator told Lerner. "Then she was coughing, and she's been really short of breath since then."

"I thought, I can't believe this just happened," Lerner recalled. "I was probably the first staff member to be exposed." He was sent home and told to monitor his temperature. He and his wife began sleeping in separate bedrooms. Five days later, the fever struck.

Meanwhile, Eustis was released after four days, still shaky. Upon returning home, he immediately went to bed. He turned out to have "long haul" COVID. "It comes in waves," he told me. "I'm struggling with extreme fatigue and continued muscle pain." Working wasn't an option in any case: every theater in New York had gone dark.

9. The Doom Loop

Vice President Mike Pence was now in charge of the task force, but Azar remained a member. Meetings were often full of acrimony. Olivia Troye, a former homeland-security adviser to Pence, told me, "I can't even begin to describe all these insane factions in the White House. I often thought, If these people could focus more on doing what's right for the country rather than trying to take each other down, we'd be in a much different place." Fauci, she recalled, was considered too "outspoken and blunt" with the media, which led such Trump administration officials as Jared Kushner and Peter Navarro to complain that he was "out of control." Troye summed up the administration's prevailing view of Birx crisply: "They hate her." At task-force briefings, Birx typically presented a slide deck, and Troye once caught White House staff members rolling their eyes. Marc Short, Pence's chief of staff, remarked, "How long is she going to instill fear in America?"

On March 11, members of the Coronavirus Task Force crowded into the Oval Office, where they were joined by Kushner, Ivanka Trump, Secretary of State Mike Pompeo, and a dozen others. According to the official who kept contemporaneous notes, Birx and Fauci pushed for shutting down European travel. "Every seed case you prevent is a cluster of cases you prevent," Birx explained.

Redfield and Azar had swung around to the idea that cutting off European travel might buy time, but Steven Mnuchin, the treasury secretary, heatedly insisted that doing so would cripple the U.S. economy and trigger a global depression. The markets would crater. "Forget about ballgames!" he said, pointedly adding, "Forget about campaign rallies!"

After an hour, the president had another obligation, and he asked Pence to keep the discussion going. The group adjourned to the Cabinet Room. Mnuchin argued that there must be ways to curb viral spread without banning travel. The elderly were at high risk—why not sequester the most vulnerable?

"It's 25 percent of the population!" Robert O'Brien, the national-security adviser, observed. "You're not going to be able to stick them all in hotels."

Fauci had recently warned the group that the outbreak was going to get far worse, saying, "There's no place in America where it's business as usual. By the time you mitigate today, we're three weeks late." Colleges were sending students home, further contributing to the spread.

Another member of the task force noted that, in a bad flu season, 60,000 Americans might die. What was the difference?

"This is *twenty* times that," Pottinger argued. "This is 2 percent dead, where the flu is .1 percent."

"If we just let this thing ride, there could be two million dead," Birx said. "If we take action, we can keep the death toll at a hundred and fifty to two hundred and fifty thousand." It was surreal hearing such numbers laid out so nakedly.

Mnuchin demanded data. He felt that the United States just had to live with the virus. It wasn't worth sacrificing the airlines, the cruise ships, the hotels. "This is going to bankrupt everyone," he said. "Boeing won't sell a single jet."

"You keep asking me for my data," Birx said, sharply. "What data do *you* have? Does it take into account hundreds of thousands of dead Americans?" In the end, her side won.

That evening, in an unusually formal speech from the White House, the president announced that he was suspending travel from Europe for the next month. "We are marshalling the full power of the federal government and the private sector to protect the American people," he promised. He had also signed a bill providing $8.3 billion to help the CDC and other government agencies fight the virus. He highlighted the danger the elderly faced and urged nursing homes to suspend unnecessary visits. He advised social distancing and not shaking hands—practices that he hadn't yet adopted himself.

Trump's speech included his usual distortions. He claimed that insurance companies had agreed to "waive all copayments for coronavirus treatments," though they'd agreed only to waive fees for tests. But, for perhaps the first time, he was presenting himself as a unifier—as a take-charge consoler in chief. If he had continued playing that role, America would have had a different experience with the contagion.

●   ●   ●

Glenn Hubbard is a conservative economist who served as the chairman of President George W. Bush's Council of Economic Advisers. Soon after the pandemic began, he became involved in discussions in Washington about how to handle the financial impact. Hubbard told me, "I and other economists had been worried about a doom loop"—a cycle of negative economic feedback. When the pandemic hit, the world suffered a supply shock: trade was disrupted; factories and stores closed. If workers didn't start earning again soon, the supply shock could turn into a demand shock, and that would further weaken supply, which would increase unemployment and further diminish demand. A doom loop.

In mid-March, Hubbard spoke with the Republican senators Marco Rubio of Florida, Susan Collins of Maine, and Roy Blunt of Missouri. The NBA had just suspended its season. Economic forecasts were terrifying. The senators were getting panicked reports from business owners back home.

Only Collins had been in office during the 2008 financial crisis, when Congress had passed a 700-billion-dollar bill to bail out troubled assets—the outer limit of what these conservatives had ever imagined spending. Now they were talking about trillions. Enlarging the deficit and expanding the federal government's reach were anathema to the Republican caucus; to some members, it smacked of socialism. Rubio indicated that he would never support such spending in normal times.

"You need to do something," Hubbard warned. "We've been having a debate for decades now about the size of government. The more interesting debate is the *scope* of government." He spoke of the first Republican president, Abraham Lincoln: "He decided to do the Homestead Act, land-grant colleges, and to lay the foundation for the transcontinental railroad. If Lincoln, in the middle of the Civil War, had the idea of using government as a battering ram for opportunity, why can't we do that today? Instead of focusing on how big government is, think about what you want it to do."

Rubio, who is the chairman of the Small Business Committee, thought about the restaurants, the travel companies, the hair salons—all of them service businesses "with the least ability to survive." The action that Congress was contemplating was heresy from a fiscal-conservative perspective, but the alternative—failing businesses, deepening poverty, boundless unemployment—was worse.

Action was necessary, the senators agreed. As it turned out, there was a surprising logistical problem: the Treasury Department had previously bailed out corporations and given checks to individuals, but it wasn't clear how to give assistance to small businesses. Collins was working on a loan-forgiveness program, and Rubio was trying to figure out how to create a new loan program through the Small Business Administration's existing network of lenders. "That's when the Paycheck Protection Program arose as an idea," Rubio told me. Loans taken out to keep people on the payroll could be forgiven, offering employees assurance that their jobs would still be there when the clouds cleared.

The Democrats were fully on board, and Congress soon approved 350 billion dollars' worth of forgivable loans to small businesses. The overall relief package was even larger. Chris Coons, a Democratic senator from Delaware, told me, "We went from 'We don't know what to do' to 900 pages and $2.2 trillion in about ten days. I've never seen anything like it."

Hubbard said, "Nothing like a big shock to help people become more bipartisan."

10. Reinforcements Arrive

On March 12, Amy Klobuchar was back in Minnesota. Her husband, John Bessler, who teaches law at the University of Baltimore, remained in Washington. He awoke that morning feeling ill. "He was going to take my place at my constituent breakfast in DC," Klobuchar recalled. "It was when he would have been most contagious, as we now know. There would have been around fifty people, in a small room. And then he was going to a faculty meeting—about sixty people, in a small room. Then he was going to get on an airplane and fly to Minnesota, with a bunch of people packed in. I was having some minor surgery at Mayo, and he was going to come there! He really would have had quite a day of infecting people." They had no idea how he'd caught the virus. He was fifty-two and, until then, in excellent health.

Bessler stayed home and steadily grew worse. For more than a week, Klobuchar kept calling, anxiously asking what his temperature was. Their only thermometer was in centigrade, so Klobuchar had to Google the conversion. Each time, it exceeded a hundred degrees. Hearing that he was short of breath, she urged him to see a doctor, worrying that "it was one of those cases where people are underestimating how sick they are, and then they die the next day." After Bessler coughed up blood, he went to the hospital to get tested. He had severe pneumonia. Doctors kept telling Klobuchar, "The oxygen is getting worse." She couldn't visit him, making the ordeal even more frightening.

Bessler spent five days in the hospital. He recuperated and was back in the couple's DC apartment when his test finally came back positive.

· · ·

Dr. Lerner's COVID case was mild. He returned to work at Bellevue after twelve days, on March 23. The city had become weirdly quiet: First Avenue resembled an abandoned set on a studio back lot. During his absence, a tent had been erected in the courtyard, for screening patients. Everyone now wore a mask.

Non-COVID patients in intensive care were shuttled to the postoperative surgical unit, which was available because all surgeries had been canceled. This freed up fifty-six ICU beds. Workers installed HEPA filters in each room, creating negative pressure that prevented infected air from escaping. Offices were turned into more patient units; as soon as carpenters walked out of a converted room, a patient was wheeled in. Twenty-five more spaces for ventilator patients were added in the ER. When all the beds filled, the ICU cubicles were doubled up. Lerner, still recovering, tended to his patients through televisits, taking hour-long naps as Bellevue whirled around him.

In mid-March, Bellevue had its first COVID death: a middle-aged patient with no preexisting conditions, who had been hospitalized for two weeks. Dr. Amit Uppal, the director of critical care, recalled, "Among our staff, we just looked at each other and said, 'OK, here we go.' And from there it just exponentially ramped up."

Uppal, the son of Indian immigrants, grew up in Northern California and did his medical training at Ohio State. He was drawn to Bellevue because he wanted to serve the disadvantaged but also because of the staff—"people that could work anywhere in the country and chose to defend this population." Uppal wanted to specialize in critical care so that he could handle the most extreme diseases. He was prepared to face the knotty ethical dilemmas at the limits of medical knowledge.

Part of the mission at Bellevue is helping patients die well. "It provides you a rare perspective on your own life," Uppal said. "Many laypeople who don't do medicine and aren't exposed to end-of-life issues may not have the opportunity to reflect on what's really important to them until the end of their own life." But COVID seemed cruelly designed to frustrate the rituals of death.

Just as Bellevue's first patients began dying, the hospital was flooded with new admissions. The ICU's typical mortality rate was far lower than COVID's, so even critical-care staff like Uppal were unsettled. Such doctors knew how to click into emergency mode. Before COVID, that might last thirty or forty minutes— say, with a heart-attack patient. After a bus wreck or a mass-casualty event, emergency mode could last a full day. With COVID, it lasted weeks on end.

During rounds, Uppal passed each of the ICU's fifty-six cubicles. The patients were all on ventilators, the distinctive gasping sound unvaried. IV lines extended outside each cubicle, so attendants didn't have to enter to administer medication. In the antiseptic gloom, the patients appeared identical. It was too easy to overlook their humanity. Uppal forced himself to examine their charts. He needed to recapture "what made them unique."

·   ·   ·

Overwhelmed hospitals in New York's outer boroughs transferred more than six hundred patients to Bellevue, knowing that nobody would be turned away. The ER became a hot zone where many people coming off the street required immediate intubation. Before COVID, the ER was always jammed, and nobody wore PPE. Nate Link told me, "When COVID hit, we made a promise to ourselves that we would not let the emergency rooms back up, and that we would keep them pristine." Staffers had to remain swathed in PPE, Link said, adding, "In the end, only 15 percent of the staff in the emergency department tested positive. That's lower than the hospital in general. It's even a bit less than the city average. The message is that PPE works."

Some doctors needed new roles to play. Orthopedic surgeons began devoting their shifts to turning patients—"proning"—to facilitate breathing. Ophthalmologists helped in the ICU; general surgeons treated non-COVID patients. "Everybody found a niche," Link said. "We were a completely different hospital for three months."

More than 20,000 New Yorkers died from COVID in the spring. As the numbers mounted, Link noticed that employees were practicing "psychological distancing." He said, "Our staff had never seen so much death. Normally, a patient dying would be such a big deal, but, when you start having a dozen patients die in a day, you have to get numb to that, or you can't really cope." This emotional remove was shattered when the first staff member died: a popular nurse, Ernesto (Audie) De Leon, who'd worked at Bellevue for thirty-three years. Link said, "His death was followed by a COVID-style 'wake,' as many of his colleagues approached his ICU cubicle in full PPE, put their hands on the glass door, and read Scripture, prayed, and wept. Because of the infection-control restrictions, staff consoled each other without touching or hugging. It was very unnatural."

When Bellevue's doctors were at their lowest ebb, reinforcements arrived: hospital workers from other states flooded into New York to help. According to Governor Andrew Cuomo, 30,000 people responded to the city's call for aid. It was a rare glimpse of national unity. "Half the people in the ICU had Southern accents," Link told me. "That's what saved us."

11. The No-Plan Plan

In mid-March, America began shutting down. The Coronavirus Task Force urged Americans to work from home. Education would be virtual. Travel and shopping would stop. Restaurants and bars would close. The goal was to break the transmission of the virus for fifteen days and "flatten the curve." Trump's impatience flared. At a press briefing, he said of the virus, "It's something we have *tremendous* control over." Fauci corrected him, observing that the worst was ahead, and noting, "It is how we respond to that challenge that's going to determine what the ultimate end point is."

Trump held a conference call with governors. "We're backing you a hundred percent," he said. Then he said, "Also, though, respirators, ventilators, all the equipment—try getting it yourselves."

Most governors had assumed that, as in the event of a hurricane or a forest fire, the federal government would rush to help. Storehouses of emergency equipment would be opened. The governors, faced with perilous shortages of ventilators, N95 masks, and nasal swabs, expected Trump to invoke the Defense Production Act, forcing private industry to produce whatever was needed. Surely, there was a national plan.

Governor Inslee, of Washington, was flabbergasted when he realized that Trump didn't intend to mobilize the federal government. Inslee told him, "That would be equivalent to Franklin Delano Roosevelt, on December 8, 1941, saying, 'Good luck, Connecticut, *you* go build the battleships.'"

Trump responded, "We're just the backup."

"I don't want you to be the backup quarterback," Inslee said. "We need you to be Tom Brady here."

Larry Hogan, the Republican governor of Maryland, was incensed. "You're actively setting us up!" he told Trump.

Matt Pottinger's brother, Paul, kept sending desperate e-mails from Seattle. He had heard about medical workers fashioning PPE out of materials from the Home Depot. Industrial tape and marine-grade vinyl were being turned into face shields. Garbage bags were serving as surgical gowns. A local health official wrote him, "We are currently drafting up guidelines for how to make homemade masks from cloth and I've asked other innovators in the community to see if they can figure out if we can do ANYTHING that would be better than nothing." Matt wrote to Paul, "Help is on the way, but it probably won't be in time—so start tearing up bedsheets and turning them into lab coats, raid the Salvation Army for garments, wrap bras around your faces in place of facemasks if you have to."

The Strategic National Stockpile existed for such emergencies, but Secretary Azar had recently testified to the Senate that it had only twelve million N95 masks—a fraction of what was needed. The storehouse had once held more than a hundred million masks, but many were used during the 2009 H1N1 flu pandemic, and the supply wasn't replenished.

After Trump made clear that the states were on their own, Ned Lamont, the gregarious governor of Connecticut, called other governors in his region: Phil Murphy, of New Jersey; Charlie Baker, of Massachusetts; Gina Raimondo, of Rhode Island; and Cuomo. The states needed to act together, Lamont said. "If I close down bars and Andrew keeps them open, that doesn't solve any problems," he said. "Everybody's going to go down there to drink, and bring back the infection."

The governors were daunted by the task facing them. Lamont imagined furious constituents: "You're going to close down the schools? My God!" Acting in concert provided political cover and a sense of solidarity.

The governors closed gyms, restaurants, and bars at the same time. Lamont, Murphy, and Cuomo prohibited gatherings exceeding fifty people. Baker and Raimondo limited them to twenty-five. Cuomo announced, "If you were hoping to have a graduation party, you can't do it in the state of New York, you can't go do it in the state of New Jersey, and you can't do it in the state of Connecticut."

Governors discovered that the Trump administration was sabotaging their efforts to protect citizens. Charlie Baker arranged to buy three million N95 masks from China, but federal authorities seized them at the Port of New York, paying the supplier a premium. In another group call with Trump, Baker, a Republican, complained, "We took seriously the push you made not to rely on the stockpile. I got to tell you, we lost to the Feds. . . . I've got a feeling that, if somebody has to sell to you or me, I'm going to lose every one of those."

"Price is always a component," Trump replied coldly.

Baker quietly secured a cache of 1.2 million masks from China and enlisted the help of Robert Kraft, the owner of the New England Patriots, who used the team plane to fly the shipment to Logan Airport, where it was received by the Massachusetts National Guard and spirited away.

At a briefing, Cuomo fumed, "You have fifty states competing to buy the same item. We all wind up bidding up each other." He threw up his hands. "What sense does this make? The federal government—FEMA—should have been the purchasing agent."

Gina Raimondo pressed FEMA, saying, "Can we tap into our national stockpile?" After days of giving her the runaround, the agency promised that a truckful of PPE was on its way. At 9 PM, she got a text saying that the truck had arrived. Raimondo told Politico, "I called my director of health. 'Great news, the truck is finally here!' She says, 'Governor, it's an empty truck.' They sent an empty truck."

Inslee told me, "Only 11 percent of the PPE we've obtained has come from the federal government."

Governors who got more had to show obeisance to Trump. Gavin Newsom, of California, praised the president fulsomely after being promised a shipment of swabs. Around this time, a reporter asked Trump, "You've suggested that some of these governors are not doing everything they need to do. What more, in this time of a national emergency, should these governors be doing?"

"Simple," Trump said. "I want them to be *appreciative*."

•   •   •

In the spring, Trump pressed the FDA to fast-track authorization of a malaria treatment, hydroxychloroquine, for COVID patients. Fox News touted the drug as a "game changer." Tucker Carlson and Laura Ingraham aired breathless interviews with Gregory Rigano, who had cowritten a "paper"—a self-published Google Doc—calling the drug an effective treatment. Rigano, a lawyer, had recently started blockchain funds that aimed to "cheat death" and "end Alzheimer's." Between March 23 and April 6, hydroxychloroquine was mentioned on Fox News nearly three hundred times. White House officials, including Peter Navarro, heavily promoted it.

At a task-force briefing, Fauci was asked if hydroxychloroquine curbed the coronavirus. "The answer is no," he said.

The president glowered and stepped toward the mike. "I'm a big fan," he said.

Three months later, the FDA withdrew its authorization. The drug was ineffective and caused "serious cardiac adverse events" and other side effects, including kidney disorders and death. When hydroxychloroquine was paired with azithromycin—a combination that Trump had publicly championed—patients were twice as likely to suffer cardiac arrest as those who took neither drug.

Fox News stopped hyping hydroxychloroquine, but Trump still wanted a quick fix. While cases in New York were doubling every three days, and doctors were treating patients in tents in

Central Park, he declared that he wanted America "raring to go" by Easter.

. . .

Over all, the case fatality rate for COVID is 2 percent. But for people over seventy-five the risk of death is hundreds of times greater than it is for those under thirty. The devaluation of elderly lives was evident in the low standard of care in many nursing homes, where 40 percent of U.S. deaths have occurred, despite accounting for only 8 percent of cases. In March, 235 military veterans were living at the Soldiers' Home in Holyoke, Massachusetts. Some had served in the Second World War. Now they were captives to a system that was failing to protect them.

According to an independent investigation commissioned by the state, family members and workers had long complained about understaffing, in part because of a 2015 hiring freeze ordered by Governor Baker. On March 17, a veteran who had been showing symptoms for weeks was tested for COVID. He lived in one of two dementia units; he wasn't isolated, not even after his test came back positive, four days later. Contagion took hold, and overburdened employees made the fateful decision to combine the two units, with beds placed in tight rows. Many disoriented veterans climbed into the wrong beds, accelerating the spread. A recreational therapist said that she felt as if she were leading her patients "to their death."

On Friday, March 20, Michael Miller, who is retired from the Army National Guard, got a call from his two sisters, Linda McKee and Susan Perez. "They're not thinking Dad's gonna make it through the night," they said. Their father, James L. Miller, was ninety-six and had been at the Soldiers' Home since 2015. The siblings drove to the facility. Only one family member could enter at a time. Mike went in while his sisters waited in the car. His father "looked like a corpse," he recalled. "He had been in that state of decay for a week, and nobody called us."

Jim Miller had landed at Normandy Beach on D Day. He had helped liberate a concentration camp near Nordhausen, Germany. After mustering out, he became a postal worker and a firefighter. He was a taciturn man who had rarely discussed his military service with his children.

Now this quiet old veteran was dying in the midst of bedlam. "Men were just wandering around," Mike said. "They were in various states of dress. There was a curtain drawn for my dad— other veterans would open the curtain and stand there. And these gentlemen I knew. They meant no disrespect." A man on a nearby bed was "just moaning—he couldn't breathe. He ended up passing away that night."

Staffers couldn't offer the dying residents anything but "comfort measures"—morphine under the tongue. Jim was so dehydrated that he couldn't swallow. "Give him an IV!" Mike pleaded. But staffers weren't authorized to do this; nor could they transport him to a hospital. Mike moistened his dad's mouth with a foam swab. Nurses broke down, Mike recalled: "They loved my dad. But they couldn't do anything." He never saw any administrators.

Mike returned each day as his sisters kept vigil in the parking lot. On Saturday, they witnessed the arrival of a refrigerated truck that had been sent to store bodies. On Monday, Jim Miller passed away. Before it was all over, at least seventy-five other veterans had died.

12. Little Africa

In the COVID world, everyone is in disguise. When Dr. Ebony Hilton enters a room, patients see wide-set, lively eyes above her surgical mask. Her hair and body are hidden by a bonnet and a gown. Her accent marks her as a Southerner. She calls herself a "country girl," which is at odds with her assured manner. When the call comes to intubate a COVID patient, "it's already a situation where somebody is dying," she told me. "The only reason I'm placing this breathing tube is because your body is shutting down, so if I don't touch you you're dead." She added, "If I do touch you, *I* could die."

Hilton, who is thirty-eight, is a professor and an anesthesiologist at the University of Virginia School of Medicine, in Charlottesville. UVA's hospital has some 600 beds, but at night Hilton often works alone: "I'm literally the only anesthesiologist attending for the entire hospital. At that moment, I can't shut down, I can't go to my room and let fear stop me." She continued, "I don't think any of us have slowed down to think that this could be the one that gets me sick. You don't have time to consider options A, B, C, and D. You've got to gown up and go."

One day in early March, Hilton got a page. A patient was septic, meaning that an infection had entered her bloodstream and was raging through her body. Her kidneys were starting to fail. Ordinarily, doctors would suspect bacteria as the cause, but the infection's spread had been alarmingly rapid, and the symptoms matched what doctors were reporting about COVID patients in China and Italy. Many health-care workers had noted the speed with which the infection killed when it made its move.

Hilton entered the room, wearing an N95 mask. The patient had no blood pressure; without intervention, her oxygen-starved brain would start dying within seconds. The procedure for intubation requires a pillow to be placed under the patient's shoulder blades, so that the head is tilted back in the "sniffing position." Hilton made sure that the patient was oxygenated and given a sedative and a muscle relaxant; then she pried her mouth open, pushed her tongue aside, and inserted a laryngoscope—a curved blade attached to a handle, which looks like the head of a walking cane. The device lifts the epiglottis, exposing the vocal cords. If the vocal cords don't readily appear, pressure on the larynx can bring them into view. Hilton slowly inserted a plastic tube through the narrow portal between the vocal cords, down into the trachea. Once the tube was secured, the patient was connected to a ventilator.

That was probably Hilton's first COVID patient, but there was no way to know. Virginia had barely any tests in early March.

•　　　•　　　•

Hilton comes from a community near Spartanburg, South Carolina, called Little Africa. After the Civil War, Simpson Foster, a formerly enslaved man, and a Cherokee named Emanuel Waddell founded the community as an agrarian refuge. "It's tiny," Hilton said. "We don't have a red light. We only have my great uncle Hobbs's store—he keeps snacks and stuff for us."

Little Africa is in the foothills of the Blue Ridge Mountains. "When you're sitting on the porch, you can see the skyline of the peaks," Ebony's mother, Mary Hilton, told me. "We have doctors, lawyers, judges—we have so many professions coming out of the Little Africa community, because we put so much emphasis on education, taking care of each other," she said. "Eb is coming from a very powerful place."

When Ebony was eight, her little sister asked Mary if they could have a brother. Mary was caught by surprise but answered honestly: her first child had been a boy. "I was seventeen," she recalled. "I had never heard of an OB-GYN. We always went to the clinic." She went alone; her mother was picking cotton. Mary suspects that, during a pregnancy exam, a technician punctured her amniotic sac. The boy was born prematurely and died after three days. "I told Eb that story, not knowing it would change her life," Mary said. The moment Ebony heard it, she announced that she was going into medicine. Her resolve must have been evident: right then, Mary began calling her Dr. Hilton.

Not long ago, Ebony and her sisters, Brandi and Kyndran, placed a tombstone for the brother they never knew. They erected it in the churchyard of the New Bedford Baptist Church, in Little Africa. "He was a fighter," Ebony told me. "He tried to beat the odds. So I try to finish out that mission for him."

Hilton's image of her future was formed by watching *Dr. Quinn, Medicine Woman*. She attended the Medical University of South Carolina, intending to become an obstetrician-gynecologist. "One night, when I was on my OB rotation, there was a lady having a seizure—she actually had eclampsia—and this guy ran into the room and started shouting orders, like, 'I'm going to do the A-line,' 'You start a magnesium.' I leaned over and asked, 'Who is *that* guy?' One of the OBs said, 'Oh, that's the anesthesia resident.'" Hilton told herself, "I want to be the person that, when there's utter chaos, you know what to do."

In 2013, she became the first Black female anesthesiologist to be hired by the Medical University of South Carolina, which opened in 1824. UVA hired her in 2018. "Growing up in medicine, what I've come to realize is that, should I have a child, it would actually be at more risk of dying than my mom's child was," she said. She cited a Duke University study that correlated race and education levels: "If you look at white women with my same level of degrees, my child is five to seven times more likely to die before his first birthday than theirs. It's been that way historically for Black women. Our numbers haven't really changed, as far as health outcomes, since slavery times."

Many minorities suffer from comorbidities. "That's where the social determinants of health kick in," Hilton said. Asthma and chronic respiratory disease can be the result of air pollution—say, from an industrial plant in a low-income neighborhood. "If you're in a gated community, you don't see smoke billowing out of these industries, because you have the money and power to influence the policy makers to say, 'You can't put that here.'" Heart failure, obesity, and diabetes are tied to whether or not there are nearby restaurants and grocery stores with healthy options. She pointed out that, in South Carolina, one in every five counties doesn't have a hospital; eleven counties don't have any OB-GYNs.

The moment the first American COVID death was announced, in February, Hilton said, she "started doing a tweetstorm to CDC and WHO, saying, 'We know racial health disparities exist, and they existed before COVID—and we know where this will end up.'" She demanded, "Tell us who you're testing and who you're not." The CDC didn't release comprehensive data until July, after the *Times* sued for it. The country, it turned out, was experiencing wildly different pandemics. For every ten thousand Americans, there were thirty-eight coronavirus cases. But, for whites, the number was twenty-three; for Blacks, it was sixty-two; for Hispanics, it was seventy-three. At Hilton's hospital, seven of the first ten COVID fatalities were people of color.

Hilton and her colleagues went to minority communities in and around Charlottesville to provide testing at churches and shopping centers. "Minorities are less likely to be tested, which means they might go back home, where they have the capability to infect their entire community," she said. People of color are more likely to be exposed because so many are essential workers. "Only one in five African Americans can work remotely," she said. "Only one in six Hispanics can."

Staffers at UVA's hospital prepared their wills. Hilton realized that she would be spending long hours away from her dog, Barkley, so she bought a puppy—"a dog for my dog"—that she named Bentley. "They barely get along," she admitted. Hilton's neighbor, a nurse in the COVID unit, has two children, and feared exposing them. The woman began living in her basement.

·　　·　　·

One of the hardest moments at Hilton's hospital came when Lorna Breen, a forty-nine-year-old doctor, was admitted to the psych unit. Her father, Philip Breen, is a retired trauma surgeon; her mother, Rosemary Breen, had been a nurse on the ward where

Lorna was admitted. Lorna had been living in Manhattan, over-seeing the ER at NewYork-Presbyterian Allen Hospital.

When COVID inundated New York, she worked twelve-hour shifts that often blurred into eighteen. She barely slept. Within a week, Breen caught COVID herself. She sweated it out in her apartment while managing her department remotely. After her fever broke, she returned to work, on April 1.

Breen was defined by her vitality. She was a salsa dancer and a cellist in an amateur orchestra. She ran marathons; she drove a Porsche convertible; in her spare time, she was pursuing an MBA. "She never left the party," her sister, Jennifer Feist, told me.

Breen told Feist that a trauma nurse was walking through the ER triaging patients based on how blue their faces were. So many doctors in New York fell ill that, at one point, Breen supervised the ERs in two hospitals simultaneously. It became too much. As her father put it later, Breen was "like a horse that had pulled too heavy a load and couldn't go a step further and just went down."

Breen called her sister one morning and said that she couldn't get out of a chair. "She was catatonic," Feist told me. "COVID broke her brain."

Feist and her husband, Corey, decided that Breen needed to come home to Virginia. A friend in Connecticut drove Lorna to Philadelphia; another friend took her to Baltimore. Feist was waiting on the side of the road to drive her to Charlottesville.

During the eleven days that Breen spent in UVA's hospital, she was terrified that her career was over. Licensing boards, she knew, might flag evidence of mental illness. Before COVID, Breen had never had a trace of instability. Feist and her husband, both attorneys, assured her that she wouldn't lose her license. Breen seemed to improve: she even tried to do her MBA homework on her phone. Feist took Breen home with her on the last Saturday in April. The next day, Breen killed herself.

The pandemic has added immeasurable stress to a public-health workforce already suffering from burnout. Feist told me, "She got crushed because she was trying to help other people. She got crushed by a nation that was not ready for this. We should have been prepared for this. We should have had some sort of plan."

13. The Mission of Wall Street

Goldman Sachs is a controversial name in high finance. Its influence pervades American economic policy. Three of the twelve presidents of the Federal Reserve have worked there. Steven Mnuchin, the treasury secretary, is a Goldman alum. The company's many critics see it as the pinnacle of avarice. They hold it responsible for contributing to the vast income disparities in America and see its alumni as manipulating government policy to further enrich the wealthy. But, in the upper chambers of power, Goldman's culture of success is revered.

In the first quarter of 2020, the Goldman view of the economy was exuberant. Jan Hatzius, its chief economist, told me, "We had come fully out of the deep downturn post-2008." Unemployment was near historically low levels; wages were creeping up. Sure, median incomes hadn't risen substantially since the seventies; the gap between the rich and the poor appeared unbridgeable. But those weren't *Goldman* problems. The company exists to make wealthy clients wealthier.

When the Wuhan outbreak began, the economic risk to America seemed low. Previous pandemics, such as H1N1 and SARS, had negligible economic impact on the United States. On February 12, with COVID already rooted in this country, the Dow Jones closed at 29,551—a record high at the time. Three weeks later, Hatzius said, "we began the deepest contraction in the global economy on record."

Hatzius compiled data for quarterly Goldman GDP forecasts. Normally, he said, "you estimate the ups and downs of a business cycle by, say, relating people's propensity to spend on consumer goods to their labor income or tax changes, or the effect of interest-rate changes on the willingness or ability to buy homes." This situation was different. "It wasn't the case that people didn't have the money to go to restaurants—they *couldn't* go to restaurants." Airlines stopped flying. Car production ceased. Entire sectors had to be subtracted from the economy: "It was more arithmetic than econometrics."

On March 27, the *Times* ran an apocalyptic headline: "Job Losses Soar; U.S. Virus Cases Top World." Curiously, by that time, the Dow had reversed its plunge and begun a long climb that was strikingly at odds with the actual economy. In November, it once again reached record highs.

Steve Strongin is a senior adviser at Goldman. Sixty-two, he wears rimless glasses that lend him the aspect of a nineteenth-century European intellectual: Ibsen without the sideburns. "Markets very often get talked about as though they're some kind of giant casino," he told me. "But they actually have a deep economic function, which is to move capital, both equity and debt, from businesses that no longer serve a purpose to businesses we need *today*."

The market's initial reaction, Strongin said, was, "Somehow we are going to freeze in place, the virus will pass, and then we'll unfreeze." During that phase, Wall Street's function was to provide liquidity as clients turned to preservation strategies—raising cash, drawing on lines of credit—while waiting out the contagion. But the pandemic settled in like a dinner guest who wouldn't leave and was eating everything in the pantry.

"The moment when everybody was forced to reassess the severity and longevity of the crisis is when people realized that asymptomatic carriers were important," Strongin said. "That meant that all the prior controls were going to fail." Thousands of businesses would close. Nobody alive had seen a catastrophe of such scale. The rules had to change. The pandemic was a historic disrupter, forcing a shift from short-term to long-term thinking. Strongin, who once wrote a paper called "The Survivor's

Guide to Disruption," said, "Once that realization came into place, you saw the rush to opportunity."

Investors pivoted to a consolidation phase: going with the winners. The market recovery was led by five stocks—Facebook, Apple, Microsoft, Google, and Amazon—accounting for more than twenty percent of the S&P. However, "the Darwinian reality of capitalism is not about this brilliant insight into the five winners," Strongin said. "It's about taking money *away* from the fifty thousand losers. It's the core of the economic system—we don't prop up failures."

The most useful thing the government can do, he said, is help people start new small businesses: "The current split between the stock market and the employment numbers is a flashing warning that the economy and the people are not the same. If we don't spend real money, the pain will be very real, and the political consequences dangerous at best."

14. The Man Without a Mask

The third and final chance to contain the infection—masks—was the easiest, the cheapest, and perhaps the most effective. But the administration, and the country, failed to meet the challenge.

On March 4, as Matt Pottinger was driving to the White House, he was on the phone with a doctor in China. Taking notes on the back of an envelope while navigating traffic, he was hearing valuable new information about how the virus was being contained in China. The doctor mentioned the antiviral drug remdesivir—which was just emerging as a possible therapy in the United States—and emphasized that masks were extremely effective with COVID, more so than with influenza. "It's great to carry around your own hand sanitizer," the doctor said. "But masks are going to win the day."

Still on the phone when he parked his stick-shift Audi, on West Executive Avenue, next to the West Wing, Pottinger forgot to put on the parking brake. As he rushed toward his office, the car rolled backward, narrowly missing the vice president's limo, before coming to rest against a tree.

While the Secret Service examined the errant Audi, Pottinger kept thinking about masks. America's pandemic response had already been handicapped by China's withholding of information about human-to-human and asymptomatic transmission. The testing imbroglio would set the country back for months. But masks offered a ready solution.

Deborah Birx had told Pottinger that, whereas mask wearing is part of Asian culture, Americans couldn't be counted on to comply. Pottinger began to see America's public-health establishment as an impediment. The surgeon general, Jerome Adams, had tweeted, "STOP BUYING MASKS! They are NOT effective in preventing general public from catching #Coronavirus." Such messages were partly aimed at preventing the hoarding of hospital-grade masks, but they dissuaded people from adopting all forms of face covering. In those early days, the U.S. medical establishment looked at SARS-CoV-2 and flatly applied the algorithm for SARS: sick people should wear masks, but for others they weren't necessary. Redfield, of the CDC, told me, "We didn't understand until mid-March that many people with COVID weren't symptomatic but were highly infectious."

Pottinger, however, thought it was evident that, wherever a large majority of people wore masks, contagion was stopped "dead in its tracks." Hong Kong was one of the world's densest cities, but there was no community spread of the virus there because nearly everyone wore masks. Taiwan, which was manufacturing ten million masks per day for a population of twenty-three million, was almost untouched. Both places neighbored China, the epicenter. Pottinger's views stirred up surprisingly rigid responses from the public-health contingent. In Pottinger's opinion, when Redfield, Fauci, Birx, and Hahn spoke, it could sound like groupthink, echoing the way that their public messaging was strictly coordinated.

Nobody in the White House wore a mask until Pottinger donned one, in mid-March. Entering the West Wing, he felt as if he were wearing a clown nose. People gawked. Trump asked if he was ill. Pottinger replied, "I just don't want to be a footnote in history—the guy who knocked off a president with COVID."

Many NSC staffers work in the Situation Room, monitoring news and global developments. They are crammed together like workers in a call center. Pottinger asked the staff virologist to teach everyone how to mask up. Some people were annoyed. Masks had become a political litmus test, with many conservatives condemning mask mandates as infringements on liberty, and to wear one in Trump's White House seemed borderline treasonous. Pottinger was shocked to learn that, in any case, the White House had no ready supply of masks.

He called an official in Taiwan and asked for guidance about controlling the virus. Masks, he was told again. Soon after that call, Taiwan's president donated half a million masks to the United States, via diplomatic pouch. Pottinger took 3,600 for the NSC staff and the White House medical unit and sent the rest to the national stockpile.

In early April, new studies showed substantial reductions in transmission when masks were worn. Pottinger put copies of the studies into binders for key task-force members. A Chinese study reported on an infected traveler who took two long bus rides. He began coughing on the first ride, then bought a face mask before boarding a minibus. Five passengers on the first ride were infected, and no one on the second. Another study failed to detect any viral particles in aerosol or droplets from subjects wearing surgical masks.

On April 3, the CDC finally proclaimed that masks were vital weapons. It was the last opportunity to do something meaningful to curb the pandemic.

The CDC's sudden reversal, Redfield admitted to me, was awkward: "When you have to change the message, the second message doesn't always stick." Worse, when the president announced the new mask advisory, he stressed, "This is voluntary," adding, "I don't think I'm going to be doing it."

. . .

Trump is a notorious germophobe. He hates shaking hands and recoils when anyone near him sneezes. He once chastised Mick Mulvaney, on camera in the Oval Office, "If you're going to cough, please leave the room." Years before COVID, Trump told Howard Stern that he had a hand-washing obsession, which "could be a psychological problem." It's one of the only frailties he acknowledges. He seems fascinated by his horror of contamination.

How could such a man refuse to wear a mask in a pandemic? It wasn't just Trump, of course; the people around him followed his example. Pence visited the Mayo Clinic without a mask, violating hospital policy. Many Republican legislators shunned masks even after members of their caucus became infected. It wasn't just Republicans, but Democrats were twice as likely to say that masks should always be worn. It wasn't just men, but women were more in favor of masks. It wasn't just white people, but they were much more averse to mask wearing than Blacks and Latinos were. If you name each of the groups least likely to wear a mask, the result roughly correlates with the average Trump voter.

Some antimaskers called the coronavirus a hoax; others believed that it wasn't all that dangerous. But the image of the maskless president spoke to people, especially his base. He appeared defiant, masculine, invulnerable. He knew that the virus was dangerous—"more deadly than even your strenuous flus," as he told Bob Woodward, in a February interview that surfaced months later. Yet he dared the virus to touch him, like Lear raging against the storm.

Tens of millions of Americans emulated the president's bravado, and the unchecked virus prolonged unemployment, upended efforts to reopen the economy, and caused many more fatalities. "I'm not buying a fucking mask," Richard Rose, a thirty-seven-year-old army veteran from Ohio, posted on Facebook. "I've made it this far by not buying into that damn hype." He tested positive on July 1 and died three days later. There are many similar stories.

It's dispiriting to think that, had such a simple precaution been broadly implemented from the start, America could have avoided so much suffering, death, impoverishment, and grief. The starkest example occurred in Kansas, when the governor issued an executive order to wear masks in public but allowed counties to opt out. It was as if Kansas were performing a clinical trial on itself. Within two months, infections in mask-wearing counties had fallen by 6 percent; elsewhere, infections rose 100 percent.

Of course, wearing a mask was a much smaller burden than self-isolating. Although CNN repeatedly ran alarming footage of people who refused to stop going to bars or malls, a far greater number of Americans had listened to the experts, sequestering themselves for months, at tremendous financial and emotional cost. My wife and I live in Austin, and, as the quarantine dragged on, we forced ourselves to take an occasional drive, partly to keep our car battery alive. We'd snake through vacant streets downtown, grimly taking note of which businesses had boarded up since the previous drive.

One April afternoon, I went for a jog on a school track near my home. A group of young women were running time trials in the hundred-meter dash. They were the fastest people I had ever seen. Occasionally, as I came around a curve, I'd pull even with one of the women just as she was taking off. It was like Wile E. Coyote eating the Road Runner's dust.

"What school do you guys run for?" I asked one of them, who was cooling off.

"Oh, it's not a school," she said. "We're Olympians."

Instead of competing in Tokyo, here they were, on a middle-school track in Austin, isolating together and trying to maintain peak condition as they waited for the rescheduled Games. So many dreams have been deferred or abandoned.

15. "I Can't Breathe"

The corpse on the autopsy bench was a middle-aged Black man with COVID-19. Six feet four and 223 pounds, he had suffered from many of the comorbidities that Ebony Hilton had described to me. The medical examiner identified signs of heart disease and hypertension. The autopsy noted the presence of fentanyl and methamphetamine, which could be considered comorbidities, although they didn't really factor into this case. The cause of death was a police officer's knee on the neck. The victim was George Floyd.

On a video seen worldwide, four Minneapolis policemen killed Floyd as he was handcuffed and lying face down in the street. It was Memorial Day. One cop stood watch as two knelt on Floyd's back and held his legs while the fourth, Derek Michael Chauvin, pressed his knee into Floyd's neck for more than nine minutes.

At a time when health officials were begging people to stay home and avoid groups, protests arose in Minneapolis, then spread across America. They called to mind the Liberty Loans parades in 1918—the ones that had served as potent vectors for the killer flu. Nevertheless, 1,300 hundred public-health officials signed a letter supporting the demonstrations.

Hilton joined a protest in Charlottesville on June 7. Hundreds of people marched to the rotunda at the University of Virginia, carrying Black Lives Matter signs and placards saying "Let My People Breathe." I asked Hilton if she was worried about the mass gatherings. She said that she expected a rise in infections. Then she added, "For Black men, one in every thousand is at risk of dying in his lifetime from an encounter with a police officer. If you think about that number, that's what leads Black people to say it's worth me dying and going out to this protest and saying enough is enough. Police brutality is almost like a pandemic, a generational pandemic. It's a feeling—I'm going to die anyway, so I might as well risk this virus that I can't see, to speak about the virus of systemic racism that I *can* see."

Surprisingly, the marches did not appear to be significant drivers of transmission. "We tested thousands of people," Michael Osterholm, the director of the Center for Infectious Disease Research and Policy, at the University of Minnesota, said. "We saw no appreciable impact." One study found lower rates of infection among marchers than in their surrounding communities. Epidemiologists concluded that mask wearing and being outdoors protected the protesters. Moreover, demonstrators were on the move. Osterholm said that people in stationary crowds are more likely to become infected. In other words, joining a protest march is inherently less dangerous than attending a political rally.

16. Thelma and Louise

The president hadn't gathered with supporters since March and was eager to dive back into the pool of adulation. An event was scheduled for June 20. "It's going to be a hell of a night," he promised. He tweeted, "Almost One Million people request tickets for the Saturday Night Rally in Tulsa, Oklahoma!"

Only 6,200 showed up. Trump was enraged by the dismal turnout but delivered his usual blustery speech. Because Oklahoma had just seen a record increase in COVID cases, attendees were required to release the Trump campaign from responsibility for any exposure. Just before Trump went onstage, two Secret Service officers and six campaign staffers tested positive.

In the audience was Herman Cain, the former CEO of Godfather's Pizza and an erstwhile presidential candidate, who had become one of Trump's most prominent Black supporters. Like nearly everyone else, he was unmasked. He flew home to Atlanta the next day, feeling exhausted—"from his travels," his daughter, Melanie Cain Gallo, believed. It was Father's Day, and she stopped by to give him a gift. They embraced. She had seen a photograph of him at the rally and wondered why he hadn't worn a mask. Cain had preached the virtue of social distancing and hand washing on *The Herman Cain Show*, a web series that he hosted, and he had usually worn a mask in public. He told her that everyone entering the Tulsa auditorium had passed a fever check—an insufficient gauge.

Gallo worked with her dad all week on his show. By Friday, they were both feeling ill, but Cain filmed another episode. Flanked by the American flag and a painting of Ronald Reagan, he looked wan, his eyes rheumy. He quoted a newspaper headline: "U.S. Death Rate Falls for Third Day in a Row." Other newscasts had hyped rising case counts, he complained, adding, "They never get to the death rate is *falling*."

On Monday, both were sick enough to go to a clinic for a test. Cain was feeling weak, so he waited by the car while Gallo stood in a long line. Suddenly, he passed out. An EMS truck took him to the ER. "They checked him out and said he was fine," Gallo recalled. They returned to the testing clinic. Both were positive.

Her case was mild. On July 1, Cain was hospitalized. That day, he tweeted an article about a forthcoming Trump rally at Mt. Rushmore. "Masks will not be mandatory," Cain tweeted, adding approvingly, "PEOPLE ARE FED UP!" It was a defiant nod to Trump's base. Cain died on July 30. He was seventy-four.

•   •   •

For some public-health officials, Deborah Birx had become an object of scorn. "She's been a disaster," a former head of the CDC told me. The Yale epidemiologist Gregg Gonsalves tweeted, "Dr. Birx, what the hell are you doing? What happened to you?

Your HIV colleagues are ashamed." Birx was accused of enabling an incompetent and mendacious president. The mortified look on her face at the press briefing when he suggested injecting disinfectant or using powerful light—"inside the body, which you can do either through the skin or in some other way"—became a meme, underscoring how much Trump had compromised scientists. The public didn't know what she was saying in private.

Birx confided to colleagues that she'd lost confidence in the CDC. She disparaged the agency's hospital reports on COVID, which relied on models, not hard data. A CDC staffer told *Science* that compiling precise totals daily in a pandemic was impossible. But hospitals quickly complied after Birx said that supplies of remdesivir could be portioned out only to hospitals that provided inpatient COVID data.

In August, Dr. Scott Atlas, a neuroradiologist, a fellow at Stanford University's Hoover Institution, and a Fox News regular, joined the task force. He was adamant that children should return to school—as was the American Academy of Pediatrics, which urged a "safe return" to schools in the fall, warning of learning deficits, physical or sexual abuse at home, and depression. That was a debate worth having, but most of Atlas's views on COVID seemed reckless. He insisted that masks did little to stop the spread, and he advocated creating "herd immunity" by allowing the virus to be passed freely among people at lower risk. Herd immunity is gained when roughly 70 percent of a population has effective antibodies to the disease, through either infection or vaccination.

Once Atlas got to the White House, Trump stopped speaking to other health advisers. Herd immunity could be achieved by doing nothing at all, which became the president's unspoken policy. Atlas encouraged Trump and others to believe that the pandemic was waning. "His voice is really very welcome combating some of the nonsense that comes out of Fauci," Stephen Moore, a White House economic adviser, reportedly said. (The

White House denies that "the President, the White House, or anyone in the Administration has pursued or advocated for a strategy of achieving herd immunity.")

Birx and Atlas had it out in the Oval Office, in front of Trump. Birx accused Atlas of costing American lives with his unfounded theories. Atlas cursed her. Birx, who spent twenty-eight years in the army, gave it right back. Atlas said that young, asymptomatic people shouldn't be tested, adding, "She just wants to lock them down and not let them live their lives." They kept shouting at each other, but Trump was undisturbed and didn't take either side. "It's all reality TV to him," one of Birx's colleagues said.

After the confrontation, Birx demanded that Pence remove Atlas, but Pence declined. The task force began to dissolve after Atlas took a seat.

.　　　.　　　.

When Birx was working in Africa, she and her chief epidemiologist, Irum Zaidi, had met with presidents and village elders across the continent, learning the value of personal diplomacy. The two scientists decided to take an American road trip together. The contagion had moved from the coasts to the heartland. In June, when the virus suddenly gripped Texas, Birx and Zaidi traveled to Dallas to meet with Governor Greg Abbott. Abbott's dithering response to the pandemic had led to attacks by Democrats—who noted that the death rate soared when he lifted restrictions too soon—and by Republicans, who called him a tyrant for imposing any restrictions at all. At a press conference, Birx urged Texans to mask up, especially young people. "If they're interacting with their parents and grandparents, they should wear a mask," she said. "No one wants to pass the virus to others." She praised Abbott for closing bars, knowing that he was being pressured to fully open the economy. Abbott soon issued a mask mandate.

Zaidi grew up in Atlanta, and her father was a CDC statistician. On vacations, they took long car trips, a passion passed along to Zaidi. She loves to drive—fast. As they were leaving Dallas, a state trooper pulled her over. She'd been doing a hundred and ten.

"Little lady, what's the hurry?" he asked.

Zaidi explained that they'd just met Governor Abbott, and New Mexico's governor was next. "Surely you recognize Dr. Birx," she said.

The trooper let them off.

Soon after their visit to New Mexico, Governor Michelle Lujan Grisham announced a hundred-dollar fine for going maskless in public. Birx and Zaidi proceeded to Arizona and met with Governor Doug Ducey. Birx explained that even a small increase in the percentage of positivity—going from 3.5 to 5 percent—could spark an unmanageable crisis. Ducey soon declared, "If you want to participate in *any* good or service in Arizona, you're going to wear a mask."

Birx and Zaidi racked up 25,000 miles as they crossed the country eight times, visiting forty-three states, many more than once. They saw the rural areas and the cities, red America and blue America. They drove past cotton farms and soybean fields, but they also saw derelict oil rigs and abandoned factories, remnants of a vanishing industrial age. There were gleaming cities, bold and glassy, with construction cranes crowning the skyline, and broken towns, tumbling in decay, with all the promise bled out of them.

The women, who got regular COVID tests, established their own protocols. They cleaned rental cars and motel rooms with Clorox Wipes. In the morning, early, they'd pick up coffee and pastries at Starbucks. Lunch was often peanut butter spread on bread with a plastic knife. Dinner was served at a drive-through window. Baristas and gas-station attendants were useful informants of community outbreaks and served as indicators of local mask compliance. Birx and Zaidi met mayors and community organizers; they visited hospitals and nursing homes; they turned HIV activists into COVID activists. In Atlanta, they urged officials to test migrants working on chicken farms. They visited more than thirty universities. Those that conducted mandatory weekly testing of students had positivity rates below 1 percent; at schools where only symptomatic people were tested, positivity rates were 12 to 15 percent. Republican and Democratic governors made the same complaint: many people wouldn't listen as long as Trump refused to set an example.

One of the most effective governors Birx and Zaidi encountered was Jim Justice, of West Virginia. He issued a mask mandate, and in press briefings he read out the names of West Virginians who had died of COVID. He urged residents to "be great, loving neighbors." The state developed a plan to safely reopen schools by constantly assessing the level of risk in every county and presenting these data on a color-coded map. "It's something that every county and every state can do," Birx said. "West Virginia represents exactly what we want to see across the country—a commonsense approach based on the data."

•   •   •

A pandemic lays bare a society's frailties. Birx and Zaidi saw a nation that was suffering from ill health even before COVID attacked, where 40 percent of adults are obese, nearly half have cardiovascular disease, and one in thirteen has asthma. They visited reservations and met with Native Americans, who have been particularly ravaged by COVID. The Salt River Pima-Maricopa Indian Community, in Arizona, gave Birx a mask inscribed with the Salt River tribe's shield. When North Dakota recorded the nation's highest rate of infection, Birx met with the governor, Doug Burgum, and with local, state, and tribal officials. Birx scolded them: "This is the *least* use of masks that we have seen in retail establishments of any place we have been." She added, "It starts with the community, and the community deciding that it's important for their children to be in school, the community deciding that it's important not to infect the nursing-home staff who are caring for their residents." Burgum eventually agreed to a mask mandate. In South Dakota, Governor Kristi Noem couldn't find the time to meet with Birx.

For nearly six months, Birx corralled politicians, hospital executives, and public-health officials, often bringing such leaders together for the first time. She took charts and slides from state to state, promoting a simple, consistent message about masks, social distancing, transparency, and responsible leadership. She was the only federal official doing so.

One day in October, Birx and Zaidi were eating lunch at a roadside stop in Utah, beside the Bonneville Salt Flats, where land speed records are often set. The salt stretched out like a frozen sea.

They'd rented a blue Jeep Wrangler. "We have to go off-road, for just a minute," Zaidi said. Birx gazed at the great white emptiness. "As long as you don't hit anybody," she said.

17. Dark Shadows

I asked Dr. Fauci about the global-preparedness study calling America the nation best prepared for a pandemic. What happened? He emitted a despairing laugh and said, "We never got back to baseline"—the point when the contagion had been reduced enough to allow contact tracing to minimize spread. "It could be the fact that we didn't have a uniform strategy," he went on. "It could be our own culture right now, of people not wanting to be told what to do. The guidelines say 'Don't go to bars. Wear a mask.' And you look at the pictures in the newspaper and on TV and you see large crowds of mostly young people, not wearing masks."

Fauci, who has led NIAID through six administrations, has never seen this level of distrust and anger in the country. "Political divisiveness doesn't lend itself to having a coordinated, cooperative, collaborative response against a common enemy," he said. "There is also this pushback in society against anything authoritative, and scientists are perceived as being authority, so that's the reason I believe we have an antiscience trend, which leads to an antivaccine trend." Even with an effective vaccine—or several of them—social resistance could delay the longed-for herd immunity.

I asked Fauci if he'd been threatened. "Oh, my goodness," he said. "Harassing my wife and my children. It's really despicable. It's this Dark Web group of people who are ultra-ultra-ultra-far-right crazies. They somehow got the phone numbers of my children, they've tracked them where they work, they've harassed them with texts, some threatening, some obscene. We have gotten multiple death threats, my wife and I." He sighed and said, "It is what it is."

. . .

"Buy ammunition, ladies and gentlemen, because it's going to be hard to get," Michael Caputo warned, in a rambling Facebook Live event on September 13. Caputo is an assistant secretary of health and human services, and focuses on public affairs. He controls the flow of information from America's public-health establishment: the CDC, the FDA, and the NIH. Trump appointed Caputo to the post in April, when COVID was out of control; competence and transparency were needed to restore public trust. Caputo had no public-health expertise, and he claimed that his best friend was the notorious political operative Roger Stone.

Evidently, all the president wanted Caputo to do was reinforce his message that the virus wasn't as dangerous as scientists claimed and that the crisis was under control. Caputo presided over interventions by HHS that meddled with the CDC's guidelines—apparently, to get case numbers down and stanch the flow of bad news. Trump asked Caputo to lead a campaign to "defeat despair," which encouraged celebrities to endorse the administration's laissez-faire approach. To fund the campaign, Caputo snatched 300 million dollars from the CDC's budget.

Meanwhile, his science adviser, Paul Alexander, a part-time professor at a Canadian university, pushed an alternative plan: herd immunity. "It only comes about allowing the non-high risk groups to expose themselves to the virus," Alexander wrote to Caputo, in an e-mail obtained by *Politico*. "We want them infected."

Caputo's efforts met with resistance from Fauci and others, and he felt under siege. In the Facebook video, he was unshaven, sitting outside his house in Buffalo. "There are scientists working for this government who do not want America to get better," he said. "It must be all bad news from now until the election." He stared into space. "This is war. Joe Biden is *not going to concede*. The Antifa attacks, the murders that have happened, the rallies that have turned into violence—this is all practice."

•   •   •

Such embattled thoughts were shared by Adam Fox. A powerfully built man with a trim brown beard and a square face, he helped lead a militia called the Michigan Three Percenters—a reference to their belief that only 3 percent of American colonists took up arms against Britain in the Revolutionary War.

In a strip mall in Grand Rapids, a shop called the Vac Shack sells and services vacuum cleaners. Fox, a former employee, had been kicked out of his girlfriend's house and was homeless. The shop's owner let Fox sleep in the basement. That's where he allegedly began plotting to kidnap Gretchen Whitmer, Michigan's governor, who had enforced tough lockdown measures.

In June, at a gun-rights rally in Lansing, Fox met with members of a militia, the Wolverine Watchmen, who planned to kill police officers. They were infuriated by Whitmer's COVID restrictions, but, even before the pandemic, they'd been prone to anger.

"I'm sick of being robbed and enslaved by the state," one of the conspirators complained, after receiving a ticket for driving without a license.

Fox allegedly told the Watchmen that he was recruiting for an operation targeting the state capitol. He needed 200 men to storm the building and abduct politicians, including Whitmer, whom Fox called a "tyrant bitch." Although the plotters were mostly unemployed or in low-paying jobs, they spent thousands of dollars on a Taser and night-vision goggles and were planning to spend thousands more on explosives. They were plainly inspired by Trump's disparaging of Whitmer for shutting down her state. "LIBERATE MICHIGAN!" the President had once tweeted.

The FBI learned of the scheme, and arrested the conspirators in October. In a statement, Whitmer singled out Trump, who, in a recent debate with Biden, had refused to explicitly condemn right-wing, white-supremacist violence. "Words matter," she said. "When our leaders meet with and encourage domestic terrorists, they legitimize their actions and they are complicit."

Trump tweeted that "My Justice Department and Federal Law Enforcement" had foiled the plot, adding, "Rather than say thank you, she calls me a White Supremacist." He commanded Whitmer, "Open up your state."

On Michael Caputo's Facebook video, he sighed deeply. "I don't like being alone in Washington," he said. "The shadows on the ceiling in my apartment, there alone, those shadows are so long."

Soon afterward, he went on medical leave.

18. The Rose Garden Cluster

On September 26, eight days after the death of Supreme Court Justice Ruth Bader Ginsburg, Trump nominated her successor, Amy Coney Barrett, in a White House ceremony. The Reverend John Jenkins, the president of the University of Notre Dame, where Barrett had taught law, recalled, "We were required to wear a mask at entry and, after going through security, were immediately taken to a room and administered a nasal swab for a COVID test." Once a negative result came back, guests could remove their masks. "I assumed that we could trust the White House health protocols," Jenkins said. He regretted his decision: "I unwittingly allowed myself to be swept up very publicly into the image of a White House that sometimes seemed to disregard scientific evidence and minimize the threat of the pandemic."

Guests were ushered to the Rose Garden, where there were 200 assigned seats. Barrett spoke briefly. "Movement conservatives were very happy," Mike Lee, the Republican senator from Utah, recalled. Friends who hadn't seen one another for months reunited, he said, which "added to the jovial atmosphere." Afterward, dozens gathered in the Diplomatic Reception Room to meet the Barrett family.

That day, 769 American deaths from COVID were recorded—down from the spring peak, on April 15, of 2,752. Despite the absence of miracle drugs, the death rate for hospitalized patients had fallen significantly. In part, this was because the average age of patients was lower, but the improved chances of survival were also the result of flattening the curve, which gave doctors and scientists the time to devise more effective treatments, such as proning. The infection rate, however, was harder to slow. The number of cases per day, which had topped 75,000 in mid-July, had faded a bit in the late summer, but it was again rounding upward. After months of being more careful, Americans had apparently let down their guard.

The White House refused to say when the president had last been tested before the Rose Garden event. He had just made multiple campaign stops, in Florida, Georgia, and Virginia. More than a dozen guests—including Reverend Jenkins, Senator Lee, the former New Jersey governor Chris Christie, and the former presidential adviser Kellyanne Conway—soon tested positive. Without knowing Trump's testing history, no one can say when he contracted the disease or how many people he might have infected. The full extent of the Rose Garden cluster will never be known. Fauci labeled it a superspreader event.

Despite his germophobia, Trump is proud of his immune system, boasting on multiple occasions that he never gets the flu. But COVID hit him hard. According to *New York*, he told a confidant, "I could be one of the diers." A friend from the real-estate world, Stanley Chera, had died from it. "He went to the hospital, he calls me up," Trump recounted after Chera's death. "He goes, 'I tested positive.' I said, 'Well, what are you going to do?' He said, 'I'm going to the hospital. I'll call you tomorrow.' He didn't call." *Vanity Fair* reported that Trump developed heart palpitations. He asked aides, "Am I going out like Stan Chera?"

Hospitals are often portals to the graveyard, and that has been especially true during the pandemic. But Trump, who received a series of cutting-edge therapies, including monoclonal antibodies, was ready to return to the White House after three days. According to the *Times*, he considered hobbling out of the hospital and then yanking open his shirt to reveal a Superman logo. In the event, he saved his drama for the moment he stood again on the Truman Balcony and ripped off his surgical mask.

"Don't be afraid of COVID," he tweeted afterward. "Don't let it dominate your life."

19. Survivors

After Amy Klobuchar dropped out of the presidential race, she was on Biden's shortlist for his running mate. George Floyd's death put an end to that. She had begun her career twenty years earlier as the district attorney in Minneapolis, earning a reputation for being tough on crime but light on police misconduct. On June 18, she asked Biden to take her name off his list and urged him to select a woman of color as his running mate.

That day, she learned that her ninety-two-year-old father, Jim Klobuchar, had COVID. He was a retired newspaper columnist, and known to everyone in Minneapolis, especially cops and bartenders. Full of adventure, he was also often full of alcohol. When Amy was a young lawyer, her father was arrested for drunk driving. In a closed hearing, she encouraged him to take responsibility and plead guilty. He did so, and finally got sober. Now this vigorous old man, so troubled and so beloved, had COVID—and Alzheimer's. When Klobuchar visited him, at an assisted-living facility, they were separated by a window, and she believed that it would be her final glimpse of him alive. He recognized her, but couldn't understand why they had to remain separated. He sang to her: "Happy Days Are Here Again." He has since recovered.

.   .   .

Among the many awful legacies that COVID will leave, one blessing is that our understanding of coronaviruses and the tools to counter them has been transformed. Much of that progress will be because of Barney Graham, Jason McLellan, and other scientists who have spent their careers building to this moment.

There has never been such an enormous, worldwide scientific effort so intently focused on a single disease. More than 200 vaccines are in various stages of development. On December 11, the FDA granted its first Emergency Use Authorization for a COVID vaccine. Created by Pfizer, in partnership with the German firm BioNTech, it uses the modified protein that Graham and McLellan designed. In its third and final human trial, it was deemed 95 percent effective. Giant quantities of the vaccine had been prepared in advance of FDA approval. "Our goal is more than a billion doses by the end of 2021," Philip Dormitzer, Pfizer's chief scientific officer for viral vaccines, told me. The first employee at UVA's hospital to get the Pfizer inoculation was Ebony Hilton.

Operation Warp Speed, the government initiative to accelerate vaccine development, may prove to be the administration's most notable success in the pandemic.

Moderna's vaccine secured approval next. Its formulation proved to be 94.1 percent effective in preventing infection and, so far, it has been 100 percent effective in preventing serious disease. Graham is happy that he chose to work with Moderna. In 2016, his lab developed a vaccine for Zika, a new virus that caused birth defects. His department did everything itself: "We developed the construct, we made the DNA, we did phase 1 clinical trials, and then we developed the regulatory apparatus to take it into Central and South America and the Caribbean, to test it for efficacy." The effort nearly broke the staff. Moderna was an ideal partner for the COVID project, Graham told me. Its messenger-RNA vector was far more potent than the DNA vaccine that Graham's lab had been using.

In another major development, Eli Lilly recently received an Emergency Use Authorization for a monoclonal antibody that is also based on the spike protein that Graham and McLellan designed. It is similar to the treatment that President Trump received when he contracted COVID.

Graham had been in his home office, in Rockville, Maryland, when he got a call telling him that the Pfizer vaccine was breathtakingly effective—far better than could have been hoped for. "It was just hard to imagine," he told me. He walked into the kitchen to share the news with his wife. Their son and grandchildren were visiting. "I told Cynthia, 'It's working.' I could barely get the words out. Then I just had to go back into my study, because I had this major relief. All that had been built up over those ten months just came out." He sat at his desk and wept. His family gathered around him. He hadn't cried that hard since his father died.

Graham and his colleagues will not become rich from their creation: intellectual-property royalties will go to the federal government. Yet he feels amply rewarded. "Almost every aspect of my life has come together in this outbreak," he told me. "The work on enhanced disease, the work on RSV structure, the work on coronavirus and pandemic preparedness, along with all the things I learned and experienced about racial issues in this country. It feels like some kind of destiny."

. . .

More than a thousand health-care workers have died while taking care of COVID patients. Nurses are the most likely to perish, as they spend the most time with patients. On June 29, Bellevue held a ceremony to memorialize lost comrades. Staff members gathered in a garden facing First Avenue to plant seven cherry trees in their honor.

As the coronavirus withdrew from Bellevue, it left perplexity behind. Why did death rates decline? Had face masks diminished the viral loads transmitted to infected people? Nate Link thinks that therapeutic treatments such as remdesivir have been helpful. Remdesivir cuts mortality by 70 percent in patients on low levels of oxygen, though it has no impact on people on ventilators. Amit Uppal told me that the hospital has improved at managing COVID. "We now understand the potential courses of the disease," he said. Doctors have become more skilled at assessing who requires a ventilator, who might be stabilized with oxygen, who needs blood-thinning medication. Then again, the main factor behind superior outcomes may be that patients now tend to be younger.

When a patient is discharged, the event offers a rare moment for the staff to celebrate. On August 4, a beaming Chris Rogan, twenty-nine years old, was wheeled by his wife, Crystal, through a gantlet of cheering health-care workers, in scrubs and masks. There were balloons and bouquets. After so much death, a miracle had occurred.

Rogan was an account manager for a health-insurance firm in midtown. Crystal was a teaching assistant. In late March, he developed a low-grade fever and stomach discomfort, but he wasn't coughing. His doctor said that he probably had the flu. Rogan grew increasingly lethargic. He developed pneumonia. An ambulance took him to Metropolitan Hospital, on the Upper East Side. He still felt OK, even when his oxygen level fell to 64 percent. An hour after he checked in, he couldn't breathe. He was placed in a medically induced coma and intubated for nine days. During that time, the ventilator clogged and Rogan's heart stopped for three minutes. When he was brought back to consciousness, a doctor asked, "Did you see anything while you were dead?"

"No," Rogan said. "I don't even remember being resuscitated."

He began experiencing what hospital staffers told him was ICU psychosis. He told Crystal that he'd been stabbed as a child. He began conversing with God. Just before he was intubated again, on April 15, he felt certain that he would die in the hospital. He didn't wake up for sixty-one days.

During that time, he was transferred to Bellevue, which was better equipped to handle him.

It's a mistake to think that a patient in a coma is totally unaware. Rogan swam in and out of near-consciousness. When his doctor came in, he tried to talk to him: "Why am I awake? Why can't I move?" He couldn't sleep because his eyes were partly open. "It's like being buried alive," he told me.

His tenth wedding anniversary passed. Sometimes he heard Crystal's voice on video chat. "I hear you," he'd say, but she couldn't hear him. "I feel the tube down my throat, tell them to take me off the vent." A machine kept pumping oxygen into his lungs; *psht! psht! psht!* The sound pounded in his head. He would dream that he had left the hospital, then wake to find himself still there, the ventilator pumping away. "It was fucking torture," he said.

He developed internal bleeding. Clots formed in his legs. He told God that he didn't want to die—that he had too much left to do. God assured him that he was going to make it.

Crystal was charged with making choices for Rogan's care. The hardest one was the decision to amputate his right leg. It took three days to get him stable enough to perform the operation, which had to be done at his bedside, because he was too fragile to move. The doctors performed a guillotine amputation, just below the knee. Eight days later, they had to take off the knee.

Rogan doesn't remember any of that. Some days, he is elated to be alive; other times, he asks himself, "What kind of quality of life is this?" Whether or not it was ICU psychosis, he's clung to the experience of talking with God.

When he emerged from the coma, he couldn't move his arms, but now his right hand is functional. After several weeks of rehab, he can walk a bit with a prosthetic leg.

When he fell ill, there were only 150,000 cases in the United States. When he left the hospital, there were more than 4 million.

.   .   .

The death toll kept mounting, surpassing 300,000 at year's end. Some victims were famous. The playwright Terrence McNally was one of the first. The virus also killed Charley Pride, the first Black singer in the Country Music Hall of Fame, and Tom Seaver, one of the greatest pitchers in baseball history. Eighty percent of fatalities have been in people aged sixty-five or older, and most victims are male. It's been strange to find myself in the vulnerable population. I'm a year younger than Trump, so his adventure with COVID was of considerable interest to me. If I get ill, I'm not likely to receive the kind of treatment the president did, but I'm in better physical condition, despite a bout of cancer. My wife, though, has compromised lungs. Even before the coronavirus put a target on our age group, mortality was much on my mind. Sometimes I'm dumbstruck by how long I've lived; when I'm filling out a form on the internet, and I come to a drop-down menu for year of birth, the years fly by, past the loss of parents and friends, past wars and assassinations, past presidential administrations.

On September 9, our grandchild Gioia was born. She is the dearest creature. We stare into each other's eyes in wonder. Even in this intimate moment, though, the menace of contagion is present: we are more likely to infect the people we love than anyone else. Deborah Birx has recalled that, in 1918, her grandmother, aged eleven, brought the flu home from school to her mother, who died of it. "I can tell you, my grandmother lived with that for eighty-eight years," she said.

·   ·   ·

Even before the election, Matt and Yen Pottinger had decided that they were tired of Washington. He was burned out on the task force, which had drifted into irrelevance as the administration embraced magical thinking. They drove west, looking for a new place to live, and settled on a ski town in Utah. Matt will join Yen there once he wraps up his job in Washington.

Pottinger's White House experience has made him acutely aware of what he calls "the fading art of leadership." It's not a failure of one party or another; it's more of a generational decline of good judgment. "The élites think it's all about expertise," he said. It's important to have experts, but they aren't always right: they can be "hampered by their own orthodoxies, their own egos, their own narrow approach to the world." Pottinger went on, "You need broad-minded leaders who know how to hold people accountable, who know how to delegate, who know a good chain of command, and know how to make hard judgments."

At the end of October, before returning to DC, Pottinger went on a trail ride in the Wasatch Range. As it happened, Birx was in Salt Lake City. Utah had just hit a record number of new cases. On the ride, an alarm sounded on Pottinger's cell phone in the saddlebag. It was an alert: "Almost every single county is a high transmission area. Hospitals are nearly overwhelmed. By public health order, masks are required in high transmission areas."

Pottinger said to himself, "Debi must have met with the governor."

.   .   .

COVID has been hard on Little Africa. "Some of our church members have passed, and quite a few of our friends," Mary Hilton, Ebony's mother, told me recently. "We just buried one yesterday. They're dropping everywhere. It's so scary." A cousin is in the hospital.

"One out of 800 Black Americans who were alive in January is now dead," Hilton told me. "There would be another 20,000 alive if they died at the same rate as Caucasians." She added, "If I can just get my immediate family through this year alive, we will have succeeded." She and two colleagues have written a letter to the Congressional Black Caucus proposing the creation of a federal Department of Equity, to address the practices that have led to such disparate health outcomes.

Infected people keep showing up at UVA's hospital at a dismaying pace. Hilton recently attended the hospital's first lung transplant for a COVID patient. He survived. Lately, more young people, including children, have populated the COVID wards. Hospitals and clinics all over the country have been struggling financially, and many health-care workers, including Hilton, have taken pay cuts.

Thanksgiving in Little Africa is usually a giant family reunion. Everyone comes home. There's one street where practically every house belongs to someone in Hilton's family; people eat turkey in one house and dessert in another. Hilton hasn't seen her family for ten months. She spent Thanksgiving alone in Charlottesville, with her dogs.

.   .   .

Thanksgiving was Deborah Birx's first day off in months. She and her husband have a house in Washington, DC, and her daughter's family lives in nearby Potomac, Maryland. During the pandemic, they have been a pod. Recently, Birx bought another house, in Delaware, and after Thanksgiving she, her husband, and her daughter's family spent the weekend there.

Her access to the president had been cut off since the summer, and, with that, her ability to influence policy. She had become a lightning rod for the administration's policies. Then, in December, a news report revealed that she had traveled over the Thanksgiving weekend, counter to the CDC's recommendation. She was plunged into a cold bath of schadenfreude. Old photographs resurfaced online, making it look as if she were currently attending Christmas parties.

Birx indicated that she might soon leave government service.

20. Surrender

Austin bills itself as the "Live Music Capital of the World," but the bars and dance halls are largely closed. Threadgill's, the roadhouse where Janis Joplin got her start, is being torn down. The clubs on Sixth Street, Austin's answer to Bourbon Street, haven't been open for months. A band I play in has performed in many of them, but for the past several years we had a regular gig at the Skylark Lounge, a shack tucked behind an auto-body shop. Johnny LaTouf runs the place with his ex-wife, Mary. It's been shut since March 15.

"All small businesses have been affected, but music venues around the country were already in a struggle," Johnny told me. He's had to let go his ten employees—including three family members. That's only part of the damage. "When the musicians get laid off and the bands disperse and go their separate ways, then you've actually broken up *their* business." He added, "COVID killed off more than people with preexisting conditions. Lots of businesses have preexisting conditions."

Lavelle White, born in 1929, was still singing the blues at Sky-lark until the doors closed. "Some of our greater musicians are older, because it takes a lifetime to master the craft," Johnny said. Skylark was a mixing bowl where younger musicians learned from their elders. "Now that pathway is broken."

When Congress passed the CARES Act, which included money to support small businesses, local bars were not a priority. "There's no money," Johnny said Wells Fargo told him. He helps several older musicians with groceries, but he doesn't know how many in that crowd will ever return. Some have died from COVID.

•   •   •

Two qualities determine success or failure in dealing with the COVID contagion. One is experience. Some places that had been seared by past diseases applied those lessons to the current pandemic. Vietnam, Taiwan, and Hong Kong had been touched by SARS. Saudi Arabia has done better than many countries, perhaps because of its history with MERS (and the fact that many women routinely wear facial coverings). Africa has a surprisingly low infection rate. The continent's younger demographic has helped, but it is also likely that South Africa's experience with HIV/AIDS, and the struggle of other African countries with Ebola, have schooled the continent in the mortal danger of ignoring medical advice.

The other quality is leadership. Nations and states that have done relatively well during this crisis have been led by strong, compassionate, decisive leaders who speak candidly with their constituents. In Vermont, Governor Phil Scott, a Republican, closed the state early, and reopened cautiously, keeping the number of cases and the death toll low. "This should be the model for the country," Fauci told state leaders, in September. If the national fatality rate were the same as Vermont's, some

250,000 Americans would still be alive. Granted, Vermont has fewer than a million people, but so does South Dakota, which was topping a thousand cases a day in November. Scott ordered a statewide shutdown in March, which caused an immediate economic contraction. Governor Noem opposed mandates of any sort, betting that South Dakotans would act in their best interests while keeping the economy afloat. Vermont's economy has recovered, with an unemployment rate of 3.2 percent—nearly the same as South Dakota's. But South Dakota has seen twelve times as many deaths.

In Michigan, the state's chief medical officer, Joneigh Khaldun, is a Black emergency-room doctor. "She was one of the first to look at the demographics of COVID and highlight that we have a real racial disparity here," Governor Whitmer told me. "Fourteen percent of our population is Black, as were 40 percent of the early deaths." The state launched an aggressive outreach to Black communities. By August, the rates of both cases and fatalities for Blacks were the same as—or lower than—those for whites. The vast differences in outcomes among the states underscore the absence of a national plan. The U.S. accounts for a fifth of the world's COVID deaths, despite having only 4 percent of the population.

In August, the Pew Research Center surveyed people from fourteen advanced countries to see how they viewed the world during the pandemic. Ninety-five percent of Danish respondents said that their country had handled the crisis capably. In Australia, the figure was 94 percent. The United States and the U.K. were the only countries where a majority believed otherwise. In Denmark, 72 two percent said that the country has become more unified since the contagion emerged. Eighteen percent of Americans felt this way.

On March 16, Trump issued nationwide guidelines for closing schools, shutting down bars and restaurants, and limiting unnecessary travel and social gatherings. But that day marked a turning point. In his conversation with governors, he abandoned any effort to coalesce a national plan, and his administration began undercutting governors' attempts to acquire PPE Then, on April 3, Trump undermined the CDC's guidance on wearing masks: "You don't have to do it. *I'm* choosing not to do it. But some people may want to do it."

Trump, by his words and his example, became not a leader but a saboteur. He subverted his health agencies by installing political operatives who meddled with the science and suppressed the truth. His crowded, unmasked political rallies were reckless acts of effrontery. In his Tulsa speech, he said that he'd asked his health officials to "slow the testing down"—impeding data collection just to make his administration look better. When the inevitable happened and he contracted the disease, he almost certainly spread it. Every guest at the Barrett reception tested negative for the virus before entering. Trump may well have been the superspreader at the Rose Garden event.

Thepresident could have tried to bring the country together. In the press conference where he said that he wouldn't wear a mask, he praised the efforts of the Democratic governors of New York and New Jersey; he expressed sympathy for Michiganders, who were "getting hit very, very hard." He announced federal efforts to aid New York City. "America is engaged in a historic battle to safeguard the lives of our citizens," he said. "Our greatest weapon is the discipline and determination of every citizen to stay at home and stay healthy." The man who said those words might have been the president the country needed. But he was not that man.

He campaigned against Biden, but mainly he campaigned against the disease. "When the year started, he appeared unbeatable," Senator Lee told me. "My Democratic colleagues were discouraged about their chances. By the end of the impeachment trial, when we began hearing about the virus, we were not sure it would be a big deal. But it put an end to one of the things the president is best at—those big rallies." When Trump finally resumed them, defying medical advice, his fury was volcanic. "People are tired of hearing Fauci and all these idiots," he grumbled on October 19, when the number of new cases exceeded 65,000. "COVID, COVID, COVID, COVID, COVID, COVID!" he said at a rally in North Carolina, five days later. "We're doing great. Our numbers are incredible." That day, nearly 80,000 new cases were reported, overshadowing the highest levels of the summer. In Omaha, on October 27, he said of COVID, "I'm here, right?. . . I had it." Hospitalizations were up 46 percent that month. He ignored the fever sweeping through the Mountain West and the Great Plains—Trump country. His slogan was both cynical and fatuous: "If I can get better, *anybody* can get better."

Infections often rose in counties where Trump held a rally. The surge in infections and deaths mocked his assertions that we were "rounding the turn." The disease stalked him; it encircled him. On October 25, Trump's chief of staff, Mark Meadows, declared, "We are not going to control the pandemic." The administration had given up.

COVID couldn't kill Donald Trump, but it could defeat him.

Five days before the election, Biden spoke at a drive-in rally in Tampa. "So much suffering, so much loss," he said. "Donald Trump has waved the white flag, abandoned our families, and surrendered to the virus." Honking cars punctuated his remarks. That day, new confirmed cases topped 90,000.

The next day, Fauci said, "All the stars are aligned in the wrong place as you go into the fall and winter season, with people congregating at home indoors. You could not possibly be positioned more poorly."

Halloween night in Austin was beautiful, graced with a blue moon. My wife and I set out a bowl of chocolate bars and Dum Dums, but there were scarcely any trick-or-treaters. As dusk settled over the city, when our neighborhood would normally be filled with fairies and vampires, a deer galloped down the street.

21. "Get Here Now"

America is full of strivers whose dreams seem just out of reach. Iris Meda was one of them. She had a big smile but sad eyes. She grew up in Harlem, the oldest of six children. Her mother was a domestic who was home only one day a week; her stepfather was a longshoreman. Meda's first bed was an ironing board.

For most of her childhood, she was the family caretaker, walking her siblings to school before she went herself. Like many of her high-school friends, she dropped out after a bout of depression. She married and had two daughters. Meda eventually got a GED and surprised herself by graduating at the top of her class from Bronx Community College. In 1984, she earned a nursing degree from City College. Medicine fascinated her. She would go home and talk about watching a surgeon massage a patient's heart. She was drawn to those who were wounded or hurting—people who felt that the world wasn't big enough for them. For years, she was a nurse at the Rikers Island jail. She cared about the prisoners, and they knew it. When her husband was transferred to Dallas, she gave notice, and on her last day the inmates clapped her out. "She was always looking for an underdog to pull up, because she was an underdog," her daughter, Selene Meda-Schlamel, said.

Meda retired in January, after two years in the North Texas Job Corps. She had been in charge of on-site care, meaning that she was on call nights and weekends, and when she turned seventy she decided that she'd had enough. She and Selene had big plans. Meda wanted to travel; she wanted to ride in a convertible for the first time; she talked about writing a book. "In March, it all came to a screeching halt," Selene told me. Her mother was still a proud New Yorker, so she spent a lot of time in front of the TV watching Dr. Fauci and Governor Cuomo. "Her knowledge of science kept her ahead of the news reports," Selene said. Meda, having worked in nursing homes, hospitals, and jails, knew that COVID would be devastating for people who were confined and for those who took care of them.

Meda couldn't stand being idle during the crisis. "She wanted to teach," Selene said. "She wanted to encourage younger nurses to continue their education. She wanted them to reach their full potential in a way she almost didn't." Meda successfully applied for a job at Collin College, in Allen, Texas. At the time, courses were being offered virtually, and Meda imagined that she would be teaching online in the fall. When the semester began, she learned that many classes were in-person. According to the local NPR station, the college's president, H. Neil Matkin, had made his views of the virus known in an e-mail to trustees: "The effects of this pandemic have been blown utterly out of proportion across our nation."

Meda hoped to be in a large classroom where students could be widely spaced, but she was assigned to teach a lab for a nurse's-aide course. There was no social distancing. On October 2, a student was coughing and sneezing, complaining of allergies. That day, Trump announced that he had COVID. Meda was repulsed when he insisted on taking a car ride to wave at his supporters outside the hospital, with Secret Service agents in the car with him. Meda texted Selene, "He's putting all those people at risk just for a photo."

On October 7, Meda learned that the student had tested positive. The college chose to continue in-person classes even after one student died. By this time, Trump was out of the hospital, saying he felt "better than twenty years ago."

Meda became feverish on October 12. Two days later, she tested positive and went to the ER, but her oxygen level was not low enough for her to be admitted. On October 17, Selene took her mom back to the hospital. Meda was seriously ill, but the staff, worried about COVID, kept her waiting outside, slumped over on a bench in the ER drive-through. When the triage nurse finally waved Meda in, Selene wasn't permitted to join her, because she had been exposed. Meda's oxygen level was now so low that she couldn't speak. Selene didn't see her again for thirty days.

During that period, Meda was able to speak only once on the phone. Most days, she texted with Selene. One day, she asked

Selene to call a nurse who she thought was doing an excellent job. "She's having a hard day," Meda texted. She worried about her students and wondered if anyone else had caught the virus. (None showed symptoms.)

The disease progressed inexorably. Selene could tell that doctors were doing everything they could, but her mother's lungs wouldn't rebound. Selene wondered if things would be turning out differently had her mother received treatment earlier.

On November 14, Selene got a call advising that her mother's blood pressure was plummeting. "Based on how she's declining, how long do we have?" Selene asked, thinking that she would pick up her father, so that he could say goodbye. "A couple hours," the doctor said. Ten minutes later, a nurse called and said, "Get here now."

"They put me in a helmet," Selene recalled. "There was a plastic flap that closed around my neck. Inside the helmet there was a fan at the top that blew air down, so that any air that got in would be flushed away. And they put a gown on me, and double gloves, and they let me go in and say goodbye to her. That was the biggest shock, to see her, and to see how she looked. She was twice her size, because she was swollen from steroids. Her tongue was swollen and hanging out the side of her mouth because she was on the ventilator—she'd been intubated. They had to brace her head to keep it straight on the pillow, and they had tape around her mouth to keep the tube in. I'll never forget it. But I think the thing that will haunt me is the smell. It's like the smell of decay, like she had already started to die.

"The thing that made it so hard to see that was to juxtapose it against President Trump out there, saying he felt like he was twenty-eight years old again and he never felt better. So how could the same thing that did this to her, how could someone ever take it for granted that this was nothing, you have nothing to be afraid of?"

Selene gathered her mother in her arms as the machines went silent.

•   •   •

My wife and I voted early, in a drop-off location in Travis County, where 97 percent of eligible voters were registered. It was a new way of voting—swift, efficient, and rather exhilarating. And yet the vote came amid a crescendo of bad news. The week before November 3, the country added half a million new COVID cases, reaching record highs in half the states. The stock market had its worst week since the swan dive in March. Eight million Americans had fallen into poverty since the summer. At least five members of Vice President Pence's staff had been infected with COVID, as the virus continued to roam the White House.

In Texas, as in many Republican states, there were naked attempts to suppress the vote. Governor Abbott restricted the number of drop-off sites to one per county, including in Harris County, which has more than four million people. The attorney general, Ken Paxton, went to court to block the enforcement of a mask requirement at the polls, endangering voters as well as poll workers, who tend to be older. For the election, Abbott readied a thousand National Guard troops in major Texas cities, in anticipation of violence. Store owners in Dallas boarded up their windows, like beach communities awaiting a hurricane.

But there was no violence in Texas on Election Day. Voting is a simple act, and an act of faith. It is a pledge of allegiance to the future of the country. Across America, people waited in long lines to vote—despite the disease, despite attempts to discredit or invalidate their vote, despite postal delays, despite Russian or Iranian meddling, despite warnings from the White House that the president would not go quietly if he lost. They voted as if their country depended on it.

ProPublica

"The Black American Amputation Epidemic" was one of two stories by Lizzie Presser that won ProPublica the National Magazine Award for Public Interest this year. The second story was "Tethered to the Machine," which, like "The Black American Amputation Epidemic," explored racial disparities in health care. The judges in Public Interest said these stories were "elegant and gripping," adding that Presser's work "pushed the American Diabetes Association—and Congress—to take immediate steps to end preventable amputations." Articles written by Presser for the California Sunday Magazine, where she was a contributing writer, were nominated for the National Magazine Award for Reporting in 2018 and 2019. Presser is now a staff reporter at ProPublica. Her story "The Dispossessed," published by ProPublica and the New Yorker in 2019, won the George Polk Award for Magazine Reporting the following year.

Lizzie Presser

The Black American Amputation Epidemic

I t was a Friday evening in the hospital after a particularly gru-
eling week when Dr. Foluso Fakorede, the only cardiologist in
Bolivar County, Mississippi, walked into room 336. Henry
Dotstry lay on a cot, his gray curls puffed on a pillow. Fakorede
smelled the circumstances—a rancid whiff, like dead mice. He
asked a nurse to undress the wound on Dotstry's left foot then
slipped on nitrile gloves to examine the damage. Dotstry's calf
had swelled to nearly the size of his thigh. The tops of his toes
were dark; his sole was yellow, oozing. Fakorede's gut clenched.
Fuck, he thought. *It's rotten.*

Fakorede, who'd been asked to consult on the case, peeled off
his gloves and read over Dotstry's chart: He was sixty-seven, never
smoked. His ultrasound results showed that the circulation in his
legs was poor. Uncontrolled diabetes, it seemed, had constricted
the blood flow to his foot, and without it, the infection would not
heal. A surgeon had typed up his recommendation. It began:
"Mr. Dotstry has limited options."

Fakorede scanned the room. He has quick, piercing eyes, a
shaved head, and, at thirty-eight, the frame of an amateur bodybuilder. Dotstry was still. His mouth arched downward, and faint
eyebrows sat high above his lids, giving him a look of disbelief.
Next to his cot stood a flesh-colored prosthetic, balancing in a
black sneaker.

"How'd you lose that other leg?" Fakorede asked. Dotstry was tired, and a stroke had slowed his recall. Diabetes had recently taken his right leg, below the knee. An amputation of his left would leave him in a wheelchair.

Fakorede explained that he wasn't the kind of doctor who cuts. He was there because he could test circulation, get blood flowing, try to prevent any amputation that wasn't necessary. He hated that doctors hadn't screened Dotstry earlier—when he'd had the stroke or lost his leg. "Your legs are twins," he said. "What happens in one happens in the other."

Dotstry needed an immediate angiogram, an imaging test that would show blockages in his arteries. He also needed a revascularization procedure to clean them out, with a thin catheter that shaves plaque and tiny balloons to widen blood vessels. His foot was decaying, fast. Though Fakorede ran an outpatient practice nearby, when doctors consulted him on inpatients at Bolivar Medical Center, the local hospital, he expected to use its facilities.

He asked his nurse to schedule the procedures. But by the time he had driven home to his ranch house on the northern edge of town, he hadn't received an answer. Nor had he when he woke up on Saturday at three-thirty a.m., as he did every morning. By sunrise, he was restless at his kitchen counter, texting the hospital's radiology director, explaining the need for an intervention on Monday, Martin Luther King Jr. Day. Within a few hours, he got a response: "I don't have the staff or the supplies. I'm sorry."

Now Fakorede was mad, walking briskly into his office, dialing friends on speaker phone, pacing around his conference room. He'd been raised in Nigeria, moved to New Jersey as a teenager, and had come to practice in Mississippi five years earlier. He'd grown obsessed with legs, infuriated by the toll of amputations on African Americans. His billboards on highway 61, running up the Delta, announced his ambitions: "Amputation Prevention Institute."

Nobody knew it in January, but within months, the new coronavirus would sweep the United States, killing tens of thousands of people, a disproportionately high number of them black and diabetic. They were at a disadvantage, put at risk by an array of factors, from unequal health-care access to racist biases to cuts in public health funding. These elements have long driven disparities, particularly across the South. One of the clearest ways to see them is by tracking who suffers diabetic amputations, which are, by one measure, the most preventable surgery in the country.

Look closely enough, and those seemingly intractable barriers are made up of crucial decisions, which layer onto one another: A panel of experts decides not to endorse screening for vascular disease in the legs, so the law allows insurance providers not to cover the tests. The federal government forgives the student loans of some doctors in underserved areas, but not certain specialists, so the physicians most critical to treating diabetic complications are in short supply. Policies written by hospitals, insurers and the government don't require surgeons to consider limb-saving options before applying a blade; amputations increase, particularly among the poor.

Despite the great scientific strides in diabetes care, the rate of amputations across the country grew by 50 percent between 2009 and 2015. Diabetics undergo 130,000 amputations each year, often in low-income and underinsured neighborhoods. Black patients lose limbs at a rate triple that of others. It is the cardinal sin of the American health system in a single surgery. save on preventive care, pay big on the backend, and let the chronically sick and underprivileged feel the extreme consequences.

Fakorede grabbed his car keys and headed to the hospital. He walked straight to the lab. As he suspected, it had all the supplies that he needed. *Why won't they give me staff?* he wondered. *They wouldn't do that to a surgeon.*

He has little tolerance for this kind of transgression. He is militaristic, to an extreme. To him, nonhealing wounds are like heart attacks. "Time is muscle," he repeats. He calls huddles when nurses forget to check a patient's ankles: "If you haven't assessed both legs, I don't want to walk into that room." He considers each of his procedures an act of war. When people stand in his way, he sends a barrage of text messages, punctuated by exclamation marks. And he uses his cell phone to collect evidence that the system is working against his patients, and his efforts.

He pulled out his iPhone and photographed the hospital's wires and catheters, IVs and port protectors. He shot the images over to the hospital's radiology director. Fakorede's private practice was closed for the holiday weekend. He calculated that he had only a few days to carry out some plan before Dotstry's remaining leg was amputated.

· · ·

Two maps explain why Fakorede has stayed in the Mississippi Delta. One shows America's amputations from vascular disease. The second shows the enslaved population before the Civil War; he saw it at a plantation museum and was stunned by how closely they tracked. On his phone, he pulls up the images, showing doctors or history buffs or anyone who will listen. "Look familiar?" he asks, toggling between the maps. He watches the realization set in that amputations are a form of racial oppression, dating back to slavery.

Fakorede was initially tempted to move to the Delta while practicing in Tennessee. He befriended a medical-device sales rep named Maurice Hampton who had grown up in the Mississippi region. Hampton talked about how black families were leery of local hospitals and how few black doctors in the Delta specialized in vascular work. "It's the norm to go to Walmart and see an amputation or a permacath in the neck," he'd told Fakorede. "If you don't see one, then you didn't stay but two minutes."

Then, a little over a year into his Tennessee job, Fakorede found himself at loose ends. He'd raised concerns that he was being billed for expenses that weren't his and asked for an audit; though the audit later found that the clinic where he worked had claimed over $314,000 in improper expenses, he was quickly terminated. Fakorede sued the clinic for retaliation under the False Claims Act and lost. (The clinic's lawyer said his client had no comment, but there were "numerous" reasons for Fakorede's departure.) In the spring of 2015, he had a mortgage, a quarter of a million dollars in student debt, and four months of severance pay. He also had an impulse to understand the Delta.

Fakorede spent four days driving through its long, flat stretches of farmland dotted with small towns and shotgun houses. The wood-slat homes and bumpy roads reminded him of his grandparents' village in the Nigerian state of Ondo, where he'd spent summers as a kid. He drove scores of miles on the Mississippi highways without seeing a single grocery store; fast-food chains lit the busiest intersections. He was startled by the markers of disease—the missing limbs and rolling wheelchairs, the hand-built plywood ramps with metal rails. He thought of amputees like "an hourglass," he said, "that was turned the day they had their amputation." Mortality rates rise after the surgeries, in part, because many stop walking. Exercise improves circulation and controls blood sugar and weight. The less activity a person does, the higher the risk of heart attacks and strokes. Within five years, these patients were likely to be dead.

Fakorede weighed taking a lucrative job up north, near his parents, who had both been diagnosed with diabetes. He had professional connections there; he'd gone to Rutgers Robert Wood Johnson Medical School and done a residency at NewYork-Presbyterian Weill Cornell Medical Center. But the South, he felt, needed him. About 30 million people in America had diabetes, and Mississippi had some of the highest rates. The vast majority had type 2; their bodies resisted insulin or their pancreas didn't produce enough, making their blood sugar levels rise. Genetics played a role in the condition, but so did obesity and nutrition access: high-fat meals, sugary foods, and not enough fiber, along with little exercise. Poverty can double the odds of developing diabetes, and it also dictates the chances of an amputation. One major study mapped diabetic amputations across California, and it found that the lowest-income neighborhoods had amputation rates ten times higher than the richest.

The Delta was Mississippi's poorest region, with the worst health outcomes. Fakorede had spent years studying health disparities: African Americans develop chronic diseases a decade earlier than their white counterparts; they are twice as likely to die from diabetes; they live, on average, three years fewer. In the Delta, Fakorede could treat patients who looked like him; he could find only one other black interventional cardiologist in the entire state. A growing body of evidence had shown how racial biases throughout the medical system meant worse results for African Americans. And he knew the research—black patients were more responsive to and more trustful of black doctors. He decided after his trip that he'd start a temporary practice in Mississippi, and he rented an apartment deep in the Delta.

He fantasized about building a cardiovascular institute and recruiting a multidisciplinary team, from electrophysiologists to podiatrists. But as he researched what it would take, he found a major barrier. Medical specialists with student debt, who graduate owing a median of $200,000, generally could not benefit from federal loan-forgiveness programs unless they got jobs at nonprofit or public facilities. Only a few types of private-practice providers—primary care, dentists, psychiatrists—qualified for national loan forgiveness. The Delta needed many other physicians. Though Bolivar County was at the center of a diabetes epidemic, there wasn't a single diabetes specialist, an endocrinologist, within one hundred miles.

Fakorede leased a windowless space in the Cleveland Medical Mall, a former shopping center that had been converted to doctors' offices. People came to him with heart complaints, but he also asked them to remove their socks. Their legs alarmed him.

Their toes were black and their pulses weak. Their calves were cold and hairless. Some had wounds but didn't know it; diabetes had numbed their feet. Many had been misdiagnosed with arthritis or gout, but when Fakorede tested them, he found peripheral artery disease, in which clogged arteries in the legs limit the flow of blood.

This is what uncontrolled diabetes does to your body: Without enough insulin, or when your cells can't use it properly, sugar courses through your bloodstream. Plaque builds up faster in your vessels' walls, slowing the blood moving to your eyes and ankles and toes. Blindness can follow or dead tissue. Many can't feel the pain of blood-starved limbs; the condition destroys nerves. If arteries close in the neck, it can cause a stroke. If they close in the heart, a heart attack. And if they close in the legs, gangrene.

Within a month, Bolivar Medical Center had credentialed Fakorede, allowing him to consult on cases and do procedures in the hospital. His most complicated patients came in through the emergency room. Some arrived without any inkling that they had gangrene. One had maggots burrowing in sores. Another showed up after noticing his dog eating the dead flesh off the tips of his toes. Fakorede took a photo to add to his collection. "It was a public health crisis," he told me. "And no one was talking about amputations and the fact that what was happening was criminal."

On weekends, Fakorede had been driving back to his five-bedroom home in Tennessee, but in August of 2015, he decided to go all-in on Bolivar County. He sold his house and black Mercedes G-Wagon and applied for funding to build a practice in the Delta: Cardiovascular Solutions of Central Mississippi. He pitched himself as a heart guy and a plumber, removing buildup in the arteries. Four banks denied him loans, so he borrowed money from friends. He gave himself a two-year window to reduce amputations and publish his outcomes.

•   •   •

The Delta flood plain runs 7,000 square miles along the north-western edge of the state, with sweet-smelling, claylike soil cordoned between bluffs and the banks of the Mississippi River. By the nineteenth century, the primeval forests had been transformed into a cotton empire; at the start of the Civil War, more than 80 percent of people in many Delta counties were enslaved. Sharecropping emerged after emancipation, and black farmers cultivated small plots in return for a portion of their crop. They lived on credit—for food and feed and clothing—until the harvest, but even then, their earnings rarely covered their expenses.

For decades, African Americans in the South struggled to find and afford health care. The American Medical Association excluded black doctors, as did its constituent societies. Some hospitals admitted black patients through back doors and housed them in hot, crowded basements. Many required them to bring their own sheets and spoons or even nurses. Before federal law mandated emergency services for all, hospitals regularly turned away African Americans, some in their final moments of life.

Fakorede was drawn to Bolivar County, in part, because of its history. He'd run out of gas there when he was first scouting the region, and later that evening, he'd Googled its background. For a brief moment, Bolivar was the center of a movement for public health care, driven by the conviction that racial equality was not possible without justice in health. In 1964, when a group of physician activists traveled to the Delta, Robert Smith, a black doctor from Jackson, saw rocketing rates of intestinal parasites and maternal death. "I understood for the first time what it truly meant to be black in Mississippi," he told a magazine. Under President Lyndon B. Johnson's War on Poverty, a Boston doctor secured funding to open a community health center in Bolivar, which he grew with the help of Smith. Clinicians worked with residents to take on housing, sanitation, exercise, and nutrition. Its success spawned a national project of more than a thousand Federally Qualified Health Centers for the underserved. But funding shrank under President Richard Nixon, and the centers' initiatives were scaled back to basic primary care.

By the time Fakorede moved to the Delta, in 2015, the state had the nation's lowest number of physicians per capita. It had not expanded Medicaid to include the working poor. Across the country, 15 percent of African Americans were still uninsured, compared with 9 percent of white Americans. That year, Jennifer Smith, a professor at Florida A&M University College of Law, wrote in the National Lawyers Guild Review what Fakorede saw firsthand: "While the roots of unequal and inequitable health care for African Americans date back to the days of slavery, the modern mechanisms of discrimination in health care has shifted from legally sanctioned segregation to inferior or non-existent medical facilities due to market forces."

Fakorede understood that to reach patients, he needed referrals, so he met primary care providers at hospitals and clinics. He asked them to screen for vascular disease, measuring blood pressure at the ankle and the arm. Many didn't have the time; given the shortage of local physicians, some were seeing up to seventy patients a day. Others didn't know much about peripheral artery disease or why it was important to diagnose. Some were offended by Fakorede's requests. Michael Montesi, a family doctor, was grateful for the help, but he found it brash for the new doctor in town to start telling the veterans what to do. He recalled thinking, "Where were you the first twelve years of my practice, when I needed a cardiologist, when I needed an OB-GYN, when I needed a surgeon, when I had to do an amputation in the ER, or deliver a baby that was twenty-three weeks and watch the baby die because there was nobody there that could take care of him?"

The brush-offs disturbed Fakorede, but when he dug deeper, he realized that the doctors weren't only overwhelmed; they had no guaranteed payment for this vascular screening. The Affordable Care Act mandates that insurers cover all primary care screenings that are recommended by the U.S. Preventive

Services Task Force, an independent panel of preventive care experts. The group, though, had not recommended testing anybody without symptoms, even the people most likely to develop vascular disease—older adults with diabetes, for example, or smokers. (Up to 50 percent of people who have the disease are believed to be asymptomatic.) As specialists, cardiologists are reimbursed if they screen patients with risk factors. But by the time patients got to Fakorede, the disease was sometimes too far along to treat. Many already had a nonhealing wound, what's known as "end stage" peripheral artery disease, the last step before an amputation.

When Luvenia Stokes came to Fakorede, she had already lost her right leg at the age of forty-eight. Like many Delta residents, she grew up in a food desert, and without money for fresh produce, she'd developed diabetes at a young age. She said that a pedicurist nicked her toe, and the small cut developed an infection. Without good blood flow, it began bubbling with pus. Stokes told Fakorede that no doctor had performed an angiogram to get a good look at the circulation or a revascularization to clean out the arteries. A surgeon removed her second toe. Without cleared vessels, though, the infection spread. Within weeks, a new surgeon removed her leg.

Stokes lived in a single-wide trailer with her mother. Her wheelchair could not fit in the doorways, so she inched through sideways with a walker. Because she could hardly exercise, she gained forty-eight pounds in two years. The amputation hadn't treated her vascular disease, and a stabbing pain soon engulfed her remaining leg, "like something is clawing down on you," she said. When she finally made it to Fakorede, she told him that one doctor had prescribed neuropathy medication and another had diagnosed her with arthritis. "I'm not letting them get that other leg," Fakorede told her. Stokes's grandmother, Annie, who lives in a nearby trailer, had lost both her legs, above the knee, to diabetes. Her cousin Elmore had lost his right leg, too.

General surgeons have a financial incentive to amputate; they don't get paid to operate if they recommend saving a limb. And many hospitals don't direct doctors to order angiograms, the most reliable imaging to show if and precisely where blood flow is blocked, giving the clearest picture of whether an amputation is necessary and how much needs to be cut. Insurers don't require the imaging, either. (A spokesperson for America's Health Insurance Plans, a leading industry trade association, said, "This is not an area where there is likely to be unnecessary surgery.") To Fakorede, this was like removing a woman's breast after she felt a lump, without first ordering a mammogram.

Nationwide, more than half of patients do not get an angiogram before amputation; in the Delta, Fakorede found that the vast majority of the amputees he treated had never had one. Now, he was determined to make sure that no one else lost a limb before getting the test. This wasn't a controversial view: The professional guidelines for vascular specialists—both surgeons and cardiologists—recommend imaging of the arteries before cutting, though many surgeons argue that in emergencies, noninvasive tests like ultrasounds are enough. Marie Gerhard-Herman, an associate professor of medicine at Harvard Medical School and a cardiologist at Brigham and Women's Hospital, chaired the committee on guidelines for the American College of Cardiology and the American Heart Association. She told me that angiography before amputation "was a view that some of us thought was so obvious that it didn't need to be stated." She added: "But then I saw that there were pockets of the country where no one was getting angiograms, and it seemed to be along racial and socioeconomic lines. It made me sick to my stomach."

Stokes wasn't at immediate risk of losing her left leg when she met Fakorede, but pain prevented her from walking. She had a severe form of the disease, and Fakorede booked her for an angiogram and revascularization. He inserted a wire into her arteries and cleaned out the clogged vessels, letting oxygen-rich blood rush to her remaining foot. While she was recovering in Fakorede's lab, she thought about her neighbors who had the same problems. "I really don't like what's happening to us," she said to me. "They're not doing the tests on us to see if they can save us. They're just cutting us off."

Patients didn't know about vascular disease or why their legs throbbed or their feet blackened, so Fakorede went to church. The sales rep, Hampton, introduced him to pastors, and several times each month, he stood before a pulpit. He told the crowds that what was happening was an injustice, that they didn't need to accept it. He told them to get screened and if any surgeon wanted to cut off their limbs, to get a second opinion. In the lofty Pilgrim Rest Baptist Church, in Greenville, he asked the congregation, "How many of you know someone or know of someone who's had an amputation?" Almost everyone raised their hands.

At first, Fakorede took a confrontational approach with colleagues. Some seemed skeptical that he could "prevent" amputations; it's a tall claim for a complex condition. Once, when a doctor had disregarded his advice, he'd logged it in the electronic health record, so the oversight would be on display for anyone who looked up his patient's chart. Fakorede could fume when people questioned his authority; self-confidence carried him, but it sometimes blinded him to his missteps. Over time, though, Fakorede tried to rein in the arrogance. "You peel off a layer that may be comprised of: I'm from up North, I know it all, you should be thankful we're here to provide services that you probably wouldn't get before." He picked up some Southern manners. Fakorede began texting doctors with photos of their patients' feet along with X-rays of their arteries, before his intervention and afterward. Referrals picked up, and within a year, he'd seen more than 500 patients.

But Bolivar Medical Center, he learned, was turning away people who couldn't pay a portion of their revascularization bill up front. Several former employees told me the same. "It's a for-profit hospital, it's no secret, it's the name of the game," Fakorede said. "But a for-profit hospital is the only game in town in one of the most underserved areas. So what happens when a patient comes in and can't afford a procedure that's limb salvage? They eventually lose their limbs. They'll present back to the emergency room with a rotten foot." And a surgeon would have no choice but to amputate. (A hospital spokeswoman said that last year, it gave $25 million in charity care, uncompensated care, and uninsured discounts. Asked if it turned away patients who couldn't pay for revascularization, she did not respond directly: "We are dedicated to providing care to all people regardless of their ability to pay.")

The practice was discriminatory, he reasoned, and also financially backward. At $237 billion in medical costs each year, diabetes is the most expensive chronic disease in the country; one of every four health-care dollars is spent on a person with the condition. Left untreated, the costs pile on. Medicare spends more than $54,000 a year for an amputee, including follow-ups, wound care, and hospitalizations; the government program is the country's largest payer. Then come the uncounted tolls: lost jobs, a dependence on disability checks, relatives who sacrifice wages to help with cooking and bathing and driving.

By the time Carolyn Williams came to see Fakorede, in 2016, she'd been uninsured with diabetes for twenty years; she'd worked at a housing nonprofit and for a food-assistance program, but neither had offered coverage. At the age of thirty-six, she'd needed a triple bypass surgery, and at forty-four, she had three toes amputated. Untreated leg pain left her needing a wheelchair; she pulled out of Delta State University, where she was pursuing a degree in social work. Fakorede reconstituted blood flow in her legs and got her walking. But the diabetes was already destroying her kidneys. She joined the government's disability rolls. She also went on dialysis, at a yearly cost to Medicare of $90,000.

On the days when Fakorede wanted to give up and leave, he drove to an Emmett Till memorial in Money, Mississippi. After fourteen-year-old Till was mutilated and murdered, in 1955, his mother had insisted on opening his casket. "Let the people see what I've seen," she said, and his image brought national outrage to racist violence in the South. Fakorede thought often about how that decision sparked the Civil Rights Movement. He thought about it as he exhibited his photos of rotten feet and limbless bodies, his own proof of what he considered a modern atrocity. He didn't want to live by Bolivar Medical's policies. He decided that in order to treat as many people as possible, irrespective of income or insurance, he needed to build a lab of his own.

. . .

This January, that lab was now Dotstry's best shot. The hospital's consulting surgeon expected to amputate his leg below the knee. He had written that because Dotstry's kidneys were impaired, the contrast dye in an angiogram would be dangerous. But Fakorede could replace the dye with a colorless gas, which wouldn't jeopardize Dotstry's health.

It would have made the most sense to perform the procedure at the hospital; Dotstry had been admitted and was occupying a bed. But after Fakorede opened his outpatient lab and hired away two techs and a nurse, a spokeswoman said the hospital stopped doing certain interventions. She told me it shouldn't have surprised Fakorede that they couldn't schedule Dotstry's case and that if he had been unable to treat a patient in his lab, the hospital could have worked with him to find another. Fakorede told me he'd never received such a message. When a doctor asks him to treat an inpatient with an acute condition, his responsibility, as he sees it, is to do it in the hospital. "If I don't have a hospital that wants to coordinate," he asked, "what do I do?"

The answer, at least this time, was to get his patient out of there. He called Dotstry's doctor and convinced her to discharge him for the intervention. Then, at noon on Saturday, Fakorede walked back into room 336. Dotstry's sister, Judy, was standing by his bed. She wore tall leather boots over acid-washed jeans, with a thick, black wig in a braid down her back.

Fakorede handed over his card. "I called the hospital to see if we can do this case on Monday," he said, "and they said no."

Judy inhaled. "What now?"

Fakorede laid out the plan for a Monday morning angiogram in his own procedure room. He would open up as many vessels as he could. If he could get circulation to Dotstry's foot, he might be able to save it. He wasn't sure about the toes.

When Dotstry had suffered his stroke several years back, Judy had become his caregiver. She'd stopped taking jobs in home care and supported her brother without pay—shuttling him to doctors' appointments, controlling his sugars, managing his medications. After his amputation, she'd helped him learn to walk again. In place of a salary, she'd drawn disability for an old work injury; she'd been electrocuted while operating a machine, and the nerves in her arm were damaged, making her hands tremble. But she couldn't stay unemployed forever. This past fall, she had gone back to work, cleaning the local post office.

After Fakorede left, Judy looked over at her brother, who sat slumped over the side of the cot, a blue gown slipping off his bony shoulders. Their father had been a sharecropper, and Dotstry had dropped out of elementary school to help on the farm, harvesting soybeans, rice, and cotton. Of ten kids, he was the oldest boy, and he took care of the others, bringing in cash and cooking them dinner. They almost never saw a doctor. Instead, they'd relied on cod liver oil or tea from hog hoofs, parched over a fire.

Dotstry had spent his career driving tractors, hauling ,crops and plowing fields, but he wasn't insured and still rarely saw doctors. At sixty, when he was diagnosed with type 2 and prescribed insulin, he didn't know how to manage the medicine properly; he had never learned to read. Insulin pumps were too expensive— more than $6,000. His blood sugar levels often dropped, and he sometimes passed out or fell on the job. Little by little, his employer cut back his duties. In 2015, he had a stroke; diabetes had raised his risk. A year later, his right foot blackened and was amputated at the ankle. The infection kept spreading, and soon, his lower leg went. He could no longer work.

Two of his sisters had died after complications of diabetes. Judy had stood over their beds like she was now standing over Dotstry's. *He's still here*, she reminded herself.

She pulled out her phone and called another brother. "They gonna amputate his foot, cause it's bad," she said. "Toe's rotted."

Dotstry looked up from the bed. "No!" he shouted. "They can't take that off. Why?"

"Why you think your foot look like that? Why you think it smells? It stinks!" she said. Dotstry reached down to unwind the gauze. Judy wondered why he hadn't told her that his foot was infected sooner. She lowered her voice. "You were doing pretty good. If you wasn't, I could have tried to get back in there and do something."

Her daughter, Shequita, ran into the room, huffing. She was loud and pissed off. "Whose foot is that?" she shrieked. She kneeled by the cot and helped Dotstry scoot up onto his pillow, stretching out his legs. He was usually a prankster, a hard-headed contrarian, the uncle who'd picked her up and spun her around like an airplane. She was thrown off by how quiet he'd become.

"Your daughter wants to know if you want to come stay with her, if you want to come to Texas," Shequita told him.

Dotstry knew the offer was on the table, but he hadn't yet accepted. A few days earlier, a tornado had torn the roof from his trailer, and he was, for the moment, without a home.

"She said it's a lot better doctors up there," Shequita continued, "and if she gotta stop working to take care of you, she can do that." She gripped her hands around the frame of the bed and leaned over it, locking her eyes with his. "I need you to be thinking hard about this, sir. This ain't you. I need you to get back to *you*."

"He ain't gotta go to Texas," Judy interrupted.

Shequita shot back: "You gonna take care of him?"

Judy was silent. She knew that she couldn't, not like before. She needed her paycheck for home repairs; a flood had warped her wooden floors. But Dotstry's daughter was younger, and Judy thought that if she quit her job at Walmart, she'd get restless. Besides, Dotstry knew no one in Texas. She pictured him in a wheelchair, staring off, confused about where he was. Judy figured if he went, he'd go on and die.

She crossed her arms. "He'll be all right if they don't have to amputate that leg," she said.

Shequita looked at her mother. She walked over to where she stood, by a shaded window, and threw her arms around her neck. Then she left the room. Judy hoisted herself up onto the foot of her brother's cot. She swung her legs up so that she faced him, and she laid herself down.

•　　•　　•

About every five years, the doctors and researchers who make up the U.S. Preventive Services Task Force reassess their screening guidelines. In 2018, the members returned to peripheral artery disease and the blood flow tests that Fakorede had asked local primary care doctors to conduct. Once again, the panel declined to endorse them, saying there was not enough evidence that the tests benefited the average asymptomatic American.

In their statement, they acknowledged that public commenters had raised concerns that the disease "is disproportionately higher among racial/ethnic minorities and low-socioeconomic populations" and that this recommendation "could perpetuate disparities in treatment and outcomes." In response, the panel said it needed better evidence. But as the National Institutes of Health has found, minorities in America make up less than 10 percent of patients in clinical trials.

Dr. Joshua Beckman, the director of vascular medicine at Vanderbilt University Medical Center, was an expert reviewer of the evidence base for the task force, and its final report struck him as irresponsible. It hardly noted the advantages of treatment after screening; the benefits were right there in the data that he saw. The panel discounted the strongest study, a randomized control trial, which demonstrated that vascular screening, for men ages sixty-five to seventy-four, reduced mortality and hospital days. (The study bundled peripheral artery disease screening with two other tests, but in Beckman's eyes, the outcomes remained significant.) He was confused about why the task force had published its evaluation of screening the general public when it was clear that the condition affects specific populations. Several American and European professional society guidelines recommended screening people with a higher risk. "You wouldn't test a twenty-five-year-old for breast cancer," he told me. "Screening is targeted for the group of women who are likely to get it."

Dr. Alex Krist, the chair of the task force, repeated the group's position in an email that the data were not strong enough to endorse screening, even for at-risk patients. "The Task Force does not do its own research, so we can't fix these research gaps, but we can—and did—ring the alarm bell to raise awareness of this vital issue among researchers and funders."

Vascular surgeons who have spent their careers studying limb salvage have come to see preventive care as perhaps more important than their own last-ditch efforts to open blood vessels. Dr. Philip Goodney, a vascular surgeon and researcher at Dartmouth and White River Junction VA Medical Center, made a name for himself with research that showed how the regions of the country with the lowest levels of revascularization, like the Delta, also had the highest rates of amputation. But revascularizations aren't silver bullets; patients still must manage their health to keep vessels open. Now, Goodney believes his energy is better spent studying preventive measures earlier in the disease's progression, like blood sugar testing, foot checks, and vascular screening. Many patients have mild or moderate disease, and they can be treated with medicine and counseled to quit nicotine, exercise, and watch their diet. "We need to build a health system that supports people when they are at risk, when they are doing better and when they can keep the risk from coming back," he told me. "And where there's a hot spot, that's where we need to focus."

Fakorede scrolled through the task force's statement. "You want more data? Really? Who has the highest amputation rates in America?" he asked. "That's your data." He had taken to the national stage, speaking at conferences about what he'd witnessed in Bolivar. On behalf of the Association of Black Cardiologists, he testified before Congress, convincing U.S. Rep. Donald M. Payne Jr., a Democrat from New Jersey, along with U.S. Rep. Gus Bilirakis, a Republican from Florida, to start a Congressional Peripheral Artery Disease Caucus. The group is pushing for the task force to reevaluate the evidence on screening at-risk patients, for federal insurers to start an amputation-prevention program, and for Medicare to ensure that no amputation is allowed before evaluating arteries. Other groups are advocating for legislation that would require hospitals to publicly report their amputation rates.

In Bolivar, Fakorede had seen more than 10,000 cardiovascular patients from around the Delta. Dr. DeGail Hadley, a primary care provider in town, told me that before Fakorede arrived, he wasn't sure what was best to do for patients with rotting feet. "It was always a process of transferring the patients to Jackson or Memphis, which can be difficult." Both cities were two hours away. Now, Fakorede was performing about 500 angiograms annually in town. Last year, he published a paper in *Cath Lab Digest* describing an 88 percent decrease in major amputations at Bolivar Medical Center, from fifty-six to seven. (Fakorede did not provide me with all of his sources.) The hospital has different internal figures, which also reflect a significant decrease. Between 2014 and 2017, the hospital recorded that major amputations had fallen 75 percent—from twenty-four to six.

Fakorede couldn't catch everyone in time, and he was haunted by the patients who got to him too late. A week before he'd met Dotstry, Sandra Wade had come in with an open sore on her right big toe. She came from a family of diabetics. Her mother had died after a diabetic coma. Her cousin had just lost a leg. Her oldest sister, who'd raised her, had given up on walking when a tired, burning, itching sensation consumed her legs. Now, Wade felt it, too.

"I don't want to give up like that," Wade had said, reclining in a cot in Fakorede's pre-procedure room. "I want my toes. I don't want to lose not one limb. I choose life." She elongated her O's. She was fifty-five and had a high, gentle voice, a wide smile, and big, curled lashes under loose, curled hair. She had spent most of her career in food service and retail, recently managing a Family Dollar, but after diabetes took her eyesight, she'd had to quit. She wondered if the sodas and chips that had fueled her at the store had accelerated her disease. Or if she'd focused so much on her son, who was developmentally disabled, that she'd neglected herself. She didn't like to offload blame onto her genes. "Somebody's gotta try to change the cycle," she'd said. "I really want to be the one."

Fakorede inserted an IV into the top of her leg. He opened up each of her blocked arteries, one at a time, until he got to the most important one, which ran along her inner calf. It was supposed to supply blood to her open wound, and she needed it to heal. Without it, she'd likely lose her toe. If she didn't control her sugars, she could lose her lower leg next. Fakorede was hopeful as he slid a wire through the vessel in her knee, and into that crucial artery in her calf. But then, about a third of the way down, it stopped. It was as if the vessel itself had evaporated.

.   .   .

Under a crisp, wide sky, on Martin Luther King Jr. Day, churches around town were opening their doors for services. Fakorede's office was scheduled to be closed, but he'd called in his nurses and radiology technicians, even those out hunting deer, to staff Dotstry's case.

"What's up, young man?" Fakorede greeted Dotstry, who was slowly fading into his Ambien, and he handed Judy a diagram of a leg. "The prayer is that we can find this many vessels to open up," he said, pointing to the paper. "As soon as I'm done, I'll let you know what I find."

In the procedure room, he put on his camouflage-patterned lead apron, and with an assistant, he inserted an IV near Dotstry's waist. He wound a wire across Dotstry's iliac artery, into the top of his left leg. The femoral artery was open, even though it had hardened around the edges, a common complication of diabetes. They shot a gas down the arteries in Dotstry's lower leg so the X-ray could capture its flow. Fakorede looped his thumbs into the top of his vest, waiting for the image. Other than a small obstruction, circulation to the toes was good. "They don't need to whack off the knee," he said, staring at the screen. Dotstry would lose one toe.

After they'd cleaned out the plaque, Fakorede called Judy into the lab and pulled up the X-rays. Dotstry snored in the background. The doctor showed Judy a playback of the blood moving through the vessels. She could tell that his foot had enough flow. She folded over, running her palms along her thighs. "Y'all have done a miracle, Jesus."

Dotstry would need aggressive wound care, help controlling his sugars and a month in rehab following his toe amputation. In the meantime, Judy and her daughter would have to learn to manage his antibiotics and find him an apartment. He'd still be able to tinker with his cars, as he did most afternoons. And as far as Judy was concerned, he wasn't moving to Texas.

Fakorede scrubbed out. He sat at his desk to update Dotstry's doctors. He called an infectious disease specialist, thirty-five miles south, to check on whether he could see Dotstry the following morning. Then he dialed the hospital and asked for one of the nurses. He explained what he'd found: that Dotstry didn't need a leg amputation.

"Oh, great," the nurse replied. "The surgeon was calling and asking about that. He called and tried to schedule one."

Fakorede had been typing up notes at the same time, but now he stopped. "He was trying to schedule it when?" he asked.

"He was trying to schedule it today."

Reveal

The Public Interest judges' citation explains nearly everything you need to know about this story: "In 2013 a ten-year-old girl from Honduras arrived in the United States—and subsequently disappeared into the federal immigration system. This heartbreaking narrative tells the story of her six years in custody. The result is a portrait of a broken, callous system that has failed countless children—none more so than one girl and the family that spent years trying to find her." Written by Aura Bogado, "The Disappeared" was published by Reveal *from the Center for Investigative Reporting, a nonprofit newsroom where Bogado is a senior reporter and producer.* Reveal *was also nominated this year for the National Magazine Award for Podcasting for three episodes of* American Rehab, *hosted by Al Letson, which showed how a well-known drug-rehabilitation organization turns patients into unpaid laborers.*

Aura Bogado

The Disappeared

O n the fifth floor of the tall glass federal building in Portland, Oregon, the immigration court hums in hushed tones, an air of reverence coming from a dozen or so fidgety children and teenagers. They sit in two long pews that line the back of the room, facing the elevated bench of the immigration judge.

A massive Department of Justice seal towers over the bench, flanked by giant windows that allow a glimpse of the downtown skyline. At one table, an attorney representing Immigration and Customs Enforcement faces the judge. Every ten minutes or so, a new young client makes their way around the table, ready to face the full brunt of the U.S. immigration system. Not one is here with an adult family member. Each time, an attorney steps forward to represent them. Sometimes it's the same attorney for several clients in a row. The room feels prim, almost quaint, dissonant for a space in which each decision can mean the difference between life and death.

On this cold afternoon in January, there is one girl in particular I've come here to see.

The girl, now seventeen, has been in U.S. immigration custody since she was ten years old. Since presenting herself at the border and seeking asylum in late 2013, she has been separated from her family, shuttled back and forth between shelters and foster homes across the United States, from Oregon to Massachusetts to Texas to Florida, and back to Texas and Oregon again, from what I've been able to piece together.

She's become a long-term resident of what's supposed to be a short-term system. I wonder if she's ever had a friend for more than a few months, if she's gotten a real education, if she's learned to speak English. I wonder when she last got a hug from anyone who loves her.

What I do know is that, after all these years, she wants out. She's come to court today to try and deport herself from the United States.

Her case is up first. Dressed neatly in a lace-trimmed blouse with her hair pulled back, the girl stands up from the second row of seats and timidly makes her way toward the respondent's table. She takes a seat next to her attorney and puts her headphones on so that an interpreter can help her make sense of the proceedings. Now, she seems excited.

Judge Richard M. Zanfardino reads out her name.

"Yes," she confirms. "Sí."

The judge notes that a letter from the girl's child advocate, whom the government has previously appointed to look out for her best interests, supports her request to leave the United States but with four recommendations. He doesn't list them all in court, but he addresses one in particular. While ICE *standards* call for the agency to provide up to a thirty-day supply of medications to people who are being deported, the advocate has recommended that ICE provide the girl with a sixty-day supply.

The ICE attorney asks for time to consider the recommendations. But the girl's attorney, Caryn Crosthwait, says her client wants to leave the country as soon as possible and rejects any proposal to extend the departure request.

Judge Zanfardino points out that he can't order ICE to do anything and can only encourage the agency to make its best efforts. It's true: immigration judges lack the autonomy of criminal and civil court judges; while they can administer oaths and interrogate witnesses, they cannot always order immigration authorities to take a particular action. Whether she would be sent away with a two-month supply of medications was entirely up to ICE.

The entire proceeding lasts around twenty minutes. At the end, Judge Zanfardino gives the seventeen-year-old what she came here for.

"You've been granted the voluntary departure request that your attorney filed on your behalf," he tells her.

The girl is clearly elated. She's grinning from ear-to-ear as she stands and turns to face the two rows of seats behind her, which are dotted with other children here for their own hearings. Then she steps outside of the courtroom to confer with her attorney.

But there is something the girl doesn't know, that I've just recently learned. She still has a family in the United States, and they want her home. It's unlikely that I'll get to talk with the girl, but her family has given me a message for her just in case. An hour or so after the judge's ruling, in the court's elevator lobby, I manage to hand the girl a few pieces of paper, just as her chaperone is rushing her away from me.

"Take them," I tell her in Spanish. She does.

Among the papers is a photograph of the relatives she hasn't seen in more than six years. She sees the photo and makes a hard stop.

"Son ellas," she says to her chaperone. It's them—her family.

She looks back at me bewildered, as if asking me to help her make sense of this almost impossible moment in the dull lobby. The last time the girl saw most of her relatives was in 2013, before the government rendered her and her brother unaccompanied minors. She was separated from him less than a year and a half later, for reasons I haven't been able to figure out. She has, on rare occasions, spoken with her brother by phone, but she's lost contact with everyone else in the family photo I've just handed her.

The women who raised her have told me they were never informed of the sister and brother's separation within the system.

•　　•　　•

The child I encountered in court that day is one of an unknown number of kids who have simply disappeared into the U.S. immigration system—specifically, into the bowels of the Office of Refugee Resettlement, or ORR, the federal agency charged with the care and reunification of unaccompanied minors. I've tried to get that figure through records requests and have been stonewalled; *Reveal* from the Center for Investigative Reporting is currently suing the government under the Freedom of Information Act. From conversations with attorneys and current and former shelter staff, a report from the California attorney general, and from a partial list obtained from ORR, I've found evidence that at least seven kids were in the system for at least two years—far longer than the two or three months ORR's director has told Congress is the average length of stay. That partial list, obtained from ORR through a previous public records lawsuit filed by *Reveal*, indicates one boy was held for more than three years. A declaration in a federal lawsuit was written by a girl who'd been in the system for four years. And the ORR list indicates another boy was in the system for five years before being discharged.

There are laws, rules, and legal settlements guiding ORR's handling of children that I had assumed would prevent something like this from happening. But I have learned through my reporting that the government can pretty much do whatever it wants. It can take a child from their family without explanation. It can detain a child indefinitely.

The girl's story would have likely gone unknown outside of a few case managers and lawyers had I not come across a scrap of information a few months ago: a child had been in the system for six years, longer than any case I'd heard of. A girl from Honduras.

I didn't have much else to go on other than her full name and the name of the town where she grew up but was told she had mentioned the first name of an aunt who had raised her.

I knew that it was ORR policy not to speak to reporters about any individual child's case. So I set out to find that aunt on my own, to see if she could help me piece together the girl's story. I searched on Facebook for women in Honduras, then in Mexico and the United States, going through hundreds of searches. But she had a pretty common name, and I came up dry. So I started searching for anyone with the girl's last name who lived in the small town where she grew up. And I finally stumbled upon a very distant relative who remembered something about a girl who'd gone to the United States and then went missing. And that person knew the aunt.

It turns out the aunt wasn't in Honduras. She was living in rural North Carolina, where I reached her by phone. She told me she was the girl's sponsor, that she had put together all the paperwork to reunify the family and take custody of both the girl and her brother all the way back in 2013. But she never got the kids. She didn't know why. Then, one day, less than a year and a half later, she couldn't get in contact with them anymore. No one answered the phone number she usually dialed to connect with the kids, which belonged, she thought, to their case worker or case manager. And she said she never got a call from that number again.

All these years, the girl didn't know what had happened to her family. And the family didn't know what had happened to their girl.

Now I could see why the girl might have chosen what's known as voluntary departure. I could see how her expectation of being reunified with her family might have turned into anger and hopelessness. I could see her choosing freedom—any kind of freedom—after being held in custody for nearly half her life.

No one from ORR, no case manager or advocate or attorney had informed the family about the girl's court date or her desire to self-deport. Her family found out from me, and I'd only found out about the hearing a day before it took place, some six weeks after I first spoke with her aunt.

Katharine Gordon, an immigration attorney who worked as a child advocate between 2015 and 2017, told me that while a birth parent would usually be told about a child's decision to choose voluntary departure, there was little clarity about whether another family member serving as a sponsor, like the girl's aunt, would typically be notified.

Fearful of traveling to immigration court and even more fearful of government agents, case workers and attorneys, the family hoped that my reporting would lead me to their girl. They had a message they wanted me to share if I got the chance: That they missed her. That they hoped they would see one another soon. And that she shouldn't sign any deportation papers because they wanted her back—not back in their hometown in Honduras, but with them in North Carolina.

They were terrified about what would happen to her if she was sent back to Honduras.

The message might have been too late: Judge Zanfardino had just granted her deportation request. She's required to leave soon. Maybe ICE will put her on a plane today, maybe they'll do so next week.

But Judge Zanfardino ruled that she must leave, to a place she hardly even knows, no later than May 15.

.   .   .

Weeks before I attended the girl's court hearing, my early conversations by phone with the aunt were bundled with emotion. Some of it was confusion. How could I, a stranger, have any information about the child she had raised? A lot of what I heard was sheer sorrow.

She told me about how Doña Amalia, the kids' grandmother and matriarch of the family, has prayed daily during all of these long years, both for the children's safety and for the family to find out what happened. She began to tell me why the family had left Honduras to begin with. It started with the story of Santos, one of her sons.

Like other family members, Santos crossed and recrossed multiple borders to get to the United States from Honduras, back when it was much easier to do so undetected in the late 1990s and early aughts. As a teenager and into his mid-twenties, he worked painting houses in North Carolina and sent money to family back home in Honduras, across the same borders he'd crossed himself.

By 2005 Santos was in his late twenties and had found something much more lucrative than painting houses: dealing cocaine. The following year, he was sentenced to prison in North Carolina for drug trafficking. He was eventually deported to Honduras in early 2012. He had just turned thirty-five and was welcomed back home to their rural hillside community. He reconnected with the girl, whom he'd previously met when she was still a baby, and met his other cousin, the girl's brother, for the first time.

By this time, the girl had grown into a spirited and inquisitive child who enjoyed helping others with whatever task they were working on. Family members describe her as deeply affectionate.

The aunt calls it one of the happiest times of her life: Her son was finally back home. Later that spring, they all got to spend Mother's Day together.

He'd be dead a week later.

Honduras—a country smaller than the state of Louisiana—had the world's highest rate of homicide in 2012. Santos was one of more than *7,000 people* killed there that year when he was gunned down while driving his truck, the one he used for his burgeoning lumber business, hauling fresh cuts to market. His killers lit his vehicle on fire, and bystanders dragged Santos' body out.

As the family made plans to bury the body, they also started to map their escape. They had gotten threats of violence before.

But they no longer felt simply like threats—now it seemed they could materialize into sexual assault or death without further warning.

Over the course of the next year, Doña Amalia, her two daughters, several grandchildren, and a great-granddaughter, Dayani, all found their way to the Honduran capital of Tegucigalpa. From there, Doña Amalia supervised the sale of the family's cows and other family possessions. What they couldn't sell they gave away.

The family used the money from the sale of the livestock to get to Mexico—some to Chiapas and others to Mexico City—a final stop before heading to the United States in small groups to claim asylum. They arrived at the U.S. border during the first year of President Barack Obama's second term.

Doña Amalia and the aunt went a few months ahead of the rest of the family so that they could set up a home to welcome the others in rural North Carolina, where several family members already lived, most working in painting and construction. Santos himself had lived there, part of a growing community with ties to Honduras.

Doña Amalia and her daughter presented themselves to immigration officials at the border so they could claim asylum. They told officials they were fleeing violence, passed their initial screening, and were released by Customs and Border Protection ahead of an unscheduled immigration court date. Then they made their way to North Carolina and found a place to live.

The girl and the boy then arrived at the border with another aunt and cousin, and likewise told officials they were seeking asylum, according to documents the aunt in North Carolina was given when she filed to be the children's sponsor.

Family members said the four were first placed in a holding cell. It wasn't too cold, as some holding cells are, and everyone was given aluminum blankets to cover themselves if needed. Within a few hours, the girl and her brother were taken away. The aunt and her daughter stayed behind and were ultimately released.

Records indicate the children were moved to the custody of ORR and into the care of a contractor called Morrison Child & Family Services in Portland, Oregon, in November 2013. They were placed in a program called Micasa, which specialized in short-term foster care for unaccompanied minors under the age of fourteen. The girl was ten, and her brother was eight.

If the government can't place children with a birth parent, it is ORR policy for shelter staff to find other relatives in the country who are fit to care for them. The family expected a short separation but was sure that the children would be with them within a few months, which government data show is about average.

ORR classifies minors into four tiers for reunification: Category 1 applies to children who have a parent or legal guardian, such as a stepparent, in the United States. Children in category 2 have immediate relatives such as an aunt, a grandparent or a cousin. Category 3 is for children with a sponsor who is a distant relative or an unrelated adult. Children with no sponsor are placed in category 4.

While ORR would not comment on how the children were formally categorized, their aunt in North Carolina seeking sponsorship would appear to put the boy in category 2 and the girl, because she is a stepchild, in either 2 or 3.

All sponsors have to prove they're suitable in the eyes of ORR by agreeing to an extensive background check, and the children's aunt was deeply engaged in that process.

She said every time a case worker or case manager made a new request, she fulfilled it: birth certificates from Honduras that required the help of people in the United States and Honduras, address confirmation for her new place in North Carolina, proof of her eleven-dollars-an-hour wage for her construction job, with which she would financially support the children. The aunt had just arrived to a new country in the wake of the gruesome murder of her son but said she did everything that was asked of her.

First through texts and later in person, family members provided me with some of these documents, along with other communications that confirm the federal government had identified the aunt as the children's sponsor.

A fax dated August 15, 2014, says that then-Morrison case manager Yesenia Avalos sent a security plan, which included guidelines for the children's release and resources that would be available afterward. The document indicates the government was, at this time, anticipating the release of the children to the family. Morrison spokesperson Patricia DiNucci wouldn't comment on the children's cases or their time at Morrison and declined the opportunity to answer general questions about Morrison's policies related to staff communication with sponsors.

"Please take the time to review and read the documents," reads the cover page, in the aunt's native language of Spanish.

The aunt said she reviewed the security plan with other family members, signed in agreement, and sent it back by fax. Three days later, Avalos sent over background check forms, which were also completed and signed by the family and later shared with me.

The aunt said she was able to talk with the children from time to time throughout this first year, usually by video call. Over the course of those calls, while the children were living with their first foster family, the Honduran family began to see the girl change. She told them that the foster family's rules were too strict and she longed to be back with the family she knew and loved.

Daisy Camacho-Thompson, an assistant professor of psychology at California State University, Los Angeles, and one of the authors of a policy brief on the effects of family separation, said that ten-year-olds, on the cusp of adolescence, are especially vulnerable to stress.

"It is harmful to children to be separated from a caring adult at any point during development," Camacho-Thompson said. "That said, because adolescence is a sensitive period in human development, trauma during this time can have long-term physical, psychological, and physiological effects, impacting cognitive and emotional development."

She said that transitions—like migrating to a new country or even moving to a new school—are tough for kids. Family support can help cushion the impact, but family separation during periods of significant change can expose children to what researchers call "toxic stress" that can result in long-term negative effects. The longer a child is separated, Camacho-Thompson said, the worse the outcomes are for that child.

.   .   .

As the children were approaching a year in the refugee agency's custody, their aunt held out hope that they'd be reunited. During this period, other children in the family who'd arrived at the border had already been processed through the system and released to other family members. The aunt believed that it was still just a matter of time.

But the siblings weren't released. Instead, they were transferred to another foster care program.

The family is unsure of when it started, but around this time the girl began to tell them that she was cutting herself; her grandmother recalls that it was the tender skin on the inside of her arms. On the video calls, she told the family she hated life without them and wanted to end hers out of desperation. One time, she rammed her head into a wall, busting it open so badly she required a brief hospitalization. Her aunt and grandmother learned this from her, after the fact; they said they were never notified by ORR. And they said their child had never harmed herself before coming to the United States.

The girl wasn't hospitalized only for self-injurious behavior. Doña Amalia and other family members recall that the girl had an operation that may have been a tonsillectomy, another procedure they learned about only afterward. The family said they weren't informed about it by ORR or given the chance to opt the girl out. They said they likely wouldn't have opposed the procedure but said case workers who were in communication with the family never informed them or gave them options when it came to medical decisions.

Gordon, the immigration attorney, told me that's not uncommon. "I wasn't aware of any policy that required consent," she told me.

With the girl's situation deteriorating, in early 2015, the process fell apart. They stopped getting calls from anyone associated with the girl's case. And their calls weren't being answered. The family wouldn't hear from the two children again—or hear anything about them—for five years.

They said they called and called the phone number that had previously connected them to the children. For months, there was no answer. Eventually, the line was disconnected. A few of the children's records were lost as the family moved around North Carolina, and some were ruined in a flood in 2016. But several were carefully saved in two plastic bags, and in one I found a document with phone numbers related to the girl's former case worker. One was out of service. Another had a new user who's unrelated to the federal shelter system.

There are some circumstances in which the government will decide not to place children with their sponsors, such as when ORR discovers that a family member has a history of abuse or a criminal record. If that happened in this case, I've been unable to find a record of it. And the family was never told. They recalled no phone call, letter, or any communication that explained why the government didn't release the children to them.

It's true that the girl isn't related to her aunt and grandmother by blood. The girl's mother gave birth to her before getting involved with Doña Amalia's son, the boy's father. But the girl was raised in Doña Amalia's household in Honduras, just like her brother, and was part of the family. Even if this detail mattered to ORR—and the family says they were forthcoming about it—it could only have shifted the girl from category 2 to category 3. And the sponsorship process had appeared to be well underway until, suddenly, it wasn't.

.   .   .

Every morning and every night, Doña Amalia prays for her two grandchildren. It's the very first thing she does when she makes her way out of bed to put a pot on for coffee. And it's the last thing she does before she lies down to rest at the end of the day. Everyone in the family pines for the children, but at ninety-four, Doña Amalia is the one most worried she'll never see them again.

It's not like Doña Amalia didn't try to find out what happened. She said she petitioned God every day.

"I'd ask, are they dead? How are they, my God? How must those children be? Suffering? Naked? Hungry?"

Other family members had come into contact with case managers like Yesenia Avalos, but no one helped them get their children back. They didn't know who to turn to and became increasingly scared that they might be targeted for deportation themselves.

The family was petrified of the government—not just of government officials but also of everyone in the whole shelter system.

For the aunt and other family members, a system that disappeared two children would most certainly disappear adults, too. Disappear them into immigration detention. Disappear them back to Honduras to face almost certain death. Or disappear them into the jaws of the unknown, just like their children.

So they prayed. And cried. And waited.

Doña Amalia made a point to name under whose leadership this happened: Obama. "They let us in," she said. "But they took our children."

Doña Amalia doesn't think about the children only on holidays and birthdays. For the matriarch, thoughts about the children are constant and all-consuming.

Tending to her hens meant thinking about how the girl used to help with the chickens back in Honduras. Putting on a pot of beans for the day would summon memories of the boy eating lunch. Taking a walk would remind her of how much the children loved to stroll the coffee fields that surrounded their childhood home. Every detail of her day evoked the children. After years of thinking about them, the girl and the boy became the permanent backdrop to her way of being.

Her husband was killed in a brawl decades ago. Her grandson was shot and set on fire. She's known hunger and experienced deep poverty. She's lived through violence and threats of violence. She may dwell upon those traumas from time to time, but she said their presence pales in the face of her constant thoughts about the children.

Doña Amalia has other grandchildren and great-grandchildren, and spending time with them brings her clear joy. But the mystery of what happened to her two missing grandchildren weighs on her. "It's as if they were dead. We knew nothing. Nothing," she said.

For the family, this isn't separation. For them, these children were disappeared.

·　　·　　·

After I reached out to ask her about the girl, the aunt wanted to know something. If I was capable of locating her in North Carolina and learning where the girl was in Oregon, was I capable of finding the boy inside the system?

It was unlikely. There are few public records about minors. Fine-toothing social media could help—but the boy's name is so common that hundreds of children popped up on social as soon as I searched. I friended and sent messages to countless fourteen-year-olds with the same name who wished me luck but said they weren't the person I was looking for. On December 11, however, I was sure I had found the right kid. I located a phone number for him, we texted briefly, and then I gave him a ring.

Yes, it was the boy. On the phone, he was surprised and suspicious but sweet. He'd been living with a foster family in Massachusetts for several years. Yes, the girl was his sister. And although he didn't acknowledge it immediately, yes, his aunt and Doña Amalia in North Carolina were indeed the ones who raised him back in Honduras. He speaks Spanish but was more comfortable in English. He rattled off his favorite and least favorite classes at school. He told me he felt loved and supported by his foster family and was happy with them. We hung up after saying we'd talk again.

"Can I call you tomorrow with my stepmom so we can keep talking more," he texted me, adding that he had to get to sleep since it was a school night.

"All good," I responded.

A couple of hours later, I heard from the woman who fosters the boy, the one whom he calls his stepmom. She was warm and communicated a clear concern and compassion for the child she says she's been raising for around five years. There wasn't too much she could share, but she had questions about whether what he had said to her was correct—if his family was really in North Carolina. I assured her that it was.

The boy gave me permission to let the family know about him, and I knew this was information I had to deliver in person. I printed out a stack of photos of the boy that I'd found online, cleared a date to meet with Doña Amalia, the aunt, and Dayani in person, and booked a flight to North Carolina. I had something I wanted to share, I told them.

A week or so later, sitting on a sectional around a coffee table, with Christmas tree lights helping to illuminate the room, I handed the family photos of their boy. I wondered if they'd know who he was.

Silence gave way to sudden gasps.

"Look at him."

"He has earrings!"

"He's so big now."

Through sobs, laughter, and near disbelief, the family confirmed that this was their boy. He was a lot taller and thinner than they remembered him—a fourteen-year-old now, whom Doña Amalia hadn't seen since he was seven years old in Chiapas.

"And these photos?" asked Dayani, who is now twenty-two. "Where is he, what state is he in?"

"He's in Massachusetts," I told her.

"Have you spoken with him?"

"Yes," I responded.

Using a tablet, I showed the family how I found him online, sharing more photos and videos he's posted over time. I let the family know the boy and his foster mom had told me he was occasionally in touch with his sister.

In the coming days, the family would get in touch with the boy and learn that he was safe and sound. Their worries now were focused on the girl.

If I managed to talk to the girl, they told me over and over again, I had to deliver a message: that they loved her, they missed her, and they wanted her to come home.

.   .   .

Last September, Jonathan Hayes, a Trump appointee who directs the Office of Refugee Resettlement, stood before a House subcommittee, raised his right hand in oath and proceeded to provide sworn testimony.

"I believe that a child should not remain in ORR care any longer than the time needed to find an appropriate sponsor," he said, adding that the agency's mission is to release children as soon as possible while also ensuring their safety. He also praised ORR's efforts in reducing lengths of stay in custody.

"As of the end of August of this year, the average length of time that a child stays in HHS custody is approximately fifty days," Hayes testified, "which is a dramatic decrease of over forty percent from late November 2018, when the average length of care was ninety days."

ORR spokesperson Lydia Holt would not tell me whether Hayes knew about the girl who'd been in custody more than 2,100 days on the day of his testimony, saying only that, "Cases are elevated to Director Hayes on an as-needed basis."

But the six-year detention of this one Honduran child exposes a system far more inhumane than what Hayes described to Congress. And those years the girl has spent in federal custody have exposed her to almost all of its cruelty.

By all accounts, the girl didn't like detention from the start. Morrison's Micasa program, her first placement, was contracted by ORR at the time to provide transitional foster care for younger unaccompanied minors.

Like so many ORR contractors, Morrison has had its share of problems. During the girl's approximately yearlong stay in Micasa, documents obtained through a federal records request by Judicial Watch indicate Morrison's transitional foster program was the subject of multiple "significant incident reports"—critical events that triggered federal government reports. Several involved alleged child abuse, according to documents that I've reviewed. In July 2014, one girl claimed her foster family was physically and emotionally abusive. Less than three months later, a different child claimed his foster family restricted him to his bedroom. A few days after that, records indicate a child and a youth care worker reported that a staffer physically disciplined a child.

In a 2018 declaration in federal court, a mother detailed how Morrison had failed to reunite her with her son. She said she was told by the Morrison case manager that she wouldn't need to provide fingerprints. Later, it turned out, she did need to provide them, but the case manager had forgotten to tell her about her fingerprint appointment. She was later told her husband's prints were lost. Meanwhile, her son was transferred to a shelter in Florida, grew ill and had to be hospitalized. According to the declaration, signed February 6, 2018, "No one from Morrison or the government has given me more information about my son's health, the studies, results or medical treatment he is receiving." At the time of the filing, related to the Flores settlement guiding the federal government's treatment of unaccompanied minors, the family had yet to be reunified; a federal filing indicates the boy was released shortly thereafter.

DiNucci, the Morrison spokesperson, did not respond to a request for comment about these allegations.

Toward the end of October 2014, sources indicate, the girl, then eleven, and the boy, then nine, were transferred to another foster home across the country in Massachusetts, this one run by Ascentria Care Alliance. Ascentria did not immediately respond to queries.

People familiar with the girl's time in Massachusetts say something serious happened there that prompted the federal government to separate her from her brother in early 2015. That was the last time the girl was in the presence of a family member since she arrived in the United States. It was also right around this time, according to Dayani, Doña Amalia, and the girl's aunt, that all contact with them ceased.

Rules governing the behavior of staff and residents in the federal shelter system stipulate that touching is strictly prohibited. If everyone's followed the rules, then the girl hasn't experienced a hug or even held someone's hand in close to five years.

Research has shown that adolescence is a critical period when bonding and affection are critical to development.

"Think about all the things that you learned about how to be a human from the people who care about you during those ages," said Camacho-Thompson, the child development researcher. "It doesn't happen at forty to forty-seven, it happens at ten to seventeen."

The years during which the girl's been isolated and alone make up the very period during which most adolescents are learning what it means to be a person in society.

"Trauma occurring while these skills are being built can lead to disorders such as depression, anxiety, and post–traumatic stress disorders," Camacho-Thompson said. "Trauma during this period can affect the way we are wired."

After the children were separated, the boy was placed into a new foster home in Massachusetts, the one where he remains today. But his sister was headed deeper into ORR's system.

When children who are alone and detained experience behavioral problems, ORR sometimes sends them to therapeutic facilities like SandyPines Residential Treatment Center in Tequesta, north of Miami. Sources indicate that the girl spent four months there.

Her transfer there coincides with the period when the girl's family says they lost contact. They do recall talking to her during a hospital stay, and SandyPines is known locally as a hospital, but it's not clear if they talked to her while she was there. They remember hearing about Oregon and Massachusetts, but no one remembers her mentioning Florida.

The girl's time at SandyPines was relatively brief. By July 2015, sources indicate, she'd be turned over to another treatment center, one that's become synonymous with the forced drugging of unaccompanied minors.

The Shiloh Treatment Center is a collection of trailers and old homes in Manville, Texas. I've talked with children and family members involved with seven separate cases of child migrants detained at Shiloh.

Their accounts, and court documents, make Shiloh sound horrific. They say children were held down and forcibly drugged with powerful psychotropic medications. According to the affidavits, children were told they would not be released or see their parents unless they took their meds. One child was prescribed a powerful cocktail of daily medications, including an antipsychotic, an antidepressant, and a Parkinson's medication commonly used to treat the side effects of antipsychotics. The drugs rendered some children unable to walk, afraid of people, and wanting to sleep constantly, court filings say.

There also have been a number of reports of violence and sexual assault.

For example, while the girl was there, local sheriff's records indicate someone made a call from the facility to report a sexual assault. The call notes include notations that "kids all speak Spanish" and that, during an interview, a child said "they had another inappropriate relation with a staff member." The Brazoria County Sheriff's Office didn't return calls for comment.

Just five days after the girl arrived at Shiloh, police received a call from someone who believed "there may be some physical abuse from a staffer," police records show.

And six months before she arrived, police recorded a call from the facility. The caller said they wanted to alert authorities that according to a new federal mandate they had to report "all contact" between Shiloh residents and staff to law enforcement. The caller went on to say there had been "three incidents involving contact between (residents) and staff" but said "they are not wanting to pursue charges on anybody." The record shows the call came from the phone number of Luis Valdez, then an administrator at Shiloh. Valdez didn't respond to requests for comment. When I called Shiloh for comment, I was cut off and told to call ORR in Washington, DC, before the person on the line hung up on me.

One year passed at Shiloh for the girl, during which she turned thirteen, sources indicate. Then another, and the girl turned fourteen. After about two years at Shiloh, in late 2017, the girl was once again transferred—this time to a shelter in New York.

The girl, sources indicate, spent about eight months at Children's Village in Dobbs Ferry, New York.

Last year, the inspector general of Health and Human Services issued a report which found an operation in disarray. "Children's Village failed to meet or properly document that it had met certain requirements for the care and release of children in its custody in 46 of the 50 case files reviewed," the report said. It included photographs of unsanitary shower facilities and plaster peeling from bedroom walls and called into question the provider's shoddy records system and substandard practices around releasing children to sponsors. The inspector general then recommended that Children's Village refund the government close to $3 million in what it called unallowable grant expenditures.

Abuse allegations at the facility date back some forty years. More recently, in 2012, a teacher was fired after sending nude photos to a fifteen-year-old at Children's Village. The following year, a therapist was accused of stomping on a child's face while that child was restrained.

By mid-2018, at age fifteen, the girl was sent back to Shiloh. She'd spend close to another year and a half there before she ever made it out again.

While she was there for the second time, in July 2018, a federal judge ruled that ORR had violated Texas laws that require parental consent for medication. Judge Dolly M. Gee said Shiloh must stop medicating children without consent and ordered all migrant children to be relocated, unless a licensed psychiatrist or psychologist had determined they were a risk to themselves or others. Under Texas law, Gee wrote, "parents have the right to consent to medical, psychiatric, or psychological treatment . . . and other adult relatives of the child have the right to consent if the parent(s) cannot be contacted." The court found that Shiloh staff improperly signed the consent forms themselves.

The family worry about whether their girl was one of the children who was medicated during her time there. But they've never been told.

In September 2019, the girl was once again transferred, this time back to the care of Morrison in Portland, where she remains today. While there, she turned seventeen; in another year she would age out, get transferred into the custody of Immigration and Customs Enforcement, and be placed into an adult detention facility.

Marcela Cartagena was a youth care worker and then an education assistant at Morrison for about a year and a half starting in late 2015. She said that while there were several individual efforts by teachers to support student learning, she characterized some of the teaching as a joke.

Sometimes, she said, a teacher would play a YouTube video about animals and call it science. Or a video about erupting volcanoes and call it geography. Even when lesson plans were more formal and adhered to, the teachers only had material for three months, as children aren't typically in ORR custody for that long. So kids who are in custody past that three-month mark have a tough time getting anything new, according to Cartagena. The system has little to offer them.

"By that point kids lose motivation," Cartagena said. "Their mental health starts declining, and they lose hope."

She remembers that a lot of children in the program arrived with few literacy skills. They'd enter the program super motivated to learn the ABCs, but anyone still in after three months would have to start all over again, learning the same basics. Spokesperson Patricia DiNucci did not respond to written questions about Morrison's educational offerings.

Daisy Camacho-Thompson, the psychology professor, studies the way academic motivation predicts achievement. When I shared details about what I knew about the girl's educational experience the last few years, she wondered what value education would even hold for the girl because of the trauma she'd experienced.

Camacho-Thompson said the constant stress the girl has endured may have diminished her motivation for learning. "Your body's learning how to react to stress, and being moved around from place to place while you think your family has abandoned you," she said.

.   .   .

Case managers tend to get the blame or praise from families in these situations. As the ones who talk most with sponsors, case managers play a significant role in communicating every step of the reunification process to family members desperate to get their kids back. Yet they have limited control over the outcome of any case. Officials within ORR are ultimately the ones who make the final decision on whether to discharge a child to their family or transfer a child within the system.

In addition to her case managers and case workers, the girl has also had a number of other people working for her—at least one child advocate and many different attorneys. But these relationships are often temporary.

The case workers and managers are typically staff members of an individual shelter or treatment center. Katharine Gordon, the immigration attorney, said in her experience, "as long as the case worker is at the organization, the case worker stays on the case. However, I've experienced times when five or more case workers were on the same case, because of case workers leaving their positions."

And every time a child is transferred to a new location in the system, they get a new case worker and a new case manager, Gordon said. The girl was transferred at least six times.

Another challenge of prolonged detention for children in federal custody is a lack of steady legal representation, which can create lost opportunities for immigration relief.

Sofia Linarte, an attorney who works with Catholic Charities Community Services of the Archdiocese of New York, was listed on the docket as the girl's attorney that January day in the Portland immigration court. But the attorney who actually represented her before Judge Zanfardino was Caryn Crosthwait, who works with Immigration Counseling Service. Virginia Maynes, a colleague of Crosthwait's, had also previously represented the girl, sources say.

All three attorneys work with organizations that are part of a national network of legal services providers funded by ORR.

．　　　●　　　●

The girl also has a child advocate named Pamela Nickell, who works with the Young Center for Immigrant Children's Rights, another ORR contractor. While the girl's attorneys represent the girl as a client, Nickell's role is to determine what's in the child's best interests—because what a child wants and what's best for her aren't necessarily the same thing.

I've tried to reach out to anyone I could find involved in this girl's case over several weeks, but no one would comment on the case.

All three of the attorneys I identified that worked on the case, Linarte, Crosthwait, and Maynes, said they couldn't speak with me because of concerns over confidentiality. Nickell, her child advocate, didn't respond to me. I called and emailed Isabel Rios, the girl's case manager at Morrison, but she didn't respond either. I asked to interview Judge Zanfardino, but the court's spokesperson, Kathryn Mattingly, wrote to me that judges don't do interviews. "Immigration judges consider all evidence and arguments presented by both parties and decide each case in a manner that is timely, impartial, and consistent with applicable law and case precedent," Mattingly wrote in a follow-up email.

The Children's Village shelter told me any questions about unaccompanied minors must be handled by ORR. When I sought comment from ORR, I initially received only a written statement from ORR spokesperson Patrick Fisher about the agency's general policies and some recent data about the agency's work on family reunification. ORR, he said, reunified 72,593 children in fiscal year 2019, which he called "the largest number ever in program history." Fisher said as a matter of policy the agency doesn't comment on specific cases—though ORR had asked me to identify the child in question, which I did.

"It must be emphasized that ORR evaluates potential sponsors' ability to provide for the child's physical and mental well-being," Fisher's statement read. "The overwhelming majority of UAC (unaccompanied minors) are released to suitable sponsors who are family members within the United States to await immigration hearings."

In a subsequent email, Lydia Holt, the ORR spokesperson, said that every case is different and that generalizing from one individual case would result in an inaccurate depiction of the agency's operations.

DiNucci, the Morrison spokesperson, said she couldn't discuss anything related to a specific youth in the program's care. ICE told me it doesn't comment on cases that involve minor children or on any individual's medical history.

If, for whatever reason, the federal government or its contractors decided the children shouldn't be reunited with their family in North Carolina, the boy was at least placed with a loving family that's ready to care for him for the long run. But his sister was moved around to seven placements in five states.

The brother has the freedom to be a child, to be good, to be bad, to make real choices. He has an engaging social media presence. He is fully bilingual, chatting easily in both languages, and enjoys reading the books assigned to him in high school English. He's had consistent schooling for the past five years and a steady mother figure and the chance to build real friendships.

But the girl told Doña Amalia that she's still unable to read in either language. She is fluent in Spanish but still knows only a handful of English-language words. For her, the window during which language is most easily acquired has closed. She's been in situations where misbehaving has meant drastic consequences, where there are no friends and no adults steadily at her side. She can't reach out to her brother on social media; she doesn't even have her own phone.

The boy has existed in the free world with a devoted family. The girl never got a chance at an ordinary childhood. With less than a year before she turns eighteen, the fleeting years of her adolescence have all but vanished in detention.

There's one line Doña Amalia said that has always stuck with me.

"They buried her," she said. "They buried her."

·   ·   ·

Not long after I passed the girl those papers near the elevator in the Portland courthouse, which included her aunt's phone number, the family finally heard from someone in the shelter system for the first time in five years. Isabel Rios, who identified herself as the girl's current case manager—the one who had chaperoned her that day in court—said the girl wanted to talk to Doña Amalia. Rios told them it had to happen sometime between Monday and Friday, they said; she didn't work on the weekends.

Doña Amalia doesn't have a cell phone. Setting up a call meant another family member had to take time off work to get to Doña Amalia's home on January 23 with a phone. Suddenly, Doña Amalia had a live video connection to the child she had longed to see for years. A week later, she recounted the conversation to me.

The girl spoke first. "Hi grandma," she said.

Doña Amalia started to cry. She told her grandchild, "I've been crying for you for seven years."

The girl said she'd been cutting herself again. She said she had asked to be deported and was going home to Honduras. Doña

Amalia warned her about what awaited her there. "What are you going to do over there? To lose yourself. To raise children. To get passed around from man to man? That's where you're headed." She told the girl not to go.

The girl told her grandmother that she thought the family had abandoned her. That she'd just called to say goodbye.

A few days later, Dayani gave her cousin an even clearer picture of what Honduras has in store. Dayani herself spent time in an ORR shelter in Texas, and she remembers the desperation she felt while she was there. She's been inside and she's been out. And, several years older than her cousin, she has a sharper memory of what Honduras was like.

Dayani told the girl that in Honduras, men would come after her, and there'd be no one to protect her. She wouldn't always have food to eat or clothes to wear. If she survived the threat of violence that often defines their little town, she'd break her back doing work for very little money. In North Carolina, meanwhile, she'd have a supportive family, her own bedroom, and her own cell phone.

After they'd spoken for a while, the girl relented and told Dayani that she'd rather go to North Carolina than Honduras now that she knew her family wanted her. But she said it was too late: Her request for voluntary departure had already been granted.

"I told her she had the right to ask for it to be canceled," Dayani told me. She said the girl told her she would talk to her attorney or find someone else who could help her stay.

Soon after, the girl's case manager asked the family in North Carolina if they had the birth mother's contact information in Honduras. Within days, the birth mother says she also got a call and talked to her daughter for the first time in eight years.

I connected with the birth mother shortly after that call. She told me her daughter had decided she wanted to stay with her family in the United States after all. The birth mother, whose husband was murdered, is raising two younger kids on her own with money she gets from washing her neighbor's clothing. She said she also wants her daughter to stay in the United States.

"The girl should be with her family," she told me. "And that's Doña Amalia."

She told the person who called her—a Spanish-language speaker who may have been the case manager, an attorney, or, she thought, someone from the U.S. government—that she wanted the girl with the people who raised her.

But the birth mother said the person on the line told her there's nothing that could be done now that the judge had granted the child's request for voluntary departure. Feeling defeated, she acknowledged that the girl could come to live with her—but said that she shouldn't expect much.

"So I said, 'Well, if that's the result, then if she comes here she's not going to have much to eat and she's going to walk around barefoot like I do here,'" she told me.

The mother said that the caller did not inform her that her daughter still has the option to petition to reopen her case.

Family members have told me that, a little over a week ago, people related to the girl's case arrived in the family's community in Honduras. The family had been told by several community members that the visitors asked questions of the birth mother and her neighbors as part of what they believed to be an evaluation of whether the girl should be returned to her home country.

Now, the family says, they're left waiting. The case manager is mostly ignoring their calls, just like before.

They don't know what's going on with their child. And they're terrified they're going to lose her again.

Reveal chose not to name the girl, her brother, or their birth mother to protect the children's privacy as minors; their aunts asked not to be named, fearing repercussions from immigration authorities.

Public Books

FINALIST—SINGLE-TOPIC ISSUE

This is the first of three articles drawn from "Preexisting Conditions: What 2020 Reveals About Our Urban Future," a collection of essays published by Public Books *that was nominated for the 2021 National Magazine Award for Single-Topic Issue (it is illustrative of the changes that have overtaken media in this century that the competition for what was once quintessentially a print award is now open to digital magazines like* Public Books*). Many of these essays, along with new and updated pieces, will be published by Columbia University Press in the collection* The Long Year: A 2020 Reader *in late 2021. Adam Tooze, who wrote this article, was born in London and educated at Cambridge, the Free University of Berlin, and the London School of Economics. He is now a professor of history at Columbia. His latest book,* Shutdown: How Covid Shook the World's Economy, *was published in September 2021.*

Adam Tooze

Global Inequality and the Corona Shock

I n the first half of 2020, as the world economy shut down, hundreds of millions of people across the world lost their jobs. Following India's lockdown on March 24, tens of millions of displaced migrant workers thronged bus stops waiting for a ride back to their villages. Many gave up and spent weeks on the road walking home. Over 1.5 billion young people were affected by school closures. The human capital forgone will, according to the World Bank, cost $10 trillion in future income.

Meanwhile, in China, economic growth had resumed by the summer. Amazon has added hundreds of thousands to its global workforce. The world's corporations issued debt as never before. And, with Jeff Bezos in the lead, America's billionaires saw their wealth surge to ever-more-grotesque heights.

In Las Vegas the painted rectangles of parking lots were repurposed as socially distanced campsites for those with no shelter to go to. Tech-savvy police forces in Southern California procured drones with loudspeakers to issue orders to the homeless remotely. Lines of SUVs and middle-class sedans snaked for miles as tens of thousands of Americans stopped commuting and queued for food. Meanwhile, in the Hamptons, wealthy exiles from Manhattan outbid one another to install luxury swimming pools on the grounds of their summer residences.

Even in a world accustomed to extreme inequality, the disparate experience of the COVID shock has been dizzying. It will be years before comprehensive data is available to chart the precise impact of the pandemic on global inequality. But what might a sketch look like?

•   •   •

In the last fifty years, we have seen national differences between rich and poor countries narrow. Around the world, a new global middle class has emerged. At the same time, as lower-middle income and working-class incomes have been squeezed and the incomes of the top 1 percent have surged, inequality has widened within the advanced economies. Viewing the situation at scale, Branko Milanovic diagnosed a move back to the world of Karl Marx and Frantz Fanon, a world organized by hierarchies of class and race, rather than by nation.[1]

This does not mean that nation-states do not matter. Inequality is not fate. Not only have some societies made huge leaps forward, but national welfare states also have the power to substantially mitigate inequality. If the distribution of disposable incomes is much less unequal in Germany than in the United States, it is not because Germany is less globalized. It is not because it is less capitalist. It is not because pretax income inequality in Germany is less—it is, if anything, slightly more unequal than in the United States. It is not even because Germany has a much more progressive tax system. It doesn't. It is because Germany's welfare system is far more generous in transferring income to the least well-off. It is a matter of political choice.

Inequality trends are best studied on a long-term basis. But large shocks, like the financial crisis of 2008, can have major impacts. The worst impact of the mortgage and banking crisis was confined to the North Atlantic. As a result, the rapidly growing emerging economies, led by China, accelerated their catch-up. In the short run, income differentials within Europe and the United States were compressed. But as the economy bounced back, the gap between rich and poor once again widened. This was compounded by policy responses to the crisis, including central-bank monetary stimulus, that lopsidedly boosted financial markets. At the world level, while the Asian middle class continued to grow, in other emerging market economies, notably in Brazil and South Africa, growth ground to a halt.

COVID-19, a disease originating in marginalized rural communities in central China, is the most sudden and savage globalization shock to date. It is the first truly comprehensive crisis of the Anthropocene era, affecting virtually everyone on the planet. It poses a far more general challenge to states and national welfare systems than 2008 did. It has confirmed familiar differences among national regimes of inequality, and it has exposed new ones.

How severe the shock on a country becomes depends on how well the public-health crisis is managed, on societal reserves and coping capacities, on the institutional and technical infrastructures that underpin solidarity, and on political will. In this respect, China, where the disease originated, and India are polar opposites.

Thanks to a dramatic collective mobilization, China managed to contain the spread of the virus by February. The shock to production and consumption was severe but short-lived. In 2020, China will probably be the only major economy to achieve any growth. In that regard its status in 2020 is even more distinctive than it was in 2008. As the rest of the world shrinks, the Chinese Communist Party moves ever closer to achieving its objective of transforming China into a "comprehensively well-off society." This does not mean that all Chinese escaped the crisis. In fact, because the average level of consumption continues to rise, it is precisely through stark disparities that the impact of the pandemic has been felt. In February, as the lockdowns hit, it was above all China's vast army of 290 million migrant workers who bore the brunt. Tens of millions are still looking for work. Government efforts to prop up small businesses with loans and a $15 billion retraining program to reskill 50 million workers have had limited success. Little wonder that open discussion of unemployment and inequality is increasingly controversial.

Whereas robust overall growth has allowed Beijing to maintain the momentum of the China Dream, the reverse is true in India. Between 2014 and 2018, India was, for a brief heady moment, the fastest-growing economy in the world. In 2019 worrying signs of fragility, particularly in the financial sector, were revealed. But the abrupt shutdown ordered by Modi's government on the night of March 24 was shattering, and the impact fell extraordinarily heavily on the least well-off. A hundred million migrant workers were left stranded. Millions were held in detention centers without adequate housing or food. Unemployment soared to a dizzying 24 percent.

GDP in the second quarter of 2020 was down by a similar percentage—by far the worst among the G20 economies. By the summer New Delhi was forced to change tack, encouraging a resumption of economic activity despite the fact that the epidemic was running out of control. The parts of India least well equipped to cope are poor rural backwaters, to which migrant workers returned in their millions, bringing the virus with them. Meanwhile, 270 million schoolchildren wait to hear when and how schooling will resume. Only 8 percent of India's households have a computer with an internet connection.

Whereas in China the narrative of national triumph over COVID "balances" the hardship of those worst affected, in India a rampant epidemic, a savage economic recession, and extreme disparities compound one another. The same is true in Latin America.

Latin America is the most unequal continent in the world. Since 2013, growth has slowed far behind the pace being set in

Asia. Both facts are reflected in the continent's failure to cope with COVID. When the virus first arrived in Mexico, it was labeled a rich person's disease. It was affluent families who had been on ski holidays in the United States that brought it home. Miguel Barbosa, the populist governor of Puebla state, rallied his supporters by declaring that "the poor, we're immune." From its initial foothold among the most affluent neighborhoods, COVID spread into the sprawling favelas. Peru imposed a determined lockdown policy. But it was near impossible to make that stick in a megacity like Lima, in which, despite two decades of unprecedented economic growth, more than 70 percent of the population lives hand to mouth, relying on street commerce and informal labor markets. The most graphic images of the entire epidemic came from Guayaquil in Ecuador, where bodies in improvised coffins were left to rot on the streets of a city whose history is one characterized by deep class and racial divides.[2]

At the beginning of the new millennium, Latin America counted alongside "emerging Asia" as an arena of the new "global middle class." The shock of 2020 raises the specter of another "lost decade."

Rich societies faced the corona shock with far greater economic and medical resources. Japan, South Korea, and Taiwan made good use of these advantages to contain the epidemic. The same cannot be said of Europe and the United States. As a result of their failure to react promptly, Europe and the United States underwent prolonged lockdowns, triggering recessions that are significantly worse than those of 2008.

But not all rich countries have done equally badly. Germany effectively contained the first wave of the epidemic without a comprehensive lockdown of its economy. Given the devastating shock suffered by Italy and Spain, there was reason to fear a widening gulf within the EU, which might even have escalated into a new crisis of the Euro area. Instead, after months of knife-edge negotiation, Europe's leaders agreed on a €750 billion program to share at least some of the cost of reconstruction and recovery.

This act of solidarity among states was impressive. But it was a long way removed from the pain suffered, in Europe as elsewhere, by low-wage workers, poor households, migrant workers, and precarious small businesses. It is Europe's uniquely extensive national-welfare and health-care regimes that have been put to the test. Reactions ranged from a rapid adjustment in workplace health and safety conditions to a strategy to address the pandemic, which in the British case revolved entirely around "saving" the National Health Service.

Europe's great welfare innovation of the crisis has been the adoption of short-time working systems on a model pioneered by Germany during the 2008 crisis. Employers are subsidized to cover the wages of furloughed workers. This system has a progressive distributional effect through providing wage support only up to an upper-income threshold. It is not just the scale of these systems that is remarkable, but the fact that they have been extended to include a variety of self-employed workers, gig workers, agency workers, and previously stigmatized groups such as sex workers.

All in all, though the pandemic was poorly handled and the economic shock in Europe (as measured by the contraction of GDP) has been worse than in the United States, the safety net of legal and social regulation has gone a long way toward absorbing the crisis's impact on the most vulnerable—so far, at least..

Since the 1970s, America's inequality dynamics along lines of both class and race have been more extreme than in any other advanced society. So, too, has been the open subordination of politics to the interests of wealth. COVID has confirmed that contrast.

New York City, the epicenter of the U.S. epidemic, was a case study in extremes. While the affluent Upper East Side emptied out, working-class Black and Latino people living in Queens suffered COVID mortality rates almost as bad as the worst of northern Italy. School closures divided the city along lines of housing and access to internet. Single parents, overwhelmingly mothers and disproportionately women of color, were left to fend as best they could. While Wall Street traders toiled to reap the profits of turbulent markets, hundreds of thousands of workers in retail, bars, restaurants, nail and hair salons, and the theater business were summarily dismissed. So dramatic was the skew in job losses toward the least well paid that, as employment collapsed, in April America's hourly average wage surged by 5.5 percent.

The sense of impending social crisis was so severe that for a brief moment the congressional Republican Party actually joined the Democrats in voting through the $2 trillion CARES Act. The United States lacks the labor-market infrastructure that would enable a European-style response to the crisis. But for a brief moment in 2020, Congressional largesse demonstrated what a welfare-driven, redistributive social policy in America might look like. With supplements to unemployment benefits and stimulus checks, disposable incomes rose even as tens of millions lost their jobs. But even at that moment, there was no let-up in the distributional struggle. Short-term relief for low-paid workers was traded for massive support for corporate America and a staggering tax cut for the wealthiest.

While small firms were battered, Amazon and the other tech giants thrived. Once again, inequality of living conditions, employment, and income was compounded by massive differences in the structure of wealth. The essential complement to congressional fiscal policy was a series of interventions by the Fed to stabilize financial markets. Without the Fed's liquidity provision, March might have seen a financial heart attack on the scale of 2008. The result would have been a disaster not only for the U.S. economy. Yet monetary largesse has side effects. While it brings interest rates down, it induces a lopsided surge in stock markets that benefits the 10 percent of the population who hold substantial wealth in the form of equity. And even among those with financial assets, not everyone gained equally. The crisis selected among firms as well as among people. The difference in fortunes between the energy and tech sectors has been huge, as has been the fate of those who work in those sectors.

Meanwhile, amid the extreme polarization of the summer and with the impending election and unemployment numbers suggesting at least some degree of recovery, that brief moment of political cohesion was soon over. Congress became deadlocked over efforts to pass a new stimulus package. The GOP went back to arguing that generous benefits rob low-waged Americans of the incentive to work. Such benefits, the thinking goes, do too much to mitigate inequality. The other sticking point has been the Republican refusal to support adequate financial assistance for the states and cities hardest hit by the crisis. As a result, America heads toward 2021 facing the prospect of an urban fiscal crisis on a scale last seen in the 1970s.

. . .

The upshot of this partial exercise in mapping is that the COVID crisis reveals a world split into five distinct regimes of inequality and growth. Europe and the United States have differed in ways that have become familiar in recent decades. What is new is that the world of emerging markets has split three ways. All three are marked by extreme inequality, but whereas China has maintained growth, India has suffered a shuddering blow that has starkly exposed its limited governance capacities. The one consolation is that India may be able to get back on track. The same cannot be said for Latin America, which is haunted by the prospect of a new "lost decade."

If 2020 will be remembered as, in President Macron's words, the moment when humanity as a whole suffered an "anthropological shock," it will also be remembered as a moment of extreme polarization, the moment that buried, once and for all, the millennial vision of a convergent future of economic globalization, growth, and social transformation.

Notes

1. Branko Milanovic, *Global Inequality: A New Approach for the Age of Globalization* (Cambridge, MA: Harvard University Press, 2016).
2. Chris Garces, "Carceral Pandemic Politics and Epidemiological Elites in Ecuador," *NACLA Report on the Americas* 52, no. 3 (2020).

Public Books

FINALIST—SINGLE-TOPIC
ISSUE

*The second of three articles from
"Preexisting Conditions: What
2020 Reveals About Our Urban
Future"—a collection of essays
that won* Public Books *a place
on the short list for the National
Magazine Award for Single-Topic
Issue—"The Limits of
Telecommuting" explores the
often-unhappy effects of what
those of us fortunate enough to
escape the more dire consequences
of the pandemic simply called
"working from home," but which
Margaret O'Mara, the writer of
this article, reminds us was an "an
extraordinary social experiment
unfurling at global scale and
astounding speed." A graduate of
Northwestern University and the
University of Pennsylvania and a
one-time policy analyst in the
Clinton White House, O'Mara
is now a professor of history at
the University of Washington.
She is the author of several books,
including most recently* The Code:
Silicon Valley and the Remaking
of America.

Margaret O'Mara

The Limits of Telecommuting

Forty years prior to COVID-19, Alvin Toffler saw the future of working from home, and it looked very good. In his 1980 best-seller, *The Third Wave*, the futurist author declared that modern economies would soon shift away from the office and toward "the electronic cottage"—a retro-utopian update of the preindustrial days of home work and piece work, now wired to the modern world via desktop computers, faxes, and dial-up modems. "The electronic cottage raises once more on a mass scale the possibility of husbands and wives, and perhaps even children, working together as a unit," he explained. This arrangement would propel "greater community stability" and "a renaissance among voluntary organizations."

Fast-forward to the great pandemic and shutdown of 2020, an extraordinary social experiment unfurling at global scale and astounding speed. By June, 42 percent of the American workforce was working from home. The benefits of the new normal became readily apparent—no commutes! comfy sweatpants!—and many relished the slowdown in the relentless pace of twenty-first-century life. As Toffler predicted, America's remote-working classes became simultaneously placeless and newly rooted in place, their mental maps shrinking to a few neighborhood blocks, the local grocery, the nearby park.

Yet Toffler's optimistic, communitarian forecast failed to perceive how this new electronic reality would exact a toll on mental and financial health; split open new fault lines of class, gender, and race; and accelerate a long-brewing social reckoning. Schools and child-care facilities shuttered, leaving working parents, especially mothers, struggling to balance professional and domestic duties. Some had to cut back work hours; others quit their jobs altogether.

Seven months into the pandemic, the U.S. employment statistics reflected the sharp inequalities of COVID's economic toll, with job losses falling disproportionately on women and people of color.

Many such losses were among those who could not stay home in the first place, on whose labor in grocery stores and Amazon warehouses and meatpacking plants all the comforts of the electronic cottage were dependent.

There already has been a great deal of speculation about the lasting effects of this information-overloaded digital year on work, schooling, and the public realm. As retailers shutter and major corporations announce they will keep workers home for good, it is clear the pandemic has already changed some things permanently. But looking backward to the roots of remote work is equally important. It turns out that these systems were never really designed to benefit the groups that could gain the most from them: working mothers, caretakers, and their children, especially those without easy access to new technology.

Perhaps the lesson to take from this year of living online is not just about making better, more humane work-and-learn-from-anywhere technology. It is about recognizing technology's limits.

Like many of Toffler's ideas, the "electronic cottage" combined ahistorical grandiosity with canny insight into emerging technological and demographic trends. By the early 1980s, a growing number of mothers of young children had entered America's waged workforce and, thanks to woefully inadequate child-care infrastructure, were struggling to balance work and family life. One job they could do from home? Code.

As the personal-computer market boomed, some employers hungry for talented programmers used telecommuting as way to recruit women back into the waged workforce. "I want to spend as much time as possible with my child and not having to commute gives me extra time," one mother and part-time programmer told the *New York Times* in 1985. Work-from-home life offered flexibility and job fulfillment even for those without children. "I have the kind of personality that likes to make my own schedule," one unmarried female programmer told the *Times*. She arranged to spend three days a week in the office and two at home.

But both the women and the men who became telecommuting's early adopters quickly saw the tradeoffs. By moving out of the office, workers lost many of the rituals and regulations that protected them from overwork and exploitation. "Whenever I'm awake," one telecommuting engineer admitted to a *Washington Post* reporter in 1980, "I'm working." Labor unions were so concerned about remote workers' susceptibility to employer surveillance and isolation that the AFL-CIO issued a resolution opposing "computer homework" in 1983.

The commercialization of the internet in the 1990s set off another wave of ebullient predictions about the work-from-home future, with little attention paid to addressing those early concerns about its impact on workers' well-being. Thus, even as work-from-anywhere information-technology jobs increased, the actual percentage of telecommuters remained vanishingly low. One 1994 survey of companies that allowed remote work found that less than 1 percent of employees took advantage of it. The chief obstacle was managerial resistance. "Managers won't give up control," one researcher noted. "They still can't trust that employees are working when they aren't present."

Stubborn insistence on face time helped explain why, even at the apex of the dot-com boom in 1999, a mere 7 percent of the American workforce worked remotely. What's more, 1990s telecommuters often were not working from home. Instead, they flocked to satellite offices built to shorten commutes in traffic-choked regions like Los Angeles and Washington, DC. Grand predictions that the average knowledge worker would soon retreat to an internet-enabled cabin in the woods never came to pass.

The case of the tech industry is particularly revealing. Even as dot-com-era leaders steadfastly preached the gospel that computer hardware and software would upend the way the world worked, played, and communicated, they too remained firmly committed to the office. Skyrocketing real-estate prices in 1990s Silicon Valley and Seattle reflected that even the builders of this miraculous new online infrastructure believed it was far better to work face-to-face.

This intensified after 2000. Instead of dispatching workers to self-directed lives in their electronic cottages, internet-age Silicon Valley traded in drab office spaces for far-grander facilities designed to make workplaces compelling playgrounds that met employees' every need. Google, founded by two Stanford graduate students, built an elaborate Silicon Valley headquarters that was a fantasy version of a richly endowed college campus, drenched with amenities like free food in the cafeteria, climbing walls, and massage rooms.

As CEO of Apple and Pixar, Steve Jobs helped popularize the gospel of innovation-by-serendipitous-encounter, facilitated by offices with open layouts and spots for impromptu connection. The perks that tech companies loaded into these campuses reflected the kind of employee they wanted to recruit and retain: young, unattached, able to put work first at any cost. Apple's new corporate headquarters, opened in 2017, featured custom-designed ergonomic desk chairs and a two-story yoga room. Missing from the $5 billion facility: a child-care center.

Even firms that once embraced telecommuting pulled back from it. IBM had made a big remote-work push at the start of the "electronic cottage" era, but slumping stock prices and employee attrition helped prompt a reversal in policy. In a preview of what many would experience in 2020, IBM found that remote work made it difficult to build strong teams and mentor junior employees. Workers could easily be lured away by superstar tech companies with glitzy campuses where they could, as Amazon's employee motto put it, "work hard, have fun, make history." By the mid-2010s, Big Blue had joined the rush to build perk-filled offices in what one executive termed "really creative and inspiring locations."

Soon after Marissa Mayer, a longtime Googler, became CEO of Yahoo! in 2012, she banned remote work altogether. "Speed and quality are often sacrificed when we work from home," the company's human-resources director said at the time. Many employees found Mayer's move particularly distressing because the CEO was the mother of young children. They had hoped she would be more sympathetic to the pressures working mothers faced.

Discouragement of telecommuting supercharged the workaholic vibe of the tech world and contributed to an abysmal record on gender diversity that has worsened over time. A 2018 survey of 80 tech companies found that women made up only 24 percent of the technical workforce, down from 36 percent in 1991. Employees—many of whom, as ever, were mothers of young children—asking for partial or full-time work-from-home arrangements found themselves sidelined from important projects or denied permission altogether. Generous parental benefits were at odds with the realities of workplace culture, one Seattle-area engineer lamented to a labor researcher in 2019. "Everyone is supported before they take maternity leave, but when it comes time to be promoted they are questioned for being absent."

·　　·　　·

Into this state of affairs came the novel coronavirus. The American workforce suddenly divided into three: those thrown out of work by the shutdowns, those deemed "essential"—from grocery clerks to surgeons—who continued to work outside the home, and those now working through screens, with nearly all human contact filtered through software. The vast majority of America's children and college-age adults abruptly began learning online as well, their teachers and professors scrambling to catch up.

The economic and psychic effects rippled outward from the electronic cottage. "Weekends and weekdays are the same," one Chicago-area mother remarked to a reporter in September. "I don't really know where I am in time, if that makes sense." Working parents, meanwhile, were not all right. "All the choices stink," one researcher was quoted in August, as schools prepared for another term of mostly remote education. "Parents tell me about not being able to sleep because they're so anxious, or tell me they've been crying a lot."

As the homebound classes logged onto Facebook, ordered necessities from Amazon, and upgraded laptops and smartphones, the quarterly earnings and market valuations of tech's largest companies soared into the stratosphere. The most popular portal for work and learning, Zoom, transformed from a software product into a verb. By the end of summer, the value of the American tech sector exceeded that of the entire European stock market.

But as public events were canceled, so too were serendipitous connections and accidental meetings. Online events meant that human experience was opted into, not happened upon. Running into strangers immediately signaled danger, whether on the subway or in the grocery aisle. City dwellers no longer wandered down the street to choose a restaurant; delivery-app algorithms chose the restaurant for you.

Even in this placeless fog, geography was destiny, perhaps more than ever. Generations of racial and economic segregation of the housing market meant that where you lived at the start of the pandemic greatly determined how well you survived its physical and economic hardships. America's pixelated portals filled with scenes of stark inequity. Hundreds of cars lined up outside food banks as the unemployment rate soared to levels unseen since the Great Depression. The toxic combination of spatial segregation, health-care inequity, and economic precarity was compounded by a profoundly bungled federal response that left Black Americans and other racial minorities more likely to fall ill and die from COVID-19.

The destiny of geography, race, and income was evident in the Department of Labor's September 2020 jobs report, which revealed that the COVID recession was starkly different from those before it. The Great Depression had generated social solidarity partly because the economic pain was so broadly felt across social classes. So too had the Great Recession of 2008–2009 left its impact on nearly every income tier.

But 2020's great disruption made already-staggering inequality even greater. Employment in upper income brackets—including and especially within the roaringly profitable tech industry—was bouncing above pre-COVID levels while employment among working-class and poor Americans spiraled down.

What comes next? The uncertain trajectory and duration of the pandemic make it particularly difficult to see what work, school, and life will look like on the other side, but clues are emerging.

It is now easier to see why earlier forecasters got the electronic revolution wrong and why telecommuting and online education never quite gained traction. Months without normal social interaction have reinforced the value of ordinary human connection and the power of place, whether it be a national park or a café table on a car-free city street. The deficit is particularly keen in education, most glaringly for younger children but even visible at the collegiate level, as professors struggle mightily to maintain student engagement via Zoom.

These trends uncovered something that information-society futurists and the techno-optimistic Silicon Valley moguls long pushed to one side: computers do *not* change everything. Digital tools and connections neither transcend society's problems nor solve them. Sometimes, in fact, they make inequities greater. Analog ways of doing things—going to work in an office, going to school in a classroom, attending college on a physical campus— have persisted not only because of technological limitations, but because they serve human needs that digital tools cannot fulfill.

Yet the great disruption of 2020 is establishing digital habits that are unlikely to disappear. It turns out that Google and Amazon can continue to generate enormous profits even while their employees work from home. Smaller companies don't need costly office leases dragging down their bottom line, nor do employees need to live in expensive places like the Bay Area, where the average home price exceeds $1 million.

Some companies have declared they are giving up the office for good. Others may return, but would only ask their workers to come in a few days per week. The partly-from-home arrangements so many workers hungered for in the past may now become commonplace. Some workdays will be spent in the office, the others in the electronic cottage. But the old, familiar issues with remote work are still with us, no closer to being addressed by employers or government regulators.

There are worrisome signs, too, that the bifurcated economy of our pandemic year may continue to intensify. The commercial-real-estate sector faces a reckoning as offices shrink or disappear, and the retailers and restaurants that depend on office-worker business will fade away with them. As the urban job base shrinks, large American cities face a possible redux of the fiscal crises of the 1970s and 1980s, with the urban working class again suffering the brunt of the pain from cuts to transit, housing, and health-care programs. Public universities, their budgets never fully restored since state legislatures slashed funding during the last decade's financial crisis, are newly reeling from the economic impact of lost tuition and the costs of online instruction.

In some ways, the nation's public realm is back to where it was at the time Toffler was writing *The Third Wave*, at the end of the stagflating 1970s: sapped of resources, riven by social discord and public distrust, unable to serve all fairly. At the time, technologists saw technology as the answer to all of America's many problems. A computer on every desk, a modem to communicate, an electronic cottage to free oneself from workplace drudgery.

But it was already clear in 1980 that the digital realm is ultimately a poor substitute for the public one. Our responsibility, after 2020, is to realize how these digital shortcomings are reflections of the analog world: job insecurity for too many, a child-care system that remains piecemeal and patchwork, standards of work performance that rarely take into account the realities and rhythms of everyday life for workers of every age, gender, and caregiving status. If we do that, we might finally create the sort of electronic cottage that works for everyone.

Public Books

FINALIST—SINGLE-TOPIC ISSUE

"Preexisting Conditions: What 2020 Reveals About Our Urban Future," the collection of essays from which this article was drawn, grew out of *"Crisis Cities,"* a public symposium on a catastrophic year, co-organized by Public Books and the NYU Cities Collaborative. *The judges who nominated "Preexisting Conditions" for the National Magazine Award for Single-Topic Issue praised these essays for "engaging with issues ranging from economic injustice to police violence to global pandemic, with a thrilling level of intellectual and emotional sophistication."* Eric Klinenberg's *"Rebuilding Solidarity in a Broken World"* is the last essay in the collection—and of course looks forward. Klinenberg is a professor in the department of sociology at New York University and the author most recently of Palaces for the People: How Social Infrastructure Can Help Fight Inequality, Polarization, and the Decline of Civic Life.

Eric Klinenberg

Rebuilding Solidarity in a Broken World

N ew York City, where I live, was one of the most dangerous places on earth during the early stages of the coronavirus pandemic. At the peak of the outbreak's first wave, hospitals were overwhelmed. There were shortages of basic health supplies, including surgical gowns, masks, and ventilators. Nurses wore garbage bags to protect themselves. A convention center, a church, a tennis complex, and patches of Central Park were converted into emergency medical facilities. So many people died that hospital morgues could not handle the bodies, and refrigerated trucks were called in to store those that remained. By mid-April 2020, New York City alone had already registered more COVID-19 cases, and nearly as many deaths, as the entire United Kingdom and more deaths than Germany, Iran, Japan, and South Korea, combined.

Like most disasters, the coronavirus outbreak hit the city's poorest people and places much harder than it hit middle-class and affluent communities. The number of cases and fatalities in the heavily immigrant, working-class neighborhoods in central Queens, the Bronx, and Brooklyn dwarfed those in Manhattan's toniest districts. The reasons were hardly mysterious. Most working-class New Yorkers had no choice but to keep working. They live in smaller residential units and are more likely to share their homes with extended family members or roommates. They also shop in smaller, more crowded commercial outlets and congregate in tighter gathering places, where viruses spread easily. They cannot spend weeks in their apartments, nor stock up on food and medical supplies. Prosperous New Yorkers, however, had resources to shelter at home, jobs that allowed them to work remotely, health care that helped them manage dangerous "underlying conditions," and second homes in the country where they could escape. The affluent shared a city with the poor and working class, but they effectively lived in another world.

New York's early and devastating outbreak transformed urban life. Orders to stay at home and maintain social distance have blocked conventional forms of democratic engagement. The traditional public sphere—libraries, plazas, university campuses, union halls, and the like—shuttered. Instead of streets and sidewalks, bookstores and dance clubs, we had Twitter, Amazon, Facebook, and Zoom.

But from the early days of the pandemic, one could also see hopeful signs of movement toward more democracy, more solidarity, and a greater recognition of how we all benefit from building common ground. Something extraordinary happened in the midst of this catastrophe. Thousands of medical workers from around the country volunteered to assist in New York City's urgent-care units, at considerable risk to their own health. Teenagers, stuck at home, began teaching elderly relatives and neighbors how to use communication technologies that ease the pain of isolation. Healthy young adults delivered meals and medications to people too old or sick to go outside. Cleaners, cashiers, grocers, police officers, and delivery workers turned out daily to fulfill responsibilities that we deemed essential. For months, each workday ended with a celebration of the city's civic culture and irrepressible will to be together. At seven p.m., New Yorkers in every neighborhood opened their windows and banged pots and pans, a brash but joyful expression of gratitude to health-care workers.

It's impossible to measure the pain and suffering we endured during 2020, and we know that more hard times are on the way. But 2020 also awakened a spirit of social solidarity that we desperately need. Reckoning with the health crisis and its aftermath will force us to reconsider who we are and what we value. In the long run, it could help us rediscover the better version of ourselves. Rekindling social solidarity will require changing the way we conceive of and organize the neighborhood, the workplace, the city, and the nation.

Neighborhood

We can begin where we live because our neighbors and neighborhoods shape us in ways that are invisible, especially when we spend so much time on our screens. If the people who live nearby are amiable, we feel safe and secure in parks and playgrounds; we socialize on our sidewalks and stoops. We develop a sense of shared responsibility and look after each other. We knock on our older neighbor's door during heat waves, drop off food during a pandemic. If the people who live near us are menacing, however, we grow cautious and distrustful. When the sociologist Elijah Anderson did fieldwork in poor, segregated neighborhoods in Philadelphia, he found that high levels of crime led old people and families with children to hunker down, even at life stages where neighborly support can help.

Children, we know, are deeply affected by local conditions. Living near high-achieving peers and having easy access to libraries, community centers, good schools, and athletic fields pave the way to successful cognitive, emotional, and physical development. Living close to violence delays child development, or worse. Parents, even the most loving and supportive, can only do so much on their own.

Today, though, poor people in segregated neighborhoods are not alone in their dissatisfaction with the social life and mutual support systems in their communities. Across the country, in cities and suburbs, residents of solidly middle class and even affluent neighborhoods complain that people don't engage with or take care of one another like they once did. Some of this is nostalgia, a longing for idealized communities that were never as tight as we imagine. But the best research on neighborhoods tells us that there is a fundamental truth behind this feeling: contemporary Americans are much less likely to spend time with neighbors. No matter how many friends we have on Facebook or how often we meet colleagues for drinks after work, there's a hole at the center of our experience.

Americans have so much to gain from building solidarity in the neighborhood, but doing this requires some critical thinking about what's wrong with the way we've been treating one another and about how our fantasies of independence compromise our well-being. Today, too many Americans feel ashamed to admit that they need anyone. They'd rather be miserable, stressed, and sick than let anyone think they can't take care of themselves.

Work

During the twentieth century, labor unions and the social contract that they won through successful organizing were the key to expanding the American middle class and the many privileges that came with it: Eight-hour workdays. Weekends off. Paid vacations. Subsidized housing. Pensions. Health insurance. As they crafted the New Deal, policy makers recognized that the United States would not recover from the Depression unless government supported workers and not just capital. The Wagner Act of 1935 established that the federal government would promote the interests of labor. A suite of legal labor protections followed, as did historic growth in the U.S. economy, increased longevity, and dramatic improvement in most Americans' quality of life.

For decades, "solidarity" was American labor's guiding principle and rallying cry. It was, at root, an expression of workers' material interest in organizing to gain power and leverage in a nation that had always privileged capital and disdained regulatory oversight. It was also based on workers' collective experiences beyond the shop floor, in the union halls, local pubs, sports leagues, and "workingman's neighborhoods" that shaped civic life and politics. On their own, as the songwriter Ralph Chaplin famously put it, in "Solidarity Forever," individual workers are vulnerable. Together, they are invincible: "The union makes us strong."

By the late 1950s, this confidence proved unwarranted. Large industrial firms discovered that they could boost profits by building factories in developing countries where workers would accept lower wages and fewer benefits than those negotiated by American unions. Millions of people and thousands of communities, especially in the rust belt, were devastated by deindustrialization. The pact among capital, labor, and the state came undone, and in place of solidarity came a renewed faith in meritocracy and free markets, the same invisible hand that led the United States into the first Gilded Age and the Great Depression.

In the late twentieth and early twenty-first century, America generated extraordinary new wealth, but it was hardly shared. The top 1 percent of Americans accumulated massive fortunes as executive pay surged. Elite professionals flourished. The middle-class population plummeted. Blue-collar communities saw conditions deteriorate dramatically. In white, working-class areas, life expectancy declined for the first time in history because of what economists Anne Case and Angus Deaton called "deaths of despair" from addiction and suicide. Black and Latinx communities were left out of the prosperity that, through the magic of regressive policies, trickled up. In 2017, Congress passed one of the steepest tax cuts in American history, with the lion's share of the benefits going to the very same people who already own the lion's share of the wealth.

Republicans in the nation's capital are not the only source of the problem. Consider liberal, enlightened Silicon Valley, where entrepreneurs build lush corporate campuses, with athletic facilities, biking paths, yoga studios, outdoor lounges, coffee bars, and gourmet cafeterias offering free food and amenities to their workers—except those who do menial jobs. At Google, cafeteria workers are not welcome to eat at the tables they serve, janitors cannot play in the game rooms they clean, drivers cannot ride the Google bus. Less educated people, primarily people of color, are Silicon Valley's second-class citizens. They get low wages. They're ineligible for high-end health-care and retirement plans, and excluded from free childcare.

It's impossible to build solidarity amid extreme inequality. Just as, during the Depression, the New Deal reset the relationship between capital and labor and evened out the distribution of American wealth, so too must the rebuilding of America after COVID-19. Solidarity will once again be essential. How do we restore it at work?

We must rebuild solidarity across ethnic, racial, religious, political, and class lines. We survived the pandemic by shifting the workplace from the office to the den or kitchen table, from the conference room and water cooler to Zoom. After the crisis, many corporations will want to keep us there—home, alone, with our own private infrastructures, not together in the shared physical spaces where relationships grow. Rebuilding solidarity requires us to resist this. In the coronavirus, we've learned to recognize the value of labor—and laborers—that many of us took for granted. Janitors. Clerks. Doormen. Delivery workers. Food servers. Farm workers. We're not only more aware of our interdependence, we're also more attuned to our shared vulnerability and strengths. Our challenge is to honor and sustain that knowledge, so that it's reflected in public policies around taxation and social protection, as well as in our interactions.

We could also adopt new models for building solidarity between workplaces and communities, so that labor unions organize to improve not only wages and working conditions but also the lives of the people they serve. In recent years, teachers' unions across the country have made surprising gains through campaigns to "bargain for the common good." In Los Angeles and Chicago, for instance, teachers' unions have partnered with community organizations to demand more resources for students in "high-needs" schools and impoverished neighborhoods. These initiatives helped teachers find new allies in their communities, new sources of collective strength. We're better off working together.

City

In the ways that matter most, the pandemic has been a divisive and unequal experience for urban residents. In New York, Chicago, Detroit, and Milwaukee, Black people and Black neighborhoods have had significantly higher incidences of the virus than white people and white neighborhoods, and higher mortality rates, too. What these and most other American cities have in common is that they are organized around segregation—by race and by class, often both at once.

Segregation is an engine for sustaining inequality of all kinds. In recent years, as the United States has grown more unequal, both class segregation and the gap between conditions in poor and wealthy neighborhoods within American cities have increased. In the COVID-19 crisis, though, segregation did not fully separate city residents from one another. Infectious diseases do not respect race and class boundaries, and dangerous conditions in one neighborhood endanger others nearby. Extremely unequal and spatially divided cities are unhealthy for everyone. That's why so many affluent urban Americans decided to flee.

After the pandemic, urban Americans will find themselves in a new state of uncertainty. Commercial corridors will be devastated. Restaurants, retailers, and long-running community organizations will be closed. Public institutions—universities, libraries, parks, playgrounds, even hospitals—will need massive bailouts to reopen. Public transit systems will face enormous deficits. Tens of millions of city dwellers will need jobs. Here, again, we can expect Silicon Valley to suggest a remedy. More online shopping. More home deliveries. Virtual libraries instead of neighborhood branches. Digital happy hour instead of drinks at the bar.

That would be a disaster. We long for our gathering places, regardless of the shape they take. If, at first, we may struggle to readjust to physical proximity, never before have we so appreciated the value of shared spaces. It's hard to imagine how we can revive our cities and our economy without investing in new infrastructure. Social infrastructure, widely and fairly distributed, must be part of that plan.

What's Next

When the pandemic ends—and it will end—we must reorient our politics and make substantial new investments in public goods and public services. We need not become less communal. Instead, we will be better able to see how our fates are linked. The cheap burger I get from a restaurant that denies paid sick leave to its cashiers and kitchen staff makes me more vulnerable to illness, as does the neighbor who refuses to wear a mask in a pandemic because our public school failed to teach him science or critical-thinking skills. The economy—and the social order it helps support—will collapse if the government doesn't guarantee income for the millions of workers vulnerable to unemployment. Young adults will struggle if government doesn't significantly reduce or, better, cancel their student debt.

There has never been a better moment for recognizing the depth and scale of our interdependence, the extent to which our fates are linked. There has never been a better time for reviving the New Deal project that rescued America from the modern historical event most similar to the current crisis, the Great Depression. But what we need now is necessarily different, because building solidarity in a society as open and diverse as the contemporary United States requires genuine inclusion, of women and people of color, of white working-class communities ravaged by suicide and addiction, of manual laborers and farm workers who are every bit as "essential" in ordinary times as they are in a crisis. It also requires revitalizing the ecosystems that sustain all life on this planet, which is why the next New Deal must be green.

The Atlantic

FINALIST—REPORTING

The word to describe this article is "prescient." Published online on September 23, 2020, "The Election That Could Break America" bore this subhead: "If the vote is close, Donald Trump could easily throw the election into chaos and subvert the result. Who will stop him?" The judges who nominated "The Election That Could Break America" for the National Magazine Award for Reporting added this: "Drawing on extensive interviews with scholars, lawyers and political strategists, Barton Gellman predicted that Trump would sow doubt about the integrity of the election results and employ arcane legal maneuvers in an attempt to hold on to power. Reading this story is like watching a train come right at you." Now a staff writer at The Atlantic, *Gellman was for twenty-one years a reporter at the* Washington Post, *where his work won three Pulitzer Prizes.*

Barton Gellman

The Election That Could Break America

There is a cohort of close observers of our presidential elections, scholars and lawyers and political strategists, who find themselves in the uneasy position of intelligence analysts in the months before 9/11. As November 3 approaches, their screens are blinking red, alight with warnings that the political system does not know how to absorb. They see the obvious signs that we all see, but they also know subtle things that most of us do not. Something dangerous has hove into view, and the nation is lurching into its path.

The danger is not merely that the 2020 election will bring discord. Those who fear something worse take turbulence and controversy for granted. The coronavirus pandemic, a reckless incumbent, a deluge of mail-in ballots, a vandalized Postal Service, a resurgent effort to suppress votes, and a trainload of lawsuits are bearing down on the nation's creaky electoral machinery.

Something has to give, and many things will, when the time comes for casting, canvassing, and certifying the ballots. Anything is possible, including a landslide that leaves no doubt on Election Night. But even if one side takes a commanding early lead, tabulation and litigation of the "overtime count"—millions of mail-in and provisional ballots—could keep the outcome unsettled for days or weeks.

If we are lucky, this fraught and dysfunctional election cycle will reach a conventional stopping point in time to meet crucial deadlines in December and January. The contest will be decided with sufficient authority that the losing candidate will be forced to yield. Collectively, we will have made our choice—a messy one, no doubt, but clear enough to arm the president-elect with a mandate to govern.

As a nation, we have never failed to clear that bar. But in this election year of plague and recession and catastrophized politics, the mechanisms of decision are at meaningful risk of breaking down. Close students of election law and procedure are warning that conditions are ripe for a constitutional crisis that would leave the nation without an authoritative result. We have no failsafe against that calamity. Thus the blinking red lights.

"We could well see a protracted postelection struggle in the courts and the streets if the results are close," says Richard L. Hasen, a professor at the UC Irvine School of Law and the author of a recent book called *Election Meltdown*. "The kind of election meltdown we could see would be much worse than 2000's *Bush v. Gore* case."

A lot of people, including Joe Biden, the Democratic Party nominee, have misconceived the nature of the threat. They frame it as a concern, unthinkable for presidents past, that Trump might refuse to vacate the Oval Office if he loses. They generally conclude, as Biden has, that in that event the proper authorities "will escort him from the White House with great dispatch."

The worst case, however, is not that Trump rejects the election outcome. The worst case is that he uses his power to prevent a decisive outcome against him. If Trump sheds all restraint, and if his Republican allies play the parts he assigns them, he could obstruct the emergence of a legally unambiguous victory for Biden in the Electoral College and then in Congress. He could prevent the formation of consensus about whether there is any outcome at all. He could seize on that uncertainty to hold on to power.

Trump's state and national legal teams are already laying the groundwork for postelection maneuvers that would circumvent the results of the vote count in battleground states. Ambiguities in the Constitution and logic bombs in the Electoral Count Act make it possible to extend the dispute all the way to Inauguration Day, which would bring the nation to a precipice. The Twentieth Amendment is crystal clear that the president's term in office "shall end" at noon on January 20, but two men could show up to be sworn in. One of them would arrive with all the tools and power of the presidency already in hand.

"We are not prepared for this at all," Julian Zelizer, a Princeton professor of history and public affairs, told me. "We talk about it, some worry about it, and we imagine what it would be. But few people have actual answers to what happens if the machinery of democracy is used to prevent a legitimate resolution to the election."

Nineteen summers ago, when counterterrorism analysts warned of a coming attack by al-Qaeda, they could only guess at a date. This year, if election analysts are right, we know when the trouble is likely to come. Call it the Interregnum: the interval from Election Day to the next president's swearing-in. It is a temporal no-man's-land between the presidency of Donald Trump and an uncertain successor—a second term for Trump or a first for Biden. The transfer of power we usually take for granted has several intermediate steps, and they are fragile.

The Interregnum comprises seventy-nine days, carefully bounded by law. Among them are "the first Monday after the second Wednesday in December," this year December 14, when the electors meet in all fifty states and the District of Columbia to cast their ballots for president; "the 3d day of January," when the newly elected Congress is seated; and "the sixth day of January," when the House and Senate meet jointly for a formal count of the electoral vote. In most modern elections these have been pro forma milestones, irrelevant to the outcome. This year, they may not be.

"Our Constitution does not secure the peaceful transition of power, but rather presupposes it," the legal scholar Lawrence Douglas wrote in a recent book titled simply *Will He Go?* The Interregnum we are about to enter will be accompanied by what Douglas, who teaches at Amherst, calls a "perfect storm" of adverse conditions. We cannot turn away from that storm. On November 3 we sail toward its center mass. If we emerge without trauma, it will not be an unbreakable ship that has saved us.

•   •   •

Let us not hedge about one thing. Donald Trump may win or lose, but he will never concede. Not under any circumstance. Not during the Interregnum and not afterward. If compelled in the end to vacate his office, Trump will insist from exile, as long as he draws breath, that the contest was rigged.

Trump's invincible commitment to this stance will be the most important fact about the coming Interregnum. It will deform the proceedings from beginning to end. We have not experienced anything like it before.

Maybe you hesitate. Is it a *fact* that if Trump loses, he will reject defeat, come what may? Do we *know* that? Technically, you feel obliged to point out, the proposition is framed in the future conditional, and prophecy is no man's gift, and so forth. With all due respect, that is pettifoggery. We know this man. We cannot afford to pretend.

Trump's behavior and declared intent leave no room to suppose that he will accept the public's verdict if the vote is going against him. He lies prodigiously—to manipulate events, to secure advantage, to dodge accountability, and to ward off injury to his pride. An election produces the perfect distillate of all those motives.

Pathology may exert the strongest influence on Trump's choices during the Interregnum. Well-supported arguments, some of them in this magazine, have made the case that Trump fits the diagnostic criteria for psychopathy and narcissism. Either disorder, by its medical definition, would render him all but incapable of accepting defeat.

Conventional commentary has trouble facing this issue squarely. Journalists and opinion makers feel obliged to add disclaimers when asking "what if" Trump loses and refuses to concede. "The scenarios all seem far-fetched," *Politico* wrote, quoting a source who compared them to science fiction. Former U.S. attorney Barbara McQuade, writing in *The Atlantic* in February, could not bring herself to treat the risk as real: "That a president would defy the results of an election has long been unthinkable; it is now, if not an actual possibility, at the very least something Trump's supporters joke about."

But Trump's supporters aren't the only people who think extraconstitutional thoughts aloud. Trump has been asked directly, during both this campaign and the last, whether he will respect the election results. He left his options brazenly open. "What I'm saying is that I will tell you at the time. I'll keep you in suspense. Okay?" he told moderator Chris Wallace in the third presidential debate of 2016. Wallace took another crack at him in an interview for Fox News this past July. "I have to see," Trump said. "Look, you—I have to see. No, I'm not going to just say yes. I'm not going to say no."

How will he decide when the time comes? Trump has answered that, actually. At a rally in Delaware, Ohio, in the closing days of the 2016 campaign, he began his performance with a signal of breaking news. "Ladies and gentlemen, I want to make a major announcement today. I would like to promise and pledge to all of my voters and supporters, and to all the people of the United States, that I will totally accept the results of this great and historic presidential election." He paused, then made three sharp thrusts of his forefinger to punctuate the next words: "If . . . I . . . win!" Only then did he stretch his lips in a simulacrum of a smile.

The question is not strictly hypothetical. Trump's respect for the ballot box has already been tested. In 2016, with the presidency in hand, having won the Electoral College, Trump baldly rejected the certified tallies that showed he had lost the popular vote by a margin of 2,868,692. He claimed, baselessly but not coincidentally, that at least 3 million undocumented immigrants had cast fraudulent votes for Hillary Clinton.

All of which is to say that there is no version of the Interregnum in which Trump congratulates Biden on his victory. He has told us so. "The only way they can take this election away from us is if this is a rigged election," Trump said at the Republican National Convention on August 24. Unless he wins a bona fide victory in the Electoral College, Trump's refusal to concede—his mere denial of defeat—will have cascading effects.

.　　.　　.

The ritual that marks an election's end took its contemporary form in 1896. On the Thursday evening after polls closed that year, unwelcome news reached the Democratic presidential nominee, William Jennings Bryan. A dispatch from Senator James K. Jones, the chair of the Democratic National Committee, informed him that "sufficient was known to make my defeat certain," Bryan recalled in a memoir.

He composed a telegram to his Republican opponent, William McKinley. "Senator Jones has just informed me that the returns indicate your election, and I hasten to extend my congratulations," Bryan wrote. "We have submitted the issue to the American people and their will is law."

After Bryan, concession became a civic duty, performed by telegram or telephone call and then by public speech. Al Smith brought the concession speech to radio in 1928, and it migrated to television soon afterward.

Like other rituals, concessions developed a liturgy. The defeated candidate comes out first. He thanks supporters, declares that their cause will live on, and acknowledges that the other side has prevailed. The victor begins his own remarks by honoring the surrender.

Concessions employ a form of words that linguists call performative speech. The words do not describe or announce an act; the words themselves are the act. "The concession speech, then, is not merely a report of an election result or an admission of defeat," the political scientist Paul E. Corcoran has written. "It is a constitutive enactment of the new president's authority."

In actual war, not the political kind, concession is optional. The winning side may take by force what the losing side refuses to surrender. If the weaker party will not sue for peace, its ramparts may be breached, its headquarters razed, and its leaders taken captive or put to death. There are places in the world where political combat still ends that way, but not here. The loser's concession is therefore hard to replace.

Consider the 2000 election, which may appear at first glance to demonstrate otherwise. Al Gore conceded to George W. Bush on Election Night, then withdrew his concession and fought a recount battle in Florida until the Supreme Court shut it down. It is commonly said that the Court's 5–4 ruling decided the contest, but that's not quite right.

The court handed down its ruling in *Bush v. Gore* on December 12, six days before the Electoral College would convene and weeks before Congress would certify the results. Even with canvassing halted in Florida, Gore had the constitutional means to fight on, and some advisers urged him to do so. If he had brought the dispute to Congress, he would have held high ground as the Senate's presiding officer.

Not until Gore addressed the nation on December 13, the day after the court's decision, did the contest truly end. Speaking as a man with unexpended ammunition, Gore laid down his arms. "I accept the finality of this outcome, which will be ratified next Monday in the Electoral College," he said. "And tonight, for the sake of our unity as a people and the strength of our democracy, I offer my concession."

We have no precedent or procedure to end this election if Biden seems to carry the Electoral College but Trump refuses to concede. We will have to invent one.

· · ·

Trump is, by some measures, a weak authoritarian. He has the mouth but not the muscle to work his will with assurance. Trump denounced Special Counsel Robert Mueller but couldn't fire him. He accused his foes of treason but couldn't jail them. He has bent the bureaucracy and flouted the law but not broken free altogether of their restraints.

A proper despot would not risk the inconvenience of losing an election. He would fix his victory in advance, avoiding the need to overturn an incorrect outcome. Trump cannot do that.

But he's not powerless to skew the proceedings—first on Election Day and then during the Interregnum. He could disrupt the vote count where it's going badly, and if that does not work, try to bypass it altogether. On Election Day, Trump and his allies can begin by suppressing the Biden vote.

There is no truth to be found in dancing around this point, either: Trump does not want Black people to vote. (He said as much in 2017—on Martin Luther King Day, no less—to a voting-rights group cofounded by King, according to a recording leaked to *Politico*.) He does not want young people or poor people to vote. He believes, with reason, that he is less likely to win reelection if turnout is high at the polls. This is not a "both sides" phenomenon. In present-day politics, we have one party that consistently seeks advantage in depriving the other party's adherents of the right to vote.

Just under a year ago, Justin Clark gave a closed-door talk in Wisconsin to a select audience of Republican lawyers. He thought he was speaking privately, but someone had brought a recording device. He had a lot to say about Election Day operations, or "EDO."

At the time, Clark was a senior lieutenant with Trump's reelection campaign; in July, he was promoted to deputy campaign manager. "Wisconsin's the state that is going to tip this one way or the other. . . . So it makes EDO really, really, really important," he said. He put the mission bluntly: "Traditionally it's always been Republicans suppressing votes . . . [Democrats'] voters are all in one part of the state, so let's start playing offense a little bit. And that's what you're going to see in 2020. That's what's going to be markedly different. It's going to be a much bigger program, a much more aggressive program, a much better-funded program, and we're going to need all the help we can get." (Clark later claimed that his remarks had been misconstrued, but his explanation made no sense in context.)

Of all the favorable signs for Trump's Election Day operations, Clark explained, "first and foremost is the consent decree's gone." He was referring to a court order forbidding Republican operatives from using any of a long list of voter-purging and intimidation techniques. The expiration of that order was a "huge, huge, huge, huge deal," Clark said.

His audience of lawyers knew what he meant. The 2020 presidential election will be the first in forty years to take place without a federal judge requiring the Republican National Committee to seek approval in advance for any "ballot security" operations at the polls. In 2018, a federal judge allowed the consent decree to expire, ruling that the plaintiffs had no proof of recent violations by Republicans. The consent decree, by this logic, was not needed, because it worked.

The order had its origins in the New Jersey gubernatorial election of 1981. According to the district court's opinion in *Democratic National Committee v. Republican National Committee*, the RNC allegedly tried to intimidate voters by hiring off-duty law-enforcement officers as members of a "National Ballot Security Task Force," some of them armed and carrying two-way radios. According to the plaintiffs, they stopped and questioned voters in minority neighborhoods, blocked voters from entering the polls, forcibly restrained poll workers, challenged people's eligibility to vote, warned of criminal charges for casting an illegal ballot, and generally did their best to frighten voters away from the polls. The power of these methods relied on well-founded fears among people of color about contact with police.

This year, with a judge no longer watching, the Republicans are recruiting 50,000 volunteers in fifteen contested states to monitor polling places and challenge voters they deem suspicious-looking. Trump called in to Fox News on August 20 to tell Sean Hannity, "We're going to have sheriffs and we're going to have law enforcement and we're going to have, hopefully, U.S. attorneys" to keep close watch on the polls. For the first time in decades, according to Clark, Republicans are free to combat voter fraud in "places that are run by Democrats."

Voter fraud is a fictitious threat to the outcome of elections, a pretext that Republicans use to thwart or discard the ballots of likely opponents. An authoritative report by the Brennan Center for Justice, a nonpartisan think tank, calculated the rate of voter fraud in three elections at between 0.0003 percent and 0.0025 percent. Another investigation, from Justin Levitt at Loyola Law School, turned up thirty-one credible allegations of voter impersonation out of more than 1 billion votes cast in the United States from 2000 to 2014. Judges in voting-rights cases have made comparable findings of fact.

Nonetheless, Republicans and their allies have litigated scores of cases in the name of preventing fraud in this year's election. State by state, they have sought—with some success—to purge voter rolls, tighten rules on provisional votes, uphold voter-identification requirements, ban the use of ballot drop boxes, reduce eligibility to vote by mail, discard mail-in ballots with technical flaws, and outlaw the counting of ballots that are post-marked by Election Day but arrive afterward. The intent and effect is to throw away votes in large numbers.

These legal maneuvers are drawn from an old Republican play-book. What's different during this cycle, aside from the ferocity of the efforts, is the focus on voting by mail. The president has mounted a relentless assault on postal balloting at the exact moment when the coronavirus pandemic is driving tens of millions of voters to embrace it.

．　　．　　．

This year's presidential election will see voting by mail on a scale unlike any before—some states are anticipating a tenfold increase in postal balloting. A fifty-state survey by *The Washington Post* found that 198 million eligible voters, or at least 84 percent, will have the option to vote by mail.

Trump has denounced mail-in voting often and urgently, airing fantastical nightmares. One day he tweeted, "mail-in voting will lead to massive fraud and abuse. it will also lead to the end of our great republican party. we can never let this tragedy befall our nation." Another day he pointed to an imaginary—and easily debunked—scenario of forgery from abroad: "rigged 2020 election: millions of mail-in ballots will be printed by foreign countries, and others. it will be the scandal of our times!"

By late summer Trump was declaiming against mail-in voting an average of nearly four times a day—a pace he had reserved in the past for existential dangers such as impeachment and the Mueller investigation: "Very dangerous for our country." "A catastrophe." "The greatest rigged election in history."

Summer also brought reports that the U.S. Postal Service, the government's most popular agency, was besieged from within by Louis DeJoy, Trump's new postmaster general and a major Republican donor. Service cuts, upper-management restructuring, and chaotic operational changes were producing long delays. At one sorting facility, the *Los Angeles Times* reported, "workers fell so far behind processing packages that by early August, gnats and rodents were swarming around containers of rotted fruit and meat, and baby chicks were dead inside their boxes."

In the name of efficiency, the Postal Service began decommissioning 10 percent of its mail-sorting machines. Then came word that the service would no longer treat ballots as first-class mail unless some states nearly tripled the postage they paid, from twenty to fifty-five cents an envelope. DeJoy denied any intent to slow down voting by mail, and the Postal Service withdrew the plan under fire from critics.

If there were doubts about where Trump stood on these changes, he resolved them at an August 12 news conference. Democrats were negotiating for a $25 billion increase in postal funding and an additional $3.6 billion in election assistance to states. "They don't have the money to do the universal mail-in voting. So therefore, they can't do it, I guess," Trump said. "It's very simple. How are they going to do it if they don't have the money to do it?"

What are we to make of all this?

In part, Trump's hostility to voting by mail is a reflection of his belief that more voting is bad for him in general. Democrats, he said on *Fox & Friends* at the end of March, want "levels of voting that, if you ever agreed to it, you'd never have a Republican elected in this country again."

Some Republicans see Trump's vendetta as self-defeating. "It to me appears entirely irrational," Jeff Timmer, a former executive director of the Michigan Republican Party, told me. "The Trump campaign and RNC and by fiat their state party organizations are engaging in suppressing their own voter turnout," including Republican seniors who have voted by mail for years.

But Trump's crusade against voting by mail is a strategically sound expression of his plan for the Interregnum. The president is not actually trying to prevent mail-in balloting altogether, which he has no means to do. He is discrediting the practice and starving it of resources, signaling his supporters to vote in person, and preparing the ground for post–Election Night plans to contest the results. It is the strategy of a man who expects to be outvoted and means to hobble the count.

Voting by mail does not favor either party "during normal times," according to a team of researchers at Stanford, but that phrase does a lot of work. Their findings, which were published in June, did not take into account a president whose words alone could produce a partisan skew. Trump's systematic predictions of fraud appear to have had a powerful effect on Republican voting intentions. In Georgia, for example, a Monmouth University poll in late July found that 60 percent of Democrats but only 28 percent of Republicans were likely to vote by mail. In the battleground states of Pennsylvania and North Carolina, hundreds of thousands more Democrats than Republicans have requested mail-in ballots.

Trump, in other words, has created a proxy to distinguish friend from foe. Republican lawyers around the country will find this useful when litigating the count. Playing by the numbers, they can treat ballots cast by mail as hostile, just as they do ballots cast in person by urban and college-town voters. Those are the ballots they will contest.

.   .   .

The battle space of the Interregnum, if trends hold true, will be shaped by a phenomenon known as the "blue shift."

Edward Foley, an Ohio State professor of constitutional law and a specialist in election law, pioneered research on the blue shift. He found a previously unremarked-upon pattern in the overtime count—the canvass after Election Night that tallies late-reporting precincts, unprocessed absentee votes, and provisional ballots cast by voters whose eligibility needed to be confirmed. For most of American history, the overtime count produced no predictably partisan effect. In any given election year, some states shifted red in the canvass after Election Day and some shifted blue, but the shifts were seldom large enough to matter.

Two things began to change about twenty years ago. The overtime count got bigger, and it trended more and more blue. In an updated paper this year, Foley and his coauthor, Charles Stewart III of MIT, said they could not fully explain why the shift favors Democrats. (Some factors: urban returns take longer to count, and most provisional ballots are cast by young, low-income, or mobile voters, who lean blue.) During overtime in 2012, Barack Obama strengthened his winning margins in swing states like Florida (with a net increase of 27,281 votes), Michigan (60,695), Ohio (65,459), and Pennsylvania (26,146). Obama would have won the presidency anyway, but shifts of that magnitude could have changed the outcomes of many a closer contest. Hillary Clinton picked up tens of thousands of overtime votes in 2016, but not enough to save her.

The blue shift has yet to decide a presidential election, but it upended the Arizona Senate race in 2018. Republican Martha McSally seemed to have victory in her grasp with a lead of 15,403 votes the day after Election Day. Canvassing in the days that followed swept the Democrat, Kyrsten Sinema, into the Senate with "a gigantic overtime gain of 71,303 votes," Foley wrote.

It was Florida, however, that seized Trump's attention that year. On Election Night, Republicans were leading in tight contests for governor and U.S. senator. As the blue shift took effect, Ron DeSantis watched his lead shrink by 18,416 votes in the governor's race. Rick Scott's Senate margin fell by 20,231. By early morning on November 12, six days after Election Day, Trump had seen enough. "The Florida Election should be called in favor of Rick Scott and Ron DeSantis in that large numbers of new ballots showed up out of nowhere, and many ballots are missing or forged," he tweeted, baselessly. "An honest vote count is no longer possible—ballots massively infected. Must go with Election Night!"

Trump was panicked enough by the blue shift in somebody else's election to fabricate allegations of fraud. In this election, when his own name is on the ballot, the blue shift could be the largest ever observed. Mail-in votes require more time to count even in a normal year, and this year there will be tens of millions more of them than in any election before. Many states forbid the processing of early-arriving mail ballots before Election Day; some allow late-arriving ballots to be counted.

Trump's instinct as a spectator in 2018—to stop the count—looks more like strategy this year. "There are results that come in Election Night," a legal adviser to Trump's national campaign, who would not agree to be quoted by name, told me. "There's an expectation in the country that there will be winners and losers called. If the Election Night results get changed because of the ballots counted after Election Day, you have the basic ingredients for a shitstorm."

There is no "if" about it, I said. The count is bound to change. "Yeah," the adviser agreed, and canvassing will produce more votes for Biden than for Trump. Democrats will insist on dragging out the canvass for as long as it takes to count every vote. The resulting conflict, the adviser said, will be on their heads.

"They are asking for it," he said. "They're trying to maximize their electoral turnout, and they think there are no downsides to that." He added, "There will be a count on Election Night, that count will shift over time, and the results when the final count is given will be challenged as being inaccurate, fraudulent—pick your word."

The worst case for an orderly count is also considered by some election modelers the likeliest: that Trump will jump ahead on Election Night, based on in-person returns, but his lead will slowly give way to a Biden victory as mail-in votes are tabulated.

Josh Mendelsohn, the CEO of the Democratic data-modeling firm Hawkfish, calls this scenario "the red mirage." The turbulence of that interval, fed by street protests, social media, and Trump's desperate struggles to lock in his lead, can only be imagined. "Any scenario that you come up with will not be as weird as the reality of it," the Trump legal adviser said.

•   •   •

Election lawyers speak of a "margin of litigation" in close races. The tighter the count in early reports, and the more votes remaining to count, the greater the incentive to fight in court. If there were such a thing as an Election Administrator's Prayer, as some of them say only half in jest, it would go, "Lord, let there be a landslide."

Could a landslide spare us conflict in the Interregnum? In theory, yes. But the odds are not promising.

It is hard to imagine a Trump lead so immense on Election Night that it places him out of Biden's reach. Unless the swing states manage to count most of their mail-in ballots that night, which will be all but impossible for some of them, the expectation of a blue shift will keep Biden fighting on. A really big Biden lead on Election Night, on the other hand, could leave Trump without plausible hope of catching up. If this happens, we may see it first in Florida. But this scenario is awfully optimistic for Biden, considering the GOP advantage among in-person voters, and in any case Trump will not concede defeat. This early in the Interregnum, he will have practical options to keep the contest alive.

Both parties are bracing for a torrent of emergency motions in state and federal courts. They have already been skirmishing from courthouse to courthouse all year in more than forty states, and Election Day will begin a culminating phase of legal combat.

Mail-in ballots will have plenty of flaws for the Trump lawyers to seize upon. Voting by mail is more complicated than voting in person, and technical errors are commonplace at each step. If voters supply a new address or if they write a different version of their name (for example, by shortening Benjamin to Ben) or if their signature has changed over the years or if they print their name on the signature line or if they fail to seal the ballot inside an inner security envelope, their votes may not count. With in-person voting, a poll worker in the precinct can resolve small errors like these, for instance by directing a voter to the correct signature line, but people voting by mail may have no opportunity to address them.

During the primaries this spring, Republican lawyers did dry runs for the November vote at county election offices around the country. An internal memo prepared by an attorney named J. Matthew Wolfe for the Pennsylvania Republican Party in June reported on one such exercise. Wolfe, along with another Republican lawyer and a member of the Trump campaign, watched closely but did not intervene as election commissioners in Philadelphia canvassed mail-in and provisional votes. Wolfe cataloged imperfections, taking note of objections that his party could have raised.

There were missing signatures and partial signatures and signatures placed in the wrong spot. There were names on the inner security envelopes, which are supposed to be unmarked, and ballots without security envelopes at all. Some envelopes arrived "without a postmark or with an illegible postmark," Wolfe wrote. (Watch for postmarks to become the hanging chads of 2020.) Some voters wrote their birth date where a signature date belonged, and others put down "an impossible date, like a date after the primary election."

Some of the commissioners' decisions "were clear violations of the direction in and language of the election code," Wolfe wrote. He recommended that "someone connected with the party review each application and each mail ballot envelope" in November. That is exactly the plan.

Legal teams on both sides are planning for simultaneous litigation, on the scale of Florida during the 2000 election, in multiple battleground states. "My money would be on Texas, Georgia, and Florida" to be trouble spots, Myrna Pérez, the director of voting rights and elections at the Brennan Center, told me.

There are endless happenstances in any election for lawyers to exploit. In Montgomery County, Pennsylvania, not far from Wolfe's Philadelphia experiment, the county Republican committee gathered surveillance-style photographs of purportedly suspicious goings-on at a ballot drop box during the primary. In one sequence, a county employee is described as placing "unsecured ballots" in the trunk of a car. In another, a security guard is said to be "disconnecting the generator which supplies power to the security cameras." The photos could mean anything—it's impossible to tell, out of context—but they are exactly the kind of ersatz evidence that is sure to go viral in the early days of the Interregnum.

The electoral combat will not confine itself to the courtroom. Local election adjudicators can expect to be named and doxed and pilloried as agents of George Soros or antifa. Aggressive crowds of self-proclaimed ballot guardians will be spoiling to reenact the "Brooks Brothers riot" of the *Bush v. Gore* Florida recount, when demonstrators paid by the Bush campaign staged a violent protest that physically prevented canvassers from completing a recount in Miami-Dade County.

Things like this have already happened, albeit on a smaller scale than we can expect in November. With Trump we must also ask: What might a ruthless incumbent do that has never been tried before?

Suppose that caravans of Trump supporters, adorned in Second Amendment accessories, converge on big-city polling places on Election Day. They have come, they say, to investigate reports on social media of voter fraud. Counterprotesters arrive, fistfights break out, shots are fired, and voters flee or cannot reach the polls.

Then suppose the president declares an emergency. Federal personnel in battle dress, staged nearby in advance, move in to restore law and order and secure the balloting. Amid ongoing clashes, they stay to monitor the canvass. They close the streets that lead to the polls. They take custody of uncounted ballots in order to preserve evidence of fraud.

"The president can't cancel the election, but what if he says, 'We're in an emergency, and we're shutting down this area for a period of time because of the violence taking place'?" says Norm Ornstein of the American Enterprise Institute. If you are in Trump's camp and heedless of boundaries, he said, "what I would expect is you're not going to do one or two of these things—you'll do as many as you can."

There are variations of the nightmare. The venues of intervention could be post offices. The predicate could be a putative intelligence report on forged ballots sent from China.

This is speculation, of course. But none of these scenarios is far removed from things the president has already done or threatened to do. Trump dispatched the National Guard to Washington, DC, and sent Department of Homeland Security forces to Portland, Oregon, and Seattle during summertime protests for racial justice, on the slender pretext of protecting federal buildings. He said he might invoke the Insurrection Act of 1807 and "deploy the United States military" to "Democrat-run cities" in order to protect "life and property." The federal government has little basis to intercede during elections, which are largely governed by state law and administered by about 10,500 local jurisdictions, but no one familiar with Attorney General Bill Barr's view of presidential power should doubt that he can find authority for Trump.

With every day that passes after November 3, the president and his allies can hammer home the message that the legitimate tabulation is over and the Democrats are refusing to honor the results. Trump has been flogging this horse already for months. In July he tweeted, "Must know Election results on the night of the Election, not days, months, or even years later!"

Does it matter what Trump says? It is tempting to liken a vote count to the score at a sporting event. The losing coach can bellyache all he likes, but when the umpire makes the call, the game is over. An important thing to know about the Interregnum is that there is no umpire—no singular authority who can decide the contest and lay it to rest. There is a series of lesser officiants, each confined in jurisdiction and tangled in opaque rules.

Trump's strategy for this phase of the Interregnum will be a play for time as much as a concerted attempt to squelch the count and disqualify Biden votes. The courts may eventually weigh in. But by then, the forum of decision may already have moved elsewhere.

. . .

The Interregnum allots thirty-five days for the count and its attendant lawsuits to be resolved. On the thirty-sixth day, December 8, an important deadline arrives.

At this stage, the actual tabulation of the vote becomes less salient to the outcome. That sounds as though it can't be right, but it is: the combatants, especially Trump, will now shift their attention to the appointment of presidential electors.

December 8 is known as the "safe harbor" deadline for appointing the 538 men and women who make up the Electoral College. The electors do not meet until six days later, December 14, but each state must appoint them by the safe-harbor date to guarantee that Congress will accept their credentials. The controlling statute says that if "any controversy or contest" remains after that, then Congress will decide which electors, if any, may cast the state's ballots for president.

We are accustomed to choosing electors by popular vote, but nothing in the Constitution says it has to be that way. Article II provides that each state shall appoint electors "in such Manner as the Legislature thereof may direct." Since the late nineteenth century, every state has ceded the decision to its voters. Even so, the Supreme Court affirmed in *Bush v. Gore* that a state "can take back the power to appoint electors." How and when a state might do so has not been tested for well over a century.

Trump may test this. According to sources in the Republican Party at the state and national levels, the Trump campaign is discussing contingency plans to bypass election results and appoint loyal electors in battleground states where Republicans hold the legislative majority. With a justification based on claims of rampant fraud, Trump would ask state legislators to set aside the popular vote and exercise their power to choose a slate of electors directly. The longer Trump succeeds in keeping the vote count in doubt, the more pressure legislators will feel to act before the safe-harbor deadline expires.

To a modern democratic sensibility, discarding the popular vote for partisan gain looks uncomfortably like a coup, whatever license may be found for it in law. Would Republicans find that position disturbing enough to resist? Would they cede the election before resorting to such a ploy? Trump's base would exact a high price for that betrayal, and by this point party officials would be invested in a narrative of fraud.

The Trump-campaign legal adviser I spoke with told me the push to appoint electors would be framed in terms of protecting the people's will. Once committed to the position that the overtime count has been rigged, the adviser said, state lawmakers will want to judge for themselves what the voters intended.

"The state legislatures will say, 'All right, we've been given this constitutional power. We don't think the results of our own state are accurate, so here's our slate of electors that we think properly reflect the results of our state,'" the adviser said. Democrats, he added, have exposed themselves to this stratagem by creating the conditions for a lengthy overtime.

"If you have this notion," the adviser said, "that ballots can come in for I don't know how many days—in some states a week, ten days—then that onslaught of ballots just gets pushed back and pushed back and pushed back. So pick your poison. Is it worse to have electors named by legislators or to have votes received by Election Day?"

When *The Atlantic* asked the Trump campaign about plans to circumvent the vote and appoint loyal electors, and about other strategies discussed in the article, the deputy national press secretary did not directly address the questions. "It's outrageous that President Trump and his team are being villainized for upholding the rule of law and transparently fighting for a free and fair election," Thea McDonald said in an email. "The mainstream media are giving the Democrats a free pass for their attempts to completely uproot the system and throw our election into chaos." Trump is fighting for a trustworthy election, she wrote, "and any argument otherwise is a conspiracy theory intended to muddy the waters."

In Pennsylvania, three Republican leaders told me they had already discussed the direct appointment of electors among themselves, and one said he had discussed it with Trump's national campaign.

"I've mentioned it to them, and I hope they're thinking about it too," Lawrence Tabas, the Pennsylvania Republican Party's chairman, told me. "I just don't think this is the right time for me to be discussing those strategies and approaches, but [direct appointment of electors] is one of the options. It is one of the available legal options set forth in the Constitution." He added that everyone's preference is to get a swift and accurate count. "If the process, though, is flawed, and has significant flaws, our public may lose faith and confidence" in the election's integrity.

Jake Corman, the state's senate majority leader, preferred to change the subject, emphasizing that he hoped a clean vote count would produce a final tally on Election Night. "The longer it goes on, the more opinions and the more theories and the more conspiracies [are] created," he told me. If controversy persists as the safe-harbor date nears, he allowed, the legislature will have no choice but to appoint electors. "We don't want to go down that road, but we understand where the law takes us, and we'll follow the law."

Republicans control both legislative chambers in the six most closely contested battleground states. Of those, Arizona and Florida have Republican governors, too. In Michigan, North Carolina, Pennsylvania, and Wisconsin, the governors are Democrats.

Foley, the Ohio State election scholar, has mapped the ripple effects if Republican legislators were to appoint Trump electors in defiance of the vote in states like Pennsylvania and Michigan. The Democratic governors would respond by certifying the official count, a routine exercise of their authority, and they would argue that legislators could not lawfully choose different electors after the vote had taken place. Their "certificates of ascertainment," dispatched to the National Archives, would say that their states had appointed electors committed to Biden. Each competing set of electors would have the imprimatur of one branch of state government.

In Arizona, Secretary of State Katie Hobbs, who oversees elections, is a Democrat. She could assert her own power to certify the voting results and forward a slate of Biden electors. Even in Florida, which has unified Republican rule, electors pledged to Biden could meet and certify their own votes in hope of triggering a "controversy or contest" that would leave their state's outcome to Congress. Much the same thing almost happened during the Florida recount battle of 2000. Republican Governor Jeb Bush certified electors for his brother, George W. Bush, on November 26 of that year, while litigation of the recount was still under way. Gore's chief lawyer, Ronald Klain, responded by booking a room in the old Florida capitol building for Democratic electors to cast rival ballots for Gore. Only Gore's concession, five days before the Electoral College vote, mooted that plan.

In any of these scenarios, the Electoral College would convene on December 14 without a consensus on who had legitimate claims to cast the deciding votes.

Rival slates of electors could hold mirror-image meetings in Harrisburg, Lansing, Tallahassee, or Phoenix, casting the same electoral votes on opposite sides. Each slate would transmit its ballots, as the Constitution provides, "to the seat of the government of the United States, directed to the President of the Senate." The next move would belong to Vice President Mike Pence.

This would be a genuine constitutional crisis, the first but not the last of the Interregnum. "Then we get thrown into a world where anything could happen," Norm Ornstein says.

.   .   .

Two men are claiming the presidency. The next occasion to settle the matter is more than three weeks away.

January 6 comes just after the new Congress is sworn in. Control of the Senate will be crucial to the presidency now.

Pence, as president of the Senate, would hold in his hands two conflicting electoral certificates from each of several swing states. The Twelfth Amendment says only this about what happens next: "The President of the Senate shall, in the presence of the Senate and the House of Representatives, open all the certificates and the votes shall then be counted."

Note the passive voice. Who does the counting? Which certificates are counted?

The Trump team would take the position that the constitutional language leaves those questions to the vice president. This means that Pence has the unilateral power to announce his own reelection, and a second term for Trump. Democrats and legal scholars would denounce the self-dealing and point out that Congress filled the gaps in the Twelfth Amendment with the Electoral Count Act, which provides instructions for how to resolve this kind of dispute. The trouble with the instructions is that they are widely considered, in Foley's words, to be "convoluted and impenetrable," "confusing and ugly," and "one of the strangest pieces of statutory language ever enacted by Congress."

If the Interregnum is a contest in search of an umpire, it now has 535 of them, and a rule book that no one is sure how to read. The presiding officer is one of the players on the field. Foley has produced a 25,000-word study in the *Loyola University Chicago Law Journal* that maps out the paths the ensuing fight could take if only *one* state's electoral votes are in play.

If Democrats win back the Senate and hold the House, then all roads laid out in the Electoral Count Act lead eventually to a Biden presidency. The reverse applies if Republicans hold the Senate and unexpectedly win back the House. But if Congress remains split, there are conditions in which no decisive outcome is possible—no result that has clear force of law. Each party could cite a plausible reading of the rules in which its candidate has won. There is no tie-breaking vote.

How can it be that Congress slips into unbreakable deadlock? The law is a labyrinth in these parts, too intricate to map in a magazine article, but I can sketch one path.

Suppose Pennsylvania alone sends rival slates of electors, and their twenty votes will decide the presidency.

One reading of the Electoral Count Act says that Congress must recognize the electors certified by the governor, who is a Democrat, unless the House and Senate agree otherwise. The House will not agree otherwise, and so Biden wins Pennsylvania and the White House. But Pence pounds his gavel and rules against this reading of the law, instead favoring another, which holds that Congress must discard both contested slates of electors. The garbled statute can plausibly be read either way.

With Pennsylvania's electors disqualified, 518 electoral votes remain. If Biden holds a narrow lead among them, he again claims the presidency, because he has "the greatest number of votes," as the Twelfth Amendment prescribes. But Republicans point out that the same amendment requires "a majority of the whole number of electors." The whole number of electors, Pence rules, is 538, and Biden is short of the required 270.

On this argument, no one has attained the presidency, and the decision is thrown to the House, with one vote per state. If the current partisan balance holds, 26 out of 50 votes will be for Trump.

Before Pence can move on from Pennsylvania to Rhode Island, which is next on the alphabetical list as Congress counts the vote, House Speaker Nancy Pelosi expels all senators from the floor of her chamber. Now Pence is prevented from completing the count "in the presence of" the House, as the Constitution requires. Pelosi announces plans to stall indefinitely. If the count is still incomplete on Inauguration Day, the speaker herself will become acting president.

Pelosi prepares to be sworn in on January 20 unless Pence reverses his ruling and accepts that Biden won. Pence does not budge. He reconvenes the Senate in another venue, with House Republicans squeezing in, and purports to complete the count, making Trump the president-elect. Three people now have supportable claims to the Oval Office.

There are other paths in the labyrinth. Many lead to dead ends.

This is the next constitutional crisis, graver than the one three weeks before, because the law and the Constitution provide for no other authority to consult. The Supreme Court may yet intervene, but it may also shy away from another traumatizing encounter with a fundamentally political question.

Sixty-four days have passed since the election. Stalemate reigns. Two weeks remain until Inauguration Day.

.   .   .

Foley, who foresaw this impasse, knows of no solution. He cannot tell you how we avoid it under current law or how it ends. It is not so much, at this point, a question of law. It is a question of power. Trump has possession of the White House. How far will he push boundaries to keep it, and who will push back? It is the same question the president has posed since the day he took office.

I hoped to gain some insight from a series of exercises conducted this summer by a group of former elected officials, academics, political strategists, and lawyers. In four days of simulations, the Transition Integrity Project modeled the election and its aftermath in an effort to find pivot points where things could fall apart.

They found plenty. Some of the scenarios included dueling slates of electors of the kind I have described. In one version it was the Democratic governor of Michigan who first resorted to appointing electors, after Trump ordered the National Guard to halt the vote count and a Trump-friendly guardsman destroyed mail-in ballots. John Podesta, Hillary Clinton's campaign chair in 2016, led a Biden team in another scenario that was prepared to follow Trump to the edge of civil war, encouraging three blue states to threaten secession. Norm-breaking begat norm-breaking. (Clinton herself, in an August interview for Showtime's *The Circus*, caught the same spirit. "Joe Biden should not concede under any circumstances," she said.)

A great deal has been written about the proceedings, including a firsthand account from my colleague David Frum. But the coverage had a puzzling gap. None of the stories fully explained how the contest ended. I wanted to know who took the oath of office.

I called Rosa Brooks, a Georgetown professor who cofounded the project. Unnervingly, she had no answers for me. She did not know how the story turned out. In half of the simulations, the participants did not make it as far as Inauguration Day.

"We got to points in the scenarios where there was a constitutional impasse, no clear means of resolution in sight, street-level violence," she said. "I think in one of them we had Trump invoking the Insurrection Act and we had troops in the streets. . . . Five hours had gone by and we sort of said, 'Okay, we're done.'" She added: "Once things were clearly off the rails, there was no particular benefit to seeing exactly how far off they would go."

"Our goal in doing this was to try to identify intervention moments, to identify moments where we could then look back and say, 'What would have changed this? What would have kept it from getting this bad?'" Brooks said. The project didn't make much progress there. No lessons were learned about how to restrain a lawless president once a conflict was under way, no alternative moves devised to stave off disaster. "I suppose you could say we were in terra incognita: no one could predict what would happen anymore," Brooks told me in a follow-up email.

• • •

The political system may no longer be strong enough to preserve its integrity. It's a mistake to take for granted that election boards and state legislatures and Congress are capable of drawing lines that ensure a legitimate vote and an orderly transfer of power. We may have to find a way to draw those lines ourselves.

There are reforms to consider some other day, when an election is not upon us. Small ones, like clearing up the murky parts of the Electoral Count Act. Big ones, like doing away with the Electoral College. Obvious ones, like appropriating money to help cash-starved election authorities upgrade their operations in order to speed up and secure the count on Election Day.

Right now, the best we can do is an ad hoc defense of democracy. Begin by rejecting the temptation to think that this election will carry on as elections usually do. Something far out of the norm is likely to happen. Probably more than one thing. Expecting otherwise will dull our reflexes. It will lull us into spurious hope that Trump is tractable to forces that constrain normal incumbents.

If you are a voter, think about voting in person after all. More than half a million postal votes were rejected in this year's primaries, even without Trump trying to suppress them. If you are at relatively low risk for COVID-19, volunteer to work at the polls.

If you know people who are open to reason, spread word that it is normal for the results to keep changing after Election Night. If you manage news coverage, anticipate extraconstitutional measures, and position reporters and crews to respond to them. If you are an election administrator, plan for contingencies you never had to imagine before. If you are a mayor, consider how to deploy your police to ward off interlopers with bad intent. If you are a law-enforcement officer, protect the freedom to vote. If you are a legislator, choose not to participate in chicanery. If you are a judge on the bench in a battleground state, refresh your acquaintance with election case law. If you have a place in the military chain of command, remember your duty to turn aside unlawful orders. If you are a civil servant, know that your country needs you more than ever to do the right thing when you're asked to do otherwise.

Take agency. An election cannot be stolen unless the American people, at some level, acquiesce. One thing Brooks has been thinking about since her exercise came to an end is the power of peaceful protest on a grand scale. "We had players on both sides attempting to mobilize their supporters to turn out in large numbers, and we didn't really have a good mechanism for deciding, did that make a difference? What kind of difference did that make?" she said. "It left some with some big questions about what if you had Orange Revolution–style mass protest sustained over weeks. What effects would that have?"

.   .   .

Only once, in 1877, has the Interregnum brought the country to the brink of true collapse. We will find no model in that episode for us now.

Four states sent rival slates of electors to Congress in the 1876 presidential race between Democrat Samuel Tilden and Republican Rutherford B. Hayes. When a special tribunal blessed the electors for Hayes, Democrats began parliamentary maneuvers to obstruct the electoral count in Congress. Their plan was to run out the clock all the way to Inauguration Day, when the Republican incumbent, Ulysses S. Grant, would have to step down.

Not until two days before Grant's term expired did Tilden give in. His concession was based on a repugnant deal for the withdrawal of federal troops from the South, where they were protecting the rights of emancipated Black people. But that was not Tilden's only inducement.

The threat of military force was in the air. Grant let it be known that he was prepared to declare martial law in New York, where rumor had it that Tilden planned to be sworn in, and to back the inauguration of Hayes with uniformed troops.

That is an unsettling precedent for 2021. If our political institutions fail to produce a legitimate president, and if Trump maintains the stalemate into the new year, the chaos candidate and the commander in chief will be one and the same.

The Atlantic

FINALIST—ESSAYS AND
CRITICISM

The Atlantic *received eight
nominations for National
Magazine Awards this year,
including two for the work of Anne
Applebaum: the first for a series of
columns on subjects ranging from
the crisis in Venezuela to the impact
of coronavirus on America, the
second for this article. Nominated
in Essays and Criticism, "The
Collaborators" was described by
the judges as "magisterial." The
judges continued by echoing
the question Applebaum sought
to answer: Why did Republican
leaders abandon their principles
to support an immoral and
dangerous president? Applebaum
found the solution in the history and
psychology of collaboration—in
her own words, "the experiences
of Frenchmen in 1940, or of East
Germans in 1945, or of [Poles] in
1947." A former member of the
editorial board at the* Washington
Post, *Applebaum won the Pulitzer
Prize in 2004 for her book* Gulag:
A History.

Anne Applebaum

The Collaborators

On a cold March afternoon in 1949, Wolfgang Leonhard slipped out of the East German Communist Party Secretariat, hurried home, packed what few warm clothes he could fit into a small briefcase, and then walked to a telephone box to call his mother. "My article will be finished this evening," he told her. That was the code they had agreed on in advance. It meant that he was escaping the country, at great risk to his life.

Though only twenty-eight years old at the time, Leonhard stood at the pinnacle of the new East German elite. The son of German communists, he had been educated in the Soviet Union, trained in special schools during the war, and brought back to Berlin from Moscow in May 1945, on the same airplane that carried Walter Ulbricht, the leader of what would soon become the East German Communist Party. Leonhard was put on a team charged with re-creating Berlin's city government.

He had one central task: to ensure that any local leaders who emerged from the postwar chaos were assigned deputies loyal to the party. "It's got to look democratic," Ulbricht told him, "but we must have everything in our control." Leonhard had lived through a great deal by that time. While he was still a teenager in Moscow, his mother had been arrested as an "enemy of the people" and sent to Vorkuta, a labor camp in the far north. He had witnessed the terrible poverty and inequality of the Soviet Union, he had despaired of the Soviet alliance with Nazi Germany between 1939 and 1941, and he knew about the Red Army's mass rapes of women following the occupation. Yet he and his ideologically committed friends "instinctively recoiled from the thought" that any of these events were "in diametrical opposition to our Socialist ideals." Steadfastly, he clung to the belief system he had grown up with.

The turning point, when it came, was trivial. While walking down the hall of the Central Committee building, he was stopped by a "pleasant-looking middle-aged man," a comrade recently arrived from the West, who asked where to find the dining room. Leonhard told him that the answer depended on what sort of meal ticket he had—different ranks of officials had access to different dining rooms. The comrade was astonished: "But . . . aren't they all members of the party?"

Leonhard walked away and entered his own, top-category dining room, where white cloths covered the tables and high-ranking functionaries received three-course meals. He felt ashamed. "Curious, I thought, that this had never struck me before!" That was when he began to have the doubts that inexorably led him to plot his escape.

At exactly that same moment, in exactly the same city, another high-ranking East German was coming to precisely the opposite set of conclusions. Markus Wolf was also the son of a prominent German communist family. He also spent his childhood in the Soviet Union, attending the same elite schools for children of foreign communists as Leonhard did, as well as the same wartime training camp; the two had shared a bedroom there, solemnly calling each other by their aliases—these were the rules of deep conspiracy—although they knew each other's real names perfectly well. Wolf also witnessed the mass arrests, the purges, and the poverty of the Soviet Union—and he also kept faith with the cause. He arrived in Berlin just a few days after Leonhard, on another plane full of trusted comrades, and immediately began hosting a program on the new Soviet-backed radio station. For many months he ran the popular *You Ask, We Answer*. He gave on-air answers to listeners' letters, often concluding with some form of "These difficulties are being overcome with the help of the Red Army."

In August 1947, the two men met up at Wolf 's "luxurious five-roomed apartment," not far from what was then the headquarters of the radio station. They drove out to Wolf 's house, "a fine villa in the neighborhood of Lake Glienicke." They took a walk around the lake, and Wolf warned Leonhard that changes were coming. He told him to give up hoping that German communism would be allowed to develop differently from the Soviet version: that idea, long the goal of many German party members, was about to be dropped. When Leonhard argued that this could not be true—he was personally in charge of ideology, and no one had told him anything about a change in direction—Wolf laughed at him. "There are higher authorities than your Central Secretariat," he said. Wolf made clear that he had better contacts, more important friends. At the age of twenty-four, he was an insider. And Leonhard understood, finally, that he was a functionary in an occupied country where the Soviet Communist Party, not the German Communist Party, had the last word.

Famously, or perhaps infamously, Markus Wolf 's career continued to flourish after that. Not only did he stay in East Germany, he rose through the ranks of its *nomenklatura* to become the country's top spy. He was the second-ranked official at the Ministry of State Security, better known as the Stasi; he was often described as the model for the Karla character in John le Carré's spy novels. In the course of his career, his Directorate for Reconnaissance recruited agents in the offices of the West German chancellor and just about every other department of the government, as well as at NATO.

Leonhard, meanwhile, became a prominent critic of the regime. He wrote and lectured in West Berlin, at Oxford, at Columbia. Eventually he wound up at Yale, where his lecture course left an impression on several generations of students. Among them was a future U.S. president, George W. Bush, who described Leonhard's course as "an introduction to the struggle between tyranny and freedom." When I was at Yale in the 1980s, Leonhard's course on Soviet history was the most popular on campus.

Separately, each man's story makes sense. But when examined together, they require some deeper explanation. Until March 1949, Leonhard's and Wolf's biographies were strikingly similar. Both grew up inside the Soviet system. Both were educated in communist ideology, and both had the same values. Both knew that the party was undermining those values. Both knew that the system, allegedly built to promote equality, was deeply unequal, profoundly unfair, and very cruel. Like their counterparts in so many other times and places, both men could plainly see the gap between propaganda and reality. Yet one remained an enthusiastic collaborator while the other could not bear the betrayal of his ideals. Why?

·　　·　　·

In English, the word *collaborator* has a double meaning. A colleague can be described as a collaborator in a neutral or positive sense. But the other definition of *collaborator*, relevant here, is different: someone who works with the enemy, with the occupying power, with the dictatorial regime. In this negative sense, *collaborator* is closely related to another set of words: *collusion, complicity, connivance.* This negative meaning gained currency during the Second World War, when it was widely used to describe Europeans who cooperated with Nazi occupiers. At base, the ugly meaning of *collaborator* carries an implication of treason: betrayal of one's nation, of one's ideology, of one's morality, of one's values.

Since the Second World War, historians and political scientists have tried to explain why some people in extreme circumstances become collaborators and others do not. The late Harvard scholar Stanley Hoffmann had firsthand knowledge of the subject—as a child, he and his mother hid from the Nazis in Lamalou-les-Bains, a village in the south of France. But he was modest about his own conclusions, noting that "a careful historian would have—almost—to write a huge series of case histories; for there seem to have been almost as many collaborationisms as there were proponents or practitioners of collaboration." Still, Hoffmann made a stab at classification, beginning with a division of collaborators into "voluntary" and "involuntary." Many people in the latter group had no choice. Forced into a "reluctant recognition of necessity," they could not avoid dealing with the Nazi occupiers who were running their country.

Hoffmann further sorted the more enthusiastic "voluntary" collaborators into two additional categories. In the first were those who worked with the enemy in the name of "national interest," rationalizing collaboration as something necessary for the preservation of the French economy or French culture—though of course many people who made these arguments had other professionals or economic motives, too. In the second were the truly active ideological collaborators: people who believed that prewar republican France had been weak or corrupt and hoped that the Nazis would strengthen it, people who admired fascism, and people who admired Hitler.

Hoffmann observed that many of those who became ideological collaborators were landowners and aristocrats, "the cream of the top of the civil service, of the armed forces, of the business community," people who perceived themselves as part of a natural ruling class that had been unfairly deprived of power under the left-wing governments of France in the 1930s. Equally motivated to collaborate were their polar opposites, the "social misfits and political deviants" who would, in the normal course of events, never have made successful careers of any kind. What brought these groups together was a common conclusion that, whatever they had thought about Germany before June 1940, their political and personal futures would now be improved by aligning themselves with the occupiers.

Like Hoffmann, Czeslaw Milosz, a Nobel Prize–winning Polish poet, wrote about collaboration from personal experience. An active member of the anti-Nazi resistance during the war, he nevertheless wound up after the war as a cultural attaché at the Polish embassy in Washington, serving his country's communist government. Only in 1951 did he defect, denounce the regime, and dissect his experience. In a famous essay, *The Captive Mind*, he sketched several lightly disguised portraits of real people, all writers and intellectuals, each of whom had come up with different ways of justifying collaboration with the party. Many were careerists, but Milosz understood that careerism could not provide a complete explanation. To be part of a mass movement was for many a chance to end their alienation, to feel close to the "masses," to be united in a single community with workers and shopkeepers. For tormented intellectuals, collaboration also offered a kind of relief, almost a sense of peace: it meant that they were no longer constantly at war with the state, no longer in turmoil. Once the intellectual has accepted that there is no other way, Milosz wrote, "he eats with relish, his movements take on vigor, his color returns. He sits down and writes a 'positive' article, marveling at the ease with which he writes it." Milosz is one of the few writers to acknowledge the *pleasure* of conformity, the lightness of heart that it grants, the way that it solves so many personal and professional dilemmas.

We all feel the urge to conform; it is the most normal of human desires. I was reminded of this recently when I visited Marianne

Birthler in her light-filled apartment in Berlin. During the 1980s, Birthler was one of a very small number of active dissidents in East Germany; later, in reunified Germany, she spent more than a decade running the Stasi archive, the collection of former East German secret-police files. I asked her whether she could identify among her cohort a set of circumstances that had inclined some people to collaborate with the Stasi.

She was put off by the question. Collaboration wasn't interesting, Birthler told me. Almost everyone was a collaborator; 99 percent of East Germans collaborated. If they weren't working with the Stasi, then they were working with the party or with the system more generally. Much more interesting—and far harder to explain—was the genuinely mysterious question of "why people went against the regime." The puzzle is not why Markus Wolf remained in East Germany, in other words, but why Wolfgang Leonhard did not.

.   .   .

Here is another pair of stories, one that will be more familiar to American readers. Let's begin this one in the 1980s, when a young Lindsey Graham first served with the Judge Advocate General's Corps—the military legal service—in the U.S. Air Force. During some of that time, Graham was based in what was then West Germany, on the cutting edge of America's Cold War efforts. Graham, born and raised in a small town in South Carolina, was devoted to the military: After both of his parents died when he was in his twenties, he got himself and his younger sister through college with the help of an ROTC stipend and then an air force salary. He stayed in the reserves for two decades, even while in the Senate, sometimes journeying to Iraq or Afghanistan to serve as a short-term reserve officer. "The air force has been one of the best things that has ever happened to me," he said in 2015. "It gave me a purpose bigger than myself. It put me in the company of patriots." Through most of his years in the Senate, Graham, alongside his close friend John McCain, was a spokesperson for a strong military and for a vision of America as a democratic leader abroad. He also supported a vigorous notion of democracy at home. In his 2014 reelection campaign, he ran as a maverick and a centrist, telling *The Atlantic* that jousting with the Tea Party was "more fun than any time I've been in politics."

While Graham was doing his tour in West Germany, Mitt Romney became a cofounder and then the president of Bain Capital, a private equity investment firm. Born in Michigan, Romney worked in Massachusetts during his years at Bain, but he also kept, thanks to his Mormon faith, close ties to Utah. While Graham was a military lawyer, drawing military pay, Romney was acquiring companies, restructuring them, and then selling them. This was a job he excelled at—in 1990, he was asked to run the parent firm, Bain & Company—and in the course of doing so he became very rich. Still, Romney dreamed of a political career, and in 1994 he ran for the Senate in Massachusetts after changing his political affiliation from independent to Republican. He lost, but in 2002 he ran for governor of Massachusetts as a nonpartisan moderate and won. In 2007—after a gubernatorial term during which he successfully brought in a form of near-universal health care that became a model for Barack Obama's Affordable Care Act—he staged his first run for president. After losing the 2008 Republican primary, he won the party's nomination in 2012 and then lost the general election.

Both Graham and Romney had presidential ambitions; Graham staged his own short-lived presidential campaign in 2015 (justified on the grounds that "the world is falling apart"). Both men were loyal members of the Republican Party, skeptical of the party's radical and conspiratorial fringe. Both men reacted to the presidential candidacy of Donald Trump with real anger, and no wonder: In different ways, Trump's values undermined their own. Graham had dedicated his career to an idea of U.S. leadership around the word—whereas Trump was offering an "America First" doctrine that would turn out to mean "me and my friends first." Romney was an excellent businessman with a strong record as a public servant—whereas Trump inherited wealth, went bankrupt more than once, created nothing of value, and had no governing record at all. Both Graham and Romney were devoted to America's democratic traditions and to the ideals of honesty, accountability, and transparency in public life—all of which Trump scorned.

Both were vocal in their disapproval of Trump. Before the election, Graham called him a "jackass," a "nutjob," and a "race-baiting, xenophobic, religious bigot." He seemed unhappy, even depressed, by the election: I happened to see him at a conference in Europe in the spring of 2016, and he spoke in monosyllables, if at all.

Romney went further. "Let me put it very plainly," he said in March 2016, in a speech criticizing Trump: "If we Republicans choose Donald Trump as our nominee, the prospects for a safe and prosperous future are greatly diminished." Romney spoke of "the bullying, the greed, the showing off, the misogyny, the absurd third-grade theatrics." He called Trump a "con man" and a "fraud." Even after Trump won the nomination, Romney refused to endorse him. On his presidential ballot, Romney said, he wrote in his wife. Graham said he voted for the independent candidate Evan McMullin.

But Trump did become president, and so the two men's convictions were put to the test.

A glance at their biographies would not have led many to predict what happened next. On paper, Graham would have seemed, in 2016, like the man with deeper ties to the military, to the rule of law, and to an old-fashioned idea of American patriotism and American responsibility in the world. Romney, by contrast, with his shifts between the center and the right, with his multiple careers in business and politics, would have seemed less deeply attached to those same old-fashioned patriotic ideals. Most of us register soldiers as loyal patriots, and management consultants as self-interested. We assume people from small towns in South Carolina are more likely to resist political pressure than people who have lived in many places. Intuitively, we think that loyalty to a particular place implies loyalty to a set of values.

But in this case the clichés were wrong. It was Graham who made excuses for Trump's abuse of power. It was Graham—a JAG Corps lawyer—who downplayed the evidence that the president had attempted to manipulate foreign courts and blackmail a foreign leader into launching a phony investigation into a political rival. It was Graham who abandoned his own stated support for bipartisanship and instead pushed for a hyperpartisan Senate Judiciary Committee investigation into former vice president Joe Biden's son. It was Graham who played golf with Trump, who made excuses for him on television, who supported the president even as he slowly destroyed the American alliances—with Europeans, with the Kurds—that Graham had defended all his life. By contrast, it was Romney who, in February, became the only Republican senator to break ranks with his colleagues, voting to impeach the president. "Corrupting an election to keep oneself in office," he said, is "perhaps the most abusive and destructive violation of one's oath of office that I can imagine."

One man proved willing to betray ideas and ideals that he had once stood for. The other refused. Why?

•   •   •

To the American reader, references to Vichy France, East Germany, fascists, and communists may seem over the top, even ludicrous. But dig a little deeper, and the analogy makes sense. The point is not to compare Trump to Hitler or Stalin; the point is to compare the experiences of high-ranking members of the American Republican Party, especially those who work most closely with the White House, to the experiences of Frenchmen in 1940 or of East Germans in 1945 or of Czeslaw Milosz in 1947. These are experiences of people who are forced to accept an alien ideology or a set of values that are in sharp conflict with their own.

Not even Trump's supporters can contest this analogy because the imposition of an alien ideology is precisely what he was calling for all along. Trump's first statement as president, his inaugural address, was an unprecedented assault on American democracy and American values. Remember: He described America's capital city, America's government, America's congressmen and senators—all democratically elected and chosen by Americans, according to America's 227-year-old Constitution—as an "establishment" that had profited at the expense of "the people." "Their victories have not been your victories," he said. "Their triumphs have not been your triumphs." Trump was stating, as clearly as he possibly could, that a new set of values was now replacing the old, though of course the nature of those new values was not yet clear.

Almost as soon as he stopped speaking, Trump launched his first assault on fact-based reality, a long-undervalued component of the American political system. We are not a theocracy or a monarchy that accepts the word of the leader or the priesthood as law. We are a democracy that debates facts, seeks to understand problems, and then legislates solutions, all in accordance with a set of rules. Trump's insistence—against the evidence of photographs, television footage, and the lived experience of thousands of people—that the attendance at his inauguration was higher than at Barack Obama's first inauguration represented a sharp break with that American political tradition. Like the authoritarian leaders of other times and places, Trump effectively ordered not just his supporters but also apolitical members of the government bureaucracy to adhere to a blatantly false, manipulated reality. American politicians, like politicians everywhere, have always covered up mistakes, held back information, and made promises they could not keep. But until Trump was president, none of them induced the National Park Service to produce doctored photographs or compelled the White House press secretary to lie about the size of a crowd—or encouraged him to do so in front of a press corps that knew *he* knew he was lying.

The lie was petty, even ridiculous; that was partly why it was so dangerous. In the 1950s, when an insect known as the Colorado potato beetle appeared in Eastern European potato fields, Soviet-backed governments in the region triumphantly claimed that it had been dropped from the sky by American pilots as a deliberate form of biological sabotage. Posters featuring vicious red-white-and-blue beetles went up all across Poland, East Germany, and Czechoslovakia. No one really believed the charge, including the people making it, as archives have subsequently shown. But that didn't matter. The point of the posters was not to convince people of a falsehood. The point was to demonstrate the party's power to proclaim and promulgate a falsehood. Sometimes the point isn't to make people believe a lie—it's to make people fear the liar.

These kinds of lies also have a way of building on one another. It takes time to persuade people to abandon their existing value systems. The process usually begins slowly, with small changes. Social scientists who have studied the erosion of values and the growth of corruption inside companies have found, for example, that "people are more likely to accept the unethical behavior of others if the behavior develops gradually (along a slippery slope) rather than occurring abruptly," according to a 2009 article in the *Journal of Experimental Social Psychology*. This happens, in part, because most people have a built-in vision of themselves as moral and honest and that self-image is resistant to change. Once certain behaviors become "normal," then people stop seeing them as wrong.

This process happens in politics, too. In 1947, the Soviet military administrators in East Germany passed a regulation governing the activity of publishing houses and printers. The decree did not nationalize the printing presses; it merely demanded that their owners apply for licenses and that they confine their work to books and pamphlets ordered by central planners. Imagine how a law like this—which did not speak of arrests, let alone torture or the Gulag—affected the owner of a printing press in Dresden, a responsible family man with two teenage children and a sickly wife. Following its passage, he had to make a series of seemingly insignificant choices. Would he apply for a license? Of course—he needed it to earn money for his family. Would he agree to confine his business to material ordered by the central planners? Yes to that too—what else was there to print?

After that, other compromises follow. Though he dislikes the communists—he just wants to stay out of politics—he agrees to print the collected works of Stalin because if he doesn't do it, others will. When he is asked by some disaffected friends to print a pamphlet critical of the regime, however, he refuses. Though he wouldn't go to jail for printing it, his children might not be admitted to university, and his wife might not get her medication; he has to think about their welfare. Meanwhile, all across East Germany, other owners of other printing presses are making similar decisions. And after a while—without anyone being shot or arrested, without anyone feeling any particular pangs of conscience—the only books left to read are the ones approved by the regime.

The built-in vision of themselves as American patriots or as competent administrators or as loyal party members also created a cognitive distortion that blinded many Republicans and Trump-administration officials to the precise nature of the president's alternative value system. After all, the early incidents were so trivial. They overlooked the lie about the inauguration because it was silly. They ignored Trump's appointment of the wealthiest Cabinet in history, and his decision to stuff his administration with former lobbyists because that's business as usual. They made excuses for Ivanka Trump's use of a private email account and for Jared Kushner's conflicts of interest because that's just family stuff.

One step at a time, Trumpism fooled many of its most enthusiastic adherents. Recall that some of the original intellectual supporters of Trump—people like Steve Bannon, Michael Anton, and the advocates of "national conservatism," an ideology invented, post hoc, to rationalize the president's behavior—advertised their movement as a recognizable form of populism: an anti–Wall Street, anti-foreign-wars, anti-immigration alternative to the small-government libertarianism of the establishment Republican Party. Their "drain the swamp" slogan implied that Trump would clean up the rotten world of lobbyists and campaign finance that distorts American politics, that he would make public debate more honest and legislation more fair. Had this actually been Trump's ruling philosophy, it might well have posed difficulties for the Republican Party leadership in 2016, given that most of them had quite different values. But it would not necessarily have damaged the Constitution, and it would not necessarily have posed fundamental moral challenges to people in public life.

In practice, Trump has governed according to a set of principles very different from those articulated by his original intellectual supporters. Although some of his speeches have continued to use that populist language, he has built a Cabinet and an administration that serve neither the public nor his voters but rather his own psychological needs and the interests of his own friends on Wall Street and in business and, of course, his own family. His tax cuts disproportionately benefited the wealthy, not the working class. His shallow economic boom, engineered to ensure his reelection, was made possible by a vast budget deficit, on a scale Republicans once claimed to abhor, an enormous burden for future generations. He worked to dismantle the existing health-care system without offering anything better, as he'd promised to do, so that the number of uninsured people rose. All the while he fanned and encouraged xenophobia and racism, both because he found them politically useful and because they are part of his personal worldview.

More important, he has governed in defiance—and in ignorance—of the American Constitution, notably declaring, well into his third year in office, that he had "total" authority over the states. His administration is not merely corrupt, it is also hostile to checks, balances, and the rule of law. He has built a proto-authoritarian personality cult, firing or sidelining officials who have contradicted him with facts and evidence— with tragic consequences for public health and the economy. He threatened to fire a top Centers for Disease Control and Prevention official, Nancy Messonnier, in late February, after her too-blunt warnings about the coronavirus; Rick Bright, a top Health and Human Services official, says he was demoted after refusing to direct money to promote the unproven drug hydroxychloroquine. Trump has attacked America's military, calling his generals "a bunch of dopes and babies," and America's intelligence services and law-enforcement officers, whom he has denigrated as the "deep state" and whose advice he has ignored. He has appointed weak and inexperienced "acting" officials to run America's most important security institutions. He has systematically wrecked America's alliances.

His foreign policy has never served any U.S. interests of any kind. Although some of Trump's Cabinet ministers and media followers have tried to portray him as an anti-Chinese nationalist—and although foreign-policy commentators from all points on the political spectrum have, amazingly, accepted this fiction without questioning it—Trump's true instinct, always, has been to side with foreign dictators, including Chinese president Xi Jinping. One former administration official who has seen Trump interact with Xi as well as with Russian president Vladimir Putin told me that it was like watching a lesser celebrity encounter a more famous one. Trump did not speak to them as the representative of the American people; he simply wanted their aura—of absolute power, of cruelty, of fame—to rub off on him and enhance his own image. This, too, has had fatal consequences. In January, Trump took Xi's word when he said that COVID-19 was "under control," just as he had believed North Korea's Kim Jong Un when he signed a deal on nuclear weapons. Trump's fawning attitude toward dictators is his ideology at its purest: he meets his own psychological needs first; he thinks about the country last. The true nature of the ideology that Trump brought to Washington was not "America First," but rather "Trump First."

Maybe it isn't surprising that the implications of "Trump First" were not immediately understood. After all, the communist parties of Eastern Europe—or, if you want a more recent example, the Chavistas in Venezuela—all advertised themselves as advocates of equality and prosperity even though, in practice, they created inequality and poverty. But just as the truth about Hugo Chávez's Bolivarian Revolution slowly dawned on people, it also became clear, eventually, that Trump did not have the interests of the American public at heart. And as they came to realize that the president was not a patriot, Republican politicians and senior civil servants began to equivocate, just like people living under an alien regime.

●　　　●　　　●

In retrospect, this dawning realization explains why the funeral of John McCain, in September 2018, looked, and by all accounts felt, so strange. Two previous presidents, one Republican and one Democrat—representatives of the old, patriotic political class—made speeches; the sitting president's name was never mentioned. The songs and symbols of the old order were visible too: "The Battle Hymn of the Republic"; American flags; two of McCain's sons in their officer's uniforms, so very different from the sons of Trump. Writing in the *New Yorker*, Susan Glasser described the funeral as "a meeting of the Resistance, under vaulted ceilings and stained-glass windows." In truth, it bore an uncanny resemblance to the 1956 funeral of László Rajk, a Hungarian communist and secret-police boss who had been purged and murdered by his comrades in 1949. Rajk's wife had become an outspoken critic of the regime, and the funeral turned into a de facto political rally, helping to set off Hungary's anticommunist revolution a couple of weeks later.

Nothing quite so dramatic happened after McCain's funeral. But it did clarify the situation. A year and a half into the Trump administration, it marked a turning point, the moment at which many Americans in public life began to adopt the strategies, tactics, and self-justifications that the inhabitants of occupied countries have used in the past—doing so even though the personal stakes were, relatively speaking, so low. Poles like Miłosz wound up in exile in the 1950s; dissidents in East Germany lost the right to work and study. In harsher regimes like that of Stalin's Russia, public protest could lead to many years in a concentration camp; disobedient Wehrmacht officers were executed by slow strangulation.

By contrast, a Republican senator who dares to question whether Trump is acting in the interests of the country is in danger of—what, exactly? Losing his seat and winding up with a seven-figure lobbying job or a fellowship at the Harvard Kennedy School? He might meet the terrible fate of Jeff Flake, the former Arizona senator, who has been hired as a contributor by CBS News. He might suffer like Romney, who was tragically not invited to the Conservative Political Action Conference, which this year turned out to be a reservoir of COVID-19.

Nevertheless, twenty months into the Trump administration, senators and other serious-minded Republicans in public life who should have known better began to tell themselves stories that sound very much like those in Miłosz's *The Captive Mind*. Some of these stories overlap with one another; some of them are just thin cloaks to cover self-interest. But all of them are familiar justifications of collaboration, recognizable from the past. Here are the most popular.

We can use this moment to achieve great things. In the spring of 2019, a Trump-supporting friend put me in touch with an administration official I will call "Mark," whom I eventually met for a drink. I won't give details because we spoke informally, but in any case Mark did not leak information or criticize the White House. On the contrary, he described himself as a patriot and a true believer. He supported the language of "America First," and was confident that it could be made real.

Several months later, I met Mark a second time. The impeachment hearings had begun, and the story of the firing of the American ambassador to Ukraine, Marie Yovanovitch, was then in the news. The true nature of the administration's ideology—Trump First, not America First—was becoming more obvious. The president's abuse of military aid to Ukraine and his attacks on civil servants suggested not a patriotic White House but a president focused on his own interests. Mark did not apologize for the president, though. Instead, he changed the subject: it was all worth it, he told me, because of the Uighurs.

I thought I had misheard. *The Uighurs?* Why the Uighurs? I was unaware of anything that the administration had done to aid the oppressed Muslim minority in Xinjiang, China. Mark assured me that letters had been written, statements had been made, the president himself had been persuaded to say something at the United Nations. I doubted very much that the Uighurs had benefited from these empty words: China hadn't altered its behavior, and the concentration camps built for the Uighurs were still standing. Nevertheless, Mark's conscience was clear. Yes, Trump was destroying America's reputation in the world, and yes, Trump was ruining America's alliances, but Mark was so important to the cause of the Uighurs that people like him could, in good conscience, keep working for the administration.

Mark made me think of the story of Wanda Telakowska, a Polish cultural activist who in 1945 felt much the same as he did. Telakowska had collected and promoted folk art before the war; after the war she made the momentous decision to join the Polish Ministry of Culture. The communist leadership was arresting and murdering its opponents; the nature of the regime was becoming clear. Telakowska nevertheless thought she could use her position inside the communist establishment to help Polish artists and designers, to promote their work and get Polish companies to mass-produce their designs. But Polish factories, newly nationalized, were not interested in the designs she commissioned. Communist politicians, skeptical of her loyalty, made Telakowska write articles filled with Marxist gibberish. Eventually she resigned, having achieved nothing she set out to do. A later generation of artists condemned her as a Stalinist and forgot about her.

We can protect the country from the president. That, of course, was the argument used by "Anonymous," the author of an unsigned *New York Times* op-ed published in September 2018. For those who have forgotten—a lot has happened since then—that article described the president's "erratic behavior," his inability to concentrate, his ignorance, and above all his lack of "affinity for ideals long espoused by conservatives: free minds, free markets and free people." The "root of the problem," Anonymous concluded, was "the president's amorality." In essence, the article described the true nature of the alternative value system brought into the White House by Trump, at a moment when not everybody in Washington understood it. But even as they came to understand that the Trump presidency was guided by the president's narcissism, Anonymous did not quit, protest, make noise, or campaign against the president and his party.

Instead, Anonymous concluded that remaining inside the system, where they could cleverly distract and restrain the president, was the right course for public servants like them.

Anonymous was not alone. Gary Cohn, at the time the White House economic adviser, told Bob Woodward that he'd removed papers from the president's desk to prevent him from pulling out of a trade agreement with South Korea. James Mattis, Trump's original secretary of defense, stayed in office because he thought he could educate the president about the value of America's alliances or at least protect some of them from destruction.

This kind of behavior has echoes in other countries and other times. A few months ago, in Venezuela, I spoke with Víctor Álvarez, a minister in one of Hugo Chávez's governments and a high-ranking official before that. Álvarez explained to me the arguments he had made in favor of protecting some private industry and his opposition to mass nationalization. Álvarez was in government from the late 1990s through 2006, a time when Chávez was stepping up the use of police against peaceful demonstrators and undermining democratic institutions. Still, Álvarez remained, hoping to curb Chávez's worst economic instincts. Ultimately, he did quit, after concluding that Chávez had created a loyalty cult around himself—Álvarez called it a "subclimate" of obedience—and was no longer listening to anyone who disagreed.

In authoritarian regimes, many insiders eventually conclude that their presence simply does not matter. Cohn, after publicly agonizing when the president said there had been "fine people on both sides" at the deadly white-supremacist rally in Charlottesville, Virginia, finally quit when the president made the ruinous decision to put tariffs on steel and aluminum, a decision that harmed American businesses. Mattis reached his breaking point when the president abandoned the Kurds, America's longtime allies in the war against the Islamic State.

But although both resigned, neither Cohn nor Mattis has spoken out in any notable way. (On June 3, after this article went to press, Mattis denounced Trump in an article on TheAtlantic .com.) Their presence inside the White House helped build

Trump's credibility among traditional Republican voters; their silence now continues to serve the president's purposes. As for Anonymous, we don't know whether he or she remains inside the administration. For the record, I note that Álvarez lives in Venezuela, an actual police state, and yet is willing to speak out against the system he helped create. Cohn, Mattis, and Anonymous, all living freely in the United States of America, have not been nearly so brave.

I, personally, will benefit. These, of course, are words that few people ever say out loud. Perhaps some do quietly acknowledge to themselves that they have not resigned or protested because it would cost them money or status. But no one wants a reputation as a careerist or a turncoat. After the fall of the Berlin Wall, even Markus Wolf sought to portray himself as an idealist. He had truly believed in Marxist-Leninist ideals, this infamously cynical man told an interviewer in 1996, and "I still believe in them."

Many people in and around the Trump administration are seeking personal benefits. Many of them are doing so with a degree of openness that is startling and unusual in contemporary American politics, at least at this level. As an ideology, "Trump First" suits these people because it gives them license to put themselves first. To pick a random example: Sonny Perdue, the secretary of agriculture, is a former Georgia governor and a businessman who, like Trump, famously refused to put his agricultural companies into a blind trust when he entered the governor's office. Perdue has never even pretended to separate his political and personal interests. Since joining the Cabinet he has, with almost no oversight, distributed billions of dollars of "compensation" to farms damaged by Trump's trade policies. He has stuffed his department with former lobbyists who are now in charge of regulating their own industries: Deputy Secretary Stephen Censky was for twenty-one years the CEO of the American Soybean Association; Brooke Appleton was a lobbyist for the National Corn Growers Association before becoming Censky's chief of staff and has since returned to that group; Kailee Tkacz, a member of a nutritional advisory panel, is a former lobbyist for the Snack Food Association. The list goes on and on, as would lists of similarly compromised people in the Department of Energy, the Environmental Protection Agency, and elsewhere.

Perdue's department also employs an extraordinary range of people with no experience in agriculture whatsoever. These modern apparatchiks, hired for their loyalty rather than their competence, include a long-haul truck driver, a country-club cabana attendant, the owner of a scented-candle company, and an intern at the Republican National Committee. The long-haul truck driver was paid $80,000 a year to expand markets for American agriculture abroad. Why was he qualified? He had a background in "hauling and shipping agricultural commodities."

I must remain close to power. Another sort of benefit, harder to measure, has kept many people who object to Trump's policies or behavior from speaking out: the intoxicating experience of power and the belief that proximity to a powerful person bestows higher status. This, too, is nothing new. In a 1968 article for *The Atlantic*, James Thomson, an American East Asia specialist, brilliantly explained how power functioned inside the U.S. bureaucracy in the Vietnam era. When the war in Vietnam was going badly, many people did not resign or speak out in public, because preserving their "effectiveness"—"a mysterious combination of training, style, and connections," as Thomson defined it—was an all-consuming concern. He called this "the effectiveness trap":

> The inclination to remain silent or to acquiesce in the presence of the great men—to live to fight another day, to give on this issue so that you can be "effective" on later issues—is overwhelming. Nor is it the tendency of youth alone; some of our most senior officials, men of wealth and fame, whose place in

history is secure, have remained silent lest their connection with power be terminated.

In any organization, private or public, the boss will of course sometimes make decisions that his underlings dislike. But when basic principles are constantly violated, and people constantly defer resignation—"I can always fall on my sword next time"—then misguided policies go fatally unchallenged.

In other countries, the effectiveness trap has other names. In his recent book on Putinism, *Between Two Fires*, Joshua Yaffa describes the Russian version of this syndrome. The Russian language, he notes, has a word—*prisposoblenets*—that means "a person skilled in the act of compromise and adaptation, who intuitively understands what is expected of him and adjusts his beliefs and conduct accordingly." In Putin's Russia, anyone who wants to stay in the game—to remain close to power, to retain influence, to inspire respect—knows the necessity of making constant small changes to one's language and behavior, of being careful about what one says and to whom one says it, of understanding what criticism is acceptable and what constitutes a violation of the unwritten rules. Those who violate these rules will not, for the most part, suffer prison—Putin's Russia is not Stalin's Russia—but they will experience a painful ejection from the inner circle.

For those who have never experienced it, the mystical pull of that connection to power, that feeling of being an insider, is difficult to explain. Nevertheless, it is real, and strong enough to affect even the highest-ranking, best-known, most influential people in America. John Bolton, Trump's former national security adviser, named his still-unpublished book *The Room Where It Happened* because, of course, that's where he has always wanted to be. A friend who regularly runs into Lindsey Graham in Washington told me that each time they meet, "he brags about having just met with Trump" while exhibiting "high school" levels of excitement, as if "a popular quarterback has just bestowed some attention on a nerdy debate-club leader—*the powerful big kid likes me!*" That kind of intense pleasure is hard to relinquish and even harder to live without.

LOL nothing matters. Cynicism, nihilism, relativism, amorality, irony, sarcasm, boredom, amusement—these are all reasons to collaborate and always have been. Marko Martin, a novelist and travel writer who grew up in East Germany, told me that in the 1980s some of the East German bohemia, influenced by then-fashionable French intellectuals, argued that there was no such thing as morality or immorality, no such thing as good or evil, no such thing as right or wrong—"so you might as well collaborate."

This instinct has an American variation. Politicians here who have spent their lives following rules and watching their words, calibrating their language, giving pious speeches about morality and governance, may feel a sneaking admiration for someone like Trump, who breaks all the rules and gets away with it. He lies; he cheats; he extorts; he refuses to show compassion, sympathy, or empathy; he does not pretend to believe in anything or to abide by any moral code. He simulates patriotism, with flags and gestures, but he does not behave like a patriot; his campaign scrambled to get help from Russia in 2016 ("If it's what you say, I love it," replied Donald Trump Jr., when offered Russian "dirt" on Hillary Clinton), and Trump himself called on Russia to hack his opponent. And for some of those at the top of his administration and of his party, these character traits might have a deep, unacknowledged appeal: If there is no such thing as moral and immoral, then everyone is implicitly released from the need to obey any rules. *If the president doesn't respect the Constitution, then why should I? If the president can cheat in elections, then why can't I? If the president can sleep with porn stars, then why shouldn't I?*

This, of course, was the insight of the "alt-right," which understood the dark allure of amorality, open racism, antisemitism, and misogyny long before many others in the Republican Party. Mikhail Bakhtin, the Russian philosopher and literary critic, recognized the lure of the forbidden a century ago, writing about the deep appeal of the carnival, a space where everything banned is suddenly allowed, where eccentricity is permitted, where profanity defeats piety. The Trump administration is like that: nothing means anything, rules don't matter, and the president is the carnival king.

My side might be flawed, but the political opposition is much worse. When Marshal Philippe Pétain, the leader of collaborationist France, took over the Vichy government, he did so in the name of the restoration of a France that he believed had been lost. Pétain had been a fierce critic of the French Republic, and once he was in control, he replaced its famous creed—*Liberté, égalité, fraternité*, or "Liberty, equality, fraternity"—with a different slogan: *Travail, famille, patrie*, or "Work, family, fatherland." Instead of the "false idea of the natural equality of man," he proposed bringing back "social hierarchy"—order, tradition, and religion. Instead of accepting modernity, Pétain sought to turn back the clock.

By Pétain's reckoning, collaboration with the Germans was not merely an embarrassing necessity. It was crucial because it gave patriots the ability to fight the *real* enemy: the French parliamentarians, socialists, anarchists, Jews, and other assorted leftists and democrats who, he believed, were undermining the nation, robbing it of its vitality, destroying its essence. "Rather Hitler than Blum," the saying went—Blum having been France's socialist (and Jewish) prime minister in the late 1930s. One Vichy minister, Pierre Laval, famously declared that he hoped Germany would conquer all of Europe. Otherwise, he asserted, "Bolshevism would tomorrow establish itself everywhere."

To Americans, this kind of justification should sound very familiar; we have been hearing versions of it since 2016. The existential nature of the threat from "the left" has been spelled out many times. "Our liberal-left present reality and future direction is incompatible with human nature," wrote Michael Anton, in "The Flight 93 Election." The Fox News anchor Laura Ingraham has warned that "massive demographic changes" threaten us too: "In some parts of the country it does seem like the America that we know and love doesn't exist anymore." This is the Vichy logic: the nation is dead or dying—so anything you can do to restore it is justified. Whatever criticisms might be made of Trump, whatever harm he has done to democracy and the rule of law, whatever corrupt deals he might make while in the White House—all of these shrink in comparison to the horrific alternative: the liberalism, socialism, moral decadence, demographic change, and cultural degradation that would have been the inevitable result of Hillary Clinton's presidency.

The Republican senators who are willing to express their disgust with Trump off the record but voted in February for him to remain in office all indulge a variation of this sentiment. (Trump enables them to get the judges they want, and those judges will help create the America they want.) So do the evangelical pastors who ought to be disgusted by Trump's personal behavior but argue, instead, that the current situation has scriptural precedents. Like King David in the Bible, the president is a sinner, a flawed vessel, but he nevertheless offers a path to salvation for a fallen nation.

The three most important members of Trump's Cabinet—Vice President Mike Pence, Secretary of State Mike Pompeo, and Attorney General William Barr—are all profoundly shaped by Vichyite apocalyptic thinking. All three are clever enough to understand what Trumpism really means, that it has nothing to do with God or faith, that it is self-serving, greedy, and unpatriotic. Nevertheless, a former member of the administration (one of the few who did decide to resign) told me that both Pence and Pompeo "have convinced themselves that they are in a biblical moment." All of the things they care about—outlawing abortion and same-sex marriage, and (though this is never said out loud) maintaining a white majority in America—are under threat. Time is growing short. They believe that "we are approaching the Rapture, and this is a moment of deep religious significance." Barr, in a speech at Notre Dame, has also described his belief that "militant secularists" are destroying America, that "irreligion and secular values are being forced on people of faith." Whatever evil Trump does, whatever he damages or destroys, at least he enables Barr, Pence, and Pompeo to save America from a far worse fate. If you are convinced we are living in the End Times, then anything the president does can be forgiven.

I am afraid to speak out. Fear, of course, is the most important reason any inhabitant of an authoritarian or totalitarian society does not protest or resign, even when the leader commits crimes, violates his official ideology, or forces people to do things that they know to be wrong. In extreme dictatorships like Nazi Germany and Stalin's Russia, people fear for their lives. In softer dictatorships, like East Germany after 1950 and Putin's Russia today, people fear losing their jobs or their apartments. Fear works as a motivation even when violence is a memory rather than a reality. When I was a student in Leningrad in the 1980s, some people still stepped back in horror when I asked for directions on the street, in my accented Russian: no one was going to be arrested for speaking to a foreigner in 1984, but thirty years earlier they might have been, and the cultural memory remained.

In the United States of America, it is hard to imagine how fear could be a motivation for anybody. There are no mass murders of the regime's political enemies, and there never have been. Political opposition is legal; free press and free speech are guaranteed in the Constitution. And yet even in one of the world's oldest and most stable democracies, fear is a motive. The same former administration official who observed the importance of apocalyptic Christianity in Trump's Washington also told me, with grim disgust, that "they are all scared."

They are scared not of prison, the official said, but of being attacked by Trump on Twitter. They are scared he will make up a nickname for them. They are scared that they will be mocked or embarrassed, like Mitt Romney has been. They are scared of losing their social circles, of being disinvited to parties. They are scared that their friends and supporters, and especially their donors, will desert them. John Bolton has his own super PAC and a lot of plans for how he wants to use it; no wonder he resisted testifying against Trump. Former speaker Paul Ryan is among the dozens of House Republicans who have left Congress since the beginning of this administration, in one of the most striking personnel turnovers in congressional history. They left because they hated what Trump was doing to their party—and the country. Yet even after they left, they did not speak out.

They are scared, and yet they don't seem to know that this fear has precedents, or that it could have consequences. They don't know that similar waves of fear have helped transform other democracies into dictatorships. They don't seem to realize that the American Senate really could become the Russian Duma or the Hungarian Parliament, a group of exalted men and women who sit in an elegant building, with no influence and no power. Indeed, we are already much closer to that reality than many could ever have imagined.

·   ·   ·

In February, many members of the Republican Party leadership, Republican senators, and people inside the administration used various versions of these rationales to justify their opposition to impeachment. All of them had seen the evidence that Trump had stepped over the line in his dealings with the president of Ukraine. All of them knew that he had tried to use American foreign-policy tools, including military funding, to force a foreign leader into investigating a domestic political opponent. Yet

Republican senators, led by Mitch McConnell, never took the charges seriously. They mocked the Democratic House leaders who had presented the charges. They decided against hearing evidence. With the single exception of Romney, they voted in favor of ending the investigation. They did not use the opportunity to rid the country of a president whose operative value system—built around corruption, nascent authoritarianism, self-regard, and his family's business interests—runs counter to everything that most of them claim to believe in.

Just a month later, in March, the consequences of that decision became suddenly clear. After the United States and the world were plunged into crisis by a coronavirus that had no cure, the damage done by the president's self-focused, self-dealing narcissism—his one true "ideology"—was finally visible. He led a federal response to the virus that was historically chaotic. The disappearance of the federal government was not a carefully planned transfer of power to the states, as some tried to claim, or a thoughtful decision to use the talents of private companies. This was the inevitable result of a three-year assault on professionalism, loyalty, competence, and patriotism. Tens of thousands of people have died, and the economy has been ruined.

This utter disaster was avoidable. If the Senate had removed the president by impeachment a month earlier; if the Cabinet had invoked the Twenty-Fifth Amendment as soon as Trump's unfitness became clear; if the anonymous and off-the-record officials who knew of Trump's incompetence had jointly warned the public; if they had not, instead, been so concerned about maintaining their proximity to power; if senators had not been scared of their donors; if Pence, Pompeo, and Barr had not believed that God had chosen them to play special roles in this "biblical moment"—if any of these things had gone differently, then thousands of deaths and a historic economic collapse might have been avoided.

The price of collaboration in America has already turned out to be extraordinarily high. And yet the movement down the slippery slope continues, just as it did in so many occupied countries in the past. First Trump's enablers accepted lies about the inauguration; now they accept terrible tragedy and the loss of American leadership in the world. Worse could follow. Come November, will they tolerate—even abet—an assault on the electoral system: open efforts to prevent postal voting, to shut polling stations, to scare people away from voting? Will they countenance violence, as the president's social-media fans incite demonstrators to launch physical attacks on state and city officials?

Each violation of our Constitution and our civic peace gets absorbed, rationalized, and accepted by people who once upon a time knew better. If, following what is almost certain to be one of the ugliest elections in American history, Trump wins a second term, these people may well accept even worse. Unless, of course, they decide not to.

When I visited Marianne Birthler, she didn't think it was interesting to talk about collaboration in East Germany because everybody collaborated in East Germany. So I asked her about dissidence instead: when all of your friends, all of your teachers, and all of your employers are firmly behind the system, how do you find the courage to oppose it? In her answer, Birthler resisted the use of the word *courage*; just as people can adapt to corruption or immorality, she told me, they can slowly learn to object as well. The choice to become a dissident can easily be the result of "a number of small decisions that you take"—to absent yourself from the May Day parade, for example, or not to sing the words of the party hymn. And then, one day, you find yourself irrevocably on the other side. Often, this process involves role models. You see people whom you admire, and you want to be like them. It can even be "selfish." "You want to do something for yourself," Birthler said, "to respect yourself."

For some people, the struggle is made easier by their upbringing. Marko Martin's parents hated the East German regime, and so did he. His father was a conscientious objector, and so was he. As far back as the Weimar Republic, his great-grandparents had been part of the "anarcho-syndicalist" anticommunist left; he had access to their books. In the 1980s, he refused to join the Free German Youth, the communist youth organization, and as a result he could not go to university. He instead embarked on a vocational course, to train to be an electrician (after refusing to become a butcher). In his electrician-training classes, one of the other students pulled him aside and warned him, subtly, that the Stasi was collecting information on him: "It's not necessary that you tell me all the things you have in mind." He was eventually allowed to emigrate, in May 1989, just a few months before the fall of the Berlin Wall.

In America we also have our Marianne Birthlers, our Marko Martins: people whose families taught them respect for the Constitution, who have faith in the rule of law, who believe in the importance of disinterested public service, who have values and role models from outside the world of the Trump administration. Over the past year, many such people have found the courage to stand up for what they believe. A few have been thrust into the limelight. Fiona Hill—an immigrant success story and a true believer in the American Constitution—was not afraid to testify at the House's impeachment hearings, nor was she afraid to speak out against Republicans who were promulgating a false story of Ukrainian interference in the 2016 election. "This is a fictional narrative that has been perpetrated and propagated by the Russian security services themselves," she said in her congressional testimony. "The unfortunate truth is that Russia was the foreign power that systematically attacked our democratic institutions in 2016."

Lieutenant Colonel Alexander Vindman—another immigrant success story and another true believer in the American Constitution—also found the courage, first, to report on the president's improper telephone call with his Ukrainian counterpart, which Vindman had heard as a member of the National Security Council, and then to speak publicly about it. In his testimony, he made explicit reference to the values of the American political system, so different from those in the place where he was born. "In Russia," he said, "offering public testimony involving the president would surely cost me my life." But as "an American citizen and public servant . . . I can live free of fear for mine and my family's safety." A few days after the Senate impeachment vote, Vindman was physically escorted out of the White House by representatives of a vengeful president who did not appreciate Vindman's hymn to American patriotism—although retired marine corps general John Kelly, the president's former chief of staff, apparently did. Vindman's behavior, Kelly said in a speech a few days later, was "exactly what we teach them to do from cradle to grave. He went and told his boss what he just heard."

But both Hill and Vindman had some important advantages. Neither had to answer to voters or to donors. Neither had prominent status in the Republican Party. What would it take, by contrast, for Pence or Pompeo to conclude that the president bears responsibility for a catastrophic health and economic crisis? What would it take for Republican senators to admit to themselves that Trump's loyalty cult is destroying the country they claim to love? What would it take for their aides and subordinates to come to the same conclusion, to resign, and to campaign against the president? What would it take, in other words, for someone like Lindsey Graham to behave like Wolfgang Leonhard?

If, as Stanley Hoffmann wrote, the honest historian would have to speak of "collaborationisms" because the phenomenon comes in so many variations, the same is true of dissidence, which should probably be described as "dissidences." People can suddenly change their minds because of spontaneous intellectual revelations like the one Wolfgang Leonhard had when walking into his fancy *nomenklatura* dining room, with its white tablecloths and three-course meals. They can also be persuaded by outside events: rapid political changes, for example. Awareness that the regime had lost its legitimacy is part of what made Harald Jaeger, an obscure and until that moment completely loyal East German border guard, decide on the night of November 9, 1989, to lift the gates and let his fellow citizens walk through the Berlin Wall—a decision that led, over the next days and months, to the end of East Germany itself. Jaeger's decision was not planned; it was a spontaneous response to the fearlessness of the crowd. "Their will was so great," he said years later, of those demanding to cross into West Berlin, "there was no other alternative than to open the border."

But these things are all intertwined and not easy to disentangle. The personal, the political, the intellectual, and the historical combine differently within every human brain, and the outcomes can be unpredictable. Leonhard's "sudden" revelation may have been building for years, perhaps since his mother's arrest. Jaeger was moved by the grandeur of the historical moment on that night in November, but he also had more petty concerns: he was annoyed at his boss, who had not given him clear instructions about what to do.

Could some similar combination of the petty and the political ever convince Lindsey Graham that he has helped lead his country down a blind alley? Perhaps a personal experience could move him, a prod from someone who represents his former value system—an old air force buddy, say, whose life has been damaged by Trump's reckless behavior, or a friend from his hometown. Perhaps it requires a mass political event: when the voters begin to turn, maybe Graham will turn with them, arguing, as Jaeger did, that "their will was so great . . . there was no other alternative." At some point, after all, the calculus of conformism will begin to shift. It will become awkward and uncomfortable to continue supporting "Trump First," especially as Americans suffer from the worst recession in living memory and die from the coronavirus in numbers higher than in much of the rest of the world.

Or perhaps the only antidote is time. In due course, historians will write the story of our era and draw lessons from it, just as we write the history of the 1930s or of the 1940s. The Miłoszes and the Hoffmanns of the future will make their judgments with the clarity of hindsight. They will see, more clearly than we can, the path that led the United States into a historic loss of international influence, into economic catastrophe, into political chaos of a kind we haven't experienced since the years leading up to the Civil War. Then maybe Graham—along with Pence, Pompeo, McConnell, and a whole host of lesser figures—will understand what he has enabled.

In the meantime, I leave anyone who has the bad luck to be in public life at this moment with a final thought from Władysław Bartoszewski, who was a member of the wartime Polish underground, a prisoner of both the Nazis and the Stalinists, and then, finally, the foreign minister in two Polish democratic governments. Late in his life—he lived to be ninety-three—he summed up the philosophy that had guided him through all of these tumultuous political changes. It was not idealism that drove him or big ideas, he said. It was this: *Warto być przyzwoitym*—"Just try to be decent." Whether you were decent—that's what will be remembered.

Vanity Fair

FINALIST—SINGLE-TOPIC
ISSUE

This letter introduces "The Great Fire," a special issue of Vanity Fair guest-edited by Ta-Nehisi Coates. "It was our shared goal," wrote Radhika Jones, the editor in chief of Vanity Fair, of her collaboration with Coates, "to make a magazine that would capture the spirit of this time, and that it would be beautiful." Their achievement of that goal was recognized by the judges who nominated the issue for National Magazine Awards in three different categories: Single-Topic Issue, Essays and Criticism, and Coverage of Race in America. "The Great Fire," as Coates explains, explores the possibility of an America in which for the first time "a legitimate antiracist majority is emerging." Coates is the author of several books, including Between the World and Me, which won a National Book Award in 2015. His article "Fear of a Black President" won the National Magazine Award for Essays and Criticism in 2013.

Ta-Nehisi Coates

Editor's Letter from "The Great Fire"

Last year Chicago poet Eve L. Ewing published *1919*, a volume that channels her city's Red Summer into blues. It is a magical work. The voices of housekeepers and stockyard hands are summoned. The thoughts of trains carrying black people north are conjured up. The doom of a black boy is told to the rhythm of a jump rope. The centerpiece of this bracing work is "True Stories About the Great Fire," a poem inspired by the belief among white Chicagoans that the first Great Migration to the city was "the worst calamity that had struck the city since the Great Fire" of 1871, which took hundreds of lives and burned out the heart of the city. The implications of this equation are haunting. Once a people become a "calamity," all means of dealing with them are acceptable. I have not yet watched George Floyd's murder in its entirety, but I have seen enough of the genre to know the belief in black people as disaster, as calamity, as a Great Fire upon the city, has not yet waned.

I don't know if there is a better way of explaining the police publicly torturing a man on a bright city street. I don't know how else to think about the killing of Walter Scott, save that an agent of the state had considered him an offense to God. I don't know what explains Botham Jean nor Atatiana Jefferson, killed in their own homes, save some perverted act of fire prevention. I see the face of Elijah McClain—his deep brown skin, his Mona Lisa smile, his eyes flush with nothing so much as the wide, willing magic of youth—and I think there can be no justification for erasing this young man, save the belief that he is not a man at all, that he is both more and less; that he is Mike Brown, bulking up to run through bullets; that he is Trayvon Martin, irradiated by Skittles and iced tea; that he is Amadou Diallo, whose wallet glinted like a gun. I don't know how else to comprehend the jackboots bashing in Breonna Taylor's door and spraying her home with bullets, except the belief that they were fighting some Great Fire—demonic, unnatural, inhuman.

The logic here is obvious. To plunder a people of everything, you must plunder their humanity first. To despoil the peasantry of Europe, it was necessary to regard them as a class condemned to "eat thistles and briars" and "go naked on all fours." Only after the English told themselves they were warring against cannibals and drinkers of blood could they devastate the Irish. To massacre the children of the Cheyenne and Arapaho would be a great crime. But to exterminate the "nits" who were to grow into "lice" was wholly permissible. And so it is with the children of the enslaved, regarded, to this very day, as a Great Fire consuming white maidenhood, immolating morality, and otherwise reducing great civilizations to ashes. There is an insidious cost to this—a man invents a monster to justify his brutality, only to find the monster is within. For fear of Fire, America has turned its worldly affairs over to a barbarian game show host, presently selling charlatanism while pandemic races across the land.

This story is old—older than 1919 and older than 1619. But if terror and self-deception explain the present craven order, they cannot explain the uprising against it. To date, that uprising, which did not begin this year, spans from Ferguson to Baltimore to Minneapolis to Salt Lake City to London to Tokyo. The implications have been profound. The killers of Corey Jones and Laquan McDonald are in prison. In India, the makers of skin lightener are being forced to face the implication of their product.

In the United Kingdom, statues of slave traders are falling. The private army sent to Portland has been defeated. Washington, DC's, football team, which once pledged itself to a racist banner, has been rendered literally nameless.

This is a movement with all the problems of any movement—surely the absurd portrait of a banker taking a knee before a vault will not be its last perversion. And yet the math is clarifying: Black Lives Matter was still meeting disapproval in the wake of Heather Heyer's murder, but by the time of George Floyd's, those trends had reversed. Large majorities of Americans now acknowledge that racism and police brutality are problems. Something is happening, and I think to understand it, we must better understand the nature of this Great Fire.

Last month Congressman Ted Yoho decided to publicly deride his colleague Alexandria Ocasio-Cortez as a "fucking bitch," and fellow congressman Roger Williams lent an assist. But more telling than the act was Yoho's denial that any such words had been uttered. For Yoho to admit that he'd committed such a vile act would have degraded him. For Williams to have stood by and watched the vile act would have degraded him further. Evil exacts a toll on both the donor and the recipient. Thomas Jefferson, oracle of American liberty, was most sublime when lamenting the effects of enslavement on enslavers such as himself. "There must doubtless be an unhappy influence on the manners of our people produced by the existence of slavery among us," wrote Jefferson. "The man must be a prodigy who can retain his manners and morals un-depraved by such circumstances."

One way to both do evil and preserve one's "manners and morals" is to emit a smog of euphemisms—*extraordinary rendition, enhanced interrogation, peculiar institution, heritage not hate.* In the wake of Bloody Sunday, a dissembling George Wallace recast native Alabaman John Lewis as an "outside agitator." But beneath a rain of blows, Lewis, blazing at the highest flame, illuminated the stark brutality of Jim Crow for the whole world to see.

Whiteness thrives in darkness. It has to—because to assert itself in full view, to admit to calling a congresswoman a "fucking bitch" to her face, is to have one's own "manners and morals" degraded. A thousand Eric Garners will be tolerated, so long as they are strangled to death in the shadows of the American carceral system, the most sprawling gulag known to man. And so evil does its business in the shadows, ever-fearing not the heat of the Great Fire but the light. To clearly see what this country has done, what it is still doing, to construct itself is too much for any human to take. So it was with the slave narrative. So it is with the cell phone. The reaction of the beholder is physical. They double over in disgust. They wail on the floor. They punch the air. They pace the room until they are at last compelled out of their sanctuary, out of their privilege, out into the streets, out into the diseased air, to face off with the legionaries who guard the power implicit in their very names.

It is an impressive thing, this Great Fire, but it is not omnipotent. It is endangered not just by corporate co-option but by those who venerate "the art of the possible" like an eleventh commandment. Even now it is said that only on November 3 will we truly know how bright the Fire burns. "Don't boo. Vote," we are told, when in reality we should do both. In 2018, New York State elected a slate of liberal legislators. The repeal of 50-a, a law which sealed police misconduct records, topped their list of reforms. But it wasn't until June 12—amid a national movement of protest—that the political will amassed to take the law off the books. Voting is civic hygiene—both essential and insufficient. And voting alone has never been enough to protect anything—least of all the vote itself. In 1868, America cried black suffrage and Reconstruction; eight years later it chose Red Shirts and Redemption. In this way the path to a postracist democracy was rejected, and America set down the dark road to 1919.

Thus from the vantage of America's own record, the question is not will the protesters get out and vote, it's will the voters continue to protest? How many navy veterans will give an arm to force their country to keep its words? When will the wall of moms be breached? How many Heather Heyers can a privileged class take? Already we hear the music—*Trump is the first racist president. This is not who we are. America is better than this*—seeking to take us back to a world where Malice Green and Eleanor Bumpurs were simply the price of doing business. I would like to think it is different this time, and indeed there is math that says so. It must be remembered that in 2016, the candidate of white supremacy lost the popular vote. It is possible, then, that for the first time in American history, a legitimate antiracist majority is emerging and thus giving birth to a world beyond Founding Father idolatry, where we can seek not merely to defeat the incumbent president but to erase his entire philosophy out of human existence.

Certainly the activists, artists, and writers assembled in these pages hope that such a world is in the offing, full knowing that we can never depend on it. We are enrolled in the longest war, ancestral, generational, impatiently waiting for the Fire to take effect. "And we can wait a long time," as Ewing tells us. "And the Fire can too."

Vanity Fair

FINALIST—ESSAYS AND
CRITICISM

Jesmyn Ward's essay "Witness and Respair" is drawn from "The Great Fire," the special issue of Vanity Fair *guest-edited by Ta-Nehisi Coates. The essay begins with the death of Ward's husband in January 2020, long before most Americans knew enough to take coronavirus seriously ("I walked into my son's room where my Beloved lay," Ward writes, "and he panted:* Can't. Breathe*") and ends with "people in the streets" after the murder of George Floyd. Writes Ward, "I recognized their action for what it was: witness." "In this searing essay," read the judges' citation, "Ward uses her personal grief to make sense of the violence done to Black bodies." Ward now teaches at Tulane University. Her second novel,* Salvage the Bones, *won the National Book Award for Fiction in 2011; her third novel,* Sing, Unburied, Sing, *won the same award in 2017.*

Jesmyn Ward

Witness and Respair

My beloved died in January. He was a foot taller than me and had large, beautiful dark eyes and dexterous, kind hands. He fixed me breakfast and pots of loose-leaf tea every morning. He cried at both of our children's births, silently, tears glazing his face. Before I drove our children to school in the pale dawn light, he would put both hands on the top of his head and dance in the driveway to make the kids laugh. He was funny, quick-witted, and could inspire the kind of laughter that cramped my whole torso. Last fall, he decided it would be best for him and our family if he went back to school. His primary job in our household was to shore us up, to take care of the children, to be a househusband. He traveled with me often on business trips, carried our children in the back of lecture halls, watchful and quietly proud as I spoke to audiences, as I met readers and shook hands and signed books. He indulged my penchant for Christmas movies, for meandering trips through museums, even though he would have much preferred to be in a stadium somewhere, watching football. One of my favorite places in the world was beside him, under his warm arm, the color of deep, dark river water.

In early January, we became ill with what we thought was flu. Five days into our illness, we went to a local urgent care center, where the doctor swabbed us and listened to our chests. The kids and I were diagnosed with flu; my Beloved's test was inconclusive. At home, I doled out medicine to all of us: Tamiflu and Promethazine. My children and I immediately began to feel better, but my Beloved did not. He burned with fever. He slept and woke to complain that he thought the medicine wasn't working, that he was in pain. And then he took more medicine and slept again.

Two days after our family doctor visit, I walked into my son's room where my Beloved lay, and he panted: *Can't. Breathe.* I brought him to the emergency room, where after an hour in the waiting room, he was sedated and put on a ventilator. His organs failed: first his kidneys, then his liver. He had a massive infection in his lungs, developed sepsis, and in the end, his great strong heart could no longer support a body that had turned on him. He coded eight times. I witnessed the doctors perform CPR and bring him back four. Within fifteen hours of walking into the emergency room of that hospital, he was dead. The official reason: acute respiratory distress syndrome. He was thirty-three years old.

Without his hold to drape around my shoulders, to shore me up, I sank into hot, wordless grief.

.　　　.　　　.

Two months later, I squinted at a video of a gleeful Cardi B chanting in a singsong voice: *Coronavirus*, she cackled. *Coronavirus.* I stayed silent while people around me made jokes about COVID, rolled their eyes at the threat of pandemic. Weeks later, my kids' school was closed. Universities were telling students to vacate the dorms while professors were scrambling to move classes online. There was no bleach, no toilet paper, no paper towels for purchase anywhere. I snagged the last of the disinfectant spray off a pharmacy shelf; the clerk ringing up my purchases asking me wistfully: *Where did you find that at*, and for one moment, I thought she would challenge me for it, tell me there was some policy in place to prevent my buying it.

Days became weeks, and the weather was strange for south Mississippi, for the swampy, water-ridden part of the state I call home: low humidity, cool temperatures, clear, sun-lanced skies. My children and I awoke at noon to complete homeschooling lessons. As the spring days lengthened into summer, my children ran wild, exploring the forest around my house, picking blackberries, riding bikes and four-wheelers in their underwear. They clung to me, rubbed their faces into my stomach, and cried hysterically: *I miss Daddy*, they said. Their hair grew tangled and dense. I didn't eat, except when I did, and then it was tortillas, queso, and tequila.

The absence of my Beloved echoed in every room of our house. Him folding me and the children in his arms on our monstrous fake-suede sofa. Him shredding chicken for enchiladas in the kitchen. Him holding our daughter by the hands and pulling her upwards, higher and higher, so she floated at the top of her leap in a long bed-jumping marathon. Him shaving the walls of the children's playroom with a sander after an internet recipe for homemade chalkboard paint went wrong: green dust everywhere.

During the pandemic, I couldn't bring myself to leave the house, terrified I would find myself standing in the doorway of an ICU room, watching the doctors press their whole weight on the chest of my mother, my sisters, my children, terrified of the lurch of their feet, the lurch that accompanies each press that restarts the heart, the jerk of their pale, tender soles, terrified of the frantic prayer without intention that keens through the mind, the prayer for life that one says in the doorway, the prayer I never want to say again, the prayer that dissolves midair when the hush-click-hush-click of the ventilator drowns it, terrified of the terrible commitment at the heart of me that reasons that if the person I love has to endure this, then the least I can do is stand there, the least I can do is witness, the least I can do is tell them over and over again, aloud, *I love you. We love you. We ain't going nowhere.*

.   .   .

As the pandemic settled in and stretched, I set my alarms to wake early, and on mornings after nights where I actually slept, I woke and worked on my novel in progress. The novel is about a woman who is even more intimately acquainted with grief than I am, an enslaved woman whose mother is stolen from her and sold south to New Orleans, whose lover is stolen from her and sold south, who herself is sold south and descends into the hell of chattel slavery in the mid-1800s. My loss was a tender second skin. I shrugged against it as I wrote, haltingly, about this woman who speaks to spirits and fights her way across rivers.

My commitment surprised me. Even in a pandemic, even in grief, I found myself commanded to amplify the voices of the dead that sing to me, from their boat to my boat, on the sea of time. On most days, I wrote one sentence. On some days, I wrote 1,000 words. Many days, it and I seemed useless. All of it, misguided endeavor. My grief bloomed as depression, just as it had after my brother died at nineteen, and I saw little sense, little purpose in this work, this solitary vocation. Me, sightless, wandering the wild, head thrown back, mouth wide open, singing to a star-drenched sky. Like all the speaking, singing women of old, a maligned figure in the wilderness. Few listened in the night.

What resonated back to me: the emptiness between the stars. Dark matter. Cold.

·   ·   ·

Did you see it? My cousin asked me.

No. I couldn't bring myself to watch it, I said. Her words began to flicker, to fade in and out. Grief sometimes makes it hard for me to hear. Sound came in snatches.

His knee, she said.

On his neck, she said.

Couldn't breathe, she said.

He cried for his mama, she said.

I read about Ahmaud, I said. *I read about Breonna.*
I don't say, but I thought it: *I know their beloveds' wail. I know their beloveds' wail. I know their beloveds wander their pandemic rooms, pass through their sudden ghosts. I know their loss burns their beloveds' throats like acid. Their families will speak,* I thought. *Ask for justice. And no one will answer,* I thought. *I know this story: Trayvon, Tamir, Sandra.*
Cuz, I said, *I think you told me this story before.*
I think I wrote it.
I swallowed sour.

·　　·　　·

In the days after my conversation with my cousin, I woke to people in the streets. I woke to Minneapolis burning. I woke to protests in America's heartland, Black people blocking the highways. I woke to people doing the haka in New Zealand. I woke to hoodie-wearing teens, to John Boyega raising a fist in the air in London, even as he was afraid he would sink his career, but still, he raised his fist. I woke to droves of people, masses of people in Paris, sidewalk to sidewalk, moving like a river down the boulevards. I knew the Mississippi. I knew the plantations on its shores, the movement of enslaved and cotton up and down its eddies. The people marched, and I had never known that there could be rivers such as this, and as protesters chanted and stomped, as they grimaced and shouted and groaned, tears burned my eyes. They glazed my face.

I sat in my stuffy pandemic bedroom and thought I might never stop crying. The revelation that Black Americans were not alone in this, that others around the world believed that Black Lives Matter broke something in me, some immutable belief I'd carried with me my whole life. This belief beat like another heart—*thump*—in my chest from the moment I took my first breath as an underweight, two-pound infant after my mother, ravaged by stress, delivered me at twenty-four weeks. It beat from the moment the doctor told my Black mother her Black baby would die. *Thump.*

That belief was infused with fresh blood during the girlhood I'd spent in underfunded public school classrooms, cavities eating away at my teeth from government-issued block cheese, powdered milk, and corn flakes. *Thump.* Fresh blood in the moment I heard the story of how a group of white men, revenue agents, had shot and killed my great-great-grandfather, left him to bleed to death in the woods like an animal, from the second I learned no one was ever held accountable for his death. *Thump.* Fresh blood in the moment I found out the white drunk driver who killed my brother wouldn't be charged for my brother's death, only for leaving the scene of the car accident, the scene of the crime. *Thump.*

This is the belief that America fed fresh blood into for centuries, this belief that Black lives have the same value as a plow horse or a grizzled donkey. I knew this. My family knew this. My people knew this, and we fought it, but we were convinced we would fight this reality alone, fight until we could no more, until we were in the ground, bones moldering, headstones overgrown above in the world where our children and children's children still fought, still yanked against the noose, the forearm, the starvation and redlining and rape and enslavement and murder and choked out: *I can't breathe.* They would say: *I can't breathe. I can't breathe.*

I cried in wonder each time I saw protest around the world because I recognized the people. I recognized the way they zip their hoodies, the way they raised their fists, the way they walked, the way they shouted. I recognized their action for what it was: witness. Even now, each day, they witness.

They witness injustice.

They witness this America, this country that gaslit us for 400 fucking years.

Witness that my state, Mississippi, waited until 2013 to ratify the Thirteenth Amendment.

Witness that Mississippi didn't remove the Confederate battle emblem from its state flag until 2020.

Witness Black people, Indigenous people, so many poor Brown people, lying on beds in frigid hospitals, gasping our last breaths with COVID-riddled lungs, rendered flat by undiagnosed underlying conditions, triggered by years of food deserts, stress, and poverty, lives spent snatching sweets so we could eat one delicious morsel, savor some sugar on the tongue, oh Lord, because the flavor of our lives is so often bitter.

They witness our fight too, the quick jerk of our feet, see our hearts lurch to beat again in our art and music and work and joy. How revelatory that others witness our battles and stand up. They go out in the middle of a pandemic, and they march.

I sob, and the rivers of people run in the streets.

. . .

When my beloved died, a doctor told me: The last sense to go is hearing. When someone is dying, they lose sight and smell and taste and touch. They even forget who they are. But in the end, they hear you.

I hear you.

I hear you.

You say:

I love you.

We love you.

We ain't going nowhere.

I hear you say:

We here.

Slate

FINALIST—REPORTING

Reporting is generally considered to be one of the most prestigious National Magazine Awards. For any journalist to win recognition in this category is more than an honor, but for a writer as young as Aymann Ismail—it was only four years ago that he won an ASME NEXT Award for Journalists Under 30—to be nominated in Reporting is remarkable. (And he was not the only ASME NEXT Award recipient to be nominated this year: another 2018 winner, The Atlantic's Vann R. Newkirk, was nominated in Podcasting, and a 2017 winner, the New Yorker's Ben Taub, was nominated in Feature Writing.) The judges in Reporting described this story as an "original, empathetic and deeply layered account of the impact of Floyd's murder on his community and especially Cup Foods, the neighborhood fixture that called 911 on May 25, 2020."

Aymann Ismail

The Store That
Called the Cops
on George Floyd

Shortly after eight p.m. on Memorial Day, May 25, Mahmoud "Mike" Abumayyaleh got a panicked phone call from a teenage employee at the store he owns with his three brothers. "Mike! Mike! They're killing him," she said. "My heart dropped. Like, it fell to the ground," Mahmoud told me. He had no clue what she was talking about. At first, he assumed a customer was accosting a worker.

Frantically, his employee explained what was happening: A police officer had pinned a customer to the ground outside the store, and that man was saying he couldn't breathe. Mahmoud manages the day shift at CUP Foods at the corner of Thirty-Eighth Street and Chicago Avenue in southern Minneapolis, but that night, young employees were working the store alone. There'd been a brief confrontation with a man accused of passing a fake bill. Then an eighteen-year-old clerk dialed 911. The man was named George Floyd, and minutes later, a cop was kneeling on his neck.

By the afternoon after Floyd's killing, CUP Foods' voicemail box was full. As the day wore on, a devastated and furious group began to gather at the intersection. They chanted, prayed, and consoled one another. Outside the shop, numbers swelled into the thousands.

In the months that followed, the intersection would become a fortress of grief and protest with sculptures, murals, and constant visitors. Armed groups would patrol the area, and police would stay on the other side of barricades. The store would be vandalized repeatedly, with "FUCK CUP FOODS" spray-painted on the exterior. Even longtime customers would question whether it ever deserved to reopen. The Abumayyaleh brothers would fret over lowball offers to buy them out after Friday prayers at the mosque in the store's basement and struggle to imagine a future for a family business with a complicated past.

But in those first days, they were only sure of one thing. "Between the phone calls, threats, the protesters outside," Mahmoud said, he and his brothers decided they had to temporarily shut down. He said he believed that most of the threats CUP Foods was getting were a form of grief, expressions of outrage from people who felt powerless after watching another Black man get killed by police. But he still didn't know what might happen. When the brothers closed the doors, they had no idea if they'd ever reopen at all.

. . .

More than thirty years ago, Samir Abumayyaleh had a choice to make. Born in Palestine, he was the oldest son of a family that arrived to the United States when he was a child. The family moved to North Minneapolis to open a small convenience store. When Samir graduated high school in 1989, he could either go to college or start his own shop like his father, Hamadeh, had and help stabilize the finances for his parents and their ten kids. He found an opportunity to lease a promising space on the other side of town, in South Minneapolis. The property had once been a drugstore and sat at the intersection of four neighborhoods. Samir went for it. He called his tiny corner store Chicago Unbeatable Prices, later shortened to just CUP. Over time, it expanded to include a deli, a cell-phone repair shop, a notary public, and MoneyGram services.

In its early years, only Samir and his parents worked in the store. They would sit outside, sipping coffee and tea, handling sporadic customers, while the kids ran around playing inside. As soon as his younger brothers were old enough—maybe before they were—they started to take shifts at the store too.

Six years ago, Samir passed off responsibility for managing the store to three of his siblings, Mahmoud, Nabil, and Ahmad, though he's still a familiar figure there, known to most people as "Sam." Samir is now forty-nine years old, and his hair is white and thick. He assertively leans forward when talking, but his voice is soft. He is eager to see business return to normal, but, he told me, as a native Palestinian, he understands the frustration coming from the protesters outside. "God made this happen for a reason," he said in Arabic. "It started a real reckoning that was needed. The way these cops treat Black people here can never be justified."

Samir's younger brothers have spent their entire lives on this corner. "I started working when I was like twelve, eleven," said Mahmoud, who is now thirty-six, and only agreed to be interviewed inside the shop if he could keep working and answering calls while we talked. "I started working full time when I was fifteen, seven days a week, during school, no breaks. And by the time I was seventeen, I was holding a shift by myself. And by the time I got to twenty-one, twenty-two, I got married, and by twenty-five, I was holding the store down by myself." Mahmoud now has four kids, one of whom, at thirteen, already works at the store.

Samir's youngest brother, Ahmad, thirty-two, manages the night shift. There are enough years between Ahmad and Samir to make him Samir's child. He was only one year old when CUP Foods opened. "A lot of customers remember me in diapers. I swear, I have pictures with them," he said. In college, he imagined a career outside of his family's business. He studied computer engineering and even got a corporate job after he graduated, still taking occasional shifts at CUP. But now, he's invested in keeping the store running and in the family.

Nabil, forty-six, once managed the store but now looks after some of the fifteen or so other properties the brothers own. Their buildings house a laundromat, a barber shop, and other businesses in neighborhoods around Minneapolis and St. Paul. Nabil has three sons who take regular shifts behind the counter at CUP Foods, and the brothers hope they will become the next generation of managers. "I'm trying to pass it on to them," he said. "They won't have to work for somebody else."

The four Abumayyaleh brothers now co-own the shop together. There are reminders of their parents everywhere. A portrait of Hamadeh, who died in 2012, hangs on the wall behind the register. A recorded recitation of the Quran plays on repeat off one of the computers, just like it did when their parents ran CUP Foods. The mosque in the basement, used by Muslims who work at local stores, auto shops, and restaurants, is dedicated to their mother's memory: It's called Masjid Ni'mat ul-Islaam. Her name was Ni'mat. "Our Mama, God rest her soul, when she was alive, she made me promise," Mahmoud said, " 'Don't ever sell this business.' "

.   .   .

During the first week after Floyd's killing, someone threw a rock through CUP Foods' window. When I first visited in late July, the brothers still hadn't fixed it. A large wooden board covered part of the storefront. As I toured the shop, a neighbor was helping with the cleanup, sweeping broken glass from the floor.

The early aftermath had been hard to fathom. As the protests went national, they intensified around Minneapolis. Two miles northeast, the Third Precinct police station was set ablaze. The authorities fired tear gas at protesters and journalists. The governor called in the National Guard. The governor and mayor also put a curfew into effect. Within the week, Derek Chauvin, the officer filmed kneeling on Floyd's neck, had been charged with murder.

Mourners brought flowers and balloons to place where Floyd died near CUP Foods' doorstep. Organizers brought markers and card stock for protesters to make their own signs. In the week after the killing, many left their signs on the ground or taped to the walls, blending in with the spray-painted graffiti that read "I Can't Breathe" and "Black Lives Matter." While other areas of Minneapolis saw looting, locals and protesters wanted to preserve the area as a place of protest, especially the space immediately in front of CUP Foods. They established a perimeter around the intersection with barricades and declared it beyond the jurisdiction of the police.

On June 15, Mahmoud and his brothers tried to open the store back up. That didn't last long. Many protesters who were holding the area down, including residents and activists from Chicago, viewed the reopening as an insult to Floyd's memory and their cause. People who were organizing around the store told the owners it wasn't safe to open—according to Mahmoud, they told the brothers, "Guys, there's too much animosity. There's too much pressure. It's not safe"—and they promptly closed back down.

Among those who warned the brothers to keep the store closed was a group called the Agape Movement, cofounded by a former gang member, who appointed themselves to keep the intersection safe. The name refers to a theological term for Christian love. When I was there, several of them were armed. I spoke with one of the Agape leaders, Steve Floyd, who said he was a distant relative of George's. ("We're from the same plantation," he told me.) Some people—Floyd described them as an angry group separate from the main protesters—"were ready to bomb that store and burn it up," he said. He'd lived in the neighborhood some forty years, a decade longer than CUP Foods had been there.

Steve Floyd doesn't blame CUP Foods directly for George's killing, but he wouldn't call the store's owners blameless. "They did what people typically don't do: pointing somebody out for something you don't even get arrested for," he said, referring to the neighborhood reluctance to call the police for nonviolent crimes.

Another local, Carmen Means, who is the executive director of a Minneapolis urban development group, told me that she believed the store should close "right now, because of the role they played—and to be clear, they did not kill George Floyd, but they did play a meaningful role in the lynching of George Floyd—that speaks to the culture of the store," she told me. "My personal experience inside the store, I didn't have any issues. I won't lie and say that I did," she said. "The challenge," she said, "is what the store represents."

•　　　•　　　•

Every time I asked the Abumayyalehs if I could meet the clerk who called 911, they said it wasn't going to happen. He's remained hidden from public view, his identity shielded by the rest of CUP Foods' staff. But on one of my trips to Minneapolis, someone close to the store put us in touch. When we finally talked, he told me I was the first reporter he'd spoken to.

Malik, who agreed to speak if I used a pseudonym, had arrived from West Africa last year to join relatives who were living in Minnesota. Malik is a U.S. citizen but had lived abroad since he was a baby. English is his second language, and even as a tall Black teenager himself, he told me that he wasn't especially aware of the dynamic between Black Americans and the police. When he dialed 911, he said he had no idea what could happen. The transcript of the call shows someone not quite used to calling the police:

OPERATOR: Is he white, Black, Native, Hispanic, Asian?
CALLER: Something like that.
OPERATOR: Which one? White, Black, Native, Hispanic, Asian?
CALLER: No, he's a Black guy.

OPERATOR: All right. (*sigh*)
CALLER: How is your day going?
OPERATOR: Not too bad.
CALLER: Had a long day, huh?

"The first week that he died, I was disturbed a lot. I couldn't sleep," Malik told me when we met in the city. "I've been thinking about it every day. Every night. Sleeping, dreaming, sitting, doing nothing."

Malik said he had barely interacted with Floyd the night he was killed. "He just came in, said, 'What's up?' to me, before everything happened. He came to all the employees, was saying 'hi' to everybody," he said. "CUP Foods is usually like that."

After Floyd paid and left, a clerk passed the bill he used through a machine that identified it as fake. Another teenage employee confronted Floyd outside the store. According to Malik, Floyd refused to return the items he had purchased and cursed them out—"basically trying to be extra on them," as Malik put it. As the other teenager returned to the store, Malik said the employee told him to call 911. So Malik did. "He [Floyd] is sitting on his car cause he's awfully drunk. He's not in control of himself," Malik told the 911 operator.

When Mahmoud got the desperate call from his employee, the police were there, and Floyd was pinned down outside. Mahmoud said he told the employee to call the police again. Specifically, he said, "call the police on the police—and make sure you record it." Mahmoud said he had been through this before. He said a police officer used to harass CUP Foods' customers around the store, so he called the cops on the cop. "It worked," he said, and the harassment stopped.

It wouldn't work this time. A 911 dispatcher who was watching a live feed of the interaction had also reported the officers' actions, to no avail. Chauvin knelt on Floyd's neck for eight minutes while onlookers pleaded with him to stop. Surveillance video I later reviewed showed one of Nabil's sons, who was at the store, trying to intervene, and the police shoving him away. An hour later, Floyd was pronounced dead. "I was in shock," Mahmoud said.

Malik slid into despair after Floyd's killing. "I was feeling that I'm done with life, and stuff. Like, why am I even living? I don't deserve to be breathing, stuff like that," he said. Malik can't take time off, because he supports himself. "I have to work because everything I'm doing in life, bills and everything, I have to pay by myself. I have to pay my own rent, take care of myself, and my family," he told me.

Things have gotten a bit easier since the early days but not by much: "I'm still working on it, but at least I sleep now three to four hours a day." The killing doesn't just follow him around in his head: "Sometimes I answer random calls from people I don't know, and they say some bad stuff, like, 'You guys killed George Floyd.'"

The Abumayyaleh brothers are worried about Malik, particularly Mahmoud. He's in regular contact with the teen's family and told me he's concerned that he's entered a deep depression.

When I talked to Malik, that concern felt warranted. "At least back home, I know how the stuff works better than the United States," he told me. "Now, if it were up to me, I'd rather live in my mom's country. It's better than the United States. I'm not having any happiness. Only darkness."

The brothers can't help but feel that if only one of them had been there that night, things might have turned out differently. "We would have just taken the fake money and [banned] him like we do all the time," Nabil said. "That's what we do. Take the fake money and tell them you can't come back in here for two years." But the teens manning the store thought they were doing the right thing. "They got fake money; they called the cops," Nabil said. "It was escalated by a piece-of-shit cop. He had no remorse for human life. None."

.   .   .

"We've kept CUP Foods from burning, that I know of personally, three times," Marcia Howard told me the first time we spoke. She's been living exactly 260 steps away from CUP Foods since 1998 and helps maintain the perimeter around the intersection. Howard calls herself the "community liaison for security." She has a roll of other members on her walkie-talkie, and she wears a GoPro on her chest. ("Pics or it didn't happen," she tells me when I ask her why.)

She's an English teacher at the local high school and has summers off, but she cites her years as a marine as her primary qualification for this role. "As the city burned, Thirty-Eighth and Chicago took care of Thirty-Eighth and Chicago," she told me—she handled breaches and threats of violence to her neighborhood from rioters, some of whom she said were from out of town. (A Black family who lives above the store would have been one unwitting target.)

Howard has an eagle-eyed view of the area. "I call it the 'five C's of the four corners,'" she said. "We've got the community, we've got the churches, we've got CUP, we've got the crooks in the alley, and we've got the cops. And if you want to know the story of Thirty-Eighth and Chicago Avenue, you have to know those five C's and how they work in concert with and opposition to each other."

With one of her C's, Howard mentioned something I'd heard a lot in the area: that CUP Foods has sometimes been a hangout for people who deal drugs on the corner. Indeed, many protesters who want CUP Foods to stay closed told me they are convinced the neighborhood would be better off without it.

The brothers don't deny that the intersection sees plenty of criminal activity, but they said that was an issue long before CUP Foods opened up. "This community right here, where we're at, it's Blood territory," Nabil said, referring to the Bloods gang. "We can't stop that. Let's see the police take that away from them. We're in their neighborhood."

CUP Foods' history with the police goes back almost to its opening. According to the brothers, in 1991, just two years after becoming a licensed grocer, the family began making formal complaints to the police about the "loitering" problem. They said they were advised to place "no trespassing" signs outside their store. In 1993, they said the city conditioned their license renewal on reducing store hours, reporting drug activity to the police, removing signs from their windows that obstruct the view from the outside, and employing off-duty police officers for security.

The corner got worse. In 1995, the murder rate in Minneapolis peaked. Reports from that year noted that the Bloods gang had taken control of South Minneapolis and gun battles had become commonplace. (Minneapolis today is safer—the homicide rate in recent years has been less than half what it once was.)

In 1998, according to court records, the police opened a file on CUP Foods in what it said at the time was a response to complaints about the store. The force surveilled the area and reported it saw people engaging in "hand-to-hand exchanges"—possible drug deals—in and around the store. An undercover cop purchased apparent crack cocaine from dealers, in what are known as "controlled buys," inside the shop. But in that investigation, none of the brothers was ever convicted on drug charges. The state charged Nabil with unlawful possession of a firearm, but that charge was later dismissed.

Ahmad said that there was a time when Nabil "got caught up in the street activities himself." Nabil told me, "I was born in the streets. I was a hustler, basically. . . . I ran the streets for many years not knowing what I was doing." He specifically said he got in trouble for buying and selling electronics that he'd been told were stolen. "I was buying from this guy who worked for the federal authorities," Nabil said. "He set me up." The police got a search warrant based on that investigation, which ultimately led to a conviction for a separate instance of unlawful possession of a firearm.

After the 1998 drug investigation, police continued to coordinate controlled buys in the store, and on several occasions, drugs were allegedly purchased from dealers inside CUP Foods. According to an archived city document, in 1999 the Hennepin County Attorney's Office commenced a nuisance-abatement proceeding against CUP Foods, which resulted in the city requiring CUP Foods employees to call the police on all illegal activities or risk losing their license.

"We did make a deal with the city because we got many citations for people loitering outside," Ahmad said. "They said that if we don't call them, we get the ticket. So we had to call the police minimum ten times a week to not get fined. We had a quota." (The Minneapolis police said it had "no knowledge" of this quota and did not respond to follow-up requests.) "If we didn't call, we get in trouble," he said. "And if we did call, we get in trouble."

•　　　•　　　•

The corner where CUP Foods sits has now been dubbed George Floyd Square. The space outside the shop, where Floyd was killed, has become a sprawling memorial. On the ground where he was pinned by Chauvin, someone painted a silhouette with angel wings. It's now a landmark, with people coming from around the world, some fresh off the plane with suitcases in tow, to see it for themselves. "Welcome to George Floyd Square," volunteers say with a smile, offering up a spritz of hand sanitizer and a mask.

Flowers, trinkets, and signs with handwritten slogans are scattered everywhere, with protest graffiti on every conceivable surface. Tourists take photos with the large raised-fist sculpture at the center of the intersection and with the wooden fist that activists bolted onto the bus stop across the street.

Over the past few months, the brothers have made several attempts to repair their relationship with the community, which are also attempts to save their business. In the immediate aftermath of Floyd's killing, they publicly offered to pay for the funeral and announced that there were going to be significant policy changes on the subject of when employees should call the police (only in cases of violence). Mahmoud told me he has met privately with different members of Floyd's family. He said the meetings included Floyd's children's mother, his brothers, cousin, and uncle. "The conversation was pleasant," he said. "No animosity at all." (I reached out to ask Floyd's family about the meetings and what they think should happen to the store several times through their lawyer but didn't hear back.)

The brothers also hired Jamar Nelson, a childhood friend, to work as a public relations liaison. (He also does consulting for local political campaigns.) Nelson has had a few ideas about how the store could reopen, including a second mural on the Chicago Avenue–facing façade of a big heart, filled with the names of the many local victims of gun violence in the area who've died before and after Floyd. When I met Nelson, he showed me a scar on his head he said came from his own inter-action with the police.

Nelson told me he believes CUP Foods has been unfairly vili-fied. "You can get angry at the Beckys or the Karens of the world because those are malicious, spiteful calls to the police," he said. "This was not that. This is a business that takes extreme caution with calling the police, period. They got raided for not calling the cops. This is a community store," he told me.

The generic Arab store owner has become a cliché in many Black neighborhoods. In my experience, interactions at stores like this tend to be short, and bulletproof glass between clerks and customers creates a barrier both real and psychic. I've heard cus-tomers call Arab clerks "ock," an affectionate term short for "akhi," the Arabic word for brother. But Arab clerks are often viewed as racist, or at the very least hostile, toward the Black com-munities they serve. I have seen the hostility myself, growing up in Newark, New Jersey, a majority-Black city where many corner stores are operated by Arabs.

That's not what it looks like at CUP—the store has photos of generations of customers on the wall. But I asked Mahmoud if he recognized that dynamic. He knew what I was getting at. "A lot of Arabs are racist, and it shows. They go in Black communities and open stores, and they don't respect [the community]," he said. "But," he insisted, "that's the opposite of us. I have confidence in our community. We're going to open, inshallah. It's just a matter of time."

Nelson also rejected the idea that this dynamic might have played a part in Floyd's death. "It's hard for me to say that someone brown is racist, especially immigrants that come from war-torn countries. Because they battle white folks, they know how the white man exerts power. It's a prejudice more than racism, because prejudice comes from ignorance. A brown man who knows what being oppressed means—c'mon, I can't call that person racist."

Outside of CUP Foods, Nelson showed me where the brothers were thinking of putting in a permanent rose garden to memorialize Floyd and victims of gun violence. "I'm fed up because so many people are misinformed," he said. "CUP didn't kill Floyd." Nelson wishes that people would focus less on blaming the store and more on "trying to worry about a kid that is forever traumatized. Because this will never go away." The community, he said, is trying to heal. And "if healing doesn't involve CUP Foods," he asserted, "then that's not real healing."

· · ·

One Friday in late July, the brothers gathered in the store's basement mosque to talk over an informal offer to buy the store. "They're trying to strong-arm us," Nabil said. "Let them know this is not a serious offer," Mahmoud said.

They walked and talked, up the stairs and into the store. Their plan had been to wait out the protests, but with the lights off and the door still locked, they knew that was a gamble. On the façade of their building, the words "FUCK CUP FOODS" were scribbled. The offers—from where, the brothers didn't say—weren't close to the store's appraised value. But even if they had been, they would have been tough to swallow. Ahmad told me, "It was never for sale anyways."

After more than two months mostly dark, CUP Foods finally reopened on August 3 to a very different neighborhood. Protesters tried to force it to close again, barricading the entrance with large trash receptacles. But this time, the Abumayyalehs decided to forge ahead. The business is now bringing in around 70 percent of the revenue it did before Floyd's killing. The streets around the store are still closed off to vehicular traffic, so the people who shop there now only buy what they can easily carry on foot, usually chips, cigarettes, or water.

Not long after the store reopened, I stood outside taking notes. A woman walked past the door and, seeing CUP Foods open for business, exploded with emotion. "There are people shopping in that store!?" she exclaimed. "Ha! That store won't last." She kept shouting as she walked down the street. "This is the motherfucker that should have burned down," she said. "Bitch-ass A-rabs."

•   •   •

Minneapolis announced plans to reopen George Floyd Square to street traffic the week of August 17. (The Minneapolis Police say they would not have forcibly removed the barricades.) About one hundred people lay down on the street that Monday to show their dissent. The barricades remained.

The protesters' goal is to have the city agree to what Marcia Howard calls Resolution 001, a list of twenty-four demands designed to improve the lives of everyone in the neighborhood. (Howard also acts as an unofficial representative of the protesters in the square to the City Council.) They're seeking local government investment in job initiatives, a "contingency fund" for small-business owners of color, and work training for the next generation.

Howard said her wishes for the store are tricky. "They are in this community, and their shoppers are in this community. You cannot protest CUP Foods without protesting the people who patronize them. That's the sticky part," she said. "And so there's work to be done with the people who find it necessary to shop there, and there's work to be done for the family of owners in this neighborhood who monopolize a great deal of businesses. Everybody is trying to be on the right side of history, and that is going to take community building and conversations."

Toussaint Morrison, a Black Lives Matter organizer in Minneapolis, said he doesn't actually see any problem with CUP Foods reopening. But he doesn't necessarily think anyone should shop there. We met in a local coffee shop a short drive away from George Floyd Square. "The first Black-owned bookstore just opened. That shows you how far behind Minneapolis is," he told me.

Morrison envisioned turning the corner of Thirty-Eighth and Chicago into a new Black Wall Street, where Black residents can get special business loans so Black Americans can be the ones earning family wealth in their own communities. "People are ready to ride for Thirty-Eighth and George Floyd, and people will fight for it," he said. "But the people have to vote with their dollars, and in the Black community, we're not used to that because historically [the ability to do that has] been stripped away from us." On CUP Foods reopening, he said, "I say get a Black-owned corner store near there, and say shop here. We'll beat all of their prices. Even if we lose money, whatever." The point, he said, is to keep Black money in the Black community: "Whether they open or not, it's on us as a community to not buy their shit. It's that simple."

Asked about it later, Nabil called that idea ridiculous: "What's the difference between having a Black corner store and an Arab corner store? If this was a white corner store, I'd say, OK, I see his point. But Arabs, we struggle just like everybody else." He added, "You're asking the only brother that has Black kids. My kids are Black." His sons are expected to take over management of the store to keep it within the family. "By them opening their own store, what do you think my kids are going to do? It makes no sense to me," he said.

Across from CUP Foods one afternoon, I met Tahasha Harpole, a graphic designer selling T-shirts from her local shop with Black Lives Matter slogans printed on them. Harpole doesn't think the Abumayyaleh family has done enough to make things right. She knows them well. Her grandmother's house, where she lives now, is one block away. When she was younger, she recalls that the owners would hang bounced checks on the wall behind the register as a scam deterrent. One of the checks had her last name on it—it was a relative's—so she gave Hamadeh the money for the check, and he took it down from the wall. The next day, she asked him for a job, and he gave her one. "I was the first girl to work there," she told me.

"Nobody saw this coming," said Harpole, who is Black. She said she could attest to the store's relationship with customers but also said it isn't enough. She suggests that the brothers could work with entrepreneurs in their vicinity, sharing space inside the store to open stalls for Black-owned businesses and maybe even offer managerial roles.

Although tension between the protesters and CUP Foods is still evident, Howard recently found reason to go inside—after a white vandal sprayed black paint over a mural on the store memorializing George Floyd. "We got together to capture Daniel the Defacer," she told me. "I got him on the phone, I said, 'Mike, do y'all have a security camera out there?' He said, 'Yeah I'll see you in the morning.' So I went back into his little security office behind the counter of CUP Foods, and I recorded while he was playing it. That's me and him on the video that just went viral."

Although they have been here for more than thirty years, Howard believes things can never return to normal for the brothers. "They have been gentrified by history," she said. "This is now, including CUP, a national historic site. How they handle that as a family, and as a corporate entity, is going to either redeem their legacy or further tarnish it. And that is still yet to come."

.   .   .

When I first met Mahmoud, I asked him if he could ever imagine doing anything else but running CUP Foods. "Absolutely not," he told me. "Never in a million years." But day by day, the idea didn't seem so foreign. Mahmoud recently laughed about the rumors that celebrities like Jay-Z and Stevie Wonder wanted to buy CUP from the family. He told me he's waiting on those offers.

Some have called for the store to become a community center. Mahmoud and his brothers aren't against the idea of turning the space into a permanent memorial for Floyd, but they say that idea doesn't require them to pack up and leave. "What we want to do is a joint venture, so we're part of the movement, not to just sell it and move on," Mahmoud said.

One of the last days I was there, Mahmoud's thirteen-year-old son was working a shift in the cell-phone repair section. With business a little slow, he was mostly walking back and forth, swinging a keychain, killing time. "I want to be an architect," he told me. I asked him if that means he'd move on from the store. "No, I can do both. I can work at the store and be an architect. I'd make mad money that way," he said.

The family remains in close touch with Malik. The last time I talked to him, he said his father kicked him out of his house in the months after the 911 call, because of what he described as a "problem between me and my parents." But he sounded slightly more upbeat and said he was managing to support himself.

"Thank God—that God is helping me to not do that bad stuff that I'd regret," he told me.

Back at the store recently, one of the customers, Sal, a tall Black man with a voice so quiet it's close to a whisper, was teasing Mahmoud's son, joking that he's gotten taller but not any stronger. He told me he's been coming in since he was a kid. "I grew up around here," he said. "It's where we can get together, conversate, run into people." I asked him what he made of the protesters outside who think the store ought to be replaced with a community center. "It already is a community center," he said.

In the basement mosque that August weekend, the imam was late, so a worshiper stepped in to give the sermon in his stead. It was focused on George Floyd. "He was a Black man, but you don't have to be Black to feel like that was you," he told the group gathered beneath CUP Foods. "He was a human being first and no human ever should die the way they killed him. No one. Not Black. Not white. Not Muslim. Not Christian. Not Jewish. Nobody." It's "terrorism," the worshiper said—"what they did to him, and to all of us."

Mother Jones

FINALIST—COMMUNITY
JOURNALISM

Samantha Jones graduated from Northwestern University with a degree in journalism in 2011 and worked in Indonesia and Myanmar before joining Mother Jones, first as an editorial fellow, in 2014. She now specializes in reporting on criminal justice. Her story "Whose Streets?" was described by the editors of Mother Jones as an account of how Oakland residents persuaded the city to rethink its approach to gun violence. "Whose Streets?" was one of three Mother Jones stories that were nominated this year in a new category, Community Journalism. Along with Edwin Rios's "How Black Oaklanders Finally Expelled the School Police" and Jamilah King's "Carroll Fife Is in the House. Now She Wants to Burn It Down," "Whose Streets?" was, according to the judges, "rigorous but sympathetic, ably detailing how communities can mobilize to challenge structural racism and move toward becoming the change they seek."

Samantha Michaels

Whose Streets?

In August 2018, a few weeks after he was shot eight times at a party in Oakland, Andre Reed was recovering at his mom's house, his wounds still open, when he got a message on Instagram. It was an old friend from his school days. She said some people were looking for him and wanted to talk.

Reed, then thirty-five, had recently been released from federal prison, after years of bouncing in and out of the criminal justice system. "Is this the police?" he asked. She said she didn't think so but would check. "They don't got nothing to do with the police, nothing like that," he recalls her saying when she messaged him back.

Reed was being sought by outreach workers who wondered if he'd like to meet with a life coach to help him get his feet back on the ground. It was the latest version of a strategy to drive down gun violence in a city with one of the country's highest murder rates. The program, called Operation Ceasefire, draws on data to identify people who are at the highest risk of shooting someone or being shot themselves. At a meeting with police and community members, known as a call-in, the recruits are told they'll be punished if they keep engaging in violence. But they're also offered access to housing, jobs, medical care, and life coaches, plus a monthly stipend if they accomplish goals like signing up for health insurance, opening a savings account, and staying in touch with probation officers. The idea is to try to prevent shootings not by flooding the streets with armed police but by connecting people with resources and helping them build relationships.

Reed seemed like a perfect candidate. For nearly his entire childhood, his dad had been in prison, and Reed himself had been in and out of juvenile detention since the seventh grade. And he'd already had run-ins with gun violence. That July, he'd gone to a barbecue outside an apartment building in West Oakland. As he polished off some Chinese food while catching up with friends, two men in black ski masks walked through the gate and opened fire, striking Reed's legs. He collapsed beside a car, his thoughts on his five-month-old daughter and ten-year-old son. The shooters fled and an ambulance arrived, rushing him to a nearby hospital, where he stayed for about a week. Now, back at his mom's house in the suburbs, he struggled to move. He slept most of the day, groggy from painkillers, or watched movies. He worried he'd have no other option but to rejoin his crew on the streets once he healed.

The question of how to reach men like Reed, who are at high risk of committing or falling victim to violence, is pressing in cities like Oakland. Nationally, murder rates have fallen since their last peak in the 1990s and are now back to their 1965 levels. But the progress has been uneven. For Black men between the ages of fifteen and twenty-four in the United States, homicide, mostly by gunfire, is still the leading cause of death by far, killing more of them than the next nine top causes of death combined. During the first few months of the pandemic, shootings crept up again in some cities, including Oakland.

Many politicians have long believed that to reduce violence, cities have to put more officers on the streets and make more arrests. President Donald Trump announced in July that he plans to send hundreds of federal officers to cities around the country, with a goal of ramping up prosecutions. Ceasefire flips that script: it calls for fewer arrests for nonviolent acts, an end to the scorched-earth tactics that fueled the drug war, and an emphasis on reaching the relatively small number of people involved in most shootings. In 2015, half of all gun homicides in the United States took place in just 127 cities and towns; more than a quarter were in neighborhoods representing only 1.5 percent of the total population, according to a 2017 report by the *Guardian*. An analysis of shootings in Oakland revealed that just 0.1 percent of the city's population was responsible for most of its homicides. But many men at the highest risk of this violence—often members of gangs, with a history of shooting or being shot—are also the most isolated from social services or the most resistant to them.

Dozens of cities have experimented with programs like Ceasefire in recent decades, starting with Boston in 1996. Yet the approach, which goes by various names, has had mixed results, partly because cities have rolled it out in vastly different ways. Some city leaders promise social services but spend more money on the policing aspect of the program: they lean on cops to track down men at risk of violence, threaten them with punishment, and arrest them if they don't get in line.

When outreach workers in Oakland first got in touch with Reed, he knew Ceasefire had a reputation in the neighborhood— guys who slipped up again could find themselves in handcuffs. And going back to prison was the last thing he wanted. Plus, he was tired of case managers. He still had flashbacks to parole programs from years earlier, where he mostly watched movies and wasted time. "I always wanted to change, but all the programs just, you know, blowin' smoke," says Reed, who has long braids and tattoos of skeletons and smoke winding up his arms.

Oakland's residents have other reasons to be skeptical of a reform effort involving the police. The city's cops have been under federal oversight for brutality and civil rights abuses for seventeen years. And Oakland tried and failed to implement Ceasefire twice before, in 2007 and 2011. In 2013, at the behest of pastors and other residents, the city rolled out Ceasefire for a third time, but with a twist: the program would scale back its emphasis on law enforcement and focus, through life coaching, on helping participants develop positive relationships with mentors who grew up in similar neighborhoods as they had.

It's working. Between 2011 and 2017, the number of shootings in Oakland dropped by more than 50 percent. Meanwhile, arrests have declined, and officers are solving more murders than they once did. Police departments in New York City, Chicago, Minneapolis, and Washington, DC, have sent officials to observe the city's alternative model. "What Oakland's doing is certainly the Ceasefire strategy, but it's a very evolved version," says Mike McLively, an attorney at the San Francisco–based Giffords Law Center to Prevent Gun Violence. Life coaches, clergy, and victims' family members all play important roles in reaching out to at-risk men. Oakland "paid much more attention to a strong community voice and to providing a more robust set of social services," says researcher Thomas Abt, a Justice Department official during the Obama administration and author of the 2019 book *Bleeding Out*.

And now, amid nationwide protests to defund law enforcement and rethink how cities handle public safety, curiosity about Oakland's strategy is growing. In Minneapolis, after protests over the killing of George Floyd sparked a debate about dismantling the police, some City Council members proposed funneling more money into a program like Oakland's.

Reed was still skeptical of Ceasefire on the warm day in September 2018 when he, his mom, and his son drove two and a half hours from her house in suburban Oroville to Oakland to get more information on the mentorship program. Leaning on a cane, Reed limped from the car into an office building and rode the elevator to the third floor. At a conference table surrounded by a handful of life coaches, he sat quietly across from Leonard Haywood, a polite man about a decade his senior. Haywood offered to work one-on-one with him as a coach. Reed recalls, "I thought he was probably full of shit."

At the end of the meeting, Reed didn't make any promises. But when he went home again, the texts started coming. "Hey Dre, how you doing?" Haywood wrote shortly afterward. "Just wanted to check in, see how everything is going. Let me know if you need anything, if there's anything we can do." Haywood kept in touch with Reed for about two months, asking how the recovery was going. "I was totally surprised," Reed recalls. The texts and calls made him wonder if Haywood actually cared. Reed said he'd consider working with him if he moved back to Oakland.

From the beginning, the call for Oakland's police to rethink their approach to gun violence came from community members— and the odds were very much stacked against them. In 2003, Oakland was reeling from a murder crisis. The city had seen an 81 percent surge in homicides over the previous four years, to 113 killings in 2002. But Mayor Jerry Brown scoffed at a City Council member's suggestion that offering better job training for people with criminal records could help prevent shootings. "Do you think if we put the Godfather and his gang in a job program, they'd change their line of work?" Brown told a reporter in 2002. He instead pushed to hire one hundred more police officers, who could flood high-crime areas of East and West Oakland in search of drugs and guns.

Then the killings came to Barbara Lafitte-Oluwole's doorstep. Lafitte-Oluwole, a community organizer originally from Louisiana, lived in a green and burgundy Victorian house in West Oakland. On June 14, 2003, her stepson, Tokumbo, was celebrating his twenty-second birthday with friends outside a KFC when a man fired six bullets into him, killing him instantly. Detectives never caught the shooter. Lafitte-Oluwole believes her stepson was targeted because he was preparing to testify against men who allegedly killed his best friend months earlier after an argument about a missing Uzi.

Steeped in grief, Lafitte-Oluwole started learning about Boston's Ceasefire program, which cut youth homicides in half before city officials lost momentum and abandoned the strategy in 2000. She began working with a group of activists from the nonprofit Oakland Community Organizations (now Faith in Action East Bay) who bombarded public safety meetings with demands that city officials try the strategy. Eventually, in 2007, Mayor Ron Dellums agreed. Under Ceasefire, police would summon men at risk of shootings to a call-in.

Or at least that was the theory. After police officers surrounded people's houses with squad cars to drop off the "invitation" to the first call-in, only two men showed up. By the end of 2010, the first iteration of Ceasefire in Oakland was dead, having done little to quell the shootings. The next year, a three-year-old was gunned down while walking with his family in East Oakland. Officials briefly relaunched Ceasefire, but it fizzled out. By then, Oakland had the third-highest murder rate of any midsize city in the country.

Not everyone was ready to give up. Ben McBride, a progressive pastor from San Francisco, had resigned from his church years earlier after watching his nondenominational congregation lose family members to gunfire. Hoping to better understand the violence, in 2008 he'd moved with his wife and three daughters to part of East Oakland known as "the kill zone." His first night there, after tucking the girls in for bed, loud bangs erupted outside their home. He dropped to his knees and started to pray, terrified. It took minutes before he realized they were fireworks coming from a baseball stadium.

His older brother, Michael, also a pastor, met one of the architects of Boston's Ceasefire program while studying divinity at Duke University and became curious about the model. The McBrides had grown up with an acute awareness of the violence inflicted on Black people: Their great-uncle had been tied to a railroad track and killed by the Klan. Their dad, who met Martin

Luther King Jr. as a boy, had been jailed for protesting during the Civil Rights Movement. And in college, Michael says he was racially profiled by two white officers who pulled him over, groped him, and forced him to lie on the ground.

Despite their misgivings about the police, the McBrides knew Ceasefire had worked in Boston. So Michael encouraged other pastors to learn about the strategy and invited clergy from Boston to come share lessons from their city's success. In 2012, about 500 local religious leaders, activists, and residents piled into an Oakland church to show their support. "He was very prophetic," Lafitte-Oluwole says of Michael, whom the Obama administration later tapped as an adviser for a council that made recommendations about how to deliver social services. The huge community turnout helped convince Mayor Jean Quan and the police chief to restart Ceasefire—this time with some bold new strategies.

Data would prove crucial. For years, the police, who helped identify the participants, believed that 10,000 people, disproportionately teens, drove homicides in Oakland, which is why previous violence-prevention programs funneled most social services to a large group of teens. During the earlier iterations of Ceasefire, officers targeted known group or gang members who were on probation or parole for weapon or violence-related offenses— a broad category. Now the city's public safety director called in advisers from the California Partnership for Safe Communities, a newly formed nonprofit, to examine data gathered from a year and a half of shootings and figure out more specifically who was involved.

The results shook police and city leaders' assumptions. Just 400 men were responsible for the majority of the city's homicides, the researchers found, and their average age was twenty-eight or twenty-nine. The discovery challenged a long-held belief that people age out of violence in their twenties. Most shooters were Black or Latino and members of a street group, a term used in Oakland instead of "gang," and they had forged strong ties with friends in their crew. They were typically fighting not over drugs, as was commonly believed, but over personal beefs. Most had a history of prison or probation, and many had been involved in a previous shooting, as either a perpetrator or a target. Because the men were older, they'd had more time to rack up bad experiences with official agencies and the criminal justice system, whether through foster care or the courts.

With the new data, Ceasefire officials could target services to those people for whom intervention might stanch the most violence. Most cities don't do this analysis, says David Muhammad, Oakland's former chief probation officer and now an adviser for the California Partnership for Safe Communities. Every week, law enforcement and criminologists review each shooting that occurred over the past seven days and refer the gunmen and victims to Ceasefire if they meet most of certain criteria: they're between the ages of eighteen and thirty-five, have an extensive criminal justice history, are part of a street group, and have a family member or friend who has been shot recently. "Data changed the whole dynamic," says Ben McBride, "because we knew we could reach around 250 individuals, versus this feeling that there's 20,000 people running around terrorizing the city and being terrorized."

After Ceasefire resumed in 2013, about twenty probationers and parolees went to the next call-in at a community center. The room was tense. Men from rival gangs eyed each other from their seats. Between them sat pastors, police, and mothers whose sons had been killed. Law enforcement officers hovered in the background. Muhammad, the technical adviser, watched skeptically as officers in tactical gear tried to convince the men that the city cared about them. He and others pushed the city to scale back the police presence at future call-ins.

At a later meeting, one of the participants pointed out that the incentives to leave their groups still weren't good enough: "When you all ask me to put that gun down, it's not just the gun I'm putting down, but my ability to be safe, my ability to belong," Ben McBride recalls a man in his late twenties saying. It got McBride thinking about how some men turned to guns because their schools, the police, or adults in their lives hadn't protected them. The question city leaders needed to ask now wasn't whether these men were ready to change. It was, McBride realized, "Were we ready to be in a deep relationship with them? Were we ready to commit resources to them? Were we ready to transform society in a way they could belong to it?"

If the answer was "yes," he knew it would take investment—voters would need to pass a ballot measure to fund Ceasefire and social services for its participants. It was a tough ask, because investing in Ceasefire also meant investing in the police. And ahead of the 2014 election, the country was grappling with the police killings of Eric Garner and Michael Brown. "There was not a lot of goodwill" between law enforcement and Black people in Oakland, says McBride, who went to Ferguson, Missouri, to protest Brown's killing. He says police officers there called him and his brother the n-word and other slurs; both of them were arrested. Passing the ballot measure "was a heavy lift," he says, because "we are working with a partner—the police department—that is very flawed."

But the McBrides tried to remind people that investing in Ceasefire could have results—homicides had already fallen by nearly a third over the prior year. With Lafitte-Oluwole, pastors, and other community members, they spoke with congregants, who then spread the word to neighbors. That November, Oakland voters overwhelmingly passed Measure Z, which would raise $277 million over a decade—60 percent of it for the police, the rest for violence prevention programs, including Ceasefire.

The spending on additional services had the potential to save the city money in the long run. It would cost less than $10,000 to put someone through life coaching, according to Muhammad. By contrast, he says, a single shooting injury can cost the city more than $1 million including medical, police, court, and prison costs. Often it's more: A 2015 analysis by *Mother Jones* and researcher Ted Miller revealed that nationally, each gun death averages about $6 million in total costs. Collectively, these killings cost the United States more than $229 billion each year—upward of $700 per person. And access to social services can help drive down shootings. In his book *Uneasy Peace*, the sociologist Patrick Sharkey examined crime in 264 cities between 1990 and 2012, and found that each additional nonprofit focused on crime and social outreach was associated with a nearly 1 percent drop in murder rates.

But throwing money or programs at a problem can only get you so far. "Part of what's been deeply disturbing about the way violence prevention has and hasn't played out in cities is that for a long time it's essentially been an inside game," driven from the top down by mayors, police chiefs, and others who might not have been personally affected, says scholar David Kennedy, an architect of the Boston model. "Communities are no longer putting up with that. Because the most powerful influencer of behavior is not the cops—it's what you and your community and your mom and your best friends and your girlfriend think about what you're doing." Since so many shootings are about interpersonal conflicts, breaking the chain of violence can be like breaking the chain of viral transmission in a public health epidemic.

In 2013, as Oakland began its third attempt with the Ceasefire program, community members pushed to be more involved. City officials decided to let volunteers help police reach out to potential participants individually rather than summoning them to group call-ins. One study by the city found that 65 percent of potential participants in Oakland accepted services when a community member was present at the ask, compared with just 25 percent who did when only police reached out. Lafitte-Oluwole, a decade after her stepson was killed, volunteered to do outreach. "A lot of people carry all these burdens," she says, "not knowing they can seek help."

City officials also started to think differently about how they offered services to the program's participants. Giving someone a phone number to call for job training wouldn't cut it. Now, life coaches, some of whom came up through street groups, would build relationships with the participants, an addition to the program other cities hadn't tried. They'd sit down with the guys and see if they wanted help with any immediate needs, like avoiding threats from a rival gang or finding housing. But the coaches' main goal would be to spend time with the participants and build trust, even with men who were still involved with a street group or didn't want a job. "Just because you aren't motivated in the beginning, it doesn't mean we give up on you," says Haywood, who has been working as a life coach for eight years. "It's not just a Monday-through-Friday, job-related thing. It's deeper than that." The life coaches work with people even if they're still involved with crime, and they don't share any information with police.

In 2018, only 10 percent of the men who went through the Community & Youth Outreach coaching program, where Haywood works, were rearrested after one year. In contrast, nearly three-quarters of men in their early twenties with juvenile records in California end up arrested again within a few years of their release from detention. Fewer than 1 percent of the Ceasefire participants who did the coaching program were rearrested for shootings in 2018.

In late 2018, Andre Reed moved into his girlfriend's house in a city near Oakland and started meeting up with Leonard Haywood, or Len, his new life coach. Haywood, forty-seven, also grew up in Oakland with a single mom. As a kid, he straddled two worlds, taking classes at a private school and then coming back to his East Oakland neighborhood, where he'd ride his blue BMX bike, rap Too $hort and Richie Rich songs, and shoot hoops. Some of his friends sold crack, but beyond the occasional fight, he mostly stayed out of trouble. His football, track, and basketball coaches encouraged him to stay in school. "Sometimes you can't see certain things in yourself," Haywood says now, reflecting on his mentors. "Thinking I can only go so far."

By the time Reed limped back to Haywood's office on the third floor of a Bank of America building in East Oakland in 2018, he'd discarded the cane and, thanks to the regular phone calls, his skepticism about Haywood. Reed appreciated that Haywood hadn't rushed him to come before he was ready. "It's all about meeting people where they are," Haywood says of his approach.

At least three times a week, Reed and Haywood met at the office, Reed's house, or out somewhere to eat burgers or burritos. Both are fathers, with boys about the same age, and they bonded over their Oakland childhoods and years playing football. Haywood told Reed about the night he spent in jail before dropping out of college. Everything about the experience—getting fingerprinted and thrown into a cell, being ordered to pull down his pants and bend and cough—felt like a violation. Reed found Haywood's honesty refreshing. "Some people will talk to you but lie to you at the same time," Reed says. "He told me the truth of everything, keeping it real with me."

Haywood coaxed Reed into naming some of his goals. Safety was one. And he wanted a steady job to support his kids. Haywood referred him to SAS Automotive in nearby Newark, where he applied to build dashboards for Tesla cars. Along with his paycheck, he would receive about $200 from the city as a monthly stipend for staying employed and meeting with his parole officer. The job left less time to swing by the life-coaching office, so Haywood sometimes drove out to see him at the auto factory. Reed eventually moved to East Oakland, where he stayed in a duplex with his aunt just a few blocks from Haywood's home.

"I think I text him 'big bro' first," Reed says. "'Big bro, do I need to come do something?' That's when he text back 'little bro,' and ever since then it's just 'big bro, little bro.'" If there was a shooting in Oakland, Haywood would reach out to make sure

Reed was OK. He texted often: *How was work, what you getting into today, you ate?* Reed knew he could call his coach anytime. It was nice, he thought. The only other person who reached out regularly to hear how he was doing was his mom.

A few months after Reed started working at the auto factory, he invited Haywood into his living room, where he showed off the pile of gifts he'd stashed beneath a Christmas tree: PlayStation games for his son, and Barbies and cooking toys for his daughter, all purchased with his own paycheck.

On a Friday night last December around seven p.m., Rev. Damita Davis-Howard spotted two figures heading down a street near her Baptist church in East Oakland. "Hey, young men. How you all doin' tonight?" she called out to them as they passed a beat-up Chevy. "You be safe out here, OK?"

They both smiled. "You too," one said, before turning to walk away.

Most Friday nights for seven years, Davis-Howard, codirector of Ceasefire, and other activists have banded together for organized walks through areas of Oakland at high risk of gun violence. Her brother was shot and killed when she was in her late twenties. Two of her second cousins were shot too, and her niece was shot on her way to a party. In 2018, four bullets hit her son while he was at a store, though he survived. Joining the Night Walks, she told me, makes her feel like maybe she can change things.

About twenty people dressed in white coats carried signs that read "Love One Another" and "Honk for Peace" as they marched past houses decorated with holiday lights along Eighty-Fifth Avenue. Two men waved and filmed the walkers on their phones as drivers honked in support.

"It's like counting the apples in a seed," B. K. Woodson, a pastor, had told the marchers at a gathering at Davis-Howard's church before the walk. "We don't know the effect that walking tonight will have. What we do know is that people see us, and they know us." The city's police chief at the time, Anne Kirkpatrick, joined the group for a prayer and clasped hands with some of the marchers. "I ask for forgiveness for what we as police have done to cause harm," she said.

The Night Walks are the public face of Ceasefire, a way for pastors and other organizers to shore up support for the program in neighborhoods where many people are reluctant to work with police. But building trust can't just fall on community volunteers. Police have to clean up their act too.

After decades of widespread sweeps for drugs and guns in Black and Brown neighborhoods, the Oakland police department scaled back arrests by 55 percent between 2006 and 2015. Ceasefire officers now say their goal is not to dismantle gangs but instead to stop gang violence, targeting behaviors as opposed to groups of people. They still arrest men who commit violence. But after they do, supervisors with the program are often required to debrief the neighbors and leave a phone number. Those debriefings are "a great idea," says Cat Brooks, cofounder of the Anti Police-Terror Project, a local group that supports families affected by police violence. "Communities should know why there was a major action on their street, because that is just as triggering as intercommunal violence is for us."

The relationship between the police and the community remains fraught. By 2016, Oakland was on track for a record-low number of homicides. The Obama administration commended its police department as an example for other cities to follow. Then, as the city was hoping to end federal oversight, at least fourteen Oakland officers were found to have repeatedly had sex with a seventeen-year-old girl, trafficking her between them. The police chief resigned, and criminal charges were filed.

After the scandal, Ben McBride and other community members debated walking away from Ceasefire because they could no longer trust the police. The city suspended the strategy. "I can tell you that the individuals on our team were embarrassed by it, wanted to throw in the towel," says Captain Ersie Joyner, who then led the police department's Ceasefire unit and who says he also felt disappointed by a lack of accountability in the department in the fallout from the revelations. In the end, most community partners stayed, and Ceasefire resumed a few months later. Oakland closed the year with an overall drop in homicides. Seventy-two people were killed in 2017, the fewest since 1999. "We were able to pull it together and save people's lives," Joyner says.

There was more evidence that Ceasefire was working. In 2018, the criminologist Anthony Braga and other researchers released a study showing that shootings in Oakland had dropped in half since 2011. Ceasefire was found to be directly associated with a 32 percent reduction in gun homicides, even after controlling for other factors like gentrification and seasonal patterns. This huge reduction, the researchers found, was distinct from homicide trends in other California cities.

It was cause for celebration, for a while. Then the coronavirus struck, and protests against police violence. Both would cast uncertainty over the future of Ceasefire and policing in general.

In late May and early June, thousands of people, including the McBrides and Cat Brooks, flooded Oakland's streets to protest police killings of Black men and women. Some protesters demanded that Oakland slash $150 million from its police department budget; some insisted on dismantling the department entirely. "Whose streets?" Brooks shouted into a microphone at a protest in Downtown Oakland that defied the city's eight p.m. curfew. "Our streets!" hundreds of people around her replied.

At first glance, demands to defund the police department seem to threaten Ceasefire's existence, given that it operates as a partnership between the community and the police. But even if cities slash funds for cops and recruit social workers to respond to noncriminal 911 calls, communities will still need to deal with deadly crimes like shootings. It's possible, even likely, that the movement to reimagine public safety in America will create more of an appetite for strategies like Oakland's Ceasefire. The

McBrides, who are now calling on police departments across the country to slash their budgets, see Ceasefire as an avenue to defund traditional law enforcement and invest in communities.

Police in other cities are taking note. "They determined you can't arrest your way out of a problem. That's something we really took away," says Andrew Shearer, Portland's assistant chief, who visited Oakland to learn about the strategy. Milwaukee's police chief, who visited before assuming his new role, has instructed his department to copy Oakland's weekly shooting reviews.

In June, after Minneapolis City Council members announced their intention to dismantle their police department, they suggested they might invest more money in a local program that resembles Oakland's. "That's the kind of work we have to get behind," council member Phillipe Cunningham said of his city's Group Violence Intervention strategy. "Because the more we can do that's community-based, the less law enforcement that we actually need."

That's not to say Oakland has everything figured out. In 2016, researchers found that its officers were four times likelier to search Black men than white men during traffic stops. Another study showed that its police made arrests in 80 percent of homicides with white victims, but only 40 percent with Black victims, a pattern that exists nationally. Ben McBride says the city hasn't been transparent enough about which men are targeted by Ceasefire. And Brooks, of the Anti Police-Terror Project, worries the strategy still leans too heavily on law enforcement. Participants have told her they believe they'll go to jail if they don't accept the program's services. "When you talk to some of the brothers," she says, "their message has been pretty clear: that if they don't play, the cops are going to make life so uncomfortable they have no choice but to play." Technical advisers for the city say the police don't arrest men for rejecting services—just for engaging in violence. "For the purpose of keeping people in our communities who we love alive, we'll continue to work with the police, but we're still a far stone's throw away from trust," says Ben McBride, who eventually wants to see the current system of policing abolished. "What we've told them is, how do we come back and sit at a table with you all when you all are shooting tear gas and rubber bullets at us?"

The McBrides are asking the city to shift much more money away from policing toward the social services that keep Ceasefire humming. For years, the two brothers have also pushed Oakland to pay the volunteers who work on the program. The city recently reached an agreement with a community-based organization to provide stipends. "If you can find the money to pay police officers up to $300,000 a year to patrol the streets with guns, why can't we find the resources to stipend community members to take time away to also reduce violence?" Ben McBride says. "We want to continue to see the kind of partnership and respect for people of color that are doing the work."

"The work of saving lives, particularly Black, Latino, and Brown lives in urban America, is largely seen as the responsibility of Black and Brown people to do by ourselves—that was a problem here in Oakland," Michael McBride said in March at a community meeting at the Allen Temple Baptist Church, the same place where he had rallied support for Ceasefire eight years ago. Men and women in the pews murmured in agreement. But saving these lives, he said, would require the city to spend more money on members of the community it had long neglected, and would require activists to hold their noses and work with the police. "We may not like each other, including the police—we'll be honest, we don't like you," McBride continued. "But we have to work together. It's important to keep reminding ourselves that collaboration is the silver bullet."

Reed graduated from the life-coaching program last November, after about a year of working at the auto factory. When I met him during his lunch break one day in December, he talked about training newer employees and working toward a promotion. He and his girlfriend had a baby boy on the way, due in January. "I look in the mirror every morning and be like, 'I'm proud of you,'" he said.

But the pandemic threw a wrench in his career plans. Shelter-in-place orders closed the production line and left him without work. When I tried to check in with him in March, he didn't answer the phone or return my calls. Haywood told me he couldn't reach him either.

Shootings, meanwhile, were creeping up in Oakland and other cities like Chicago and Baltimore. Maybe it was because of the warmer weather or the fact that people were unemployed and stuck at home. Oakland had entered March on track to hit a record-low number of annual homicides, but by summer that goal seemed unlikely, according to Muhammad, though homicides were still half their pre-Ceasefire levels. Haywood wondered if the pandemic was to blame for the rising violence. He kept in touch with his clients by Zoom and FaceTime and sent them care packages with wipes, hand sanitizer, and masks. But it was harder to build a connection virtually. Community organizers paused their Night Walks to maintain social distancing.

Reed and I eventually reconnected after I tracked him down on Facebook. I wondered if he worried about finding a new job in the middle of a recession, with a criminal record. But he said he was motivated to look for something better. Though his life coaching was technically over, Haywood had called just a couple of hours earlier, with phone numbers of contacts who might be hiring. Reed got to work filling out applications. "It felt good" to talk again to Haywood, Reed told me, "because he's there for me."

For a while, Reed was trying to convince his younger brother, who got out of prison late last year, to seek out a life coach too. "He's still thinking about it," Reed says. Almost every day, Reed texts his brother to check in. *How you doing, what are you up to?* "He want to do the same, but he want to do it on his time," Reed says. "So I just wait. I just tell him, 'When you ready, you just let me know. We can go from there.'"

New Yorker

Elizabeth Alexander begins this essay with a list—an elegantly constructed list but a list nonetheless—of Black men, Black women, and Black children murdered, lynched, for no other reason, no other real reason, than the color of their skin. "I call the young people who grew up in the past twenty-five years the Trayvon Generation," writes Alexander. "They always knew these stories. These stories formed their worldview." The judges who chose "The Trayvon Generation" as the recipient of the National Magazine Award for Essays and Criticism—one of six National Magazine Awards won by the New Yorker this year—said that "in this anguished, erudite essay, Alexander links her fears for her own sons with the politics and music that reflect both the despair and resilience of a generation." Poet, essayist, and playwright, Elizabeth Alexander was named president of the Andrew W. Mellon Foundation in 2018.

Elizabeth Alexander

The Trayvon Generation

This one was shot in his grandmother's yard. This one was carrying a bag of Skittles. This one was playing with a toy gun in front of a gazebo. Black girl in bright bikini. Black boy holding cell phone. This one danced like a marionette as he was shot down in a Chicago intersection. The words, the names: Trayvon, Laquan, bikini, gazebo, loosies, Skittles, two seconds, I can't breathe, traffic stop, dashboard cam, sixteen times. His dead body lay in the street in the August heat for four hours.

He was jogging, was hunted down, cornered by a pickup truck, and shot three times. One of the men who murdered him leaned over his dead body and was heard to say, "Fucking nigger."

I can't breathe, again. Eight minutes and forty-six seconds of a knee and full weight on his neck. "I can't breathe" and, then, "Mama!" George Floyd cried. George Floyd cried, "Mama . . . I'm through!"

His mother had been dead for two years when George Floyd called out for her as he was being lynched. Lynching is defined as a killing committed by a mob. I call the four police officers who arrested him a mob.

·   ·   ·

The kids got shot and the grownups got shot. Which is to say, the kids watched their peers shot down and their parents' generation get gunned down and beat down and terrorized as well. The agglomerating spectacle continues. Here are a few we know less well: Danny Ray Thomas. Johnnie Jermaine Rush. Nania Cain. Dejuan Hall. Atatiana Jefferson. Demetrius Bryan Hollins. Jacqueline Craig and her children. And then the iconic: Alton Sterling. Eric Garner. Sandra Bland. Walter Scott. Breonna Taylor. Philando Castile.

Sandra Bland filmed the prelude to her death. The policeman thrust a stun gun in her face and said, "I will light you *up*."

. . .

I call the young people who grew up in the past twenty-five years the Trayvon Generation. They always knew these stories. These stories formed their world view. These stories helped instruct young African Americans about their embodiment and their vulnerability. The stories were primers in fear and futility. The stories were the ground soil of their rage. These stories instructed them that antiblack hatred and violence were never far.

They watched these violations up close and on their cell phones, so many times over. They watched them in near-real time. They watched them crisscrossed and concentrated. They watched them on the school bus. They watched them under the covers at night. They watched them often outside of the presence of adults who loved them and were charged with keeping them safe in body and soul.

This is the generation of my sons, now twenty-two and twenty years old, and their friends who are also children to me, and the university students I have taught and mentored and loved. And this is also the generation of Darnella Frazier, the seventeen-year-old Minneapolis girl who came upon George Floyd's murder in progress while on an everyday run to the corner store on May 25, filmed it on her phone, and posted it to her Facebook page at 1:46 AM, with the caption "They killed him right in front of cup foods over south on 38th and Chicago!! No type of sympathy </3 </3 #POLICEBRUTALITY." When insideMPD.com (in an article that is no longer up) wrote, "Man Dies After Medical Incident During Police Interaction," Frazier posted at 3:10 AM, "Medical incident??? Watch outtt they killed him and the proof is clearlyyyy there!!"

Darnella Frazier, seventeen years old, witnessing a murder in close proximity, making a record that would have worldwide impact, returned the following day to the scene of the crime. She possessed the language to say, precisely, through tears, "It's so traumatizing."

In Toni Morrison's *Sula*, which is set across the bleak black stretch of Ohio after the First World War, the character Hannah plaintively asks her mother, Eva Peace, "Mamma, did you ever love us?" To paraphrase Eva Peace's reply: *Love you? Love you? I kept you alive.*

I believed I could keep my sons alive by loving them, believed in the magical powers of complete adoration and a love ethic that would permeate their lives. My love was armor when they were small. My love was armor when their father died of a heart attack when they were twelve and thirteen. "They think black men only die when they get shot," my older son said in the aftermath. My love was armor when that same year our community's block watch sent e-mails warning residents about "two black kids on bikes" and praising neighbors who had called the police on them. My love for my children said, *Move.* My love said, *Follow your sons*, when they ran into the dark streets of New York to join protesters after Eric Garner's killer was acquitted. When my sons were in high school and pictures of Philando Castile were on the front page of the *Times*, I wanted to burn all the newspapers so they would not see the gun coming in the window, the blood on

Castile's T-shirt, the terror in his partner's face, and the eyes of his witnessing baby girl. But I was too late, too late generationally, because they were not looking at the newspaper; they were looking at their phones, where the image was a house of mirrors straight to Hell.

My love was both rational and fantastical. Can I protect my sons from being demonized? Can I keep them from moving free? But they must be able to move as free as wind! If I listen to their fears, will I comfort them? If I share my fears, will I frighten them? Will racism and fear disable them? If we ignore it all, will it go away? Will dealing with race fill their minds like stones and block them from thinking of a million other things? Let's be clear about what motherhood is. A being comes onto this earth and you are charged with keeping it alive. It dies if you do not tend it. It is as simple as that. No matter how intellectual and multicolored motherhood becomes as children grow older, the part that says *My purpose on earth is to keep you alive* has never totally dissipated. Magical thinking on all sides.

I want my children—all of them—to thrive, to be fully alive. How do we measure what that means? What does it mean for our young people to be "black alive and looking back at you," as June Jordan puts it in her poem "Who Look at Me"? How to access the sources of strength that transcend this American nightmare of racism and racist violence? What does it mean to be a lucky mother, when so many of my sisters have had their children taken from them by this hatred? The painter Titus Kaphar's recent *Time* magazine cover portrays a black mother cradling what should be her child across the middle of her body, but the child is literally cut out of the canvas and cut out of the mother, leaving a gaping wound for an unending grief that has made a sisterhood of countless black women for generations.

My sons were both a little shy outside of our home when they were growing up. They were quiet and observant, like their father, who had come to this country as a refugee from Eritrea: African observant, immigrant observant, missing nothing. I've watched them over the years with their friends, doing dances now out-moded with names I persist in loving—Nae Nae, Hit Dem Folks—and talking about things I didn't teach them and reading books I haven't read and taking positions I don't necessarily hold, and I marvel. They are grown young men. With their friends, they talk about the pressure to succeed, to have a strong public face, to excel. They talk their big talk, they talk their hilar-ity, and they talk their fear. When I am with them, I truly believe the kids are all right and will save us.

But I worry about this generation of young black people and depression. I have a keen eye—what Gwendolyn Brooks called "gobbling mother-eye"—for these young people, sons and friends and students whom I love and encourage and welcome into my home, keep in touch with and check in on. How are you, how are you, how are you. How are you, baby, how are you. I am interested in the vision of television shows like *Atlanta* and *Inse-cure*, about which I have been asking every young person who will listen, "Don't you think they're about low-grade, undiag-nosed depression and not black hipster ennui?" Why, in fact, did Earn drop out of Princeton? Why does Van get high before a drug test? Why does Issa keep blowing up her life? This season, *Insecure* deals directly with the question of young black people and mental-health issues: Molly is in and out of therapy, and we learn that Nathan, a.k.a. LyftBae, who was ghosting Issa, has been dealing with bipolar disorder. The work of the creative icon of their generation often brings me to the question: Why is Ken-drick so sad? He has been frank about his depression and sui-cidal thoughts. It isn't just the specter of race-based violence and death that hangs over these young people. It's that compounded with the constant display of inequity that has most recently been laid bare in the COVID-19 pandemic, with racial health dispari-ties that are shocking even to those of us inured to our dispro-portionate suffering.

·   ·   ·

Black creativity emerges from long lines of innovative responses to the death and violence that plague our communities. "Not a house in the country ain't packed to its rafters with some dead Negro's grief," Toni Morrison wrote in *Beloved*, and I am interested in creative emergences from that ineluctable fact.

There are so many visual artists responding to this changing same: Henry Taylor, Michael Rakowitz, Ja'Tovia Gary, Carrie Mae Weems, lauren woods, Alexandra Bell, Black Women Artists for Black Lives Matter, Steffani Jemison, Kerry James Marshall, Titus Kaphar. To pause at one work: Dread Scott's "A Man Was Lynched by Police Yesterday," which he made in the wake of the police shooting of Walter Scott, in 2015, echoes the flag reading "A man was lynched yesterday" that the NAACP flew outside its New York headquarters between 1920 and 1938 to mark the lynchings of black people in the United States.

I want to turn to three short films that address the Trayvon Generation with particular power: Flying Lotus's *Until the Quiet Comes* (2012); his *Never Catch Me*, with Kendrick Lamar (2014); and Lamar's "Alright" (2015).

In *Until the Quiet Comes*, the director, Kahlil Joseph, moves us through black Los Angeles—Watts, to be specific. In the fiction of the video, a boy stands in an empty swimming pool, pointing his finger as a gun and shooting. The bullet ricochets off the wall of the pool and he drops as it appears to hit him. The boy lies in a wide-arced swath of his blood, a portrait in the empty pool. He is another black boy down, another body of the traumatized community.

In an eerie twilight, we move into the densely populated Nickerson Gardens, where a young man, played by the dancer Storyboard P, lies dead. Then he rises and begins a startling dance of resurrection, perhaps coming back to life. The community seems numb, oblivious of his rebirth. That rebirth is brief; he gets into a low-rider car, that L.A. icon. The car drives off after his final death dance, taking him from this life to the other side. His death is consecrated by his performance, a ritual that the sudden dead are not afforded. The car becomes a hearse, a space of ritual transport into the next life. But the young man is still gone.

What does it mean to be able to bring together the naturalistic and the visionary, to imagine community as capable of reanimating even its most hopeless and anesthetized members? What does it mean for a presumably murdered black body to come to life in his community in a dance idiom that is uniquely part of black culture and youth culture, all of that power channeled into a lifting?

A sibling to Joseph's work is Hiro Murai's video for Flying Lotus's "Never Catch Me." It opens at a funeral for two children, a black boy and girl, who lie heartbreak-beautiful in their open caskets. Their community grieves inconsolably in the church. The scene is one of profound mourning.

And then the children open their eyes and climb out of their caskets. They dance explosively in front of the pulpit before running down the aisle and out of the church. The mourners cannot see this resurrection, for it is a fantasia. The kids dance another dance of black L.A., the force of black bodily creativity, that expressive life source born of violence and violation that have upturned the world for generations. The resurrected babies dance with a pumping force. But the community's grief is unmitigated, because, once again, this is a dreamscape. The children spring out into the light and climb into a car—no, it is a hearse—and, smiling with the joy of mischievous escapees, drive away. Kids are not allowed to drive; kids are not allowed to die.

·   ·   ·

What does it mean for a black boy to fly, to dream of flying and transcending? To imagine his vincible body all-powerful, a body that in this society is so often consumed as a moneymaker and an object of perverse desire, perceived to have superhuman and thus threatening powers? In the video for Kendrick Lamar's "Alright," directed by Colin Tilley, Lamar flies through the

California city streets, above sidewalks and empty lots, alongside wire fences.

"Alright" has been the anthem of many protests against racism and police violence and unjust treatment. Lamar embodies the energy and the message of the resonant phrase "black lives matter," which Patrice Cullors, Alicia Garza, and Opal Tometi catapulted into circulation when, in 2013, they founded the movement. The phrase was apt then and now. Its coinage feels both ancestral in its knowledge and prophetic in its ongoing necessity. I know now with certainty that there will never be a moment when we will not need to say it, not in my lifetime, and not in the lifetime of the Trayvon Generation.

The young black man flying in Lamar's video is joyful and defiant, rising above the streets that might claim him, his body liberated and autonomous. At the end of the video, a police officer raises a finger to the young man in the sky and mimes pulling the trigger. The wounded young man falls, slowly—another brother down—and lands. The gun was a finger; the flying young man appears safe. He does not get up. But in the final image of this dream he opens his eyes and smiles. For a moment, he has not been killed.

Black celebration is a village practice that has brought us together in protest and ecstasy around the globe and across time. Community is a mighty life force for self-care and survival. But it does not protect against murder. Dance itself will not free us. We continue to struggle against hatred and violence. I believe that this generation is more vulnerable, and more traumatized, than the last. I think of Frederick Douglass's words upon hearing slaves singing their sorrow songs in the fields. He laid waste to the nascent myth of the happy darky: "Slaves sing most when they are most unhappy." Our dancing is our pleasure but perhaps it is also our sorrow song.

My sons love to dance. I have raised them to young adulthood. They are beautiful. They are funny. They are strong. They are fascinating. They are kind. They are joyful in friendship and community. They are righteous and smart in their politics. They are learning. They are loving. They are mighty and alive.

. . .

I recall many sweaty summer parties with family friends where the grownups regularly acted up on the dance floor and the kids DJed to see how quickly they could make their old-school parents and play-uncles and aunties holler "Aaaaayyyy! That's my jam!" They watched us with deep amusement. But they would dance, too. One of the aunties glimpsed my sons around the corner in the next room and said, "Oh, my God, they can dance! They've been holding out on us, acting all shy!"

When I told a sister-friend that my older son, during his freshman year in college, was often the one controlling the aux cord, dancing and dancing and dancing, she said, "Remember, people dance when they are joyful."

Yes, I am saying I measure my success as a mother of black boys in part by the fact that I have sons who love to dance, who dance in community, who dance till their powerful bodies sweat, who dance and laugh, who dance and shout. Who are able—in the midst of their studying and organizing, their fear, their rage, their protesting, their vulnerability, their missteps and triumphs, their knowledge that they must fight the hydra-headed monster of racism and racial violence that we were not able to cauterize—to find the joy and the power of communal self-expression.

This essay is not a celebration, nor is it an elegy.

We are no longer enslaved. Langston Hughes wrote that we must stand atop the racial mountain, "free within ourselves," and I pray that those words have meaning for our young people. But our freedom must be seized and reasserted every day.

People dance to say, *I am alive and in my body.*

I am black alive and looking back at you.

Marie Claire

Anthologies like these are usually devoted nearly exclusively to literary journalism—reportage, feature writing, essays. But service journalism is one of the foundations on which print magazines were built, and its importance only continues to grow on digital platforms. "Marie Claire*'s Guide to Protecting Yourself Online" is a near archetype of the form, helpful, insightful, and entertaining. But let the judges who gave this series the National Magazine Award for Personal Service explain:* "Marie Claire*'s rich and riveting package launches in print with a warning—'By turning the page, you agree to forgo your right to blissful ignorance'—and then seductively draws us ever deeper into an understanding of why the stakes are so high and what we can do to protect ourselves. The proto-cyber design is delightful, the advice expansive and authoritative, the writing so good it's addictive. Turns out, information can be bliss."*

Edited by
Megan DiTrolio

Excerpts From "*Marie Clarie's* Guide to Protecting Yourself Online"

Invasion of Privacy

Don't Look Now, but You're Being Watched

All around you, snoops are compiling every fact about you: Your name—child's play. Your occupation—just as easy. Where you live, yes, but also if you tend to spend nights at your we're-not-defining-it's place. What you buy, who you'll likely vote for in the presidential election, and the exact distance between your eyes. Who are these spies? Your phone. Your computer. The smart home device that tells you the weather.

Don't Look Now, but You're Being Followed

Across the Internet, trackers are in hot pursuit of your information, trailing behind in the virtual shadows every time you add a blouse to your shopping cart, angry Tweet, or search an embarrassing medical question—collecting bread crumbs to take advantage of you later.

Your private, personal data is under attack. It's being tracked, mined, archived, shared, and sold. In 2020, each and every tidbit about you—all of your intimate details and idiosyncrasies—is currency that can be more valuable than the dollar, the way it's gathered more obscure than Bitcoin. Some companies (apps, search engines) have it—often, you give them access without realizing—and others (marketers, consumer brands) want it desperately.

The collecting of personal data isn't always nefarious, and you may be just fine blindly and blithely giving it away. In fact, companies can use your data to make your life easier and more convenient, creating tailored shopping suggestions, navigating you to the closest coffee shop, and recommending videos you might enjoy. Innocent enough. Except that certain entities don't just use your data; they abuse it.

No one is safe. But for some—especially women and those in minority groups—this surreptitious infiltration results in more than annoying ads: It could mean being denied housing. It could mean some of your sensitive health info, like HIV status, is spilled. It could mean losing your job for being pregnant. Women drive the majority of U.S. purchasing power, making their data prized and more likely to be hunted. If their information is sold or stolen, they face increased risks, like being stalked by an abusive ex. For women and people of color, the ubiquitous and unregulated invasion of privacy happening in the United States could mean life or death.

It's all quite Orwellian, but you don't have to surrender to Big Brother. Ahead, we explore and expose privacy's darkest secrets. What we found may be shocking, but it's also illuminating. With a few swipes, taps, keystrokes, and perhaps strongly worded emails to your elected representatives, your personal information can be returned to its rightful owner: you.

Your Data Is Discriminating . . . Against You

Prachi Gupta

In 2016, Carmen Arroyo's twenty-two-year-old son, Mikhail, regained consciousness from a six-month coma. He had been electrocuted while atop an electrical pole and had fallen nearly thirty feet, leaving him unable to walk, speak, or take care of himself. Arroyo, then forty-four, filed an application with her landlord requesting permission for her son to move into her apartment in Willimantic, Connecticut, with her. According to court records, the application was quickly denied without explanation, and Mikhail was sent to a rehabilitation facility, where he would remain for more than a year while his mother searched for a reason why.

Arroyo contacted the Connecticut Fair Housing Center (CFHC), a nonprofit that provides free legal services to alleged victims of housing discrimination. In the process of filing a complaint against the landlord, Arroyo and her lawyers discovered that the landlord didn't know why Arroyo was denied either; the decision hadn't been made by him but by an algorithm used by CoreLogic, a software company he had enlisted to screen potential tenants. After Arroyo filed her complaint, the landlord allowed Mikhail to move in with his mother. Arroyo's lawyers kept digging and ultimately determined what caused the rejection: a citation for shoplifting from 2014 (which has been withdrawn), according to court documents. "He was blacklisted from housing, despite the fact that he is so severely disabled now and is incapable of committing any crime," says Salmun Kazerounian, a staff attorney from CFHC who represents Arroyo.

What happened to the Arroyo family is just one example of data leading to discrimination. Automated data systems—technology like CoreLogic's—use collected intel (public data, such as DMV and court records, that may also be packaged with information scraped from the internet, like social-media activity) to make life-altering decisions, including whether applicants get jobs, the cost of their insurance, or how a community is policed. In theory, these systems are built to eliminate bias present in human decision-making. In reality, they can fuel it.

That is in part because algorithms are made up of biased data and often don't consider other relevant factors. Because low-income people have more contact with government agencies (for benefits like Medicaid), a disproportionate amount of their info feeds these systems. Not only can this data fall into corporate hands but the government itself uses it to surveil. For example, when UC Berkeley law professor Khiara Bridges interviewed pregnant women applying for prenatal care under Medicaid, she found that they had to reveal their sexual histories and incidences of domestic violence—details that can then be shared with other public agencies. "I talked to pregnant women who came to the clinic just to get prenatal care, and then the next day they would get a call from Child Protective Services," Bridges says. When people seek support from the state, "that can end up penalizing them later," adds University of Baltimore law professor Michele E. Gilman. A person applying for a public benefit can be flagged as a risk, which limits future housing or employment opportunities. People who don't need to apply for public benefits are exempt from these injustices.

The problem is pervasive, invisible, and cyclical: biased data is used to justify surveillance, creating an endless feedback loop of discrimination. In 2012, the Chicago Police Department began using predictive analytics, reliant mostly on arrest-record data, to increase surveillance on certain individuals it considered more likely to commit or be victims of gun violence. The program was shelved in 2019 after findings showed it was ineffective at reducing homicides. Civil-rights groups said it perpetuated racial bias. "The algorithm is developed from what you give it," says Brandi Collins-Dexter, senior campaign director for racial-justice-advocacy group Color of Change. "If you give it trash, it's going to give you trash." Feed an algorithm biased information and it will enable future bias.

This reality is the crux of the Arroyo case, the first of its kind: Mikhail, who is Latino, is one of the nearly one-third of working-age Americans who have a criminal record, a disproportionate number of whom are Black or Latinx. His lawyers are suing CoreLogic, arguing that, under the guise of neutrality and efficiency, its software reinforces discriminatory policies. (The lawsuit is still pending, and CoreLogic has denied any wrongdoing.) If Arroyo wins, it will be a small step forward. But unless the United States adopts stronger data-privacy legislation, these life-altering structures will go largely unchecked, as they are both "powerful and invisible," according to Jennifer Lee of the ACLU of Washington. Her organization is just one pushing for regulations. Until that happens, we will continue to be watched by discriminatory systems unseen—and minority groups will feel those eyes most of all.

Yikes, There's More

Algorithms can use data to make decisions about a specific person, like Arroyo, but some use it to make inferences on entire groups. This can lead to sweeping, discriminatory generalizations: Facebook has come under fire for showing different housing and job ads to different users based on race and gender; in 2018, Amazon discovered that its automated hiring tool picked male candidates over female ones. In these instances, bias was baked into decision-making tools. Even if the data is not specifically about race or gender, data points—like a person's music interests or zip code—can become "proxies," according to Collins-Dexter.

I Escaped My Abuser. He Found Me Through My Computer

As told to Megan DiTrolio

Greg (name has been changed) and I had been acquaintances for nearly a decade, but it wasn't until February 2016 that we developed a romantic relationship. At first, he took me to fancy dinners and showered me with gifts, weaving himself into my life. Despite my instincts that something was off—the relationship was moving so quickly—I gave him the benefit of the doubt because I had known him for years. I wanted to believe it was just the kind of person he was. I'd soon find out, it wasn't.

About four months in, I started to notice Greg's erratic behavior. If I tried to address an emotional concern, Greg would fly into an explosive rage. Once, he threw a boot at me; it hit a potted plant on the table next to me and smashed it into pieces. Another time, he flung a sixty-pound piece of wooden art in my direction, narrowly missing my head. As these situations became more frequent, we started sleeping in separate rooms. (He put a hole through a door once, trying to get to me.) If I tried to leave the house, he'd threaten to hurt himself (once, even hiding my car keys so I couldn't go). Then he'd beg for forgiveness and the cycle would start all over again; when someone is abusing you psychologically, it erodes your sense of self-worth. After about seven months, we got engaged—but I immediately felt nauseous about it and called off the engagement two weeks later. A month after he proposed, I found out I was pregnant, but I knew I was in an unsafe environment for a baby.

I was eight months along when Greg left for a business trip. I called a few close friends and finally opened up about my fears.

They encouraged me to leave. That night, I started packing. Soon after, I left our apartment in California, and I emailed Greg and his family to tell them I didn't feel safe and that I needed to be in peace to deliver my child. I didn't tell them where I was going. Then, I flew to New York City, where my mother lives. Over the following weeks, Greg reached out to me about 350 times via email, calls, texts, and Facebook messages. He also slandered me publicly, posting on Facebook that I'd left because I had psychiatric disorders or that I'd gone missing.

I was sitting in my mother's home, my due date approaching, when I opened an email that was seemingly from Los Angeles child services. In reality, the email wasn't from child services but from Greg. I believe this because within twenty minutes of when I opened it, Greg sent me a Facebook message that thanked me for confirming his case with child services and said he now knew I was in New York City. [Editor's note: *Marie Claire* independently confirmed that the email address used is not associated with the Los Angeles County Department of Children and Family.] I suspect that by simply opening the email, I must have inadvertently installed a tracking bug on my computer, enabling Greg to use my computer's IP address to determine my exact location. Inside the email was an embedded link that said, "Please click to get information on your case." I worried that the link was a keylogger. If I had clicked it (which I didn't), there's the chance he could have monitored everything I was typing. I was terrified.

That's when I filed a criminal report for aggravated harassment with the police. I reported his use of unauthorized technology to track my location and his ability to use that to harass me. It can be difficult to prove this type of case: Typically, the cops will tell you there's nothing they can do; the technology is somewhat uncharted territory. Additionally, it can turn into a case of he said, she said. I was referred to family court and told to seek an order of protection.

I went to the hospital two weeks before giving birth for a check-up. My fear was visible: I was skinny and pale. I hadn't slept. I was referred to a social worker who helps women in distress, and I told her what was going on. She advised me to turn off my location services on my phone; I access my email on my phone, so there was a possibility Greg could track me and know when I was going into labor. She also recommended that I file for a restraining order.

When it comes to cyberstalking cases, the best thing to do is document every instance of harassment. The night before I gave birth, I stayed up until 4 a.m. printing everything Greg had posted or sent me. It was scary because I understood that he possibly knew when I was opening those emails (the infected email I had opened might have had the capability), but I needed evidence. By the end, I had a stack the size of a college textbook.

I went to court ten days after I delivered my son and submitted a petition that detailed the aforementioned abusive behavior, including the unauthorized tracking. This convinced the judge, who granted me a temporary restraining order that same day. At that point, the restraining order was served to Greg, who accepted it, which meant he couldn't come near me, contact me, or post about me on social media. The full restraining order was granted and in effect through March 2018. He chose to leave the country. I have not seen him since.

Rebuilding my life has been one of the most difficult things I have ever done, but it's worth it. Today, my son and I are doing well. I volunteer with Safe Horizon, the largest victim-services nonprofit in the United States, to educate people about abuse and cyberstalking. I encourage anyone who can to come forward; we need to hear more of these stories. The internet has become a tool abusers can use against victims, but there are some ways we can protect ourselves. I now use a VPN server to mask my location to potential hackers. Personally, I feel like after three years, I'm finally safe.

Is My Workplace Watching Me?

Kate Dwyer

Everyone has bad days at work. When you need to vent, you angrily type a screed to your work wife on Slack. When you need to cry (we've all been there), you seek out the third bathroom stall. When you need to send a quick personal e-mail or order something on Amazon, you tilt your screen a touch to shield it from the peering eyes of your cubicle-mate. You do these things to maintain a level of privacy at the office. But in our data-driven era, how much privacy do we really have at work? For those of us working remotely, are our employers monitoring us . . . at home?

While the Wild West of the internet is still largely lawless, there are a few pieces of legislation that cover the Venn diagram of our jobs and our private data: the Americans with Disabilities Act requires employers to keep medical information confidential, even if the information does not relate to an ADA-covered disability. Health information that an employer seeks as part of the benefits onboarding process may be protected by the Health Insurance Portability and Accountability Act (HIPAA) in some instances. As for protecting employee privacy in the workplace, each state has either its own laws related to employee privacy or a general consumer-protection law that covers employee privacy or both.

If an employee uses his or her company's IT systems—whether that's through a desktop computer at the office or a work-issued laptop—such use can most likely be monitored. That shouldn't be surprising; cyber threats are pervasive, and a company needs to know what's happening on its own systems. But does that mean your employer knows *everything* you're doing online? Can people at the company read your vent-Slacks, scan your e-mails, or creep on your search history? Can they tell if you're applying to other jobs? And if they can, can they use that information against you?

Here's What You Need to Know

*Everything You Do on Your Work Computer
Can Be Accessed by Your Employer*

"If it's a work-issued computer, you should expect to have no privacy whatsoever," says Rita Heimes, the general counsel and chief privacy officer of the International Association of Privacy Professionals, an education nonprofit for privacy professionals. "Many employers have policies that explicitly say: Do not have an expectation of privacy on your work-issued computer." That's partly for security reasons; work-issued laptops likely contain the company's intellectual property and proprietary data, so those computers are often preloaded with security mechanisms that prevent employees from accessing certain websites or downloading malware and flag when they receive messages or e-mails that may contain a virus.

"To the extent that you're using a company-issued device for the purposes of browsing the web, your entire web-browsing history is going to be accessible to the employer," says lawyer Heather Egan Sussman, head of law firm Orrick's Global Cyber, Privacy, and Data Innovation Practice Group. "I choose that word *accessible* very carefully. Just because it's available does not mean the employer is then going back and checking the sites that you're visiting."

You'll enter a gray area if you start to use your personal computer for work activities, according to Ann Bartow, a professor of law at the University of New Hampshire. Her advice? "Don't use your home computer for work activities and vice versa, because the boundaries get blurry, depending on the laws in your state and the policies of your company."

The same goes for your work-issued cell phone. Even if it's inconvenient, Bartow recommends carrying a second phone for personal use only, to prevent your employer from having access to your personal data, photos, and text messages.

Companies Are Most Likely Monitoring Employees for Productivity Purposes . . .

A 2018 survey by the research firm Gartner found that 50 percent of the 239 large corporations surveyed were using monitoring techniques such as "analyzing the text of emails and social-media messages" and "scrutinizing who's meeting with whom." According to the *Wall Street Journal*, Microsoft tracks data on "the frequency of chats, emails, and meetings between its staff and clients using its own Office 365 services to measure employee productivity, management efficacy, and work-life balance"; then it allows some employees to see how they spend their time each week and offers suggestions on how to better spend their time the following week. A 2019 Accenture report found that 62 percent of C-suite execs said their organizations are using new technologies to "collect data on their people and their work" to gain insights on productivity and collaboration; only 30 percent were "very confident that they are using the data responsibly."

Such monitoring could erode trust between employees and their companies, so it's important that companies are honest about whether they're watching and, if so, what they are monitoring and why, according to *Harvard Business Review*.

Especially While So Many of Us Are Working from Home

When the pandemic started, employers hunted for new ways to make sure employees were doing their work. Software like Hubstaff—which takes screenshots of worker's screens and shares phone location data with managers (*with* the employee's knowledge)—rose in popularity, according to the *New York Times*. At the end of the newspaper's own three-week experiment, tech correspondent Adam Satariano and his editor Pui-Wing Tam decided it was "overly intrusive."

It's not illegal for employers to start monitoring their employees in real time if the employees consent (though in some states, employers do not need that consent). "Typically what we're defaulting back to are specific laws applying to employee privacy or a general consumer-protection law," Sussman says, explaining that most states' consumer-protection laws read similarly to section 5 of the Federal Trade Commission Act prohibiting unfair or deceptive acts or practices. "To the extent that the conduct of an employer is unfair or is deceptive, then it's potentially subject to scrutiny and review by the FTC," she adds. However, employees may unknowingly consent to surveillance when they sign their onboarding paperwork, according to Bartow. "If you get dumped with a bunch of paperwork when you start the job, you may not notice," she says. "They're probably not going to make a big point of it: 'Hey, we're tracking you!' But probably somewhere in your contract, you've agreed that they're going to track you, and they are."

Your Employer Probably Isn't Always Watching
Without Explicitly Telling You

"Generally speaking, they're not monitoring your data as it goes out through Google," Heimes says. "Ethically, they really shouldn't be, and most employers know that."

"I think there's a lot of misperception out there about the degree to which the employer is surveilling employees and their activities," Sussman adds. "I think a lot of those [monitoring] products and services are still in a nascent form where there's not particularly widespread adoption, and surveillance is being used for the purposes of ensuring things like productivity." An example of this could be speed and location data of a delivery vehicle for safety monitoring and real-time package tracking. "You want to make sure when the work hours end, [employers] stop collecting that information," she says.

There are legitimate reasons for collecting and analyzing employee data. Large corporations may study trends in employee behavior in order to make tech-purchasing decisions, cut costs, or identify new ways to boost productivity. "Sometimes when we all get together, our security people will say, 'Some of you are going to have to watch fewer YouTube videos because our bandwidth is stretched,'" says Heimes.

... but It Can Pull Data If There's an Investigation

However, since web browsing, e-mail, Slack, and other real-time data is typically *accessible* to employers, they'll definitely take a look at your history if you're suspected of or being investigated for fraud, violating an NDA, or sexual harassment in the workplace, and possibly if there are complaints against you.

Or, Heimes says, an employer "might actually watch you very actively for a period of time in order to gather evidence" if it has reason to believe that you were doing something nefarious, like committing a crime, stealing intellectual property, or otherwise colluding with a competitor.

Your Company Is Probably Not Using Your Home Wi-Fi to Spy on You

Let's say you bring your work-issued laptop home with you. If you connect your work laptop to your home Wi-Fi network, could your employer access your personal computer or your smart appliances? No, but your employer could potentially learn some things about your home and your home network, although it's unlikely.

"They should not be able to do that. I can't promise they can't— there's all kinds of skullduggery that happens—but as a legal matter, my first impression is no, that's too far. The government can do it, but the government would probably have to get a warrant for that," Bartow says, generally speaking. "Under basic Fourth Amendment analysis, your employer shouldn't be able to get to your personal computer through your Wi-Fi without notice, at the very least." (The Fourth Amendment protects "against unreasonable searches and seizures.")

Don't Say Anything in Slack You Wouldn't
Want Your Boss to See

Slack, Jabber, corporate Google Chat, and other office messenger services are not private channels, even if you're chatting one-on-one with another employee. "If you are using a corporate account, I think you need to assume that everything you put on there is accessible by the employer, and employees should conduct themselves accordingly," Sussman says. However, in the rare case there is someone monitoring the channels for keywords, it's probably not for water-cooler gossip. "That's not what they're looking for. Typically, they're looking for fraud, insider threats, and security threats," she adds.

"I would say that [office messenger services] should never be used for personal communication of any kind," Heimes says. "That's the employer's account. It is not your account. So if you are Slacking with another employee, anything that you say could be stored, it could be discovered in litigation, it certainly could be used against you if there was a harassment suit."

When you sign that onboarding paperwork, you're likely signing off on your right to privacy on these platforms. "Somewhere buried in your contract or terms of service, it's probably all been disclosed, but new hires are often rushed to sign without enough time to read through the long, dense documents," Bartow says.

In some cases, private Slack messages have been used against employees. The most egregious example is probably Away, which implemented a company policy that nearly all communication between coworkers must happen openly on Slack, according to The Verge's investigation. Although it was against the rules, employees created a private channel called #Hot-Topics for LGBTQ folks and people of color. #Hot-Topics was used mostly for venting and commiserating, and when CEO and cofounder Stephanie Korey found out about it, she fired six marginalized employees for "racist" language and "hate speech," though she's since denied using those terms.

Your Personal Calendar Might Be Viewable,
but It's an Easy Fix

Let's say you've synced your personal and work calendars so your meetings autopopulate on your phone. Does that mean that your employer can see that therapy appointment you have booked or your date on Friday? The answer is yes, but only if your calendar settings allow it. "It is possible to configure your work calendar so that it looks blocked, but what you're doing is not visible to others," Heimes says. "Check your settings for your calendar within your e-mail client and [change] to private. Set it so that it's not possible to see your descriptions, or, if necessary, just use nonidentifying descriptions of how you're spending your time."

If your company mandates that this isn't an option, it makes more sense to keep your work calendar totally separate from your personal calendar, keeping your personal calendar local to your personal phone or getting into the habit of using an old-school spiral planner.

VPNs Protect Company-Wide Security, Not Individual
Employees' Privacy

Many employers use a virtual private network (VPN) to access their work network securely and to protect company data (including proprietary data like trade secrets and customer data) from external cyberattacks. But that doesn't mean an individual employee's privacy is protected from monitoring by IT within the company. "[Companies] are going to take pretty extreme measures to support the security of their network," Heimes says. "When you're connected to your employer's VPN, it's the same as if you were sitting in your office. As is, the same level of rules and monitoring applies for activity that goes against company policy." Even if employees have good intentions, browsing certain websites and downloading software could create a vulnerability in the company's system. By restricting employees from accessing those sites or downloading questionable software, companies are keeping the entire network secure.

Ultimately, There's No Federal Law Governing Privacy in the Workplace

If you've traveled in Europe and gone on the internet, you've definitely encountered pop-ups asking for permission to track your data. (Recently, we've started seeing them in the United States too.) Those consent pop-ups exist because of General Data Protection Regulation (GDPR), an all-encompassing EU privacy law that applies to the processing of personal data. Since it applies to the processing of *all* personal data, the GDPR also applies to the privacy of employees who work for European businesses, even if they don't live in Europe.

There's no equivalent of the GDPR in the United States. Instead, there are hundreds of state and federal laws that address privacy and cybersecurity, including a handful that apply specifically in the employment context and the general business context.

Right now, there is no federal law governing the way that employers do or do not monitor their employees in the workplace, or the way data is used once it's gathered. Most privacy experts and consumer-rights groups agree that a federal law is long overdue. "The issue I see with having different states enacting differing laws—it's this concept of a patchwork of laws—is that in many cases, it's a challenge to do business and to support innovation when you have competing regulatory regimes," Sussman says. "Data travels across state lines. Data really knows no bounds."

At the end of the day, you should never expect privacy on your work-issued devices, and your first act of defense is to understand the way your company accesses and uses your data. Until then, write your e-mails and Slack messages like they'll end up in court someday—and save your weirdest Google searches for your non-work-issued phone.

Nancy Grace Wants You to Take Your Cyber Safety Seriously

Maria Recapito

TV true-crime avenger and former prosecutor Nancy Grace does not want you or anyone you love to end up on one of her productions. Not on Oxygen's *Injustice with Nancy Grace* or the breaking-news site Crime Online. Especially not on her daily podcast, *Crime Stories with Nancy Grace*. In her new book, *Don't Be a Victim: Fighting Back Against America's Crime Wave*, she shares insider knowledge on how to stay safe, pointing out that, increasingly, danger comes to us through losing control of our private data via technology. "It's just like drinking from a fire hydrant," she says. "When it comes to the type of potential harm that can find you online—because you have no idea who you're letting into your life—there's just so much to digest at once." Here, we chat with Grace about putting safety first, especially in these virtual times. Plus, her best advice for protecting yourself online.

MARIE CLAIRE: Why did you want to write a book about not being a victim?

NANCY GRACE: We live in this day of "It won't happen to me" thinking, because who wants to live in constant fear? I don't. That's why I wrote this book. I don't want to live in fear. I don't want anybody to live in fear, but

I want that to be backed up. To be safe, I want to know I am doing everything I can to protect myself and my family. Obviously, I'm coming from a women's point of view: protecting their children in all sorts of situations, protecting the elderly, protecting yourself [while] traveling. Long story short, I want to know how to stay safe.

I have prosecuted so many cases and covered so many cases, I can't even count them all. When I began covering cases and reporting on crimes, I kept an investigative element where I would continue to investigate them on air. But more and more, I longed to actually try to make a difference. Writing the book helped me do that. I thought back over cases I've tried, cases I investigated, cases I covered and came up with an amalgamation, a grouping of cases and lessons learned and how that could be used to help other people. I wanted to not just report on crimes but actually help people prevent crimes.

MC: In your book, you describe being at the scene of a terrible crime where there was "malice hanging in the air." What is it like to be around crime so much?

NG: In layperson talk, it's like you get a chill down your spine or the hair stands up on the back of your neck. I don't really discount those "feelings." I believe that when we have hunches or, as people say, premonitions, I think that it is because we have evolved over millions of years and our bodies and our psyches are fine-tuned to pick up on certain things we may not be able to intellectually digest.

MC: With working from home and quarantining, we are increasingly living online. Does being socially distanced make us safer?

NG: It will go back to a version of normal at some point, but during COVID you cannot let your guard down. You

can't. There is going to be a light at the end of the tunnel.
Across the country, lockdowns are being relaxed, but
you've got to keep the same rules in play, the same safety
precautions in place, even though you're online more,
because this is a perfect time for [hackers] to take advantage of you.

MC: You say going with your gut instinct is harder, in a
digital world, for people who always wear headphones and
think the best way to meet someone is through an app.
How can digital natives stay safe?

NG: I think that we are so desensitized to everything
around us. There are many types of potential harm
because, online, you have no idea who you're letting into
your life. When you meet people in person, you assess
them in ways that I cannot even articulate—from the
way they look, their shoes, their clothes, their hands, the
way they speak, their mannerisms, their habits. Are they
rude? Do they drink too much? Do they smoke? Do they
do drugs? Are they arrogant? Are they mean to the
waitress? [There are] a million things you take in
without ever realizing it, and it makes you say, "I'm not
going out with him again," and there's a reason for that.
If somebody asks, you go, "I don't know why"; you say it
just didn't click. That's not entirely accurate. It's an
instinct. You are assimilating thousands of clues that
you don't even realize you're taking in.

Online, you can't feel any of that out. You can't analyze
any of that. You see what that person wants you to see.
The next thing, they somehow have gotten their hand into
your digital wallet or purse. When you date online, it's
like you're going to a potluck dinner. You don't know
what you're getting. Now, does that happen all the time?
No, it doesn't—but it happens enough that you've got to
exercise safety precautions.

You heard it from a true-crime expert. Now read Grace's tips for staying safe online

Admit It Could Happen to You

"Don't be lulled into a false sense of complacency," writes Grace in her book. You may think that hackers wouldn't bother with little old you, but they will and do. She suggests that, at home, you should focus on your wireless router since it allows multiple devices around your house to connect without being plugged in to a socket. Change the name on the router from the factory setting, but don't make it so obvious (like "Nancy's Wi-Fi") that it can be traced back to you.

In Fact, Don't Keep Any Factory Settings

Evildoers spend time sweeping the internet just to find unsecured cameras and cameras that are still using the original user code and password, according to Grace. When they find one, they can hack in and retrieve your private data, photos, and videos. Change your password from the factory settings as soon as you start using your device. And change it regularly going forward.

Always Update Your Devices

Tech companies try to stay a step ahead of hackers by patching up flaws in their security systems, she says. Grace's solution is to keep her devices set to receive automatic software updates, which include security enhancements.

Sometimes, You've Got to Pull the Plug

When your Nest or baby monitor is not in use, unplug it. Put a sticky note over the camera lens (don't forget your computer monitor too) to remind yourself that someone might be watching. In the book, Grace tells of a case in which private video from a baby monitor was shared online by a hacker.

Add More Security

Two-factor authentication (TFA) may sound high-tech, but it's really not, she explains. This gives your web services secondary access to the account owner (you) to verify when you log in. Look for it under the privacy or security settings of Apple ID, Instagram, Facebook, Twitter, Amazon, Google, WhatsApp, Nest, and Ring, or check to see if it's offered on a particular app you use. Using an email address or mobile number, an authenticator sends you a link to click or a code to input to make sure it's really you signing on. You could also activate the WPA2 encryption codes on your router or subscribe to a virtual private network (VPN). If you suspect someone has tampered with a wireless device, look at your access log for entries at times you definitely were not home. Turn on the firewall that comes with your operating system or security software.

Be Smart About Your Smart Devices

Don't leave your devices lying around, says Grace. Digital security is important, but so is physical security. When it comes to phones, tablets, and smartphones, lock them up, shut down screens, and keep sensitive data (like bank account numbers or your social security number) off of them—as in, don't keep a list of passwords or important numbers in your Notes app. And don't plug in any random USBs; they could contain harmful malware.

Don't Take the Bait of Phishers

Bad actors will try to steal from you via legit-looking emails and other communications—trying to scoop up your credit card info,

Social Security number, secret codes, usernames, and other data, she says. If you're hearing from a major company, watch for misspellings of the company name, grammatical errors, or an email address that seems random (like if a supposed Netflix query uses a non-Netflix domain). A phisher may ask you to "confirm" personal info (by entering it) or may try to make you act in a panic by claiming that you will be billed or an account will be closed.

Weed Out Fake Profiles

Grace says in the book that she "hates fakers"—because she's met enough of them in her time on TV sets and in court. You can verify a social-media profile by doing a reverse image search. That can tell you if the account is using a stock photo or one that belongs to someone else's profile. Never accept friend requests from people you don't know.

Do Not Overshare on Social Media

What do your home address, DOB, astrological sign, and kitty cat's name have in common? They can all be used against you, Grace says. Hackers collect any details shared on social media to create, she writes, "a fake identity, a fake *you*." Keep the personal details offline.

Don't "Check in" on Social Media When You Drop by a Restaurant or Are in a Taxi to the Airport on Your Way out of Town

Picture Grace's signature "Are you kidding me?" face here: How better to tip off thieves that you're not home? That is why, she writes, "smart geotagging is no geotagging." You can configure settings to approve all attempted tags. It's not too late to delete prior locations on your posts. Then turn off location information for posts still to come.

Download Your Apps from Legitimate Sources,
and Delete Apps You Don't Use

Apps that just hang around on your phone and sit on your home screen untouched (she likens it to digital hoarding) can still collect your data, even if you're not using them. Scrap old apps; keeping them leaves an opening for hackers to sneak in.

Date Safely

Grace's book is full of horror stories of what can happen when you meet up with a cyber con looking for love. In addition to the usual caveats (such as meeting in a public place, not revealing where you work, etc.), be stingy with personal info—and remember that photos can divulge things like a license-plate number or home address. Instead of giving out your cell number or email address, create a free Google Voice number. That way, if your connection goes badly sideways, you can block unwanted calls and move on to a new swipe. As she explains in the book: "The right one is out there. Make sure you live to find them."

New York

"Graham Court: The Gilded Age Rental" and the following article, "One Fifth: The Downtown Co-op of All Downtown Co-ops," are both drawn from the New York magazine series "Biography of a Building," which, along with "Villa Charlotte Brontë: A Clffside Co-op in the Bronx," won the National Magazine Award for Leisure Interests. There is nothing quite like New Yorkers' interest in real estate or, rather, apartments. The judges in Leisure Interests summed it up rather neatly in their citation: "In a year that leisure largely forgot, voyeurism counts, right? Of course, it does. The 'Biography of a Building' series explores some of New York's most fascinating residential buildings. There's lore. There's rumor. There's innuendo. Plus, there's tons of useful advice, from the easiest way to win over a co-op board to how to make one of these places your forever home."

Matthew Sedacca

Graham Court

The Gilded Age Rental

This past February, those trawling StreetEasy for a Harlem apartment may have scrolled straight past a listing for a three-bedroom in Graham Court. The unit, 5G, has all the trappings of an uninspired twenty-first-century gut—jet-black bathroom-floor tiles; cheap-looking, stark-white kitchen cabinets. It would be impossible to tell from the pictures that almost all the other units in the building are time capsules of early-twentieth-century Harlem—with original high ceilings, claw-foot tubs, oak pocket doors, and brass sconces.

Graham Court is an eight-story apartment building that takes over the entire east side of Adam Clayton Powell Jr. Boulevard between 116th and 117th Streets. It was completed in 1901 for the real-estate tycoon William Waldorf Astor by the architectural firm Clinton and Russell, which also built the Apthorp on a full block in the West Seventies. Both were constructed in the Italian Renaissance style, and both feature lush interior courtyards, arched entryways, and iron gates. (Graham Court also shares a spiritual connection to another Upper West Side landmark; in 1987, the *New York* Times called it Harlem's equivalent to the Dakota, which has stuck as a nickname.) The Apthorp, though, announced a $95 million renovation in 2007 and, in 2008, went condo (with a handful of $10 million four-bedrooms for sale). Some two and a half miles uptown, Graham Court remained—and remains—a decidedly nonluxury rental.

In the very beginning, the apartments—suites of six-to-eleven rooms fitted with servants' chambers—were home to oil-company presidents and other types one might have found in the *New-York* Tribune's society pages. But then the real-estate bubble burst. Between 1910 and 1930, Central Harlem's black population surged from 10 percent to 70 percent. The Astor estate cut ties to its investment, and the new management decided to open the building to black residents (many of whom, some tenants say, were the maids of the previous wealthy white tenants). Decreased services followed. Graham Court's owner-ship was passed from person to person, including the heir to a clothing fortune, then to a group of real-estate investors who let the building fall into receivership.

The tenants were treated negligently. Besides the crime, which was by all accounts rampant—everything from hallway drug deals to numbers rackets to, supposedly, apartment-run brothels—the condition of the building continued to spiral. A handful of apartments were chopped up by management to fur-ther squeeze rent, the elevator was constantly broken, water often stopped running, and heat was unpredictable. By the midseven-ties, the neighborhood was in a similar state of disrepair. "Junk-ies lining the street, burned-out buildings, vacant lots," long-term tenant Margaret Porter Troupe recalls.

Before the crack epidemic and the national Carter-era reces-sion, though, Harlem in the early eighties seemed on the verge of major change. Redevelopment ramped up, and a crop of black artists and actors—Marcella Lowery, Danny Glover, Hugh Masekela—moved into Graham Court. But most of them left soon after, unable to tolerate the lack of services and the rela-tive unsteadiness of the neighborhood.

In 1987, with the city set to foreclose on the building for delin-quent taxes, tenants finally had the opportunity to purchase their apartments for $250. But mere hours before the foreclosure was to become final, the building's owner (Mohammed Siddiqui, a pharmacist whose license was later suspended for "negligence in handling prescription drugs") paid the outstanding taxes and reclaimed the building—a sharp blow for long-term tenants.

It wasn't until the early nineties (as fleets of young African American lawyers, doctors, and bankers began moving to Harlem and other historically black neighborhoods), when a group of eleven Ivy League graduates moved in, that it began slowly transforming into the more prosperous place it is today. The state of the building was another story—one of the eleven, Kathy Frazier, then a trader on Wall Street, describes stepping over passed-out bodies on her way to get to work—but most stayed, entranced with the space. And by the early aughts, the neighborhood began to gentrify in earnest. A handful of yoga studios opened. So did a Whole Foods.

A rapidly gentrifying Harlem gave Graham Court's ownership financial incentive to renovate its vacant apartments to rent at market rates. This has created what some residents see as a two-class system: New renters speak of hearing back swiftly from the management company when they voice concerns while legacy tenants in rent-controlled units say their problems go unchecked. Others feel that management is not interested in renting to black people. "I have friends who've applied who would have been qualified financially and otherwise who weren't allowed in," says Sheila Bridges, an interior designer and long-term tenant. (Management claims, "We have never denied an application based on color.")

Regardless of who you are, getting one of the apartments that maintain the charm of Gilded Age Graham Court, if you don't have a family member already living there, is a fairly epic undertaking. New tenants who succeeded in doing so dedicated at least a year to their hunts, relying on insider contacts. And many of the tenants promise that the only way they're leaving is on a stretcher. "My grandmother came in, in 1929, and she lived and died here, and my father lived and died here," says Pat Knox Horne, a former assistant fashion buyer. "And I'll live and die here."

Building Basics

- Address: 1921 Adam Clayton Powell Jr. Boulevard
- Apartments: There are one hundred in the building, spread out over eight floors and four distinct structures. Likely a few dozen are rent controlled and rent stabilized.
- Prices: $3,094 a month is the average current rate for an apartment. (Four hundred a month was the typical rent-stabilized cost for a tenant in the nineties, per one resident, and $900 a year was the starting rental price for an apartment with six-to-eleven rooms when it opened in 1901.)
- Notable residents, past and present: Zora Neale Hurston, Danny Glover, Hugh Masekela, Earl "the Pearl" Monroe, Marcella Lowery
- Landmark Status: The outside was landmarked in 1984; the inside never was. "So the apartment below me has the same layout but looks wholly different," says tenant Yvonne Stafford. "Sheetrock walls, a drop ceiling. And it's $5,500 a month. Mine is nowhere near that."
- Current owner: Graham Court Owners Corp.

Plus: A Dozen Pieces of History

The Case of the Missing Copper Cornice

Apparently, the top story of the building once had a copper cornice, just like the Apthorp. "At some point before 1987, it was removed," says long-term tenant Terry Williams. "And it was never replaced. Why didn't they do that to the Apthorp?"

William Waldorf Astor's monograph is still etched into the exterior.

The Smokestack

It was damaged in 1977, which forced management to shut down the heating system. Laconia Smedley says his apartment got so cold that winter that he had to wear his friend's fur coat to sleep.

The Top-Floor Apartments

"Let's be realistic—if this place ever went co-op, ours is probably at least a $6 million apartment, with the square footage, the seven windows facing Central Park."—Jonathan Solars, rare-violin dealer

The Wrought-Iron Gates

Topped with a Palladian arch, the gates were allegedly once the site of a shooting in the early 2010s that prompted the building's real-estate agent, Ignazio Leone, to quit. "After that, I gave up the exclusive," says Leone.

The Elevator Clash

During an elevator-service strike in the thirties, there was a tussle between the strikers and service operators. Two men were shot. One was bashed in the head.

Fraught Window Frames

Around 2001, the wooden frames were replaced with aluminum. Said the architectural historian John Tauranac: "It's contrary to all the preservation movement holds dear."

The Grand Interior Courtyard

"The landlords put barely any money into the courtyard. About ten years ago, when I noticed it started looking like a jungle, I started weeding, pruning. I put in drought-tolerant perennials that don't take a lot of maintenance—rhododendrons, hostas, a nice Japanese maple tree." —Duane Harper Grant, filmmaker and photographer

The Fire Hydrant on 116th Street

"In the seventies, elevator service and running water were fickle. We'd have the kids run down the stairs to the fire hydrant, fill up the buckets, and hoist them up via a makeshift pulley system."
—Margaret Porter Troupe, executive director of the Gloster Arts Project

A Very Suspicious Dentist

In 1947, a thirty-nine-year-old Bronx man died in the dentist office of Dr. Subbeal S. Anderson during a run-of-the-mill molar extraction. Anderson left town within two days.

Toni Morrison Read Here

"We've been running an arts salon out of our apartment since the eighties. It's a private event. We get artists, writers, musicians in our home for conversation—Toni Morrison, Ta-Nehisi Coates, Will Calhoun, Ishmael Reed."—MPT

Movie Blood

"Jungle Fever was filmed in my apartment. When I moved in, there was blood on the floor from the scene where Samuel L. Jackson was shot." —Sheila Bridges, interior designer

The People Who Live There: Inside Nine Apartments

Lucius Laconia Smedley, former music teacher

Moved in 1960

> Through the choirmaster of Metropolitan Baptist Church, who I accompanied on piano for years, I met Pearl Thornwell, who

lived in Graham Court. She was an old lady, a cook-maid, and she asked me to give her piano lessons in her home. She was renting out rooms, and I asked if I could move into one. My rent was about $203 then; I've been here since. Renting out rooms to folks in the neighborhood is how people who had these big apartments survived through the years.

Quincy Troupe and Margaret Porter Troupe, poet and executive director of the Gloster Arts Project

Moved in 1979

QT: We were living on West End Avenue at the time, and my friend told me about Graham Court. When I came to see it, the courtyard was full of drug dealers. I went to meet Laconia Smedley; when he came to the door, I saw his place had fireplaces. I asked him if all the apartments had fireplaces, and he told me some had four. I said, "If an apartment with eight rooms comes up, call me up." Eventually, he did.

MPT: When I visited, my knees were knocking: The area was very, very scary. But once I got inside, the apartment was so beautifully restored, and you couldn't hear anything from outside—it was like being in Europe.

Pat Knox Horne, former assistant fashion buyer

Conceived in the building circa 1940, moved in after her father died in 1995

My grandmother Ethel came in 1929—she had a friend who knew the Astors, and the building was almost entirely white. They were probably the second black family to move in. I was conceived right here, in my office. It was my father's room—he and my mother were only sixteen, but they were in love. I found that out when I was thirty-nine; they took me to dinner, and I said, "Was I a love child?" They told me they were in love, sneaking around when my grandmother wasn't home. It's my charge to take care of this home, and that's what I've been doing. There were no amenities around here when I moved back in—you couldn't even buy a newspaper in Harlem. When my grandmother was here, it was grand. The elevator used to have a sliding gate door with a guy there turning the wheel. We had claw-foot benches in each building in the lobby, and they took those out. We had glass chandeliers in the hallway; I kept one until I decided, What am doing?

William Allen, national crisis and service director of National Action Network, Democratic district leader for 70th Assembly District

Moved in December 1991

In 1990, I was living in New Jersey. I was in a meeting with my pastor and my friend, [former Graham Court tenants-association president] Greg Watson. I was telling the pastor, "My sister's driving me crazy. I've got to get my own place." He said, "You've had family and friends in Graham Court. Maybe somebody will rent." It's true: I had relatives who lived there dating back to my great-grandmother; we've been in Harlem seven generations. Next thing you know, I'm moving in myself. Historically, southern blacks came to Harlem and families in Graham Court would host them until they could find their own place. The whole community knows about this place, and the whole community is in love with this place. Still, today, it's Old World here. It's one of the most neighborly places you could ever want to live. When you walk inside the gate, people say "Good morning," "Good afternoon," "Good evening." If you ignore them, they inquire if you're okay.

Duane Harper Grant, filmmaker and photographer

Moved in 1993

I took over my mother's lease; she moved in in the late seventies. Luckily, the tenants association has had some very good representation, because about fifteen years ago, the landlords started trying to get rid of me. They tried to bully me and work with attrition. They didn't think I'd put up a fight, and I did. I'm still here.

Marita Green Monroe, sports marketer

Moved in 2002

In 2000, me and my husband, Earl, were living in New Jersey, and my college roommate, who lived in Graham Court and knew I'd always loved the building, told me an apartment had opened up. Earl said, "I"m not moving there." But I wanted it. Every day, still, Earl says, "I"m getting out of here." We"ve had floods, fires, mice. But where else am I gonna get a place like this? We have a house in an apartment, and people are living in a box and paying thousands in rent.

Clyde Williams and Mona Sutphen, public-affairs adviser and senior adviser at an investment firm

Moved in 2010

CW: I came to Harlem to work for Bill Clinton. Someone had a party at their place in Graham Court—I walked in and was like, Holy crap. When my wife and I went to DC to work for President Obama, we said if we came back, we'd live here. Soon after we moved in, I was blown away when I turned my head in the elevator and saw Earl "the Pearl" Monroe, a

Knicks Hall of Famer—turns out he lives right under us. My mind was blown.

Jonathan Solars and Katie Thomas, rare-violin dealers

Moved in November 2012

JS: When I brought my contractor to the apartment, he was shocked I wanted to put so much into a rental. He had never seen a rental client do that, he said. But I have customers coming in for multi-million-dollar instruments, and I intend to be here for the long haul. I mean, there are three Strads in this house. So it can't be shabby.

Kevin Harter and Jangir Sultan, VP of integrated marketing and fashion direction for Bloomingdale's and founder of Patient Advocates of NY

Moved in 2016

KH: we were living in Dumbo and were looking for a new place. Our twin boys were getting bigger. The apartment we took over was in awful condition, but between the fireplaces and the floors, I knew there was something spectacular. The sense of community in this place is crazy. Not only does everyone know everyone's kids' names—everyone knows everyone's dogs' names.

How to Get an Apartment Here

The last available unit was apartment 5G—a $4,850 three-bedroom (with two fireplaces), which was temporarily taken off the market on March 13. The real-estate agent who has rented many of the recently available apartments is Jason Lax, who posts them on StreetEasy. The more coveted apartments—the ones that retain their full Gilded Age charm—rarely make it on there. For access to those, you'll have to be more resourceful. Clyde Williams, who moved into a three-bedroom in 2010, "called everybody under the sun: the property manager, the owners. Finally, somebody called us back." Kevin Harter, the VP of integrated marketing and fashion direction for Bloomingdale's, describes a similar process when he started trying to move in, in 2016. "I had to work it," he says. "I gave gifts. There are people in the building wearing Bloomingdale's cashmere who weren't before."

The Ivy League Eleven

They came in 1993 and set the gentrification wheels in motion.

> A friend of mine from Brown lived in Graham Court, and he was able to convince the owners of the building to rent a number of apartments that they were warehousing for photo shoots and film production to all these young black professionals who would be willing to pay market rent. That's how I got here.
>
> —Sheila Bridges, interior designer and author

> Our friend from Brown organized it. Eleven of us moved in with Ivy League degrees—five of us still live here today—and the change probably began then. I don't want to sound saviorish, but when eleven black Ivy League graduates move into a building at the same time, it denotes something. We hoped to purchase our apartments once the building went co-op—our goal wasn't to be lifetime renters. What we've missed out on is the price appreciation; when we leave, there's no payout.
>
> —Kathy Frazier, wealth adviser

Building Blind Items

Anonymous tidbits from the tenants.

Of the new families flooding Graham Court in recent years, one tenant says, "They don't have money for Westchester, so this is the new place."

According to court records, former Knicks player Melvyn Davis is embroiled in a long-lasting litigation with the landlord and his own subtenants.

When tenants need "someone with power to get anything done in the neighborhood," they'll go, says one, to Clyde Williams, the former national policy director of the DNC.

One resident lives down the hall from what he believes to be the apartment of an heir to the Cabot Creamery fortune. "He got his lease for next to nothing," the tenant says, "then did a massive renovation." Plus: "He has parties, and I haven't been to one, but I hear they're amazing."

Graham Court Since March

How the tenants are faring.

Many of the drug addicts in the park across the street, which was closed because of COVID-19, were camping out in front of our gate—then the drug pushers joined them and were using it as a drug-selling station. It was like the Harlem of the seventies and eighties on steroids. The pushers and the addicts were not distancing, many were sickly. In mid-April, it got a bit better—we think people got word that the city was fining.

—William Allen

I've been inside for about two months—my niece is incarcerating me here. She brings me food from a Spanish restaurant— yellow rice, beans. The tenants seem all right. One woman's in the hospital. You can't help but run into people, but they're sensible, so they follow the rules.

—Laconia Smedley

Some folks from the building have been calling the police on the people that have come over from the park, who are maybe doing drugs. I'm not one to participate. I saw someone out front, ready to sit down. I didn't yell at him. I told him, "I know you're tired."

—Yvonne Stafford

You don't see the neighbors [as much]. We do have a tenants' page on Facebook. Yvonne posted to ask if anybody needed anything, and we have extra gloves that we've been sharing with our neighbors. The courtyard lets us get some sun on our face. It gives a sense of security.

—Jonathan Solars

New York

WINNER—LEISURE
INTERESTS

This is the second of three articles from the series "Biography of a Building," which won New York *the National Magazine Award for Leisure Interests for the fifth time in the history of the publication.* New York*'s focus on the way people live in the city dates back to the earliest days of the magazine—"What Does It Take to Get a Decent Apartment in the Year of the Great Apartment Squeeze?" reads the cover line of one issue from 1968, the year the magazine was founded—and* New York*'s lifestyle coverage has proved to be perhaps as influential as its literary journalism (1968 was also the year* New York *published what would become* The Electric Kool-Aid Acid Test*). The writer of "Biography of a Building," Matthew Sedacca, is a freelance journalist who, besides real estate, also covers that other major interest of New Yorkers, restaurants.*

Matthew Sedacca

One Fifth

The Downtown Co-op of All Downtown Co-ops

The Art Deco building has long been an expression of a certain type of New York–ness—where artists who have been here for decades live alongside investment bankers, the doormen leave out cookies, and intrabuilding relationships and tensions play out in the lobby (and don't get anyone who lives here started on the lobby).

For almost a century, One Fifth Avenue has quietly loomed over Greenwich Village. The address itself carries gravitas, and the building, a twenty-seven-story ziggurat, has long dominated the local skyline, lurking in the background of tourists' photos of the fountain and marble arch in Washington Square Park. And the goings-on inside its setback walls have, practically since its inception, been a thing of fascination for the rest of the city. It was in One Fifth that Robert Mapplethorpe shot the album cover for Patti Smith's *Horses*; where Norman Mailer's editor committed suicide; and Tim Burton and Helena Bonham Carter lived together before they split in 2014. The building is now home to both art collectors who bought apartments for under $8,000 in the 1970s and, more recently, CEOs happy to pay millions for a penthouse. Over the years, One Fifth has become as much an idea as it is a real building. "It just said New York to me," says the novelist Lesley Dormen, "the New York of a time and period that probably every writer idealizes to some extent."

One Fifth was completed in 1927 by developer Joseph G. Siegel. He recruited the architectural firms Sugarman & Berger and Helmle & Corbett, which had designed such Goliaths as the thirty-story Bush Tower in midtown. The idea, in essence, was to build an apartment-hotel that would cater to the wealthy, who were drawn to the counterculture that had recently emerged in the area. In the early days, tenants and guests passed through the building's Doric lobby to attend art auctions, benefit luncheons, and socialites' crowded salons filled with discussions of *Finnegans Wake*. Outside, curmudgeonly neighbors complained that the new building was an eyesore, as did the *New Yorker*, which called it "a pompous shaft." Still, it was a success: market-exchange presidents and lawyers looking to live like (or, at least, near) Allen Ginsberg moved en masse into the building's two- and three-room apartments, many of which featured serving pantries, private roof terraces, and views of the river.

By 1966, NYU was expanding and, looking "to preserve the character of the neighborhood," purchased the building outright to use as student and faculty housing. So families and other long-term renters lived in the hotel alongside undergrads who walked their neighbors' dogs for extra cash and called many of the onetime luxury suites home. But in August 1974, the university—which was nearing the brink of bankruptcy—unloaded One Fifth. Not long after, in 1976, the building went co-op. It was around this time that a handful of artists began moving in. One Fifth was situated blocks from the burgeoning Electric Lady Studios and the newly opened Grey Art Gallery. Plus there was the restaurant on the ground floor, One Fifth. "When I first came to this country, One Fifth bar was like *the* place to hang out," says Adam Tihany, a hospitality designer who later purchased a pied-à-terre in the building. Anna Wintour and Lorne Michaels were among the regulars, and the cast of *SNL* descended weekly from Rockefeller Center after wrapping up the show with stars like David Bowie in tow. Upstairs, the art collector Sam Wagstaff bought a twenty-seventh-floor penthouse for less than $26,000, where he slept on a mattress on the floor, as well as a unit on the eighth floor that he used as a repository for his collection, according to his biography. Patti Smith and her then-partner, Allen Lanier of Blue Öyster Cult, shacked up below, where Smith wrote *Babel* during her recovery from a near-fatal fall off a stage in Tampa in 1977. In the 1980s, Courteney Cox auditioned for her "Dancing in the Dark" music-video role in Brian De Palma's duplex apartment, and *The Heidi Chronicles* author, Wendy Wasserstein, called a two-bedroom on the sixth floor home.

The spirit of One Fifth has changed over the years, and so too have the actual apartments. That's because more and more residents have scooped up and combined two, three—in some cases, even five—of these slim, former hotel units into 2,700-square-foot four-bedroom Franken-apartments with bamboo flooring and cabinetry, gold-trimmed bathrooms, and unobstructed views of the Freedom Tower. And though their apartments have appreciated by, in some cases, millions of dollars (and as neighbors eager for more space are standing by, ready to pounce), many who bought into the building decades ago say they have no plans to leave anytime soon.

"I moved in twenty-six years ago, and I think I was too young to realize the magnitude of it," says Laura Pedone Evans, an art therapist. "It's special. People knock on my door all the time. My neighbor, who has since passed, wouldn't even knock—she'd just walk right into my apartment and leave me a plate of Persian rice. Once, it was Brian De Palma. He was asking if he could borrow a lemon."

More Pieces of History

In the 1830s, a four-story red brick townhouse stood at this address. It changed hands between various wealthy society types, and, most notably, it housed Misses Green's School for girls. Winston Churchill's mother, Jennie, was a student there. Elihu Root, who would later become secretary of state, and Andrew H. Green, who steered the construction of Central Park and the New York Public Library, were both teachers.

The Brickwork

Design architect Harvey Wiley Corbett originally used both light and dark bricks on the outside of the building to mimic 3D masonry work, a visual trick that was considered novel. In the early nineties, the co-op board spent over $1 million repairing the brickwork, which *Times* writer Christopher Gray was not fond of: "Now the building has an odd, spotty effect."

Patti Smith's Old Place

This ninth-floor apartment is owned by Jessica Salzer's family. She says that when her parents first went to look at it, around 1986, "there were industrial moving blankets hanging over the windows as curtains, pizza boxes everywhere, stains all over the carpetings, a pool table in the middle of the entryway, and—my mom said—gold records on the wall."

The Lobby Loiterers

"We always have people sitting down there," says Diana Oberlander, a resident and media-and-content strategist. "There was a woman who passed away about a year ago, a psychiatrist named Joan. She'd sit in the lobby, really old, all dressed up, and talk to the doormen for hours and hours."

According to lore, Jimi Hendrix used to stay in One Fifth when it was still a hotel. Some say there is a secret lobby that he would walk through to meet his dealer on Eighth Street.

The Steam-Pipe Incident

In 1988, the board was none too pleased when plastic surgeon Ronald Levandusky was planning to move a steam pipe while renovating his kitchen, so it forced him to halt the work. Levandusky was not pleased either: he sued the board, claiming it had a vendetta against him. (He would later sell the apartment to James Burrows, a director and cocreator of *Cheers*.)

The Broker Barrier

"There was a rumor," says Ann Weintraub, a longtime broker for the building, "that in the eighties, the doormen were physically throwing brokers out of the building—right out the front door—if they dared to come in."

The Lone Elevator Bank

There's only one—unusual for a building of One Fifth's size.

There's Something About Apartment 25b

A commercial starring the actress Shirley Jones was shot in the apartment. And, in 1980, a scene for Brian De Palma's *Dressed to Kill* was shot there, too, according to neighbor Joe Novak's memoir.

The Two-Apartment Filmmaker Family

In 2008, filmmaker Ira Sachs, who has lived on the sixth floor for over two decades, and his partner, the artist Boris Torres, asked filmmaker Kirsten Johnson, to have (and coparent) a child with them. They had twins and all lived in the same apartment—until the one next door became available and Johnson moved in.

Washington Mews

The private cobblestoned lane between Fifth Avenue and University Place abuts the building. "In the first few years we lived here," says resident Lesley Dormen, "no one was in the Mews. Now it's tons of NYU kids taking pictures. We hate NYU."

The People Who Live Here: Inside Six Apartments

Phyllis Spaeth and Julius "Jay" Novick, former Legal Aid Society attorney and former Village Voice *theater critic*

Moved in 1983

A friend of mine had just recently moved out of One Fifth, and he just couldn't stop singing its praises. There was an apartment for sale, so we went to look. We were so taken by the size of it, by how interesting each room was. Nothing was cookie-cutter; there were French doors, little Juliet balconies. The neighborhood was perfect—as my husband said before my daughter was born, "Oh, look! She could go buy drugs without having to cross a major thoroughfare." I have seen fights in this building, suing of people on the board by other people on the board. When we moved in, the board interview was so perfunctory—like, hysterical. I think it's much different now. Everything really is about the money. I mean, "Can you pay?" I understand. Very honestly, we never could've come in here now. We bought it for $200,000; now it's probably worth around $2 million.

—P.S.

Danya Labban and Tina Chandna, current board president and spouse

Moved in 1979

> Tina and I started living in One Fifth full time right after 9/11. This place knows how to respond to crises. During Sandy, the elevators weren't working, and the lights were out, and the staff were running up and down the stairs, putting out glow sticks and sleeping in the lobby.
>
> —D.L.

Lesley Dormen and Quentin Spector, writer and former executive director

Moved in 1993

> We were very close to closing on a loft in Tribeca, and suddenly I was mugged walking into the door of my Eleventh Street apartment on Christmas Night. It was a push-in thing. After that, I said, "Doorman. I must have a doorman." The second I saw our apartment, it was that magical moment of home. It was a gray January day, but the apartment was still flooded with light because it's southwest-facing. We've been here since. It has become a bit like a compound. At the end of our hall, there is a filmmaker and his husband, and the mother of their kids moved into an apartment next door to theirs. Sometimes, when the twins were toddlers, I'd hear a little knock on the door, and I'd open to see these little post-shower darlings wanting to say good night. Just before the recession, when real-estate prices were at an all-time high, suddenly these very wealthy older people were buying pieds-à-terre or moving in. It definitely started skewing a little less . . . the building was never raffish, exactly, but it

definitely seemed more artsy. Then, it became, Oh my God, all this wealth.

—L.D.

Shivashish Chatterjee and Jeannette Vargas, cofounder of a financial company and assistant U.S. Attorney for the Southern District of New York

Moved in 2003

So we've been here for seventeen-odd years. The first time we walked in, it was clear that it's not overbearing; you're in a full-service building, but it's not in your face. When you step out of the cab, you don't have three people rush out the door to help you. We found that to be quite to our taste.

—S.C.

Jason Dietz and Katie Fleischer, voice-over artist and actor and screenwriter-director

Moved in 1996 and 1995

What's interesting about the building, for me, is that I can literally look out my back window and see the apartment where I was conceived. My parents used to live at 11 Waverly Place way back when, so I guess I'm a little like Jesus; I don't go that far from home. We were able to get into the building when it was . . . manageable, because everything around here has gotten so exceedingly expensive that it's difficult now to get into any of these buildings unless you're making a whole lot of money.

—J.D.

Juliet and Dale Ponikvar, psychotherapist/couples therapist, retired lawyer

Moved in 1998

I started the renovation, a gut renovation, in '97, and it took a good year and a half. I hired the Hariris—they're two Iranian-born architects, Mojgan and Gisue. They were young then, so a One Fifth apartment was a challenge for them, and what they did was, to me, completely remarkable.

When the apartment next door to me on twenty opened up, I wanted to buy it, but my neighbor was a real sharp cookie, and she was basically using me as a stalking horse to up the price. I think Lois Gould, the fiction writer, was also a bidder, but eventually Alan Belzer, this retired COO of Allied Signal, swooped in and bought it—it was chump change for him. He apologized to me afterward, but I told him, "Don't be sorry." But then I bought the apartment below. And then the other two adjacent apartments on twenty-one became available, and I bought them.

—D.P.

Building Blind Items

Anonymous tidbits from the tenants.

"There was one time when a woman living on my floor—who was divorced—was having an affair with one of the doormen. I kid you not."

"Jessica Lange is still here and is apparently gonna stay, because she bought an apartment on the floor above hers, and she's combining them."

"We have die-hard Republicans, surprisingly, and arguments in the lobby about protesters."

Everyone Has Something to Say About the Co-op Board

As one might imagine.

People Campaign

"When Wendy Wasserstein and Michiko Kakutani both still lived in the building, I'd tell them who they should vote for. People would slip flyers under people's doors telling them who to vote for." —Phyllis Spaeth

And Complain

"The board is an oligarchy. If you're the president and say you want the water fountains to have soda, the water fountains would actually have soda, and we would be paying for it. There are always people who are on the board because they're renovating their apartment. Because we're a landmarked building, it's hard to get the paperwork approved. But if you're on the board, it doesn't have to be approved; you're the approver." —Anonymous resident

They Used to Put Out a Newsletter

"At the very beginning, I remember there was a newsletter that the board sent out . . . it satisfied a certain gossip hunger for what was going on, like whose terrace was still leaking." —Lesley Dormen

And There's the Famous Keith Richards Story

"Keith Richards lived here. He made a bid on this gorgeous duplex—over $10 million. At the end of the process, Keith and Patti Hansen come to meet the board. Apparently, it starts out collegial. They sit at the table; it's friendly. The board president is like, 'Keith, Patti, it's so nice to meet you. It's a thrill. I'm a big

Stones fan. So, Keith, why'd you pick One Fifth?' And Keith goes, 'Well, it was an address my wife thought I could remember.'"
—Anonymous resident

The Lobby's a Constant Source of Kvetching

"There has been a lot of resistance to the renovation campaigns in the lobby over the years," says resident (and former board member) Dale Ponikvar. "But a prior chairman pushed through a renovation of the mezzanine, which was aesthetically a great success, because it recaptured the original spirit of the place. The original Art Deco chandeliers were taken out and put in a hotel in the Poconos, but we replaced them with an Art Deco–esque light. People complain, of course, but it has been spruced up." Some residents, though, like Diana Oberlander, are less impressed. "The bones of the building are amazing," she says. "But then you'll have some random co-op president that decides the lobby needs to be redone, and for ten years the place looks like a Hilton hotel." Lesley Dormen says she hoped it might look "less like a doctor's waiting room."

But No One Complains About Nick's Cookies

"I started leaving out food the second year I worked here. They like the butter cookies and fig cookies, and, of course, they love Oreos. If my wife makes something special—lasagna or chicken-cutlet parm, homemade pizza—I bring it in. Over the years, I've brought in fried chicken, wine. Sometimes, at one or two a.m., people come down in their nightgowns looking for a sweet."
—Nicholas Mistretta, doorman

There's a Crew of Dog Owners That Meets in the Mews

For a while, ten or so residents would meet in the evening in the Mews and let their dogs off their leashes. "When you have a dog, you really get to know everybody," says resident Laura Pedone Evans. "Jessica Lange and I walked together with our dogs. Diana had a vizsla, so her dog had red hair; my dog was black and white; and Lesley Dormen's dog was blonde, so we started calling them the Charlie's Angels of One Fifth." Dormen adds, "They would run madly up and down the cobblestones. It was so fun. Then, this man moved into the Mews. He has four dogs and was very strict about not letting dogs off leash. So everything comes to an end."

. . . And a Wine Club

Dale Ponikvar, who lives on floors nineteen, twenty, and twenty-one, says it was founded a few years after his neighbor Shivash-ish Chatterjee moved in, in 2003. They unofficially call themselves the Gang of Eight. "It's Shiv and his wife, Jeannette Vargas; this retired finance guy and his wife; and my next-door neighbor, Susan [Martin], and her husband, Alan Belzer," says Ponikvar. "We get together three or four times a year, and we usually bring two bottles of wine to share. Susan has proposed that, until we can get together in person, we do a virtual dinner, where each of us will leave a Mason jar of wine at each other's doors. If Susan and Alan do that, that means we're all getting some twenty-year-old Bordeaux—because Alan actually bought a separate apartment on the nineteenth floor and converted it into a wine cellar."

How Do You Get Your Own One Fifth Apartment?

Ann Weintraub has been the de facto broker for the building for nearly four decades. "I've sold some apartments three, four times over," she says. The film producer Peter Newman, who bought his first One Fifth apartment from Weintraub, says, "Ann was always in the lobby and always knew what everyone's business was. She knew who was sick, who needed a room for a baby, and was just that go-to person." There are currently nine apartments for sale in One Fifth—including a three-bedroom, three-bath that hasn't been on the market in twenty-odd years. Considering that listings have proliferated during the pandemic (the latest numbers from StreetEasy say the city's inventory has nearly 30,000 listings more than last year) and the number of apartments sold in Manhattan in the past three months was down 46 percent, many of the units have seen significant price drops ($1 million off a penthouse; $450,000 off that three-bedroom). Still, the process is the same as it has always been: You apply through the board, which reviews your information. Though Weintraub says, "there are no set rules about liquidity, employment, or salary" for applicants, others in the building say that's not always the case. At one point in the not-so-distant past, says resident Oberlander, the board "required you to have something like fifty times the liquid amount of the value of your apartment in your account."

The Restaurant Downstairs

Probably cursed.

For decades, the first floor of One Fifth has housed a restaurant. In the thirties, there was the supper club #1 Bar that launched the careers of Dorothy Lamour and Paul Lynde. By 1976, George Schwarz and his wife, Kiki Kogelnik, opened One Fifth, where brothers Keith and Brian McNally worked before they went on to open the Odeon. Per building lore, hostesses were occasionally dispatched to send drunken patrons-slash-residents back up to their apartments. Throughout the nineties, though, no one was able to stay open for long. Alfred Portale, the celebrated chef of Gotham Bar & Grill, tried his hand at a seafood restaurant, named One Fifth Avenue, in 1992, which failed in less than two years. That was later followed, unsuccessfully, by Vince and Linda, where Anthony Bourdain ran the kitchen. In 1997, Ruth Reichl asked in her *Times* review if the space's newest restaurant,

Clementine, would be able to outlast the others. (Her takeaway: maybe.) But it was only with Mario Batali and Joe Bastianich's Otto Enoteca e Pizzeria in 2003 that something finally stuck—until Batali was accused of sexual misconduct in 2017 and, earlier this year, when the restaurant was forced to close permanently owing to COVID-19.

Paris Review

These three articles—"Ladies of the Good Dead," "On Immolation," and "On Doulas"— are drawn from Aisha Sabatini Sloan's column for the Paris Review, "Detroit Archives," which, in the words of the editors of the magazine, "explores her family history through iconic landmarks in Detroit." The judges who selected this work as the winner of the 2021 National Magazine Award for Columns and Commentary explained their decision in these words: "In a tense and difficult year for America, Aisha Sabatini Sloan's columns offered a celebration of the nation's most misunderstood city. These pieces display an art historian's depth of reference, a journalist's curiosity, and a novelist's attention to detail." Sabatini Sloan's most recent collection of essays, Dreaming of Ramadi in Detroit, was published in 2017. She is currently an assistant professor of creative writing and English at the University of Michigan.

Aisha Sabatini Sloan

Ladies of the Good Dead *and* On Immolation *and* On Doulas

Ladies of the Good Dead

My great aunt Cora Mae can't hear well. She is ninety-eight years old. When the global pandemic reached Michigan, the rehabilitation center where she was staying stopped accepting visitors. There were attempts at FaceTime, but her silence made it clear that for her, we had dwindled into pixelated ghosts. She contracted COVID-19 and has been moved again and again. When my mother calls to check on her every day, she makes sure to explain to hospital staff that my great aunt is almost deaf, that they have to shout in her left ear if they want to be heard.

Cora Mae has a bawdy sense of humor. Most of the time when she speaks, it's to crack a joke that would make most people blush. She wears leopard print and prefers for her hair to be dyed bright red. I have tried to imagine her in the hospital, attempting to make sense of the suited, masked figures gesticulating at her. She doesn't know about the pandemic. She doesn't know why we've stopped visiting. All she knows is that she has been kidnapped by what must appear to be astronauts.

The film *The Last Black Man in San Francisco* begins with a little black girl gazing up into the face of a white man wearing a hazmat suit. A street preacher standing on a small box asks: "Why do they have on these suits and we don't?" He refers to the hazmat men as "George Jetson rejects." It feels wild to watch the film right now, as governors begin to take their states out of lockdown knowing that black and brown residents will continue to die at unprecedented rates, taking a calculated risk that will look, from the vantage point of history, a lot like genocide. The film's street preacher sounds obscenely prophetic. "You can't Google what's going on right now," he shouts. "They got plans for us."

•   •   •

Under quarantine in Detroit, my father, a photographer, has been sifting through boxes of slides in his sprawling archive. Each image unleashes a story for him. Last week, he told me about arriving in Sarajevo while covering the Olympics. He stayed with a family of friendly strangers eight years before the war. "I wonder if they survived," he mutters to an empty room.

When my cousin was a police lieutenant, she told us about getting a call for someone who had died. At first glance, they thought the man had been hoarding newspapers or magazines, but then his daughter explained that he was a composer. The papers in those leaning stacks were original compositions.

When we hear on the news that Detroit is struggling, that people are dying, do we imagine composers? Do we imagine a man who sifts through photographs of Bosnia before the war?

In a painting by Kerry James Marshall, *7am Sunday Morning*, a long, horizontal city street appears mundane on one side, but morphs into hexagons and prisms and diamonds as the eye moves right, as if the block is being seen through multiple panes of differently angled glass. If you peer closely at the building on the left, what look like wisps of smoke wafting out of a brick building can be discerned as delicately rendered musical notes. They curve underneath a flock of birds that flutter over a beauty school and a liquor store. The almost unbearable majesty of this ordinary city block evokes Detroit for me. Some summer afternoons, a lens between me and the world gets cracked, and the light and the people and history and the sky go wonky and the moment feels achingly eternal.

.   .   .

Last year, the Detroit Institute of Arts mounted an exhibition called "Detroit Collects," featuring mostly black collectors of African American art in the city. One room was lined with giant photographs of well-dressed collectors. Immediately I recognized the wry smile of a woman named Dr. Cledie Collins Taylor.

My parents have been telling me about Dr. Taylor for years. "You're going to love her." "Her house is a museum." "She used to live in Italy." "She loves pasta." When a friend came to town, we thought we would go to the Detroit Institute of Arts, but my father took us to Dr. Taylor's house instead. The sun was spilling across the horizon, raspberry sherbet bleeding into orange, and the temperature was in the low teens. A handful of houses along the street had big paintings integrated into the architecture of a porch or a window. We knocked on a security gate and a woman in her nineties welcomed us inside.

"Every February, someone discovers me," Dr. Taylor joked, nodding at the coincidence of receiving extra attention during Black History Month. I felt a twinge of embarrassment. Here I was, encountering one of Detroit's most important artistic matriarchs for the very first time.

Art in this city is on display at the Detroit Institute of Arts, one of the most gorgeous, palatial museums I've ever visited. Spectators can gawk at Diego Court, their faces striped with sunlight, imagining the ghost of Frida Kahlo off to the side of the room. But art also bursts out of the city's residential neighborhoods. You can find paintings by one of the city's biggest rising stars, Tylonn Sawyer, tucked inside a gallery like N'Namdi Center or projected onto a screen at the DIA, but you are even more likely to see it flash like an apparition in your periphery (two children gazing upward, golden orbs radiating behind their heads) as you drive past a nondescript building near the warehouses surrounding Eastern Market.

At Dr. Taylor's house, we sat in the living room and talked for a while. The impeachment hearings were playing loudly on a television in her bedroom. "A lot of my collection is upstairs, why don't you go take a look." We crept carefully through a room that seemed to be fitted with exactly as many books as it could tastefully hold, toward a narrow stairway. Upstairs, canvases leaned against the walls. A figurine stood, stark, in a room off to the left. There was a photo-realistic painting of a black woman with short hair, in profile, wearing a pink turtleneck and sitting on a white couch. A black-and-white print of a man with hair like Little Richard peeked out from behind a stack of frames. In a round canvas, a man with an afro slouched behind a shiny wooden table, seated in front of geometric panes of blue, including a massive window framing a cloudy blue sky—as if Questlove were relaxing to "Kind of Blue" inside a Diebenkorn painting. Ordinary scenes of black life, exquisitely rendered, were scattered across the room, a collection relaxing into itself with a kind of easeful, dusty abundance. We were called back downstairs.

Dr. Taylor walked us through the house and took us on a tour of the basement. African masks, sculptures, shields, and figurines were pinned to pegboard the way other basements showcase drills and rakes. I placed my hand on the baby bump of a pregnant wooden figure. "Somewhere along the line, the collecting idea just catches you," Dr. Taylor said, humbly.

"You could tell where the problems were because you'd get a lot of things from that place," she said of collecting work from Africa. "I realized that people were responding to what they needed; certain things in their family shrines they could part with, just to eat." She told us about her friend, a playwright who convinced a general not to kill her family during the Biafran War.

Dr. Taylor tried to hold items and then give them back when wars had ended, once she realized why they'd become so available, but she struggled to get past corrupt middlemen.

She told us story after story about the objects in her home, rendering details of character and plot to bring each item alive— "she got some men who carry lumber to carry her under their wagon," and "he was a smooth talker, very good looking."

Dr. Taylor has been around the world twice. A trip to Iran ended early when the shah fell ill. She has spent entire years on sabbatical living in Italy, often bringing young members of her family along to learn the language. She was a teacher at Cass Tech, a Detroit public high school. She taught fashion design and made art out of gold in her spare time. "Do you still?" we asked. "I don't go near the fire because I can't run fast," she explained.

"Do you want to see the gallery?" She offered. It seemed unthinkable that there might be more.

We walked down the steps of her porch and immediately up the stairs of the house-cum-gallery next door. Arts Extended Groupe was established in Midtown Detroit in 1950 by Myrtle Hall, along with Dr. Taylor and a group of other artists and teachers . They wanted a space that could serve as an educational tool, not simply catering to the art market or to the growing air of elitism infecting the art world. Later, Dr. Taylor moved the space to her neighborhood. We stood underneath a small painting called *Ladies of the Good Dead* and listened to her describe an old Brazilian tradition of displaying fabrics upon the occasion of somebody's death. It was a way of collecting funds to buy young men out of slavery. The day outside darkened, slipped closer to single digits. We prepared our coats to go.

·   ·   ·

After we've been in lockdown for a while, I call to find out how Dr. Taylor is faring. She is doing fine, she tells me. She talked to her friends in Italy just last week. There is a woman on staff who goes to the gallery every so often to let in light and water the plants. There is a new show up for no one to see, photo-realistic drawings of the tales of Osei Tutu, detailing the founding of Ghana. She is making plans for the gallery's next phase: a turn away from brick and mortar, in the direction of something more like a foundation.

The doorbell rings and she excuses herself. When she gets back on the phone, she says, "You can't see the smile on my face. It's big, I can assure you." Two of her great-grandsons had just come by, and when she got to the door they were standing on the sidewalk, waving. "That was so nice!" Her voice conveys a haze of emotion so palpable it catches in me, too. "The second from the oldest, he calls me on his phone sometimes to tell me he misses me." Their father, her grandson, is a phlebotomist who lives next door, she tells me, and he takes care to strip down and shower before greeting his family when he comes home. As I imagine the scene playing out, I visualize a kind of Charlie Chaplain figure, or a magician. Her tone is so infused with wonder. It takes her a moment to compose herself.

A curator chose a painting from Dr. Taylor's collection to hang at the Detroit Institute of Arts. It's titled *Little Paul*. It is a portrait of her grandson, the phlebotomist, that she commissioned from a little-known painter named Robert L. Tomlin years ago. A boy sits in a chair wearing a gray blazer, jeans, and tennis shoes, gazing intently at the corner of the room. In an article about the exhibition, a curator from the museum muses about the life behind the painting, notes how it intrigues her.

In *The Last Black Man in San Francisco*, the sidewalk preacher shouts: "I urge you. Fight for your land. Fight for your home." The protagonists of the film fly by on a skateboard, passing frozen scenes of black life, scenes of a city that is disappearing in real time.

I remember, years ago, watching an interview with Kerry James Marshall, in which the painter carefully confronts two white art collectors who have amassed an impressive collection of contemporary black art, including his own, and exhibited it as part of a highly regarded traveling exhibition. He brings up the fact that no black art collector could do what they have done. His words are delivered as a statement, but in my mind, they hang in the air like a question.

When I think about the specific importance of a black art collector, I think about the moment we are living, or not living, through. There are stories inside every black life lost to the virus in Wayne County. I think of my great aunt, who, bafflingly, just tested negative, and was released from the hospital last night. I think of Dr. Taylor's attic full of artwork, which remains precious to her whether it falls in or out of fashion. I think about the affection that radiates from her voice. How it lingers. It is infectious.

On Immolation

For a period of time in 2014, I couldn't stop watching the surveillance video of a person setting fire to the *Heidelberg Project*, a world-renowned art installation by Tyree Guyton in a residential area of Detroit. The recorded arson struck me as a performance piece in itself. In what appears to be the very early hours of the morning, a figure approaches the threshold of a structure called "Taxi House," a home adorned by boards of wood that have been painted with yellow, pink, green, and white vehicles labeled "taxi." There is a painted clock, real tires, and toy cars. A meandering, peach colored line has been painted along a sagging corner of the roof, then it comes down onto the siding, where it moves geometrically, like Pac-Man.

The installation as a whole is like a painting brought to life, imbued with the spirits of Kea Tawana, Jean-Michel Basquiat, and Robert Rauschenberg. In a recent profile in the *New York Times*

Magazine, Guyton describes how he began the installation with his grandfather, an act of reinvention rooted in nostalgia. M. H. Miller describes the collection of carefully planned assemblages as "an act of Proustian reclamation, as if Guyton were creating a new neighborhood out of the one he'd lost, embellishing his and Grandpa Mackey's memories out of the wreckage that surrounded them." In the video of the fire that destroys "Taxi House," the figure holds something that resembles a gallon of milk; after a short time, a fireball blooms, and the figure runs away.

The *Heidelberg* installation has the vibe of Plato's lost city of Atlantis, the mythic civilization that sank into the ocean overnight after its people lost their sense of virtue. It also brings to mind Jason deCaires Taylor's undersea sculptures, human figures engaged in activities like typing, playing the cello, or watching TV; cement bodies surrounded by schools of fish. What's so remarkable about Guyton's effort is that he's constructed a frame around the present moment. The collapse he draws our eye to is not a myth or a dream of the future; it's now.

Though Guyton had originally hoped for the installation to be a solution of sorts, the traffic it brings (around 200,000 people a year) also serves as a reminder of the tension inherent to a city undergoing gentrification. In a book written about the project, *Connecting the Dots*, one neighbor explains, "Every summer night we've got people riding up and down looking at what we're doing. It's an invasion of privacy. They look at us like we're animals on display."

From what I can tell, no motive ever emerged for the arson, and no arrests were made. The one person who checked into an emergency room for severe burns on the day of the fire had been trying to deep-fry a turkey. More fires have been set at the installation in years since.

Guyton exhibits widely and has a special fan base overseas. Recently, he has decided to take the *Heidelberg Project* down. According to M. H. Miller, Guyton and his wife plan to "transform the buildings that still stand into a series of cultural and educational centers dedicated to the arts, and then build housing and work spaces marketed for artists out of this central core."

As buildings around the country were set on fire in the aftermath of George Floyd's murder, I thought about the *Heidelberg* arsonist. Widely dispersed memes featuring the Martin Luther King Jr. quote "The riot is the language of the unheard" have encouraged more and more people to see fire in the context of social upheaval not merely as an act of destruction but as an act of ritualized desecration. What language looks like at wit's end. A kind of screaming.

So what did we learn in the wake of the *Heidelberg* blaze? For one thing, the firefighters who came to put out the fire were delayed because none of the hydrants in the area were working owing to widespread water shutoffs across the city. But, also, the fire begs some of the same questions that Guyton's work elicited when he first began in the eighties: Who is the artist? Who is the criminal? Who is the bystander? Who is the institution? Can you occupy more than one role at once?

•　　•　　•

The first photograph my father took for *Newsweek* magazine was of the 1967 uprising in Detroit. In the image, a young man looks toward the camera as a warehouse burns bright orange behind him under a dark night sky. My father likes to point out how he caught the boy in a moment of bewilderment, of total awe. Recently, I asked my dad to take my wife and me to the place where the image was taken. My mother came along, too.

My dad begins the journey by veering into oncoming traffic, because the street has gone two-lane; a street construction project that has turned the neighborhood into an obstacle course. As we make our way down East Grand Boulevard, a painted storefront next to Flamin' Moez Soul Food reads US AND THEM. The grandiosity of what my parents call the Boulevard clears, and now we are passing grassy fields. We are taking a detour from our detour toward another detour.

We drive past the Packard plant, which has become a kind of unofficial graffiti museum. The British artist Banksy consecrated the space a few years back with a painting of a black boy in a strange black suit holding a can of red paint, next to the message "I remember when all this was trees." I can't say I get it, given that the area is and long has been surrounded by overgrown lots. Banksy's arrival prompted a minor controversy when local gallerists removed the section of concrete he'd spray-painted and sold it for over $100,000. A bit farther down the block, a huge sign promises COMING SOON! PACKARD PLANT BREWERY. I think about the way that ruin is being involved, here, in a kind of transaction. The image that comes to mind is Goya's painting of Saturn devouring his son.

We pass a public art installation featuring white figures kneeling. On Woodward, a billboard shows a black cop with his arms crossed and it reads: ANSWERING THE TOUGHEST CALL. Later, we will find out that the night before, Detroit cops, "fearing they were under fire," drove into a crowd of protesters.

Our plan is to first find the site of the Algiers Motel, where a group of police and National Guard killed three people and tortured several others in the midst of the 1967 uprising. My mom says, "On the map it looks like an empty field." Up a ways, there is a sizable gathering of Black men on the steps of a church, with signs that say GOD BLESS OUR FATHERS. Black men and boys are holding their hands in the air in surrender or praise.

The site of the motel is now a well-cared-for park, gated, mostly empty and surrounded by brick walls. We pause, then turn back into traffic.

Next, we attempt to find the place where my father took the photograph that began his career. After getting caught in a loop in a fancy neighborhood and circling a beautiful garden where a white man in a fedora appears to be considering purchasing the property, we turn in a direction my father hadn't planned to take. My mother says she's "going to call Rodney," my father's best friend, which is a euphemism for "we're lost."

At a red light we find ourselves staring at the bottom of a toppled SUV. It takes a moment to decipher the car's undercarriage, a desert-colored thing at an odd angle. At the intersection, people are streaming across the street like liquid, despite oncoming cars, toward what we now understand to be an accident, endangering themselves in the effort to find out what's going on. I peer more closely into the window of the toppled car but can't make anything out. A man holding a baby keeps darting toward it. There are fire trucks and a police car, city officials wearing masks and looking at the vehicle, but no one is touching anything. The plan of action seems to be hanging, still, in the air.

I request that we end the tour. I'm not sure what meaning we can make of the site of a long-ago fire when all this emergency is unfolding in real time.

·　　·　　·

On the way back home, my wife and I tune in to the end of an episode of *This American Life*. The story is about a community leader in Detroit who recently hosted a pancake breakfast, putting cops in conversation with the communities they are meant to protect. He talks about bringing people into difficult conversation with one another across the city. The breakfast took place just as coronavirus began to spread, and afterward, several people became ill.

It takes us both by surprise to realize that the man whose voice we've been listening to, Marlowe Stoudamire, just died of COVID-19. Many lament that he would have been a natural leader in the protests against police brutality that sprang up shortly after his death. Voices attempt to describe him, only to break. His wife tells the story of watching him tear up on a recent family vacation to the site of the Colosseum, a place he never expected, in his lifetime, to see.

My wife and I don't talk much for the rest of the day. Not until debriefing that night do we realize that we've both spent the past few hours replaying the scene of that horrible accident, replaying the moment when we realized that Stoudamire was dead. Even though we're inundated with bad news all day, every day, there is weird relief in the specificity of this sadness. At least we are not numb.

Later, I look up Stoudamire to see what else of his story I've missed. He was the director of an exhibition for the Detroit Historical Society called *Detroit 67*. The project features a wide swath of voices that collectively tell the story of the Detroit Rebellion of 1967. There are hundreds of collected oral histories. One woman recalls walking around with her father on mornings after nights of unrest. He would take photographs as they processed what they saw. Another woman, a professor of anthropology, talks about how the uprising reminded her of the time she spent studying in the Middle East, and compares the situation to the Arab-Israeli War, which took place that same year. A man who served on the National Guard says that there are things he saw during his deployment at the uprising, things that the police did, that he'd rather not share. The fact that he is being invited to revisit a memory that he'd like to keep to himself gives the whole project a new kind of valence for me. It reminds me of the Truth and Reconciliation Commission.

In reflecting on his career, my father talks about how he often had to argue with white editors who saw the Black subjects of his photographs as criminals and perpetrators. Meanwhile, when he looks at the photo he took of the boy and the burning building, my father sees a bystander, an innocent. He is trying to defend the young man from an accusatory, racialized gaze. But lately, I've wondered how else to interpret what's captured there. What if he did set the fire? What might he have been trying to say? On the Solange song "Mad," which has served as a much-needed balm for Black listeners since 2016, Lil Wayne says, "Now tell 'em why you mad, son."

During his own interview for *Detroit 67*, Marlowe Stoudamire says, "It's important that nobody gets their story left out."

On Doulas

In 2016, Erykah Badu performed at Chene Park, now called the Aretha Franklin Amphitheatre, a beautiful, outdoor waterfront venue in Detroit overlooking Canada. Badu donated proceeds from that concert to the African American 490 Challenge, an organization trying to raise money to process 11,341 untested rape kits that had been abandoned for years at a Detroit police department storage facility. The initiative was named 490 after the dollar amount needed to test a single kit, each of which represents, the organization's president Kim Trent emphasized, "a living, breathing victim." Four years later, thanks to their work, 11,137 kits have been tested, and there have been 210 convictions. Eighty-one percent of the victims were Black women. You could call this an archive of negligence.

Recently, my great aunt Cora Mae joined a similar sort of archive. A few months ago, she shocked us all by surviving COVID-19 just shy of her ninety-ninth birthday. But afterward, she lost her appetite and, a few weeks ago, we lost her. Her body was held at a funeral home while my parents kept sending in requests for court permission to bury her. She was terrified by the idea of burning. After a maddening couple of weeks of sending and resending forms, converting Word docs to PDFs, getting things notarized, being sent back to square one again only to be told by the funeral director, "If this isn't resolved by 4 PM I'm going to cremate the body," we finally got my great aunt a proper resting place. She was buried in a plot at Mt. Elliott Cemetery on one of the first days of fall. "That's the fastest I've seen anyone go through probate to bury a family member," the hospice social worker told my mom. "I've seen it take years." We thought our experience was an aberration, but apparently it's common for bodies to wait in funeral homes—on ice or forced into ash—in a kind of limbo that must devastate so many families.

Cora Mae loved to chew tobacco. She kept a covert spit cup in her hand like someone might hold a handkerchief. She'd often summon somebody over by curling her pointer finger, and give them money to go buy her more chew. Her voice was raspy, as if the effort to propel air through her throat took great effort, but there was also a honeyed quality that came through when she told a joke or a story or claimed innocence about something illicit. Both she and my grandmother began to tell stories toward the end of their lives about the men who had hurt them when they were young. Both she and my grandmother had in their arsenal a particularly childish mode of speaking, a gentle croon, a not-quite whine, though they were always also grasping their fingers around a more lethal, hidden option, just in case things got nasty. A story I've heard my great aunt tell over and over again involved her first and only husband and an ice pick. The doctor asked, "Cora, how'd this ice pick end up in Mr. Andrews's foot?" As she reenacted the moment, she would shrug her shoulders and make her voice go up an octave: "I don't know." Then her tone would drop again, coming close to a growl: "I guess he stepped on it."

Aunt Cora Mae survived life after Mr. Andrews by sporting jars of lye in her purse and stashing a gun underneath her pillow, but most useful to her, I imagine, was that girlish voice. This is how my Black female elders responded to the fact of being a particular kind of silenced, a particular kind of unseeable. In a society that recognizes Black females as neither fully adult nor ever truly innocent, they found a way to weaponize girlhood. That coy effect communicated both a sweetness and an edge. We often laughed when they spoke about their fondness for weapons, but never for a second did we doubt them.

In the second trimester of my pregnancy, I was having a difficult professional interaction over email. I felt distraught, like I couldn't get this person to pay attention to me, and their silence hurt me more deeply than I could understand. I began to grind my teeth at night and would wake up in excruciating pain. One night, my wife tried to talk me through it. I told her, as an afterthought, about an article I'd read while unable to sleep, about how the reason Black women die more frequently during childbirth is simply because people ignore them. She wondered aloud if the reason I was so frustrated was because this email exchange triggered in me the much more paralyzing fear of being ignored during or after labor. As soon as she said it the throbbing stopped. When I finally went to the dentist, it turned out that I'd split my molar completely in two.

·　　·　　·

In the video for her song, "Window Seat," Erykah Badu walks the route John F. Kennedy drove before he was assassinated. First, she takes off her shoes. A blurry man standing half a block behind her begins to look around, then follows her, collecting her things as she disrobes. She unzips her purple hoodie. She takes off her pants. She slips her thumbs underneath the waist of her underwear and pauses before bringing them down. Every time she takes something off, she seems to get a new rush of energy. She begins to run a little. Parents usher their children away as she passes.

The act was completely impromptu. On her Twitter feed, Badu said, the video was "shot guerilla style, no crew, 1 take, no closed set, no warning, 2 min., Downtown Dallas, then ran like hell."

This context makes the reactions of those around her all the more captivating. People peek at her while pretending not to care. She seems to be coasting a wave of adrenaline, coaching herself to keep going, committed to the act of becoming completely nude. At the end, she falls, as if struck by an assassin. This is not unlike the act of giving birth, during which, especially if you are able to labor naturally, you move through waves of adrenaline and oxytocin, toward an unthinkable act of opening. Though the video has its own themes and theses, stated explicitly at the end, what I've always been preoccupied by is the way her nakedness is an act of speech on behalf of black womanhood that nobody around her is able to ignore.

I've wanted to write about "Window Seat" as it relates to Detroit for years. I am drawn, perhaps, to the uncanny patriotism of this black woman retracing the last moments of a fallen president's life, stripping her way toward an irrefutable and radical Americanness. It's like Marvin Gaye's rendition of the "Star-Spangled Banner" at the 1983 NBA All-Stars game—that exquisitely relaxed beat and altered tune were a way of claiming a country that tries at every turn to refuse us. Implicit in both actions is the importance of slowing, of prompting a kind of deescalation for the observer, entering us into a new somatic rhythm.

Badu's walk reminds me of a performance by the conceptual artist William Pope.L, in which he crawls on hot cement through New York City, holding a yellow flower. And also it reminds me of a piece wherein the artist Gabrielle Civil holds a red rimmed mirror toward her audience as she reclines in the ocean surf, inviting viewers to see themselves attached to her body. A few years ago, I started to paint black performance artists. Amateur depictions of both these scenes live on canvases in my office. This allows me to ritualize and more fully enter into their chicanery. To feel into these ways of being heard by a world that will not listen.

Badu's guerrilla walk beckons to mind, more recently, the protests that have been taking place in Detroit and other cities around the world for the last hundred days since George Floyd was murdered. The most obvious comparison would be the white woman who showed up naked to a protest in Portland, known as "Naked Athena," facing her vagina squarely at a police line. I am moved by the bombastic nature of this action, by what so many have gleefully hash tagged, "pussy power." But it's the endurance and constant vulnerability of a community that shows up, night after night, in the face of increasing police violence, that astonishes me most.

My fears around the pandemic and my pregnancy have kept me from protesting with my body this year. I've been surprised to see that the marches in Detroit are largely absent from the national news—a grand gesture that has managed to evaporate into thin air, to be ignored or forgotten. But if you follow "Detroit will Breathe" on Instagram, there are black and white photographs of protester's faces broken open in laughter and shouting and song. They have walked in solidarity with Yemen and Palestine. There are images of ocular bones bruised and broken by batons, swollen with tear gas. Calls for donations, a lawsuit against police brutality. Mostly this feed is full of photos torn through with joy. It is a spiritually indelible archive. Proof of life.

• • •

Erykah Badu was a doula and is now a certified midwife. In one video online, she supports the performer Teyana Taylor while she moves through contractions in a bathtub. The two take turns singing and rhyming, even while Taylor's eyes drift back in pain. Badu also sits with people in hospice, singing gospel hymns and playing Richard Pryor performances so they can laugh one more time. In the attempt to assuage my anxiety, I've found a Black doula to work with, who also works with incarcerated women. I've been lucky enough to take a birthing and prenatal yoga class with a queer Black doula, surrounded by other pregnant people of color. These efforts have helped me to cope with the intense fear of being forgotten. It has done incalculable good for me to weep and breathe and feel held by a group of people who know the same fear in their bones.

My aunt Katherine flew from Detroit to Los Angeles to help my mom after I was born. My great aunt Cora Mae moved to Detroit to live with my grandmother after my grandfather died. Both aunts acted as postpartum doulas of a kind. We lost them both this summer. There is something especially cutting to me about losing these aunties while awaiting the birth of my child, like some sort of cosmic test. On FaceTime, I told my aunt Katherine how much I loved her as her head craned backward, looking toward some unseen presence. As if reporting from another dimension, she told my cousin, "I'm washing the baby's feet!"

We were granted access to visit my great aunt Cora Mae weeks after she recovered from COVID. I am convinced that the time she spent without seeing us in person took a toll on her spirit, prompting her to stop eating. Guilt made me obsessed with the idea that she should make it to the age of one hundred, and I rallied like a cheerleader. I showed her my belly. I tried to use the baby as bait. "We're having a baby?" Her voice sang out as I revealed the bump. Later, she told me, in what felt like a goodbye, "You take good care of that baby." The last time I saw her, she was deep asleep. I put the TV on mute and placed a photograph of her with my grandmother in her line of sight. I paced around her body, humming softly the songs that came into my head: "God Only Knows" by the Beach Boys and Smokey Robinson's "Ooh Baby Baby." My wife said a prayer quietly to herself and soon after, the sun burst through the blinds, covering Cora Mae's body as if in music, silver keys of light. My great aunt's remarkable voice emerged only through periodic puffs and sighs. Her leg was curled up like a wing.

American Scholar

FINALIST—ASME AWARD
FOR COVERAGE OF RACE IN
AMERICA

Farah Peterson's essay "The Patriot Slave" was nominated in a new category, for coverage of race in America. ASME believed it was especially important in 2021 to recognize the ways magazines addressed the racial reckoning that gained new force in the United States after the death of George Floyd. But race and racism have been central concerns of the National Magazine Awards for decades. The first National Magazine Award was presented to Look *in 1966 for "its treatment of the racial issue in 1965." The same year* Ebony *received a Certificate of Special Recognition for its issue titled "The White Problem in America." According to the judges, " 'The Patriot Slave' deftly dismantled the narrative that enslaved Americans chose loyalty to their masters over freedom." Farah Peterson is a professor of law at the University of Chicago. She is now working on a book about the law in antebellum America.*

Farah Peterson

The Patriot Slave

During the American Revolution, four times more black Americans served as loyalists to the crown than served as patriots. They joined the British in high numbers in response to promises of emancipation. And yet the enduring memory of black participation in that war would become the image of the faithful slave. The fact of black self-determination during the Revolution and the bizarre cultural memory that developed to suppress and obscure it inaugurated a powerful and enduring American theme. The fantasy of the patriot slave continues to haunt us and to limit us. It is a tendency to think of black people as supporting characters in the national drama—not so much as a selfless people (on the contrary, we are often smeared as freeloaders) but as people without any real selves worth bothering about.

The truth is that black people, like all people, tend to act out of personal hopes and personal fears and not solely to fulfill the wishes or confirm the fears of whites. This may sound obvious, but it has often come as a surprise. White America seems trapped in a dream only occasionally disturbed by dramatic proofs of black agency or of black indifference to its priorities. But soon the default view reestablishes itself: that blacks are the white man's boogeyman or burden, his "original sin," his project for personal moral salvation, or his tool.

W. E. B. Du Bois observed, in 1903, that white interlocutors were always curious about how it felt to be part of what they then termed "the Negro problem." "Being a problem is a strange experience," he reflected, "peculiar even for one who has never been anything else." It is no less strange to be looked upon as a solution—a dumb instrument waiting for the right hand and the right task. The view of the black American as a subsidiary character in the white man's epic, whether cast in the role of villain or of friend, denies us our own personhood. It also denies all Americans the joint strength of a truly shared national vision and the stability of a course directed by mutual concern, respect, and concessions.

In this critical election year, candidates are once again vying for the "black vote." At the same time, some states, bowing to political and economic pressure, have begun to ease the stay-at-home restrictions that diminish the spread of COVID-19, a disease that is far from contained and that has proved disproportionately deadly to black Americans. It may therefore be time to review the history of a persistent national delusion: that blacks are happy to die for the liberty and prosperity of those who would keep us powerless and poor. We are not.

Watson and the Shark, a 1778 painting by the Anglo-American artist John Singleton Copley, provides an early moment of clarity on race in American life. It features a rowboat heavy with men working desperately. Some of them are employed with the oars while another stands wild-eyed, aiming a harpoon at a shark circling the little craft. Three other men almost tilt the boat toward the viewer in their efforts to save a young man in the foreground, a pale, naked figure sinking into the water, but the victim's shocked gaze fails to connect with them.

This monumental work established Copley's reputation on the London art scene in the years after he moved his family to England to escape the Revolutionary War. It captures the moment when Copley's patron, Englishman Brook Watson, lost his leg to a shark while swimming in the Caribbean in his youth. But perhaps unintentionally, the painting captures another story, too, one that an expatriate American artist would have been uniquely positioned to tell. It expresses a moral tale about race and American destiny that, in one guise or another, has haunted this nation since its founding.

One man in the boat is *not* bending his efforts toward the rescue: a black man. His portrait is striking for this era of Western painting, in part because he appears to be a real person, an individual, and not the kind of comic caricature so much more common in eighteenth-century depictions of Africans and African Americans. In the boat, he is the only figure standing still, his stance heroic, even messianic, posed in white, windblown clothing at the pinnacle of the composition. The naked form of the youthful Watson with his streaming blond hair catches the eye, as it was meant to—artists of this era considered the classical Greek male nude one of the highest aesthetic accomplishments in painting. But of all the figures in the painting, only that of the black man would make a complete composition on its own.

That is not to say he is disconnected from the action: in his left hand, he grasps the end of a thick rope, which falls in a looping path down over the side of the boat to loosely encircle Watson's arm before disappearing into the water. The rope is like nothing so much as an umbilical cord. The black man's other hand, outstretched and palm down, is in tension with—is definitely in communication with—the upturned white hand of the drowning Watson. And his face is serious. One reads ambivalence there and also trepidation. Although this figure holds the rope, and although he is positioned as the hero of the composition, he has not yet committed to saving the drowning man.

This is a portrait of a man in crisis. Conventionally, the painting is about Watson's crisis, in the moment of his maiming. But the black man's crisis at this moment of decision is more severe and more touching. And the artist, a worldly, wealthy refugee from America's Revolution, could also be communicating an urgent message to the London viewer. The message is that "we"—white, European, Anglo people—cannot make it in the dangerous New World without "them." That is, without the New World man, this person with African skin in European clothing. It is in the black man's hands to effectuate the birth of the naked, classical Greek figure into the time and place of his new life in America. And, the artist seems to worry, it may be in the black man's hands to refuse that birth.

·   ·   ·

American slavery, before and after the American Revolution, was a relationship of intimate violence. When I teach the history of slavery, that intimacy surprises students, as do the pervasive and explicit acknowledgments by whites, in slave codes, in trial transcripts, and in memoirs, of the enslaved person's intellect and humanity. This surprise is a product of the current moment in American history, not of the facts of life in a family or on a plantation that included both enslaved and free people. Looking back on antebellum slavery from the perspective of the twenty-first century requires looking through the distorted lens of almost a hundred years of Jim Crow. The sensibility of the twentieth century's laws forbidding touching, forbidding "miscegenation"—a sensibility that meant that if a black child accidentally dipped his toe into a whites-only swimming pool, management might drain the pool before opening it for use again by white people—reflects a culture of fastidious separation that developed only after slavery's end, an anxious reaction to the loss of a more brutal racial hierarchy.

But the experience of slavery was one of closeness, not separation. Black people worked as head planters, expert agriculturalists, foremen and overseers, skillful artisans in white-owned factories. They ran white households as butlers and worked as chefs, huntsmen, midwives, and breeders of livestock. White masters turned to these black people for advice about their businesses, their laborers, the methods of production. An enslaved man might be the master's half-white uncle or cousin or even his brother. A white man's black property might be the friend he had grown up playing and squabbling with, before one was trained for tyranny and the other for subjugation. For that matter, enslaved women breastfed white children, provided the difficult and intimate care the white elderly required in their failing years, and were involved in long-term sexual relationships with white men whose dominion over their bodies the law confirmed and protected.

These relationships must have involved a constant tension and, on the part of the white owner, tremendous fear of the resentful impulses of the people who prepared his food and cared for his dependents. On large plantations, the master's fear of the enslaved people in his household would have joined with a sense of profound alienation from the enslaved families he kept working in his fields. In spite of laws like one in South Carolina outlawing drumming and black social gatherings, there was no way to prevent slave quarters from becoming places where black people might experience, in moments of exhausted respite, their own relationships and forms of spirituality, and the comforts of the music and other forms of cultural expression from the unimaginably distant homelands of their forebears. A white master could not help but fear that behind those unlocked doors, enslaved men and women might even engage in dangerous conversations and nurse private hopes and yearnings.

The British understood these fears and tried to exploit them. In 1775, Lord Dunmore, the royal governor of Virginia, became frustrated with the resistance to imperial tax laws and angry that some Virginians had begun to stockpile weapons. He decided to teach them a lesson by issuing a proclamation promising freedom to any slave who left a rebellious master and came ready to bear arms in defense of the crown. Many slaves flocked to his banner. In Virginia, where it was illegal for masters to emancipate their slaves, Dunmore's Proclamation held out what must have seemed a unique chance for self-determination. And the psychological effect of this "Ethiopian Regiment," marching to war wearing sashes proclaiming "Liberty to Slaves," was profound for black Americans throughout the colonies. In Philadelphia that year, when a white woman "reprimanded" a black man for not jumping into the street so that she could use the sidewalk, he replied, "stay you d[amne]d white bitch, 'till Lord Dunmore and his black regiment come, and then we will see who is to take the wall."

Historians have long argued over whether the American Revolution destabilized slavery, and whether so-called charters of freedom like the Declaration of Independence and the Constitution committed the new nation to emancipation. Edmund Morgan, Sean Wilentz, and Gordon S. Wood, among others, have eloquently argued that the Revolution and those early documents created a nation based on the principle of (eventual) equality. There is doubtless some truth to that. In the North, where whites enslaved people in fewer numbers and where slavery was far less important to the economy, the Revolution ushered in real and lasting change. Some states, like Rhode Island, took a lesson from Dunmore and promised emancipation to slaves who agreed to join the militia. Other northern states, like Massachusetts, allowed men to avoid military service by sending a servant to fill their place. Some men sent their slaves, offering freedom as compensation. Historians estimate that 5,000 black men fought for the patriot cause. But black Americans living in, say, Washington and Jefferson's Virginia experienced the Revolution differently. To an enslaved American in the South, trying to make choices about his life, it would have seemed that he could grasp freedom for himself, his children, or even his great-great-grandchildren only by joining the British side of the fight—or by taking advantage of the chaos of war to disappear.

Indeed, in the South, the Revolution was fought in part to protect slavery. According to historian Douglas Egerton, Lord Dunmore's 1775 Proclamation helped to convince "irresolute masters to join the call for Independence." For these incipient patriots, Dunmore's threat to the institution of slavery was the one insult they could not bear. The following year, Jefferson made this point explicitly. We all remember the part of the Declaration of Independence proclaiming that "all men are created equal" and "that they are endowed by their Creator with certain unalienable Rights," including "Liberty." Less well remembered is an item among the complaints the Declaration listed to justify independence from Britain: Americans were rebelling, it said, because the British crown had "excited domestic insurrections amongst us"— insurrections of slaves. This statement, and many others like it, undergird the argument of historians who hold that in spite of all the liberty talk of this period, the Founding Era wasn't about freedom or equality at all. As the historian Alan Taylor put it, some Americans, while demanding liberty from the British, simultaneously felt that "white men could be free only if allowed to hold blacks as property." Although never implemented, a law passed in Virginia to promote enlistment would have granted "one able bodied healthy negroe Slave between the age of ten and forty years" to each new recruit.

And so, even though the Revolution inspired white northerners to move toward emancipation, and even though Virginia changed its law after the war to allow masters the discretion to emancipate their own slaves, it's important to see these changes soberly, from the perspective of a contemporary black American observer. To a person whose fate was on the line, it would have been clear that the new nation had no intention of ending the system of kidnapping, family separation, rape, theft, and forced labor that the economy of the South depended on. No fatal misgivings prevented northern representatives to the Constitutional Convention from founding a nation in partnership with representatives from the southern states committed to the position that it was fine to torture other human beings for personal profit. As the historian Paul Finkelman has persuasively argued, the antislavery arguments of such prominent delegates as George Mason and Luther Martin did not carry the day. Although some northerners grumbled about the additional voting power the three-fifths clause gave southern states, aside from one moving speech by Gouverneur Morris, most of the qualms that northerners expressed concerned sectional power and economics, not morality. As Elbridge Gerry of Massachusetts put it, "Blacks are property, and are used to the southward as horses and cattle to the northward; and why should their representation be increased to the southward on account of the number of slaves, than horses or oxen to the north?"

Indeed, by protecting the political power of the states most dependent on it, the new Constitution tended to strengthen the institution of slavery, at least in the near term. Historical counterfactuals are difficult, but it is possible that if the American colonies had remained in the British Empire, black Americans could have benefited from Britain's 1833 law abolishing slavery. But because American patriots had, in the old cliché, "struck a blow for liberty," they were not in the empire in 1833. And as a result, after the enslaved people of Britain's Jamaican colony were formally freed, another entire generation of black men and women remained in bondage and penury under American constitutional government.

And the experience of slavery remained one of both violence and intimacy. White Americans spoke of slaves with pity, for example, when the Virginia legislature threatened to execute those "unfortunate people" who had been "seduced" by Dunmore's promises. There was pity in these relationships—how could there not be? Again, the humanity of their bondsmen, the unfairness of their fate, would have been obvious to most slave owners. There was also a great deal of shame. Jefferson frequently lamented slavery, which he called a cause for "heavy reproach," a system that by "permitting one half the citizens thus to trample on the rights of the other, transforms those into despots, and these into enemies." In his *Notes on the State of Virginia,* he admitted: "I tremble for my country when I reflect that God is just: that his justice cannot sleep for ever." But the proof the Revolution gave, that enslaved men and women would grasp freedom and take up arms if they could, only amplified white Americans' enduring fear of "insurrection." That is one reason why, in spite of their regret over the situation, these Founders did not contemplate emancipation. Their pity and shame were limited by a horror of receiving a just return on their investment. Masters feared the vengeance a black population might exact if not continually beaten into submission. In Jefferson's words, "We have the wolf by the ear and we can neither hold him, nor safely let him go."

Their pity was also limited by greed and ambition—and not just personal ambition, but their patriotic hopes for national greatness. When Americans won the war for independence, the former colonies were left alone on a continent with powerful imperial rivals for territory and dominion, including the British to the north and the Spanish to the south and west. Americans feared that without the economic power the enslaved workers produced, the new nation could not possibly remain independent and thrive. They feared, in other words, that "we," white Americans, could not make it without "them," the half brothers they stole from and savaged.

Like all intimate relationships that involve force, that between master and slave relied on a great deal of fiction: the master told the slave that ownership was benevolence; the slave performed fidelity for the master. The American Revolution forced a reckoning. Slave owners looking to rebuild their lives after the dislocation of war faced a double deprivation. They had, of course, lost all of those black men and women who had escaped or died in the attempt. A provision in the Treaty of Paris addressed this, demanding that Britain's fleets withdraw "without causing any

Destruction, or carrying away any Negroes or other Property of the American inhabitants." Perhaps more serious, however, was the slave owner's loss of those tacit narratives—including the fiction of the slave's resignation to his condition—that had made the master's own crimes bearable and helped to dull his rational fear.

A comforting fable developed in response to this anxiety. In the wake of the Revolution, Americans wanted to believe in an archetype of the loyal black servant, happy to support the nation in any capacity, content with his half life in the white man's shadow. So even though four times as many black men had joined the British side, an image of the patriot slave became part of how Americans remembered the Revolution and how, through the cult of George Washington, they constructed a national identity.

The 1780 portrait of Washington by John Trumbull helped establish this theme by prominently featuring Washington's slave, William Lee. Indulging an affectation common to that era, the artist put Lee in a feathered turban. Washington stands centered on a rocky promontory against a backdrop of storm clouds and a distant sea scene. Taken together with the clouds, the red notes on a ship in the distance, on the horse's bridle, and in the leaping flame of the turban feather give the impression that Washington is encircled by the fire and smoke of war. The victorious general points toward the only area of clear sky, his finger indicating a planted flag. The figure meant to represent Lee stands behind Washington's horse, gazing toward Washington for direction.

Lee is also prominent in Charles Willson Peale's 1779 *George Washington at Princeton*. Peale's is another triple portrait of the general, his horse, and his slave, although here the horse may have received higher billing. And this work was also popular—Peale reproduced it to order at least twenty times. The best versions of the painting, including the original in the collection of the Pennsylvania Academy of the Fine Arts and the copy hanging in the U.S. Senate Gallery, show a brown-skinned Lee in profile. His shadowed figure is part of a visual pile of the accoutrements of war, including horseflesh, weapons, and flags. Although both Peale and Trumbull purport to depict the same historical figures, their versions of Lee do not resemble each other. Unlike Washington's, Lee's actual features were not important to the portraitists. He is present in these images not as a person but as one of the tools of Washington's greatness and as a symbol of the essential fidelity of the black American.

The image of Washington with Lee beside him appealed strongly to the American psyche. It reappeared in moments of anxious reflection on the national character, when Americans looked back to Washington to find a paragon of public virtue. In 1859, *The Constitution*, a Washington, DC, newspaper, published an article titled "The Personal Appearance of Washington," in which an anonymous author described likely made-up encounters with the "chief." One of those memories was from the summer before Washington died: "He rode a purely white horse" that "almost seemed conscious that he bore on his back the Father of his Country." (Pause a moment—the *horse* had a country?) After dwelling on Washington's horsemanship, the author continued, "Behind him, at the distance of perhaps forty yards, came Billy Lee, his body servant, who had periled his life in many a field, beginning on the heights of Boston in 1775, and ending in 1781, when Cornwallis surrendered, and the captive army, with unexpressible chagrin, laid down their arms at Yorktown."

Although the article was about Washington's appearance, the author lavished attention on his companion: "Billy rode a cream-colored horse of the finest form, and his old revolutionary cocked hat, indicated that its owner had often heard the roar of cannon and small arms, and had encountered many trying scenes. Billy was a dark mulatto. His master speaks highly of him in his will, and provides for his support."

During the nineteenth century, many Americans felt that Washington represented the nation at its greatest and that by emulating his strengths and virtues, the country could achieve its highest destiny. Among his admirable attributes was the fact that he had a very faithful slave. Lee's loyalty was something that Americans knew and valued about the first president, just as they knew how well Washington sat a horse, maintained camp discipline, and guarded his personal character. Indeed, it was something that helped to define him and, through him, the nation.

Lee was a real man, but it is difficult to get to know him. No historian has written a book-length biography of him. It seems unlikely that this would be true of any white person who rode with Washington to battle, stood at his side during wartime councils, and traveled with him to Philadelphia for the Constitutional Convention. For Lee, as with so many of our black ancestors, there is not enough documentary evidence to reconstruct a full life story. Instead, we are left to catch glimpses of him through stray papers. Washington's cash accounts show that the year after the death of William Lee's first master, Colonel John Lee, the colonel's widow hastened to sell off two half-white teenagers: "Mulatto Will" and his brother Frank. She received a good price for them. George Washington's papers show that he trained Frank as a butler and William in horsemanship and hunting.

Washington's papers tell us that William Lee then went to war as Washington's personal valet. An eyewitness to the Battle of Yorktown remembered that "when the last redoubt was captured, Washington turned to Knox and said, 'The work is done, and *well* done;' and then called to his servant, 'Billy, hand me my horse.'" This recollection punctuates the decisive battle of the war with a reminder that Washington's slave stood on hand, ready to serve. These occasional mentions by other men give Lee's experience in the war some color, but through a veil of white contempt. An army physician recalled that he saw Lee halting at an overlook "and, having unslung the large telescope that he always carried in a leathern case, with a martial air applied it to his eye, and reconnoitred the enemy." Note that he said "with a martial *air*," as though Lee were a child playing at war.

We also know that Lee fell in love with and married a black woman while living with Washington in Philadelphia. We know this because Washington wrote to his business manager that he felt obligated to gratify Lee's request to bring his wife to Mount Vernon when the war ended, "if it can be complied with on reasonable terms"—although in truth, said the great man, he had "never wished to see her" again. One wonders what the free woman did, or if it was just the fact of her freedom, that made her so obnoxious to the general. Washington's letters and papers also tell us that after the war, in the course of his servitude, Lee fell twice, breaking both of his kneecaps. Disliking the idea of an idle slave, Washington converted his old campaign companion into a shoemaker, work Lee could do sitting down, and expected him to make enough shoes to keep the plantation well supplied.

Washington did leave a final note about Lee in his will, a document widely reproduced in national newspapers. The will granted William "(calling himself William Lee)" a pension and also his freedom, *if he wanted it*—a tacit acknowledgment that the deathbed emancipation may have come too late for its beneficiary to enjoy it. And even these small gestures seemed to have earned Lee some resentment. In a recollection of Washington's life, one of the general's descendants painted Lee as "a most interesting relic of the chief"—that is, a leftover thing from Washington's life suitable for a tourist to gawk at. Yet, noting that Lee had a house and a pension, he spoke disapprovingly of Lee's turn to alcoholism. A home to live in and a guaranteed income had made "Billy" "a spoiled child of fortune. He was quite intemperate at times." Charles Willson Peale, who had been propelled to fame in part by his early portrait of the general and his slave, used a visit to Mount Vernon to lecture Lee "on the subject of health and right living."

But let's allow the man, William Lee, to rest. In this case, it was not the person who made the greatest impact on American culture but the idea of him. Lee was hardly unique in this. It was likewise the *idea* of the slave rebels at Stono in 1739, of Denmark

Vesey in 1822, and of Nat Turner in 1831 that created terror in the white imagination, justifying cruelties toward other black people far out of proportion to the real accomplishments of those freedom fighters. The terrifying image of the vengeful slave was one side of a coin. On the other side was Billy Lee, the docile creature depicted by Trumbull and Peale. So powerful was the idea of Billy that it was not undermined by the fact that many of Washington's slaves fled Mount Vernon during the war. It survived even as, the historian Erica Armstrong Dunbar has shown, George and Martha Washington spent decades pursuing a woman who had managed to escape the executive mansion in Philadelphia. It endured undiminished by the ever-present genre of the runaway slave announcement, advertisements scattered through any nineteenth-century newspaper, offering rewards for slaves who had taken advantage of a moment of inattention or trust to steal themselves away.

The myth remained potent even to describe people such as Christopher Sheels—like Lee, one of Washington's body servants—who had failed in an attempt to free himself. Washington discovered Sheels's plot to escape with his fiancée in a boat docked at Alexandria. A surviving letter shows how Washington kept his discovery of their plans secret while colluding with the fiancée's owner to foil their attempt. The next mention of Sheels in the documentary record is from three months later, in a diary account by a witness to Washington's last moments. The recollection, first published in 1837, mentions that Sheels remained standing for many hours by Washington's bedside as the general slowly expired. A Currier and Ives print made much of this detail. The firm's *Death of Washington* print featured a slave standing by Washington's bed at mournful attention. Some renderings also show another slave kneeling, distraught, or a cluster of slaves, visible through an open doorway, weeping and consoling each other. These figures stood as a symbol of national sentiment—the way this era of portraiture often included a dog gazing at the master to symbolize loyalty. This is not to say that Sheels did not care for George Washington; people often love their abusers. It's just to point out that what the public wanted—and these inexpensive prints were so popular that the firm printed eight different versions of this scene—was the reassurance that the image offered. There was an appetite for an exaggerated show of a slave's love for the man who personified the nation, a love that proved itself anew in that man's most vulnerable moment.

That southerners had convinced themselves of this fable is evident in the way they talked about slavery. Northerners were wrong to grumble about the South's additional representation in Congress due to the three-fifths clause, said South Carolina congressman Charles Pinckney in 1820. The only thing unfair about it was that black slaves were not counted *more*. Slaves had always been "more valuable to the Union . . . than any equal number of inhabitants in the Northern and Eastern states," the congressman said, pointing to the work slaves had done during the Revolution to build patriot fortifications and fill out the ranks of the northern militias. And, "notwithstanding in the course of the Revolution the Southern States were continually overrun by the British, and that every negro in them had an opportunity of leaving their owners, few did; proving thereby not only a most remarkable attachment to their owners, but the mildness of the treatment from which their affection sprang."

In fact, 20,000 enslaved people responded to the 1775 Dunmore Proclamation and the even broader 1779 Philipsburg Proclamation and served with the British forces. This striking figure, historian Maya Jasanoff has noted, made the American Revolution "the occasion for the largest emancipation of North American slaves until the U.S. Civil War."

But southerners persisted in this fantasy. Slaves and masters complemented each other, they explained, to the benefit of each. In the words of a University of Virginia professor in the 1850s, while the black man "is naturally lazy, and too improvident to work for himself, he will often labor for a master . . . because he feels that, in his master, he has a protector and a friend." Among slaves' essential strengths, said the South Carolina politician William Harper, were his "fidelity—often proof against all temptation—even death itself," along with "a disposition to be attached to, as well as to respect those, whom they are taught to regard as superiors." There might be some unpleasantness between master and slave, admitted another politician, James Henry Hammond, but the same was true of all loving relationships. "Slaveholders are kind masters, as men usually are kind husbands, parents and friends," he explained. "In each of these relations, as serious suffering as frequently arises from uncontrolled passions, as ever does in that of master and slave, and with as little chance of indemnity. Yet you would not on that account break them up."

This story was so consistent and so pervasive that in the 1850s, an Englishman traveling through the southern states ventured to ask a slave to confirm it. The enslaved man explained to him that he had been born in Virginia, sold "on account of the bankruptcy of his owner," and had then been "parted from a sister" and had "never heard of her since." In the face of this tale of helplessness and heartbreaking loss, the Englishman thought to "try him" by saying he "supposed the slaves were pretty well treated." The enslaved man replied that their "treatment depends entirely . . . on the person they belong to. Indeed, how can it be otherwise?"

"But," said I, "we are told that you prefer slavery, and would not be free if you could." His only answer was a short, contemptuous laugh.

The Englishman reflected that he "almost felt ashamed of having made so silly an observation." But he could have been forgiven for his mistake, since Americans in the best position to know better held onto that silly idea even through the Civil War. One southerner admitted, as late as 1864, to the belief "that a very large number of the negroes will not accept their freedom and that, by one name or another, pretty much of the old relations will be re-established." According to the historian Eugene Genovese, when black people disappointed this expectation by embracing freedom, it left a class of former masters resentful and traumatized.

The story that these Americans wanted to believe, that they resisted giving up even in the face of all the contrary evidence, is beautifully captured in another painting, the antebellum masterpiece *Washington Crossing the Delaware*. The 1851 canvas by Emanuel Leutze shows General Washington standing heroically in the center of a boat, crossing the frozen river by night to surprise a Hessian encampment and accomplish a victory that would prove a turning point in the war. This painting could be the next panel in the story that begins with Copley's *Watson and the Shark*. It is white America's answer to the warning implicit in the earlier painting, a white man's fantasy about how the narrative must unfold. Certain details are the same: both are monumental water scenes featuring a pyramid of earnest figures in nearly identical wooden boats. But in the later image, the black figure has rescued the white man, who now occupies the place where he once stood. The white titular subject of the painting now commands the little craft, clothed in military glory, while men of all races ply the oars, helping him toward his destiny. As for the black man—well, William Lee is also there. But in strong contrast to the humanity and individuality of the black figure in the Copley painting, the black figure in *Washington Crossing the Delaware* has his face turned away and in shadow. He has made his choice, throwing his lot in with the group. Now he sits anonymously at the oar, more a symbol than a man, and almost under Washington's foot.

•   •   •

The patriot slave still exercises a powerful sway over the American imagination. This is the character Donald Trump refers to when, in the midst of his rallies, he tells the crowd to "look at my African American!" It is not the person himself, that lonely black attendee, but the *idea* of him. Indeed, without understanding the pull of this old fable, it is difficult to explain the common spectacle of Trump's white supporters displaying "Blacks for Trump" paraphernalia at his rallies.

And the delusion of the patriot slave is not partisan. Some Democrats also see the black voter as an anonymous figure who can be counted on to toil away at the oar, asking nothing for himself. It is a self-defeating attitude. If black turnout in 2016 had matched that in 2012, Hillary Clinton would have won the Electoral College. And yet many Democrats continue to take black voters for granted, entertaining the idea of nominating candidates who cannot connect with black communities or who have used prior public office to harass and disparage us.

In reality, we black Americans see ourselves as the protagonists in our own story and not merely as the helpmeets to others. There is a message in the poll numbers from the last election: to paraphrase James Baldwin, I am not *yours*. White Americans ignore this message at their peril. Like Copley's central figure in *Watson and the Shark*, the black voter asked to rescue this country may well pause a moment to wonder which is the more dangerous monster in the water. It is a painful fact, but one that cannot be brushed away, that history has taught us to doubt whether our participation will ever earn our welcome as full members of our nation. White Americans must learn to close this gap, and quickly. Reach out and grasp our hands as equals—or we both drown together.

New York Times Magazine

FINALIST—PROFILE WRITING

Who doesn't love Weird Al Yankovic? Or at least reading about him? Apparently, no one—or at least no one who reads magazines. As the judges who nominated this story for the National Magazine Award for Profile Writing said: " 'The Weirdly Enduring Appeal of Weird Al Yankovic' demystifies a seemingly baffling pop icon in prose as nimble and playful as its subject's music, making a droll and persuasive case for the artist's genius." Sam Anderson is a staff writer at the New York Times Magazine. His piece "David's Ankles," about Michelangelo's sculpture, won the National Magazine Award for Essays and Criticism in 2017. His book Boom Town: The Fantastical Saga of Oklahoma City, Its Chaotic Founding, Its Apocalyptic Weather, Its Purloined Basketball Team, and the Dream of Becoming a World-Class Metropolis was published in 2018.

Sam Anderson

The Weirdly
Enduring Appeal
of Weird Al
Yankovic

L ast summer, in the middle of what struck me as an otherwise very full life, I went to my first Weird Al Yankovic
concert. Weird Al, for anyone reading this through a
golden monocle, is the most renowned comedy musician in the
history of the multiverse—a force of irrepressible wackiness who,
back in the 1980s, built a preposterous career out of song parodies and then, somehow, never went away. After forty years,
Yankovic is now no longer a novelty but an institution—a garish
bright patch in the middle of America's pop-cultural wallpaper,
a completely ridiculous national treasure, an absurd living
legend.

I have spent much of my life chortling, alone in tiny rooms, to
Weird Al's music. ("I churned butter once or twice living in an
Amish paradise"—LOL.) And yet somehow it had never occurred
to me to go out and see him live. I think this is for roughly the
same reason that it has never occurred to me to make my morning commute in a hot-air balloon or to brush my teeth in Niag-
ara Falls. Parody is not the kind of music you go out to see in
person—it's the joke version of that music. A parody concert felt
like a category error, like confusing a mirror for a window. To me,
Weird Al had always been a fundamentally private pleasure; I was
perfectly content to have him living in my headphones and on

YouTube and—very occasionally, when I wanted to aggravate my family—out loud on my home speakers.

The show was in New York, at Forest Hills Stadium—a storied outdoor arena that once hosted the U.S. Open, as well as concerts by the Beatles, Jimi Hendrix, and Bob Dylan. It was late July, the hottest weekend of a punishingly hot summer, and the humidity was so thick it felt as if gravity had doubled. The backs of my knees were sweating onto the fronts of my knees. A performance in this context struck me as a heavy lift, even for a normal rock star. For a parody rock star, it seemed basically impossible. Deep in my brain, a blasphemous little wrinkle kept wondering, secretly, if the concert might even be sad. Weird Al was on the brink of turning sixty, and his defining early hits ("Eat It," "Like a Surgeon") were several decades old, which means they were made for a version of the culture that is now essentially Paleolithic. Down in my sweaty palm, every ten seconds, my phone dosed out new shots of racism and bullying and disaster and alarm. I felt exhausted, on every possible level, and I assumed everyone else did, too. Would anyone even show up?

The answer, to that at least, was yes. Long before showtime, the Weird Al fans started streaming in. The vibe was lighthearted reverence. It was a benevolent Weird Al cosplay cult. There were so many Hawaiian shirts that it felt like an elaborate code, some secret language composed entirely of loud patterns: parrots, hot dogs, palm trees, flowers, cars, accordions, pineapples, whales, bananas, sunsets. Everyone was so floridly mismatched that they seemed, paradoxically, to be matching—a great harmony of clashing. I saw Weird Al T-shirts from ten tours ago, Weird Al hats covered with Weird Al pins, every possible colorway of checkerboard Vans. Down toward the stage, hard-core fans greeted one another like relatives reunited at a wedding. Ages seemed to range from eighty to four.

When Weird Al appeared, waggling his arms zanily, long hair flapping in the hot wind, the crowd greeted him with a surge of joy. Yankovic's Hawaiian shirt was black and gold, traced with a pattern of tropical fronds. He still looked oddly young, as if his face had been locked into place, for copyright reasons, in 1989. Although he no longer sports a mustache or wears glasses—he shaved and got Lasik surgery more than twenty years ago, to the dismay of some fans—the other essentials remain. Weird Al has a face designed for making faces: large nostrils, wide forehead, bendy mouth, chin like a crescent moon. His eyeballs seem somehow double-jointed, able to bulge wide or disappear into a squint. His cheekbones pop like crab apples. He uses that face to mimic music-world clichés: rock-star sneer, boy-band smolder, teen-pop grin, gangsta-rap glower.

Onstage, Weird Al sat on a wooden stool and started to snap like a lounge singer. With an orchestra swelling behind him—the tour was called "Strings Attached"—he kicked into a soulful medley of 1980s parodies. If that does not sound great to you, if it in fact sounds like a very particular flavor of sonic hell, I am here to tell you something. Weird Al was absolutely belting. He was singing the bejesus out of this ridiculous music. I leaned back in my chair, reassessing core assumptions I had made about life. Was this somehow part of the joke—that Weird Al was an amazing singer? His voice was athletic and precise; he was rippling through intricate trills and runs. By the time he reached the medley's climax—"Like a Surgeon," his 1985 parody of Madonna's "Like a Virgin"—Yankovic was stretching for high notes and holding them over his head for the crowd to admire, like an Olympic weight lifter who had just snatched 500 pounds.

The show went on for two hot hours. The concrete theater was a convection oven powered by body heat, and Weird Al stomped and strutted and danced through the crowd, occasionally kicking his leg straight up, like actually vertical, 180 degrees. Sometimes he disappeared for thirty seconds and then came bursting back onstage in a costume: Kurt Cobain, Amish rapper, Devo. During "White & Nerdy," he did doughnuts all over the stage on a Segway. Before long, the masses of Weird Al's famous curls were stuck to his face, and if you looked closely you could see sweat pouring off his elbows. The parody songs, live, were tight and hard and urgent, supplemented occasionally by video clips, projected onto a giant screen, of Weird Al cameos on *30 Rock* and *The Simpsons* and the old *Naked Gun* movies. It felt less like a traditional concert than a Broadway musical crossed with a comedy film festival crossed with a tent revival.

The crowd was rolling through tantric nerdgasms, sustained explosions of belonging and joy. It felt religious. Near the end of the show, during the chorus of "Amish Paradise," as the entire stadium started swinging its arms in rhythm, I unexpectedly found myself near tears. Weird Al was dressed in a ridiculous black suit, with a top hat and a long fake beard, and he was rapping about churning butter and raising barns, and everyone was singing along. I could feel deep pools of solitary childhood emotion—loneliness, affection, vulnerability, joy—beginning to stir inside me, beginning to trickle out and flow into this huge common reservoir. All the private love I had ever had for this music, for not only Weird Al's parodies but for the originals—now it was here, outside, vibrating through the whole crowd. Weird Al had pulled off a strange emotional trick: He had brought the isolated energy of all our tiny rooms into this one big public space. When he left the stage, we stomped for more, and he came back out and played "Yoda," his classic revision of the Kinks' "Lola," and then he left again, and I decided that this was the single best performance of any kind that I had ever seen in my life. Weird Al Yankovic was a full-on rock star, a legitimate performance monster. He was not just a parasite of cultural power but—somehow, improbably—a source of it himself.

. . .

Once upon a time, there was a boy who wet his bed. He wet every kind of bed available: bunk beds, water beds, blowup beds, foldout beds. At sleepovers, he wet sleeping bags. If he didn't have a bed handy, sometimes he just wet his pants. He was fluent in that terrible feeling: warm relief at the wrong time, in the wrong place, turning into cold shame. So many mornings were so shameful.

This was not the boy's only problem: He also threw up in cars, sometimes in such pungent floods that it would ruin the upholstery forever. Occasionally he would cry at school, for no obvious reason, baffling his teachers and classmates.

The boy's family moved a lot, which meant that he wet beds in many different houses, threw up in many different cars and cried in many different school districts. When kids played kiss tag at recess, the boy would not be kissed—if a girl accidentally cornered him, she would realize who it was, then turn and run away. And so the boy spent many recesses alone, on the edge of the playground, picking up trash to earn the whole class bonus points so the teacher would allow them to watch a special movie together at the end of the year. Sometimes he would stand near the play structure, hiding his uncool shoes behind a metal pole, watching the other kids play, and he would repeat a mantra in his head: "I wish I could just be normal."

The idea of normalcy, to the boy, came mostly from television. It was some vague constellation of money, crowds, hair gel, brand-name jackets, and confidence—the kind of glittering ease that animated the great American mainstream, visible in its sitcoms and movies and slow-motion basketball highlights and, perhaps most of all, in its music videos. Weirdness, by contrast, meant everything in his own life: chubbiness, loneliness, boredom, clunky glasses, off-brand clothing, frozen bananas dipped in carob, lawn darts in his grandmother's backyard.

The bed-wetting boy, dear reader, was me. And I tell you this story not just for sympathy (although there is that) but because it was in this era that I first encountered the music of Weird Al Yankovic.

Weird Al, it seemed to me, had a perfect sense of humor. He shrieked on MTV, squeaked rubber chickens, and punctuated his songs with percussive belching. But he was more than just funny. Even as a child, I understood on some intuitive level that Weird Al was not merely the Shakespeare of terrible food puns ("Might as well face it you're addicted to spuds") or an icon of antistyle (poodle fro, enormous glasses, questionable mustache, Hawaiian shirts) but a spiritual technician doing important work down in the engine room of the American soul. I could not have said why, but I felt it.

As his name suggested, Weird Al's comedy operated right at the hot spot of my childhood agonies: weirdness versus normalcy, insider versus outsider. What a Weird Al parody did was enact a tiny revolution. It took the whole glamorous architecture of American mainstream cool—Michael Jackson's otherworldly moves, Madonna's sexual taboos—and extracted all of the coolness. Into that void, Weird Al inserted the least cool person in the world: himself. And by proxy, all the rest of us weirdos, along with our uncool lives. "Beat It," a ubiquitous superhit about avoiding street violence, became "Eat It," a nasally monologue about picky eating. ("Have a banana, have a whole bunch—it doesn't matter what you had for lunch. Just eat it.") "I Love Rock 'n Roll," a churning anthem of hard living and the devil's music, became "I Love Rocky Road," a squawking paean to stuffing your face with ice cream. It is no accident that much of Yankovic's music was about food—everyone ate food, every day, celebrities and nerds alike. It was the great equalizer.

This switcheroo was, for me, thrilling. I would sit there with my brother in our unglamorous living room, in a town where Michael Jackson would never even consider performing, and I would feel dorkily empowered. Weird Al had flipped the polarities of weirdness and normalcy. We had made it into the TV. We were normal.

Weird Al has now been releasing song parodies for seven presidential administrations. He has outlasted two popes and five Supreme Court justices. He is one of only five artists (along with his early muses, Michael Jackson and Madonna) to have had a top-forty single in each of the last four decades. Yankovic has turned out to be one of America's great renewable resources. He is a timeless force that expresses itself through hyperspecific cultural moments, the way heat from the center of the earth manifests, on the surface, through the particularity of geysers. In 1996, after Coolio's "Gangsta's Paradise" became a national earworm, Weird Al took its thumping beat and its heavenly choir and turned it into "Amish Paradise," a ridiculous banger about rural chores. When Chamillionaire's "Ridin." hit number one in 2006, Weird Al took a rap about driving in a car loaded with drugs and translated it into a monologue about the glories of being a nerd. Whatever is popular at the moment, Yankovic can hack into its source code and reprogram it.

His work has inspired waves of creative nerds. Andy Samberg, the actor and a member of the comedy group the Lonely Island, told me that he grew up having Weird Al dance parties with his family. "Each new generation of younger kids is like, 'Wait, this can exist?'" Samberg said.

Lin-Manuel Miranda, a Weird Al obsessive, credits Yankovic as an influence on *Hamilton*. Miranda once lip-synced "Taco Grande" (a Mexican-food-themed parody of the 1990 hit "Rico Suave") in front of his sixth-grade class, He told me that he prefers many Weird Al songs to the originals. "Weird Al is a perfectionist," Miranda said. "Every bit as much as Michael Jackson or Kurt Cobain or Madonna or any artist he has ever spoofed. So you get the musical power of the original along with this incredible twist of Weird Al's voice and Weird Al's brain. The original songs lose none of their power, even when they're on a polka with burping sound effects in the background. In fact, it accelerates their power. It's both earnest and a parody."

Michael Schur, the creator of *The Good Place* and cocreator of *Parks and Recreation*, remembers the force of Weird Al's 1992 parody of Nirvana.

"'Smells Like Teen Spirit' comes out, and it's like the perfect voice for all the simmering anger of an entire generation of kids,"

Schur said. "That song is vicious and angry and aggressive but also laconic and disaffected and scary. And it was immediately a gigantic thing in American culture. Then Weird Al does 'Smells Like Nirvana' and completely deflates it—the importance and seriousness and angst. That's a service he has always provided: to remind people that rock is about grittiness and authenticity and finding your voice and relating to an audience, but it's also fundamentally absurd. Being a rock star is stupid. We as a culture are genuflecting at the altar of these rock stars, and Weird Al comes out with this crazy curly hair and an accordion, and he just blows it all into smithereens by singing about Spam. It's wonderful."

Schur paused. He said there were heated debates, sometimes, in comedy writing rooms, about the merits of Weird Al's work—some cynics argue that his jokes aren't actually great, that people overrate them because they're nostalgic for their childhoods. But Schur insisted that, regardless of what you think about this lyric or that lyric, Weird Al represented the deep egalitarian spirit of our culture.

"It's a truly American thing, to be like: Get over yourself," Schur said. "Everybody get over yourselves. Madonna, get over yourself. Kurt Cobain, get over yourself. Eminem, get over yourself. No one gets to be that important in America."

. . .

Weird Al lives in Los Angeles, up in the Hollywood Hills, in a house that, he was told, once belonged to the rapper Heavy D. The house is clean, minimalist, sophisticated—the opposite of Weird Al's public persona. There are no Twinkie-shaped lounge chairs or florid shag carpets. It is high-ceilinged, full of gliding California light and beautiful furniture. Imagine a house where successful L.A. rappers would have partied in 1991: this is literally that house. It is so quintessentially L.A. that it has been used for film shoots, which means that sometimes the Yankovics—Weird Al; his wife, Suzanne; and their daughter, Nina—will be watching TV and, out of nowhere, they'll see their house onscreen: Andy Garcia will be standing in their living room or Eazy-E will be floating in their pool. Yankovic's friend Joel Miller insists that he has seen pornography set in the Yankovics' living room. To which Weird Al responds, with polite embarrassment, "I'll take his word for it."

The Yankovic family is wonderfully wholesome. Al and Suzanne met fairly late in life, when both were established in their careers. Suzanne was a high-powered marketing executive at 20th Century Fox, and she was skeptical, at first, when a friend tried to set them up. She worried that Weird Al would be wacky, loud, shrill, insufferable, exhausting, always "on."

He turned out to be the opposite. Offstage, in his civilian life, Yankovic is shy, introverted, extremely private, and unfailingly polite. Among the big personalities of the Los Angeles comedy world, his quiet decency is legendary. "He is so, so incredibly nice," Samberg (among many others) told me. "He is the nicest person you will ever meet, exactly what you're dreaming he'll be like." No one has ever heard Weird Al raise his voice in anger. He doesn't swear. When a script comes to him with a bad word in it, he politely asks for revisions. Sometimes, experimentally, Suzanne will try to get him to say a curse word at home. "C'mon, honey, it's just us!" she'll say. But he refuses.

On a bright Saturday morning, the Yankovics invited me to join them for a family hike. Weird Al wore jeans, a large floppy hat and a muted Lacoste polo. (He avoids Hawaiian shirts in everyday settings, not wanting to draw attention to himself.) Suzanne, an avid photographer, seemed to notice every plant and bird we passed. She and Al are classic opposites: he is internal and unobservant and can disappear into his head for days at a time; Suzanne is chatty and social and hyperpresent. Their daughter, Nina, is a precocious sixteen-year-old who looks uncannily like the actor Elliot Page. She and her father share a talent for math—sometimes he invents trigonometry problems for her—and she also has his sense of humor. (Once, when her school had an eighties-themed dance, Nina showed up in a pilgrim dress, like someone from the 1680s.) At one point on our hike, Nina scampered off the trail, disappeared behind a tree and returned with a time capsule that she has been stocking and reburying since she was little. Inside was a feather, dried leaves, old Polaroids, a Swiss Army knife, and a handwritten note from her dad: "It's a beautiful day and I'm going for a walk with my wonderful family and our little poodle Sandy. If you find this note, we hope you're having a lovely day too." Nina added a rock, then closed it back up and reburied it.

After the hike, the Yankovic family took me to their favorite vegan Mexican restaurant and then drove me around L.A. We passed a man who was trying to attract Instagram followers by playing guitar solos on top of a parked car. When we stopped at a red light, a film crew went rolling by, hauling a vintage car, shooting a driving scene. It occurred to me that Weird Al might be comfortable in Los Angeles because the place is already a self-parody. He is off-duty, liberated.

Back at the house, Yankovic showed me his accordion collection—two large piles of cases—and some old costumes, including the original "Eat It" jacket: red leather, zippers everywhere. It still fit him perfectly. He showed me a walk-in closet that contained more Hawaiian shirts than I have ever seen in one place. ("This represents a very small percentage of them," Yankovic said.) He showed me the corner where he composes music: a nest of keyboards and computer equipment underneath a wall of gold and platinum records. In the middle of it all, flopped like a beached jellyfish, sat an old Kurt Cobain wig.

When I asked about his writing process, Yankovic took out his laptop, sat down at a big wooden table and told me to pick a song. I chose "White & Nerdy." It is archetypal Yankovic: a parody rap that captures all the musical energy of the original while nerdifying its lyrics. ("First in my class there at MIT / Got skills, I'm a

champion at D and D / M. C. Escher, that's my favorite MC.")
"White & Nerdy" went viral in 2006, in the early days of YouTube, and drove the album *Straight Outta Lynwood* into the top ten, rekindling Weird Al's popularity for the new millennium.

At his dining-room table, Yankovic clicked around on his laptop. He has a file for every song, and each file is many levels deep. At the top stands the finished lyric. Below that, like archaeological layers beneath the surface of an ancient city, descend all the stages of writing it took to get there.

Perhaps you have always imagined that Weird Al tosses off his lyrics while juggling rubber chickens on a unicycle. I mean, this is a man who once recorded a parody of Huey Lewis and the News's "I Want a New Drug" called "I Want a New Duck," the first verse of which goes: "I want a new duck / One that won't try to bite / One that won't chew a hole in my socks / One that won't quack all night." He also converted "She Drives Me Crazy" into "She Drives Like Crazy" and "Addicted to Love" into "Addicted to Spuds" and "I Think We're Alone Now" into "I Think I'm a Clone Now" and "Zoot Suit Riot" into "Grapefruit Diet" and "Girls Just Want to Have Fun" into "Girls Just Want to Have Lunch" and—honestly, the list could go on forever.

But it turns out that Weird Al approaches the composition of his music with something like the holy passion of Michelangelo painting the ceiling of the Sistine Chapel. Looking through the "White & Nerdy" file felt like watching a supercomputer crunch through possible chess moves. Every single variable had to be considered, in every single line. The song begins with a simple sentence—"They see me mowing my front lawn"—and even here Yankovic agonized over "lawn" versus "yard" and "my" versus "the." He sifted through phrases in gradations so small, they were almost invisible:

Escher's really still my favorite MC.
Tell ya Escher's still my favorite MC.
Escher is my favorite MC.

Escher's still my favorite MC.
MC Escher's still my favorite MC.
MC Escher is my favorite MC.
Y'know Escher is my favorite MC.
Y'know Escher's still my favorite MC.

For weeks at a time, Yankovic told me, he goes into a creative trance—what he calls "the zombie phase." "I walk around the house with a thousand-mile stare," he said. "My wife asks if I'm OK."

He's fine. In fact, in some ways he's in his favorite place: three leagues deep in his head, building an alternate universe entirely out of jokes. He lines up phrases next to one another—fragments and couplets, nerd brags and white jokes, most of which will never reach the final lyric sheet:

In snowstorms it ain't easy to be seen.
I know a tangent from a vector. I love mayonnaise, that
    sweet nectar.
I ate an enormous amount of dairy while I watched *Little
    House on the Prairie.*
I know all the RadioShack employees by name.
Got an Ethernet jack inside my shower.
I can calculate how much water a sphere displaces.
I know the molecular weight of magnesium.
I know the proper names of all the Smurfs.

He reads these options again and again, agonizing, putting his current preference in bold and then changing his mind and putting something else in bold to see how it feels. He spent a long time, for instance, deciding what book would be funniest for his nerd narrator to brag about having in his library: J. K. Rowling, Douglas Adams, Stephen Hawking or hardbound comics. (He chose Hawking.) He composed whole stand-alone quatrains that were later thrown out:

I'm so white I'm almost translucent
Check out the SPF I'm usin'
In my hooptie I go cruisin'
I find Jay Leno amusin'.

"I could have written a whole second 'White & Nerdy' based on the alt lines," Yankovic said. "I figure I'm going to be living with this song for a long time. We'll probably be doing it onstage for the rest of my life. It's got to be right."

After ten minutes of staring at this verbal barbed wire, my brain felt as if it were starting to cramp. I told him I didn't know how much longer I could take it. "We're not even halfway through," Yankovic said. We had yet to reach, for instance, his encyclopedic lists of possible rhymes, all categorized by syllable count, running on for page after page like Homer's list of ships in the *Iliad*: "Polar bear / Voltaire," "my back is peeling / Darjeeling." At one point, he lined up thirty-five potential rhymes for the word "geek."

Yankovic has done a version of this process for just about every song he has ever written, parody and original, from "Eat It" to today. In the years before computers, he would do everything by hand, sifting and sorting in a binder with color-coded tabs. He used to spend weeks roaming through the West Hollywood Library, compiling facts and keywords about cloning for "I Think I'm a Clone Now" or hospitals for "Like a Surgeon." Songs that may seem dashed off are in fact the product of months of self-imposed hard labor—lonely, silent, obsessive world-building.

. . .

Alfred Matthew Yankovic grew up not in Los Angeles proper but outside of it, near Compton, in the working-class suburb of Lynwood. He was an only child, a miracle baby, born late in his parents' life near the tail end of the baby boom, in 1959. His father, Nick, was a beefy, goofy man who served as a medic during World

War II, where his heroism earned him not only two Purple Hearts but also an appearance in the syndicated newspaper comic "Combat Spotlight." ("No one dared go for a wounded man left on the field—'Hell,' said Yank, 'I'll get him.' And he did.") Weird Al's mother, Mary, was a stenographer from Kentucky. She was quiet, shy, and guarded. She made casseroles, had an iron sense of propriety, and loved her son nearly to the point of suffocation. She would devote her life to protecting him from all the many dangers of the world, real and imaginary. Although the Yankovics didn't collect art, they kept a single oil painting hanging in their living room, right above the mantel, like a shrine: a framed portrait of their son.

Alfred was a blend of his parents. He was eccentric like his dad—the two of them used to dig tunnels around the foundation of the house together, just for fun—but he was also painfully shy. He started kindergarten a year early, and at the beginning of second grade his teacher decided he was overqualified and sent him up to third grade. This meant that, for most of his life, he was two years younger than the rest of his classmates. Although Alfred's grades were perfect and he could solve any math problem you threw at him, his social life was agonizing. Imagine every nerd cliché: He was scrawny, pale, unathletic, nearsighted, awkward with girls—and his name was Alfred. And that's all before you even factor in the accordion.

It came from a door-to-door salesman. The man was offering the gift of music, and he gave the Yankovics a simple choice: accordion or guitar. This was 1966, the golden age of rock, the year of the Beatles' *Revolver* and the Beach Boys' *Pet Sounds* and Bob Dylan's *Blonde on Blonde*. A guitar was like a magic amulet spraying sexual psychedelic magic all over the world. So Yankovic's mother chose the accordion. This was at least partly because of a coincidence: Frankie Yankovic, a world-famous polka player, happened to share the family's last name. No relation. Just a wonderful coincidence that would help to define Alfred's entire life.

He took his first accordion lesson the day before his seventh birthday and progressed quickly. He had plenty of time to practice. Mary Yankovic was so overprotective that her son spent much of his life alone in his room. He never played at friends' houses, never had sleepovers, never explored his neighborhood on his bike. The farthest he was allowed to ride was half a block, to his Aunt Dot's house, and his mother would stand on the lawn and watch. For Alfred's protection, she would censor the mail, sifting through catalogues page by page with a black marker in hand, scribbling out anything inappropriate: bra ads, pictures of women in bikinis.

Alfred's bedroom was his own little kingdom, devoted entirely to his enthusiasms. If he wanted to collect and organize dozens of license plates from all over the country—which he absolutely did—there was nothing stopping him. If he wanted to rig a contraption involving pulleys and string so he could flip on the light switch without leaving his bed, he could do that too.

The years passed. Alfred sat in his room, wheezing away on his accordion, diddling its buttons, dutifully memorizing polkas and waltzes and marches and the "Mexican Hat Dance." All of his classmates hit puberty before he did. He never had a girlfriend, never went to a party or a dance. His parents never taught him about sex. "Stay away from women," his father once told him. "They have diseases and stuff." Lynwood High School was directly across the street from the Yankovic home, and when Alfred went there his mom would sometimes watch him during gym class, through binoculars, just to make sure he wasn't being bullied.

As a teenager, Yankovic's enthusiasms began to widen. He became obsessed with Elton John. He would grab his accordion and play along with *Goodbye Yellow Brick Road*, the whole double album, start to finish, memorizing it. He watched *Monty Python* and amassed stacks of *Mad* magazines, in which he would read parodies of movies he was not allowed to see. Comedy, for a smart, sheltered kid, was a cheat code—a way to use his intelligence to rearrange the world, to build pleasure out of drudgery. He loved George Carlin's album *FM & AM* so much that he transcribed it on a manual typewriter.

One night, Alfred's passion for music and comedy came together in the form of a radio DJ named Dr. Demento. Every Sunday, Demento played four hours of novelty music, both from absolute comedy legends (Spike Jones, Allan Sherman, Stan Freberg) and from nobodies who sent in unsolicited cassette tapes. Alfred Yankovic wanted, desperately, to escape his room and live in this world. He started writing his own comedy songs. One night his mother overheard the show, decided it was inappropriate and said he couldn't listen anymore. But this tide was rising too fast for even her to stop. Every week, Alfred would huddle under his blankets and listen to Dr. Demento. And it would not be long before he heard his own voice coming back at him out of the speakers. In 1976, Demento picked out "Belvedere Cruising," a song Yankovic wrote about his family's jalopy of a car, and played it on the air.

At sixteen, Alfred Yankovic graduated high school. He was valedictorian, and his speech at the ceremony was dutiful, serious, and formal—except for one passage in which he described the future destruction of the world, how the polar ice caps would melt and civilization would be drowned. As he described this hypothetical apocalypse, his voice rose to a grating shriek, until he was suddenly screaming about humanity's imminent doom. The crowd roared with laughter, interrupting his speech with a round of applause.

And then Yankovic finally escaped his lonely bedroom: He packed up his things, loaded up the junky old family car and drove off—alone—to start a new life. He would study architecture at California Polytechnic State University, about four hours north of home. As he drove off, Alfred's parents got in their new car and followed directly behind him. Alfred watched them in his rearview mirror. As soon as he hit the freeway, he gunned the engine and lost them.

．　　　．　　　．

The nickname "Weird Al" started as an insult. It happened during his first year of college. This was a fresh start for Alfred—a chance to reinvent himself for a whole new set of people. He had no reputation to live down, no epic humiliations. And so he decided to implement a rebrand: He introduced himself to everyone not as Alfred but as "Al." Alfred sounded like the kind of kid who might invent his own math problems for fun. Al sounded like the opposite of that: a guy who would hang out with the dudes, eating pizza, casually noodling on an electric guitar, tossing off jokes so unexpectedly hilarious they would send streams of light beer rocketing out of everyone's noses.

The problem was that, even at college, even under the alias of Al, Yankovic was still himself. He was still, fundamentally, an Alfred. He was, in all kinds of excruciating ways, not your average freshman. He was sixteen. He wore thick glasses and had a regrettable mustache. He was skinny and pathologically shy. He had the social skills of a ceramic frog. He didn't drink, smoke, party, date, or swear. He still felt most comfortable alone in his tiny room.

The other guys on his dorm floor knew Al Yankovic only as this mysterious oddball haunting the place like Boo Radley. They would all be hanging out, sprawled around in someone's room, door open, laughter spilling into the hallway—when suddenly this pale kid would come slumping by, off to class or to the library, saying nothing, casting a shy glance in the door. He often wore a variation on the same outfit: a striped shirt, a floppy bucket hat, like Gilligan on *Gilligan's Island*, and flip-flops even when it was raining outside. The guys would watch him pass, only very slightly interested, like a pack of lions watching a distant ibis, and Al would look in through the open door, and there would be this moment of mutual regard: the in-group and the outcast, staring each other down.

Over time, this silent encounter became a ritual, awkward but familiar. Eventually, Yankovic started to play variations: as he walked by he would stare inside and make a face—screw his eyes up, lower his eyebrows, seriocomically glower. It was the weird guy being weird, silently acknowledging his weirdness, performing it to entertain himself.

Once, in the fateful silence that followed, a guy in the room spoke up.

"Hey," he said, "It's [expletive] Weird Al!"

This was not meant as a compliment. It was an attempt to return, in words, the strange energy Yankovic was pouring into the room through his eyes. The nickname got repeated every time he went shuffling past—"Hey, Weird Al!"—and so it stuck. And slowly Al began to embrace it, to reclaim the insult as a badge of honor.

It took him a long time to make a real friend. One day, Joel Miller, one of the normal guys in the dorm room Yankovic stared into, walked into the communal bathroom to find a group of kids laughing. He asked them what was up. Turns out they had just pulled a prank on Weird Al: Knowing how cringingly awkward he was, they had sneaked in while he was showering and stolen his clothes. In his panic Weird Al had ripped down the shower curtain, wrapped himself in it, and sprinted off to his room, soaking wet. Miller threatened to bash the guys over the head with a chair, got Weird Al's clothes, and returned them.

This was the beginning of the longest close friendship of Al Yankovic's life—a friendship that still endures. Miller noticed the accordion in Yankovic's dorm room and asked if he actually knew how to play. Yankovic said yes—he could play any song anyone wanted to hear. Miller, trying to stump him, said how about Elton John's "Funeral for a Friend / Love Lies Bleeding," an eleven-minute piano-rock dirge. Al strapped on his accordion and played the song, note for note, all the way through. This earned Weird Al an invitation to hang out in the dorm room, where he played his accordion for everyone else. Miller grabbed his bongos and the two of them jammed for hours.

.   .   .

If, in the superhero narrative of Weird Al Yankovic, there is a radioactive spider-bite moment, it has to be open-mic night at Cal Poly in 1977. Imagine the scene: a bunch of longhaired idealists with banjos and acoustic guitars, ready to shock the world with the beauty of their fingerpicking. And then Weird Al steps onstage. He brought with him not only his accordion and his large glasses and his little mustache but his whole awkward chaotic energy. Miller set up his bongos, and together the pair launched into the exact opposite of earnest folk music. Yankovic played "Wipeout" and "Also Sprach Zarathustra" and a ten-minute medley that he claimed covered every song ever written in the history of the world.

Before that night, Yankovic's public performances included childhood accordion competitions and a cousin's wedding. Now he was sharing his own music, the essence of himself, with a roomful of strangers. The odds were high that he would bomb, then disappear back into his tiny room forever.

Instead, the opposite happened: The crowd went crazy. Weird Al's ridiculous music got a standing ovation. The applause would not stop. People hollered for more.

For a kid who had spent his whole childhood being either ignored or bullied, that sudden validation was transformative. Miller remembers looking over at his shy friend and seeing Yankovic's face lit with total joy. "It was glowing," he once said, "like Chernobyl melting down."

"I think it was the first time I'd ever had that kind of positive reinforcement," Yankovic told me. "It probably did flip a switch somewhere in my head."

That Chernobyl moment changed everything. Yankovic's schoolwork began to recede. He was on fire with dumb music. Weird Al wrote new songs constantly and played them at every venue that would have him. He and Miller were once heckled at a fraternity barn dance. But success was coming. In 1979, during his junior year, Weird Al stood in a men's bathroom at Cal Poly (he liked the acoustics of the tile) and recorded a parody of the number-one song in America, the Knack's "My Sharona": a lusty, humpy, cringe-y ode to seducing a teenage girl. Weird Al's version was a two-minute romp about lunch meat called "My Bologna." It had a crazy, DIY, nerd-punk energy—you could hear Yankovic committing every fiber of his lonely soul to the bit, crooning and grunting like a man driven insane with desire. It didn't matter that the pun was bad, that the singing was raw—all of that was exactly the point. Dr. Demento's listeners went crazy for it, and radio stations picked it up nationwide, and the lead singer of the Knack urged Capitol Records to release the song as a 45—and suddenly Weird Al had his first recording contract. To this day, Cal Poly marks that bathroom with a plaque as the birthplace of Weird Al Yankovic's career.

In underground comedy circles, the legend of Weird Al began to grow. He became a staple on Dr. Demento's show, answering phone lines and playing his accordion in studio and generally hamming it up. He turned Queen's "Another One Bites the Dust" into "Another One Rides the Bus." By the time Yankovic graduated from college, joke music was all he cared about. He hardly had time for anything else. He moved to Los Angeles, slept on a couch, briefly lived in his car. He got a minimum-wage job in a mailroom. He moved into a tiny apartment with a Murphy bed and a view of the Hollywood sign. He sat there by himself, recording music, building his oeuvre joke by joke. Sometimes he taped silverware all over the walls, just to be weird.

On April Fools' Day, 1984, MTV did something preposterous. The network, back then, was influential but also desperate for content, and Yankovic's outsider weirdo shtick killed with its audience, so the network gave Yankovic four hours to fill with whatever he wanted. He created *Al TV*, a parody of MTV. The conceit was that Weird Al had taken over the station with a pirate transmitter. Hour after hour, he made fun of music videos, read fake fan letters, announced fake contests, and spliced together footage of celebrities into preposterous fake interviews. (Weird Al: "Mr. George, if you were on an Arctic expedition and you got stranded, who would be the first people you'd eat?" Boy George: "Housewives, young kids.") This made Weird Al a brand name on the network—a sort of stand-in for the audience itself.

Yankovic used *Al TV* to promote the video for "Eat It"—a nearly shot-for-shot parody of Michael Jackson's original. The song would make him a true international star. The single reached number twelve on the Billboard Top 100 and won Yankovic a Grammy. Its album, *"Weird Al" Yankovic in 3-D*, went platinum. When the video first aired, Yankovic was out on a very modest tour—he and the band traveled together in a blue station wagon pulling a trailer—and in Virginia they stopped at a fast-food restaurant for lunch, and suddenly Yankovic was mobbed. "You're the 'Eat It' guy!" everyone shouted. It happened just like that, overnight. Weird Al had discovered some secret wormhole in pop-cultural space-time that sent a portion of Jackson's mega-fame dumping onto his own dorky head. After the success of "Eat It," Madonna wondered aloud to a friend when Weird Al would turn "Like a Virgin" into "Like a Surgeon," and word got back to Weird Al, and he did. In 1988, he turned Michael Jackson's megahit "Bad" into "Fat." (Last year, after more public allegations of child sexual abuse against Michael Jackson emerged, Yankovic announced that he would temporarily stop performing his Jackson parodies.)

Weird Al likes to say that every one of his albums is a comeback album. That's because a parody career is not like a normal career. It has no internal momentum. Everyone always expects you to go away. Yankovic's lowest point came in the early 1990s: It had been years since his last big song, and his attempt at a movie—1989's *UHF*—had bombed, and his phone had stopped ringing. Out of desperation, he decided to settle back into his old shtick, writing a food-based parody of Michael Jackson's latest hit, the racial-harmony anthem "Black or White." Yankovic's version was going to be called—I would prefer not to tell you this, but this is actually what it was going to be called—"Snack All Night." And it was about—well, it was about snacking all night.

The only thing that saved him was that Jackson, for the first time, said no. (Technically, a parodist does not need permission, but it is a legal gray area, and Weird Al prefers to have every artist in on the joke.) This was a reprieve, because it set up the success of "Smells Like Nirvana." Weird Al actually loved Nirvana— the music hit him deep in his soul—and before the band performed "Smells Like Teen Spirit" on *Saturday Night Live* in January 1992, Weird Al called the set and managed to get Kurt Cobain on the phone to ask his permission to do a parody. "Is it gonna be about food?" Cobain asked. No, Yankovic said: It was going to be about how no one could understand Nirvana's lyrics. Cobain thought that was hilarious.

Once more, Weird Al had caught the wind of a new phenomenon, and so his career took back off. He has been around ever since. In 2014, thirty years after "Eat It," his album *Mandatory Fun* debuted at number one on the Billboard charts. National economies collapse; species go extinct; political movements rise and fizzle. But—somehow, for some reason—Weird Al endures.

. . .

I am writing this profile, and you are reading it, in an impossible world. Comedy, a disembodied spark between distant people seems more crucial than ever. Over the last several weeks, from his house, Weird Al has been posting jokes online: a video of his (increasingly agitated) face being assaulted by tiny hands; a photo urging people to resist hoarding accordions. He recently performed a song on *The Tonight Show* in his robe. These virtual appearances are funny and sweet—little notes of solace in a wide landscape of devastation. But I keep returning, in my mind to the before times, to the summer when I not only saw Weird Al in concert but joined him on tour for a couple of days. I hung around empty arenas as his crew lugged equipment up ramps and tested lighting rigs and stocked the merch tables: Weird Al lunchboxes, Weird Al stickers, an old Weird Al T-shirt that was suddenly popular again because it had been worn by a character on *Stranger Things*. Sometimes I watched the actual shows from backstage, where I could see spit-mists blowing from Weird Al's mouth when he hit high notes; other times I watched from so deep in the venue that Weird Al looked like a small particle in a sea of waving arms. Late one night, on the tour bus, I drank from a bottle of Crown Royal that had been signed by the members of Lynyrd Skynyrd (long story) and got into a deep debate with a backup singer about the plausibility of chemtrails. When I finally fell asleep it was inside the bus, in what everyone refers to as a "coffin bunk," and all night long I could feel the bumps and swells of I-94 as it unspooled a section of the Great Plains beneath us. I woke up in a whole new place, under a whole different sky, and watched the crew set up a fresh stage.

During all of this, I saw almost nothing of Weird Al. He was like a ghost haunting his own tour: there but not there. On the road, Yankovic is reclusive, obsessed with saving his voice and life force for his fans. He spent all his free time holed up in his own small room at the back of the bus, keeping strange private hours—falling asleep at seven a.m., waking up midafternoon. Seeing him anywhere before showtime felt like seeing a panda out in the wild. He moved in a bubble of hushed, exotic, respectful excitement.

The only real exception to Weird Al's self-isolation came late at night, after the shows, when he would interact with fans in elaborate VIP sessions: photos, autographs, chats. Yankovic would do basically anything fans wanted. He would mug for the camera or flex like a bodybuilder or sign people's arms. He signed posters, cassette tapes, action figures, accordions, spatulas, glow-in-the-dark snorkels. I saw him sign a package of bologna and an exact replica of a Star Wars storm trooper helmet. These were not autograph hounds but true devotees, exactly the kinds of people Yankovic placed at the center of his songs: nerds, misfits, weirdos. Many fans seemed to have just emerged, for the first time in forever, from tiny rooms of their own. They were less interested in a photo op than in a sort of spiritual transfer.

Most of all, the fans thanked Weird Al. They thanked him for his music, for not dying of heatstroke onstage, for voicing the character Banana Man on the cartoon *Adventure Time*, for helping them survive cancer, for helping them survive their mother's cancer.

"I got introduced to your music when I was going through—struggles—in my life," said a young, balding man wearing a brown suit, and the word struggles was surrounded on all sides by an unfathomable gulf of feeling. "You helped me pull through."

Weird Al listened with deep eye contact. "Thank you," he said. "That means a lot to me."

"Thank you for all the joy you bring to the world," said a woman in Minnesota.

"Thank you for making my best times brighter with your songs," said a young man in North Dakota.

"Thank you for letting us all be ourselves."

"Thank you for being you."

Weird Al's bond with his fans is atomic. He will stop and speak with them anywhere—at airports, outside the tour bus—for so long that it becomes a logistical problem. The fans approach him like a guru, and Weird Al responds with sweet, open, validating energy.

Joel Miller, the friend who defended Yankovic from college bullies, said the relationship between Weird Al and his hard-core fans is deeply personal. "He's giving them validation," he told me. "They feel a kindred spirit. When they're at his concerts, they are in a safe space. They are able to be stupid or outlandish or whatever, exactly as they want. And nobody judges them. In fact, it's the opposite. People appreciate them for what they are, not for what they aren't."

The connection is so deep that it is more like a merging, and after a while it struck me that Weird Al has spent basically his whole life making his music for exactly these people, which is to say for his childhood self. For many decades, he has been trying to delight Alfred Yankovic, the bright, painfully shy kid who grew up alone in his tiny bedroom. For the benefit of that lonely boy, he reshaped the whole world of pop culture. His ridiculous music sent out a pulse, a signal, and these were the people it drew: the odd, the left out. A crowd of friends for that lonely kid. As I watched him with his fans, sometimes I felt as if Weird Al was multiplying all around me, multiplying inside of me. We were one crowd, united in isolation, together in a great collective loneliness that—once you recognized it, once you accepted it—felt right on the brink of being healed.

ESPN.com

FINALIST—FEATURE WRITING

This is the second story about Michael Jordan by Wright Thompson to be nominated for the National Magazine Award for Feature Writing. Thompson's article "Michael Jordan Has Not Left the Building" was published by ESPN The Magazine *in 2013 and nominated for the Feature Writing award in 2014 (it was also included in that year's edition of* Best American Magazine Writing*). So the question the judges asked about "Michael Jordan: A History of Flight" seems especially apt: "How do you write about one of the most-profiled people ever?" The answer: "You go back to the beginning, to uncover the story of 'Mike,' the person Jordan was before he became famous." Born in Clarksdale, Mississippi, and educated at the University of Missouri, Wright Thompson is a senior writer at ESPN.com. His book* Pappyland: A Story of Family, Fine Bourbon, and the Things That Last *was published in 2020.*

Wright Thompson

Michael Jordan

A History of Flight

Act I

Years ago, after a bad hurricane hit Wilmington, North Carolina, Michael Jordan came back to help the recovery effort. Jordan doesn't go home very often, but he had some friends with him on that trip and wanted to show them where he'd grown up while they were in town. The house, a middle-class split-level, is at 4647 Gordon Road, near U.S. Highway 117. It's the address where Dean Smith sent recruiting letters. Out front, Jordan seemed sentimental. One of the friends with him said later they didn't feel comfortable describing the scene. It felt private. "How do most people feel when they go back to see their childhood home?" the person explained. "MJ is human."

Someone suggested ringing the doorbell, but they worried about disturbing the current occupants, so his friends just stood there a moment with him, watching Michael Jordan look at the house where he used to live.

"Very early I had a personality split," Jordan told me once. "One that was a public persona and one that was private."

·   ·   ·

U.S. 117 is the mother road of Michael Jordan's past. It runs from Wilmington to Wilson. There have been Jordans living along that corridor since the Civil War. Al Edgerton, a longtime engineer in the North Carolina Department of Transportation and a grade school classmate of Jordan's, was part of a crew that resurfaced 117 less than a decade ago. The highway cuts through fields and little towns.

"A lot of agricultural type equipment is running up and down that road," Edgerton says. "When you get around Wallace, where Mike's dad was from, that's an ag-type county. You have a lot of farm trucks and tractors, pulling trailers of tobacco."

Al met Mike in the third grade and they were teammates in three sports growing up. They competed against each other in Babe Ruth baseball in the brutal North Carolina summers. It's hard to fathom July heat in New Hanover, Pender, and Duplin counties if you don't live there. During Al's road crew days, he would go home and his boots would be soaked from all the sweat. He'd leave them out on the porch, but the next morning when he slipped them back on, they'd still be wet. That's how hot it was. Checking asphalt reminded him of sweltering long-ago baseball games.

"We had field days in elementary school where in May you'd go out and have a hundred-yard dash," he says. "Even then, Mike, he hated losing. Some of the memories I have on activity buses going to football, basketball, baseball games. There was many times we'd have a game of cards on the activity bus. And we'd get to the school we were playing, and Mike hadn't been winning the last few hands? He wouldn't let anybody get off the bus."

Al says he met Michael Jordan only once. It must have been thirty years ago, when the Bulls star came back to his hometown to put on a basketball clinic. They ran into each other afterward and laughed and told stories for a good half-hour. They knew the same people. Their fathers had sat together at their games. They'd driven the same roads to and from school.

"I don't know Michael," Al says. "I've always known him as Mike."

•　　•　　•

Once more he is the center of our sporting lives. Michael Jordan wasn't destined to just fade away. After the 1997–98 season, which we have been reliving in *The Last Dance*, Phil Jackson looked into the future: "I know I will be forgotten as soon as this is over. All of us will. Except Michael. Michael will be remembered forever." Jackson was right. Such is the power of Michael Jordan that ESPN's prime-time ratings are up versus last year, in a time with almost no live sporting events.

The documentary tells the familiar story of Michael. Cut from his high school basketball team to six-time champion of the NBA. It is a story about will and work, and nearly every viewer knows how it ends. But still they're compelled because even though he is among the most known people on the planet, he remains a mystery. We know the whats but not the whys.

North Carolina coach Roy Williams is watching *The Last Dance* and remembering when he recruited Mike Jordan. Roy grew up in the Blue Ridge Mountains, raised in poverty by a single mom. A few years ago, he found himself driving from Chapel Hill to play golf in Wilmington. He was alone and he slipped off the interstate and drove over to the house on Gordon Road. If you're driving down Interstate 40, there's a sign at the Pender–New Hanover county line announcing that this stretch of road is named in honor of Michael Jordan. But if you're Roy Williams pulling off 117, your mind's eye focuses on Michael's father working out front of Gordon Road. Most likely on a car engine, his tongue stuck out in concentration, a habit he acquired from his grandfather and his son acquired from him. "Every single time I go down there," he says, "I drive down Michael Jordan Highway. It just reminds me of those times. James and Deloris were so good to me. You can't give the parents all the credit, but they led him by example. They taught him hard work."

Michael Jordan has become so public it can seem as if he were born fully formed. Of course, that's not true. His family spent at least six generations in one small patch of swamp and cropland in the rural outskirts and farm towns near Wilmington, on and around Highway 117. He remembers his grandparents still eating dirt and clay—a now little-known practice brought to the South from Africa—getting needed iron from the land. Michael used to eat the orange and red clay for dessert when he'd visit them.

He grew up not only hearing about a vanishing world, but he saw the last pieces of it too, a kind of life that died for much of America at the turn of the century but somehow kept going around U.S. 117 for seventy more years. He left that history behind and yet carries it all inside him too. Which means maybe the way to unravel Mike from Michael is to look at where and when his rural North Carolina roots quietly molded his career and to consider how the land where he grew up shaped his ancestors, who shaped him.

.   .   .

Five Sundays ago, in the last hour before *The Last Dance* premiered, Michael Jordan got a text message. He looked down at his phone and saw it was from the son of one of his old security guards. Those guys cross Michael's mind a lot. During the pinnacle of his fame, a group of retired and off-duty Chicago cops kept him both insulated and connected. The Sniff Brothers, they jokingly called themselves. As in jock sniffers. There were five or six core guys. Jordan took care of them long after his playing career ended, and he deeply misses the three who have died in the years since: Gus Lett, Clarence Travis, and John Michael Wozniak, whose son Nicholi sent the text. Nicky sent a picture of Michael holding the NBA championship trophy, and there, in the background as usual, was his father. The Sniff Brothers were always around. On family vacations, in hotel suites playing cards, out in Los Angeles shooting *Space Jam*, hiding out beneath the United Center in the hours before a game.

Nicky wished Michael luck and thanked him for all the support over the years. Michael wrote back immediately: "I love it. I will watch with him, Gus and CT on my heart!!!!!!!!!!!!"

The public Jordan, the symbol, needed constant security protection as the game's greatest player. The private person felt most at home around a bunch of middle-class Chicago cops, guys who'd worked narcotics and gang squad, who'd taken bullets and kicked in doors and who knew what it meant to work for a living and to live by a simple code. Guys who reminded him of home.

"They became my best friends," Jordan told me years ago.

The Sniff Brothers helped him keep one foot in the striving world of his past while the other leapt into the air. One of them, Bob Scarpetti, remembers the surreal week in 1996 when he protected Princess Diana, who was visiting Chicago, during the day and Jordan at night. In preparation for the launch of *Space Jam*, Warner Brothers commissioned research to determine the reach of Jordan's fame. The study revealed that the three most famous people on the planet at the time were Princess Di, Jordan, and the pope. That kind of fame scared Michael's father, who worried about what it might do to his son. The crowds scared Michael too, he sometimes admits.

"A normal guy," his friend Fred Whitfield says. "A country boy."

A year after *Space Jam* came out, Michael and his consigliere Estee Portnoy were in a hotel room in Las Vegas when they heard Diana had died in Paris—actually had been killed while being stalked by cameramen, by fame itself. Portnoy turned to Jordan, both of them reeling.

"You're the most famous person on the planet now," she said.

·　　·　　·

Seven years ago, Michael Jordan drove me through the streets of Charlotte in a V-12 Mercedes. The enormous engine sounded like a spaceship, and the glow of the interior lights felt like one too. The odometer showed 497 miles. I can remember the new-car smell. Soul music played through Bang & Olufsen speakers, "Black Rose" by the English R&B group Hil St. Soul.

Normally Jordan travels in the back seat of chauffeured cars. Except in North Carolina, his friends told me. In North Carolina, he drives.

"He knows his way to all the Hardee's," Whitfield said, laughing.

His faithful driver, George Koehler, grinned.

"It's good to come home."

The sun was going down.

"My parents used to live here," Jordan said as he watched people cross the street in front of him.

Lots of people know that Michael broke his foot three games into his second NBA season in 1985. Almost nobody knows that his parents sold the home where he'd grown up, where James and Deloris raised their family, just ten days after that injury happened. Charlotte was the beginning of a new kind of life to them, just as Chicago was to Michael.

"He was so wide-eyed," then-Bobcats exec Rod Higgins said.

"He was scared to death when he got to Chicago," Koehler said.

Jordan's sudden wealth changed the arc of his family. No Jordans had truly left the small patch of North Carolina near 117 before Michael. James and Deloris moved to New York for a spell, where Michael was born, but moved back to rural North Carolina before he was out of diapers.

They were tied to the country.

The Mississippi writer Kiese Laymon was thinking about that journey a few days after the first episode of *The Last Dance* aired. He smiled at the long suits and the bright colors of Jordan's wardrobe. They took on an air of sophistication in the glare of Jordan's fame, but in Laymon's mind they also called back to Deep South Sunday mornings. MJ dressed like he was walking into a Missionary Baptist or AME church. "If you look at early Jordan and listen to early Jordan," Laymon says, "I definitely see a country black boy trying hard to be accepted by the black city of Chicago."

That conflict between the lessons taught to him in the country and the way the city expected him to act would follow Jordan through his career: his unwillingness to endorse Harvey Gantt; Republicans buying sneakers; the attacks he took for not doing more to help stop the poverty and crime at the Henry Horner Homes, just blocks from the old Chicago Stadium. A local high school principal called him out to the *Washington Post* in 1992 for catering to suburban shoe buyers and not the kids trying to navigate the turf wars in gangs like the Renegade Vice Lords and the Four Corner Hustlers. Nothing in Jordan's past prepared him to understand urban decay and poverty. Jordan's experience was rooted in a different kind of decay—the pervasive feeling many country folks, especially country black folks, carry in their chests. Only the altar of hard work can offer a way out of this dirt.

"I can hear it in how his mother calls his father 'Mr. Jordan,'" Laymon tells me. "And I actually think Jordan's kind of politics of working hard versus a politics of public critique is rooted in that countriness."

·　　·　　·

Seeing Michael Jordan as from a specific place, as part of a specific family and history, is maybe the first step toward really seeing Michael Jordan at all. His people hunt deer, fish for catfish and bream, raise hogs and chickens, and regularly attend church. Jordan grew up with a military father and a New Testament mother, both of whom grew up in Old Testament homes. Hard work as the only portal from one plane of existence to another was perhaps the first lesson James and Deloris Jordan ever learned and one they passed on to all five of their children.

So in light of that, reconsider, if you will, the famous "Flu Game."

It's almost impossible to remember that there was a moment when Michael Jordan existed in the culture as a high-flying loser, an also-ran who soared individually but never led a team. That's laughable now, but it's true. Or, rather, it was. If his free-throw-line dunk is the apogee of one version of him, then the night he dragged himself into an arena, near ready to pass out, was the peak of what he'd made himself become. It was the 1997 NBA Finals. Game 5, Jazz versus the Bulls, series tied at two games each. Tipoff was seven o'clock.

Utah Jazz ball boy Preston Truman got to the arena that day around two p.m., filling fridges, restocking shelves, washing towels, hunting down applesauce, a Jordan favorite. The Delta Center is a concrete bunker, so it was eerily quiet beneath the stands.

"We were hearing rumors," he remembers.

Michael was sick.

The Bulls' bus pulled up to the northwest corner of the Delta Center. Preston rushed out to help bring in bags. "You could visibly tell there was something wrong with him," Preston says. "Any time Michael is in a room, it's like Elvis. There's so much energy around. He was not himself. Usually he's smiling. He walked into the arena very slowly."

Preston followed Michael as he inched through the concourse past the north end of the court and into the hockey locker room the Bulls had been assigned for the playoffs. Jordan went straight to a private room in the far back right corner. Only the trainers and Preston were in there. Someone turned off the lights. Michael took off his suit and lay down on a taping bench. Sometimes he curled up in the fetal position. Doctors came in and out. Preston just watched.

He overheard conversations about Jordan not playing until the second half. Nobody knew what would happen.

Preston kept looking at the digital clock that hangs in all locker rooms, connected to the game clock, counting down the minutes. The teams usually went onto the floor for warm-ups with around twenty minutes to go. Preston watched the clock and looked at Michael, just lying there in the dark with his eyes closed.

It's been twenty-three years and Preston can still picture him. Not the high-flying MJ but a vulnerable human being. The scene remains so clear, especially what Jordan was wearing on that table in the dark. He wore the same shorts he wore underneath his uniform in every one of the 1,251 NBA games he played.

They said North Carolina.

. . .

Michael might not be the most famous person on the planet anymore, decades after he last put on those shorts and took the court, but as the person has faded, the idea of him has somehow remained powerful and bright. The myth grows as the human being recedes. Here's an example: Stripped across the top of eBay's homepage a few weeks ago was a banner ad linked to everything the auction site had for sale related to Michael Jordan—both rare sneakers and pieces of memorabilia. It's a seller's market. A signed basketball goes for six grand. A signed North Carolina jersey goes for eight. Not that long ago, his 1984 Olympic uniform went for more than $200,000. Michael Russek from Grey Flannel Auctions sold that piece and said it is now in a case in the buyer's home.

The shoes Jordan wore the night of the Flu Game hit the open market a few years ago. They broke the record at the time for the highest price ever paid for game-worn shoes. Russek sold those too. Here's how it went down. A Utah businessman creeping up on middle age realized it was time to let go of childish things. It was time to go down to his safe deposit box and collect the most famous pair of sneakers in the world. That man was Preston Truman, the Utah Jazz ball boy who followed Jordan into the Delta Center.

Michael liked him because Preston always had applesauce and graham crackers waiting for him when the Bulls would roll into the Delta Center. At halftime of the Flu Game, Michael needed food but couldn't find a spoon for his applesauce, so Preston sprinted down a corridor and found one in the media dining room and rushed it back.

Earlier, as Michael gave Preston the names for his will call tickets and told the kid he could use some of them to invite his family to the game, Preston had blurted out, "Hey, MJ, you think I could get your kicks after the game?"

Michael stared at him. It's a terrifying look to receive.

"You want them?" he asked.

"I'd be honored," Preston said.

"They're yours."

Jordan started the game looking weak and out of place. The Jazz rushed to a sixteen-point lead. Then Michael began chipping away, seventeen points in the second quarter alone, finishing with thirty-eight—including a three-pointer with less than a minute left that gave the Bulls the lead for good. Michael had willed his team to victory, collapsing in Scottie Pippen's arms as he left the court with 6.2 seconds on the clock. After the game, the visitors locker room was chaos. Preston found Michael hooked up to IVs, surrounded by friends. Charles Barkley was back there. Lots of people came and went. Preston kept watching the shoes. At one point, the Bulls' equipment manager went to pick them up.

"No, no," Michael said. "Leave those there. I'm doing something with them."

He pointed at Preston.

"That's how Michael is," he says. "If he tells you he's gonna do something, he does it."

Jordan picked up the sneakers.

"Here you go, man," he said. "You worked hard for these."

.   .   .

There were woods all around Jordan's house. That means he knows the wild pleasure of playing beneath their shade, of inventing whole worlds, becoming a cowboy or a cavalryman, his brother the sworn enemy. Mike and his brother Larry had BB guns. They shot them out in the country at their grandparents' place and in the small patches of trees that pass for wilderness inside the city limits, always feeling bigger than they were, like farm kids who call a nearby ditch something grand like the Canyon.

One day Mike and Larry shot up a wasp nest and the swarm descended upon them, stingers out. They took off running, screaming, throwing water on themselves trying to make the stinging stop. Their parents were furious at the boys for shooting toward the house, but the boys just laughed and laughed. They carried the guns with them like explorers or buck private infantrymen. Playing cowboys and Indians, Larry knelt down, aimed and shot Mike in the leg. So Mike shot Larry in the face—just missing blinding him with a hit to the eye. There were a thousand close calls like that.

Hours burned away like morning mist until dinner hit the table and the mosquitoes swarmed the outdoor lights. A Southern night comes alive with strange noises and the low disembodied buzz drone of insect life. It's as dark as the deepest ocean floor. The woods always held their secrets close once the sun went down. Michael knows that too, the shadows that can lurk around old trees at night, how the thin membrane between the land of the living and the land of the dead seems porous, holes opened up by the same imagination that created the daylight play.

·   ·   ·

The land where Mike grew up is the skeleton key—the way to unlock many of the Jordan stories, myths and legends. He comes from a singular place with its own history, codes, and traditions— all of which gave him his greatest weapon: his own sense of himself and his deep reservoir of strength. The people who've gone back with him to see that old house can tell it when he gets sentimental parked out front. Anyone who's seen *The Last Dance* can hear it when he chokes up talking about his father, and about the cost of his competitiveness, those two ideas forever connected. What if *The Last Dance* is really a document for his six-year-old twins? Maybe he's crying in that interview because he's tired or even a little drunk, but perhaps he cries too because he feels like the documentary is his last chance to tell people what he thinks the highest expression of a person truly is.

Now look again at the Flu Game shoes he gave Preston. A mad genius at Nike named Tinker Hatfield designed those shoes. Tinker is now a grandfather who is riding around his Portland neighborhood on a skateboard during these days of quarantine. He says his family of loggers arrived in Oregon timber country from the hills of Kentucky and West Virginia, leaving back east their feud with the neighboring McCoys. He's from *those* Hatfields.

With his past steeped in feuds and hard work, Tinker styled himself as a futurist. He helped Michael walk a similar line between his own past and future. Together they invented a new way of being a famous athlete in the world, of representing two halves of the same man.

"He understands a process," Hatfield says of Jordan. "A process of creating something new and different. He's able to conceptualize."

The Jordan Brand is the central creation—and now the central creator, in a nifty trick—of the public Michael Jordan, the symbol, the global citizen. While cultural critics rapped Jordan for selling shoes to Republicans, folks who lived in the same part of the world he came from, the midlevel Southern cities like Wilmington and the little towns out in the nearby countryside like Burgaw and Teachey, saw not who was buying the shoes but who was selling them. Who did all these kids of every race and class want to be like? "That was a significant transformation," says Imani Perry, a professor at Princeton and one of America's leading thinkers on race, "to have the entire nation say they want to be like a black man from rural North Carolina."

Michael turned his own last name into a synonym for greatness. Nike does a lot of research about this. They've got deep data. Right now, Jordan Brand sells more than $3 billion a year of apparel and footwear, mostly to people who never saw him play. The Jumpman logo isn't identified in focus groups as a silhouette of an actual person, even though that person's actual name is often printed right above or below it. The logo has become like golden arches or an apple. Responders say it has come to mean, simply, excellence. That was Barack Obama's take on Jordan when he introduced him at the Presidential Medal of Freedom ceremony in 2016. When someone is the best, Obama joked, they are called "the Michael Jordan of rabbis or the Michael Jordan of outrigger canoeing."

Everyone in the room laughed.

Sitting in his chair, Michael leaned over to the woman sitting next to him, who'd just received the honor on behalf of her late great-aunt, and he whispered, "Were you nervous?"

Then he stood up and walked past fellow recipients Tom Hanks and Bruce Springsteen and Diana Ross and Vin Scully and Robert Redford. A soldier read out his citation. His mother was in the crowd. For the first time in a long time, he wasn't bigger than the moment. It showed in his body language and on his face. When we see the famous shots of Jordan clutching the Larry O'Brien Trophy, he's often cradling it, almost wrestling it, the man and his prize intertwined. His grip is aggressive. That's not how he looked standing next to Obama receiving his medal. He bowed his head so the shorter man could drape it over his neck. He *received* it. This was an object placed on him—not one he took. A grace, not a demand. Something he earned. Instead of hunching over and hiding his spoils, he stood there with the medal hanging on his chest. He looked out at the gathered crowd with something like humility and gratitude on his face. It's one of the few moments in his public life when he seemed to consider and appreciate how long and unlikely his road had been. In that moment of holstered guns, the work it must have taken to keep them up and loaded every other minute of every other day felt heavy and real.

.   .   .

In the last week of his presidency, Obama got a special gift: a custom pair of retro Jordan IVs with the presidential seal and his campaign logo on them. But those shoes and every following pair of iconic Jordans almost never existed. Two people saved the brand: Tinker Hatfield, a man who looked to the future, and Michael's father, James, a man who understood the past.

Hatfield came on board to run the Jordan design team starting with the Jordan IIIs. Let's go back to the mideighties. Even then Tinker looked good in flamboyant hats. He'd need all the mojo he could muster, sartorial and otherwise, because he'd been assigned an unhappy client. Jordan had broken his foot wearing Nikes, just three games into the 1985–86 season.

"It soured him," Hatfield says.

Now Jordan was entertaining offers from other shoe companies. The competition was whispering in his ear that Nike didn't have the design chops or the marketing expertise to actually deliver on the forest of promises it had made him. Even then Jordan scared people. He held the power. In the future, whenever the Nike executive suits would start complaining about how Hatfield was disrespecting the corporate culture, he'd slide a piece of paper with Jordan's cell number onto the table and dare the executives to call him and tell him why he and Tinker were wrong. Nobody ever dialed the number. But that kind of trust had to be earned, and for Hatfield, it started with a trip to Chicago.

He arrived at Michael's condo. Jordan knew he was coming. Tinker and Nike colleague Howard White knocked on the door. Nobody answered. They knocked louder, and that's when they heard a rumble and crashing coming from the basement. Hatfield thought it sounded like a pro wrestling match. He hit the doorbell. No answer. He hit it again. Finally, they heard a faint voice yell for them to come in. Tinker and Howard followed the noise downstairs.

"Michael was engaged," Hatfield says now, "in a knockdown drag-out no-holds-barred trash-talking crazy table tennis match with then-teammate Charles Oakley. They were playing table tennis like it was the Finals, Game 7. It was incredibly competitive, and there was trash-talking. It was physical. They weren't talking to us. They finally resolved the match. Michael won. He hardly ever lost at anything."

Michael and Tinker talked a little. Then they went down to Bigsby & Kruthers, where tailors were fitting Michael for a new suit. Just an hour earlier, Michael had been cursing and swinging a pingpong paddle like a battle ax, and now he engaged in thoughtful, high-level design conversation with the men bringing out bolts of fabric and showing him various cuts they could do for the lapels. If there was a moment when Tinker Hatfield first understood the direction his life would take, it happened there surrounded by tailors who were scurrying around Michael Jordan.

He went back to Portland and worked around the clock.

Jordan arrived in town to play the Trail Blazers and stopped at Hatfield's office. Tinker showed him a stack of leather, mostly sourced from furniture makers. The one Michael liked most was elephant-patterned. Tinker liked it too. So while the Nike bosses fretted about losing their new, vital client, Hatfield and his team worked with their factory in Asia to create a mock-up to present to Jordan.

There was a meeting scheduled at a hotel conference room in Orange County, California.

"Phil Knight was pretty well convinced that Michael was gonna leave Nike," Hatfield says. "Phil was very, very concerned. I think he thought for sure we had lost him. There was this one last meeting. It was in this hotel."

Everyone filed in.

Knight sat down. The Nike marketing head took a seat. So did Tinker, along with Michael's agents. James and Deloris Jordan came into the room.

Then they waited.

Hours passed.

Jordan's parents looked mortified.

"They are sitting there very respectful and quiet," Hatfield says. "You could tell they were a little steamed. They were his parents left waiting in this room for so many hours."

Nobody knew if Michael was going to even show.

"We waited for four hours," Hatfield says, "which is about how long it takes to play eighteen holes of golf. From what I understand, Michael was out on the golf course with some prospective partners, and Howard was with them but he was trying to get Michael to leave the golf course and go to the meeting."

Finally, Michael showed up.

He was in a bad mood, sulking, disinterested—until Tinker pulled out the Air Jordan III. That changed the whole tenor of the meetings, as did the models who came through wearing the corresponding apparel, and the rest is history. Jordan stayed with Nike and made enough money to buy a basketball team. For years, Hatfield thought his shoe design saved the company. Then he heard about what happened after the meeting ended.

Michael went outside and his father grabbed him in the parking lot.

"Son," he said, "that was embarrassing to your mother and I."

Michael apologized.

"What do you think I should do?" he asked.

His dad said that Nike's commitment was on display because Phil Knight had waited so long and its design skills were on display in the IIIs and that this seemed like the right move for his future. Michael listened. That's where the legend began—with North Carolina exerting its pull outside an Orange County hotel. From that parking lot to recognition from the president not just of his athletic prowess or his marketing savvy but of his drive, his competitiveness, his essential greatness. It could be seen as a culmination of a life spent escaping a past, or a postracial brand strategy anomaly, an American unicorn, or it could be seen in another way: a man actually fulfilling a destiny, carrying his family with him on his rise, coming from somewhere. Michael Jordan didn't just appear. He was raised—by his parents, by a community, by the stories of those who came before.

Act II

One of the great unexpected joys of these five weeks has been the rediscovery of the pregame theme music the Bulls used, "Sirius." You know the song. Makes your hair stand up on your arms when the synth kicks in with its tumble of sixteenth notes. A heavy bass undercurrent makes the same kind of noise a big ship propeller does beneath the black waves, a diesel engine thump. The public address announcer, Ray Clay, has made a life out of his Jordan introduction. He's done it for free in grocery stores shopping for vegetables, for money at bar mitzvahs and weddings. He even did it in Chapel Hill once at a Tar Heels event. A speech teacher helped him learn to push the air out with his stomach muscles instead of his chest and to manage the air in his lungs. Early in his career, he almost passed out after his opening, "AND NOW . . ."

"Breathing is very important," he says.

The first few notes of the song are enough to make players and coaches from that era break out in hives. It really is menacing to listen to even now. "I always can remember that damn song playing," Pat Riley told me recently. "It definitely alerted the opposition that a battle was about ready to begin, for real."

There's a version online I've been playing over and over, from Game 4 of the 1998 Finals. The crowd is as loud as the big arena speakers. The top comment on the video says, "Karl Malone hears this in his nightmares." It's thrilling even all these years later. After Clay announces the fourth starter, Ron Harper, the crowd gets louder—because he's also six-foot-six. They know what's coming. Every child of the 1990s can almost recite Clay's next words by heart, how he says Jordan's home like he's talking about Sparta or something: *FROM NORTH CAROLINA* . . . That signifies many worlds. Not just North Carolina but coastal Carolina, always different than the mountains or the Piedmont plain, and not just coastal Carolina but Wilmington, and not just Wilmington but the rural riverbank swamps stretching out from the edge of town. And not just generic swamps but two in particular. Holly Shelter and Angola Bay. That's where the Jordans come from. A tight wedge of brackish land outside Wilmington bordered by Highways 17 and 24 to the south and north, and Highways 117 and 50 to the west and east. Keep drilling down, before names and roads and any of that, go all the way back, because these 560 square miles of land tell you as much about the man as a story about being cut from a basketball team ever did. "There is a lot of power in staying connected," says Zandria Robinson, a Georgetown professor studying race, gender, popular culture and the U.S. South. "There is power in that particular kind of rearing too—all that work. This is why they stayed connected to that land."

Long before Michael Jordan came into the world, this is where he was born.

.　　.　　.

The land existed before humans ever took from it, carved homesteads from it, stalked its bounty for food and pleasure. Time moves differently back in the woods. Progress is a word that means fancier surfaces on the roads and pickup trucks instead of horse-pulled chairs with leather straps instead of springs. Before Highway 117 was a concrete road covered with asphalt, resurfaced seven years ago by a high school teammate of Jordan's, it was a wide dirt path that mirrored the Northeast Cape Fear River, running past a dozen or so plantation homes. And before that, it was nothing. A rut for deer maybe. Or a footpath used by the band of Iroquois who lived there first.

The first plantation up the Northeast Cape Fear River was called Stag Park.

The land was named on a Monday afternoon, November 12, 1663, when a group of white Englishmen from Barbados explored the river for the first time and came upon a tract of land without many trees and covered in lush, long grass—perfect for clearing. They saw turkeys and ducks. Several wolves howled. They stopped and watched a wolf tear an animal to pieces. They picked and ate wild grapes. On the northwest side of the river, they saw an enormous deer, with a mighty spread of points, and that's where they got the name for the land.

Governor George Burrington lived there first.

Samuel Strudwick got it after his death.

Ezekiel Lane Sr. got it from his family.

Upon Ezekiel's death, his granddaughter Mary Elizabeth Lane inherited Stag Park and sixteen slaves. She married a Georgia preacher, and together they ran Stag Park until around 1880.

The preacher's name was Jesse Jordan.

All that's left of the Stag Park empire is a silver historical marker on the side of 117. The land was cut into smaller and smaller pieces with each passing generation. Some of Jesse Jordan's descendants still live there. But the land always remains. Nearly four hundred years later and in the dark woods, no time at all has passed. Maybe the light now comes from million-candle-power Q-Beams instead of whale oil lamps. But it remains wild territory. These are gothic inland narrows. "Gothic" is the adjective Martin Scorsese used with his director of photography when they wanted to re-create the Wilmington coast for the film *Cape Fear*. The movie is composed so that the actual light degrades over time, to reflect the inner turmoil of the characters and to mirror the way the humidity and weird ocean currents can make the tidewater air shimmer sometimes. Black bears still hunt through these swamps. Vast woods of longleaf pine and 800-year-old cypress-tupelo trees tower over this landscape. Songbirds fill the air with sweet noise. Big whitetail deer, heads crowned with enormous medieval-looking racks, still move like shadows in and out of the forest. This is where five generations of Jordan men lived and died.

"The kind of mystical ways that people have described Jordan over the years can be frankly connected to what it is like to be on ancestral land," Zandria Robinson says. "They are living on Southern ancestral land. It's rare that it's physical in this kind of way—these multiple generations lived in this same area. Our ancestors walked their land, they buried s—— out here, worked out here, died out here, buried each other out here. . . . This is ancestral land."

The land is never just dirt and loam and clay and slate. It contains everything that has ever lived on or in it, fossils of tiny animals, the spirits of the people who tried to make their agrarian's stand, and the evil men have done to one another to control a piece of paper filed in something called a courthouse that the law says gives them title. And when the laws are corrupted and the courthouse collapses, the land will remain. Every man and woman, every race and tribe and family, makes their own history, on their land, in their dirt. They bury things that mean something only to them.

Every history is deeply personal. Every history is unique.

•   •   •

Five generations of Jordan men came before Michael, and he knew three of them: his father, James; his grandfather William; and his great-grandfather Dawson. Dawson's father was born a slave in 1862, and everyone called him Dick. In the sixty-four years he lived, before his heart and kidneys failed and he died in a Wilmington hospital, he went from slavery to owning his own home. He learned to read and could borrow the supplies needed to farm vegetables on his own credit. Like the men in a lot of families, he was a truck farmer. On Dick's death certificate, filled out with a typewriter, is the only evidence that *his* father ever lived. John Jordan and his wife, Alice, came and went from this earth and left virtually no trace of themselves behind. Think about that in the context of *The Last Dance*.

There's no history showing where John Jordan was born or where he was held captive as a slave. Based on his research into property and burial records, the Pender County historian Mike Taylor says John likely worked the fields at Jesse Jordan's plantation. New documents are being found all the time, old wills and business papers, even maps of the swamps to the east of Highway 117. "The Angola Bay map that is attached was made in 1883," Taylor says, "and was discovered in a cache of surveys found in an old barn in a neighboring county only this past year. Michael Jordan's ancestry in America is rooted in this region going back to Colonial days. They are rooted to land, first enslaved working on land in Stag Park. I believe some of his enslaved ancestors are likely buried on this land."

There's one piece of old paper that *might* have John Jordan's name on it. When Ezekiel Lane died and his granddaughter Mary Jordan inherited those sixteen slaves, their first names were listed in the probate documents, filled out by hand. First names only. Old Sam and his wife, Beck. Little Sam, Little Moses, and Ben Judge. Plato and his wife, Amy. There is only one listing for a mother and child, according to the custom of listing a woman first and a man second only if the male was actually an infant or a toddler. Too young to work. The document lists, among the sixteen, a woman named Molly or Millie and a John. That's probably Michael Jordan's great-great-great-grandfather. Probably. There's no way to ever know for sure.

That's not an accident.

Historians and genealogists talk about the difficulty of cracking "the 1870 brick wall," because census takers didn't record even the first names of slaves. It wasn't because they didn't know the names. Census takers were locals, and as court and probate records from that time show, nearly everyone knew the names of local slaves. The U.S. Congress forced census takers *not* to write down names or place of birth, which created the wall—which erased them from history but not from the land.

.　　　.　　　.

Consider where this family history is leading. Leave Stag Park and go a century into the future for a moment. Sit with James and Deloris Jordan on Gordon Road, after their kids had gone to bed, the summer air hot and humid outside. When they wanted to go commune with the past, they sometimes went inland toward the swamps and farms. But when they wanted to dream, they went the other direction. They slipped out of the quiet house and got into their car, making the drive from memory: Gordon Road to Highway 117 until, not even fifteen minutes later, they parked at the Atlantic Ocean. The smell of salt hung in the air. Sometimes they just sat in the car beneath the moonlight, and sometimes they walked hand in hand along the sandy dunes. The conversation inevitably turned to the dreams they shared for all of their five children. They wanted them to be men and women of integrity and work. They put that dream into action. James and Deloris Jordan created the America they wanted in how they taught their children to move through the world.

They told Michael to turn all negative events into positives, which later became his armor made of slights. Michael's mother wrote children's books after he got famous, and in one of them, her parenting philosophy was revealed: saying you want something is fine and well, a good start, but doing something about it is what really counts. At the end of that book, when the mother puts her son to bed after his first successful basketball game, she tells him with pride, "I guess you aren't just a dreamer but a doer, Michael."

That idea is what this ground was nurturing for all those years. It's what Zandria meant when she talked about the power of Southern ancestral land.

.   .   .

Every ten years, when the census takers would fan out around the countryside, when roads were makeshift things and not codified government projects, they'd find a Jordan man living in the same pie-slice-shaped wedge of land where they had always been. Dawson lived on Holly Shelter Road in 1920, Bannerman's Bridge Road in 1930. Both of those are tucked into bends in the river, where the old Stag Park plantation used to be, where Dawson used to work a boat.

By 1940, Dawson Jordan lived between the swamps, Holly Shelter to the south and Angola Bay to the north. The year before, he'd worked fifty-two weeks straight and made $300. His son, William, and grandson lived with him too. The boy's name was James R. Jordan. James was four years old and twenty-three years from the birth of his son the basketball star, Michael Jeffrey Jordan, living back near the swamp with the son of a former slave—seventeen miles northwest of Highway 117 where it intersects Burgaw and a half-hour drive, looping to either the north or the south of the Angola Bay swamp, from that house to the cemetery where James Jordan would one day be buried.

There are a lot of people still around those rural counties who remember the sound of Dawson's deep bass voice. He drove a mule-drawn cart even after the first rocket sent a man into space. He made and sold moonshine out in the swamps and made extra money as a cook at the Wallace Hunting Club, the kind of hand-me-down place that shows up alongside church memberships and military service in small-town obituaries. They kept a low-slung camp, covered in unpainted clapboard, fronted by a porch with no railing. The front door led to a dining room with one long table taking up most of the space.

An old man named Frank Futch used to go there with his grandfather as a young hunter and still remembers Dawson sitting on a box collecting money or on a nearby bench with one of his great-grandsons—most likely Michael's oldest brother, Ronnie. Dawson liked to mix vodka and Coca-Cola and sip while he cooked deer meat or pork chops or chicken. He made a pot of rice with every meal. Sometimes, when he'd doze off, one of the hunters, an undertaker in one of the nearby towns, would tiptoe over and pretend to start measuring the sleeping man. Dawson would startle awake, laugh, and yell at the man, "Get away from me! I ain't dead!"

• • •

Michael Jordan grew up with all these stories. He knew Dawson, who died in 1977—the year Michael started high school at Laney—and would later describe the old man as "tough," tearing up at the memory.

His childhood lives in the back-home stories he tells. There's the pig story and the ax story and the BB gun story and the horse in the cornfield story, to name a few. Unlike the usual greatest-hits montage he spins for interviewers, these remain personal to him, and he gets wary if you bring them up—*like, who in my life is talking out of school?*

Mike used to ride horses around his family's land until one threw him off and drug him through a cornfield. His foot got caught in the stirrup, and for a quarter of a mile, he bounced on the tilled ground and got ripped through the stalks. It was thirty-eight miles from the Jordan boys' house to the grandparents' place out in the country. Every weekend they went out there and just roamed around.

At six or seven, Mike went outside with an ax, mainly because his parents had told him not to play with it, and started chopping up wood and little branches, like he'd seen the grown-ups do. Then he misjudged and caught his big toe with the ax. There was blood everywhere, and he went screaming into his parents' house. His mom took him to a local doctor, and a lady there put kerosene on his foot to disinfect it. To this day, he's missing a quarter of an inch of his big toe.

Around the same age he had another brilliant idea: slip beneath the electric wire surrounding the hog pen and aggravate some of the pigs. The Jordan boys thought it was hilarious to dance in the mud and make the pigs chase them around honking and snorting. A particularly annoyed sow disagreed. She chased Mike toward the fence, and as he prepared to leap over the top wire to safety, he tripped. Caught the electric wire right across his chest. About had his teeth chattering, he got shocked so bad, and left him with a burn across his chest. When he went inside for some sympathy, his parents told him, "You shouldn't have been out there messing with the pigs."

One time, Larry wrecked a Yamaha 60 dirt bike with Mike on the back of it. Both of 'em got all skinned up but feared the wrath of their father even more. So they wrapped their cuts in tissue and then put on long-sleeve shirts to hide their arms. In the North Carolina summer. James got suspicious, eyeing the boys as they sat at the dinner table, trying to figure out what they were up to. Right about then is when Michael's elbow started bleeding— through his shirt.

"Take off that damn long-sleeve shirt," Mr. Jordan commanded.

Mike complied, revealing the disaster of his arms. His dad sold the bike.

Another time, some neighborhood kids were throwing footballs and shoes and stuff at the family's electric meter. One connected and broke it. Mike's grandmother was furious and told Mike's father, who said he'd take care of it.

He called all the neighborhood kids over to the garage.

"One way in, one way out," Michael foreshadows when telling the story later. He's a good storyteller. Mr. Jordan told the kids he wanted to give them some cake and ice cream, and like suckers, they all bought it. Mike's grandmother saw what was coming and pulled him in to help her in the kitchen, keeping him out of the line of fire. That's when they heard the screaming. Mike's dad was in there giving out whippings to all the kids, not just his own. They all ran crying to their parents, who then went over to confront Mr. Jordan.

They found him on the porch, smoking a cigarette.

"You beat my kid?" they asked.

"You damn right," he replied.

.   .   .

It was 1977 when Jordan's life got divided into two halves. One potential, one kinetic. A past full of spirits and ancestors, influences and guides, a future full of choices and conflict, dead ends and golden roads. Ninth grade really pissed him off. He got suspended on the first day of school, breaking a record of perfect attendance. All his discipline problems were driven by this sense of unfairness that had taken up residence inside him. It started with the miniseries *Roots*. The racial injustice that had shaped his family suddenly became real to him. He raged against anything he couldn't control. He'd prove himself to everyone.

That carried over to the next year, when he tried out for varsity basketball for the first time. This is where the myth of Michael Jordan was born, and in nearly all retellings of his life, including in *The Last Dance*, all roads lead back to this tryout and this rejection. The mother road is erased and a new path is laid out. That's almost true. The mother road is erased for the public but not for him. He never forgets. Anything.

On the day he didn't make the varsity basketball team as a sophomore, he stood in the school gymnasium that would one day bear his name, and he scrolled down one of two lists hung on the door, and when he didn't see his name but did see the name of his classmate Leroy Smith, he rushed home in a rage. The road that took him home that afternoon in November of 1978 was Highway 117.

In that moment, he began to understand the focus he could find by turning everyone and everything into an adversary. Like when he told the story, to himself and everyone else, that he was cut from the basketball team by a coach who doubted his talent. Turns out, he wasn't really cut at all. No, he didn't make the team. But according to a famous *Sports Illustrated* story, that's because the coach recognized his immense talent and put him on junior varsity, where he'd get more minutes a game. Clifton "Pop" Herring, that coach, later found himself taunted by Michael's story about what happened for decades.

"The thing is, people in Wilmington who knew the story," says Pop's daughter, Paquita Yarborough, "they didn't hate that Michael was a hometown hero, but they hated the story was never set straight. That's what people's irritation really was. Part of the story was for his brand. Part of the story was to sell shoes and products and 'You can be like me, I got cut. Then after that I became the greatest basketball player who ever lived.' It is annoying. It's very annoying. I have intentionally not watched Michael Jordan things. I had no clue there was a documentary."

When Pop died last December, the Jordan family sent flowers. Paquita wrote her father's obituary. Four hundred and twenty-two words and not one of them was "Michael" or "Jordan."

•　　　•　　　•

The Jordan family and the Herring family are connected by a shared history that goes a lot deeper than one basketball tryout—that history is reflected in the Pulitzer Prize winner David Zucchino's new book, *Wilmington's Lie*. It's about an organized and violent white coup of the city in 1898—exactly one hundred years before the events of *The Last Dance*. The two stories were released within months of each other and are interesting to consider together. One describes the fall of black Wilmington, and the other chronicles the rise of the most successful black Wilmingtonian.

Wilmington on the eve of the twentieth century was a model for an American city three decades after the guns of the Civil War fell silent. Zucchino paints a picture of an integrating city. Three of the ten aldermen were black. Ten of the twenty-six policemen. Black merchants were free to set up in the city market. There was a black coroner and jailer, and the only daily Negro paper in the world, as its masthead said. The paper had white advertisers. Black men didn't need to look at the ground when they passed a white man on the street. In 1880, Wilmington had the highest share of black residents of any Southern city, 60 percent, as compared to Atlanta's 44 percent and New Orleans's 27 percent. The neighborhoods were integrated. The courts were integrated. Black magistrates sentenced white defendants. A black middle class grew with each year. In 1898, Zucchino writes, the American Baptist Publication Society called it "the freest town for a negro in the country."

That didn't mean everyone in the city accepted what Wilmington was becoming.

There were two cultures living side by side, competing for the future of their home. Blacks and white Republicans, for instance, celebrated Memorial Day, laying wreaths at the American military cemetery in town. White Democrats, the political party of the slave-owning class, refused to honor American dead. They even tried to have Market Street moved so they wouldn't have to suffer the indignity of walking past the soldiers' graves. Earlier in May, they celebrated Confederate Memorial Day instead.

That was Wilmington as the 1898 election approached.

There are two great books on what happened next, but basically two groups of elite white citizens formed secret committees to overthrow the government if the election didn't go as they wanted. The mostly Irish immigrants were enlisted as muscle. The treasonous army called itself the Red Shirts. So many white people bought guns in the lead-up to the election that the stores in the city ran out and had to request an emergency restock from dealers in Richmond and Baltimore. Like the Ku Klux Klan thirty years before or again thirty years after, the Red Shirts rode in the night, yanking outspoken black citizens from their homes.

Two days after the election, the Red Shirts went looking for blood. A crowd of black longshoremen and stevedores who loaded cotton on the docks came back to their neighborhood to protect their families. A black store owner tried to reason with men to leave before the whites arrived.

"For the sake of your lives, your families, your children, and your country, go home and stay there," he begged. "We are powerless."

They faced a choice. They chose to stay.

That's when the shooting started.

The Red Shirts killed a still unknown number of people. At least sixty black people died. As Zucchino reported, the mob forced the resignation of the mayor, all of the aldermen, and the chief of police. The black newspaper was burned down. Many black residents with money, power, or education were forced to leave the city, along with white politicians who supported equality—in some cases at gun point. Three days later, the white preachers of Wilmington told their congregation they'd done the Lord's work.

"God from the beginning of time intended that intelligent white men should lead the people and rule the country," said a Baptist minister named James Kramer, who'd carried a rifle into the streets.

No conspirator was ever charged with a crime.

North Carolina's Jim Crow laws grew out of this moment. Its aftermath can be seen in the generations of stagnated lives, yes, but perhaps the cold arithmetic of numbers reveals the terrible legacy of the coup most pointedly. In 1896, according to the

New Yorker, there were 126,000 registered black voters in the state. Six years later, there were only 6,100. Black families fled the city, some moving north, others hunkering out in the swampy longleaf pine forests like the Jordans. On the morning of the coup, 56 percent of Wilmington's citizens were black. Two years later, the majority of citizens were white. Today, 76 percent of the city is white, and only 18 percent is black.

The African American population living in and around Wilmington for the past 120 years has internalized a lesson that parts of America have too often tried to ignore. Michael learned it early. Once, he and his white best friend, David Bridges, went swimming at a friend's house. The parents weren't home. The boys were around twelve. When the parents returned and saw a black kid in the pool, they ordered everyone out. Michael and David walked away, and as David tried to comfort his friend, they heard everyone jump back in the pool.

Michael has never told the story in public, just as he's never publicly commented on the 1898 massacre in Wilmington, not once, even in passing. Michael's great-grandfather Dawson was six in 1898 and didn't die until Michael's fourteenth birthday. He didn't need to read a book. He knew someone who lived through it. "I'm sure the family was aware and just laid low," Zucchino says. "A lot of people didn't talk about it. It was too painful and it died out after a few generations."

This history stayed buried for a long time, and when it did get passed down in words, it was usually told as a "war" in black homes and washed over as a "riot" in white ones. Two important books prior to Zucchino's exposed that history. One, by Helen Edmonds, was published in 1951 and enraged the Wilmington establishment by calling out their lies. The second was by H. Leon Prather Sr. His came out in the winter of 1984, on the same day Michael Jordan scored nineteen points as the Tar Heels beat Clemson to extend a winning streak to eighteen games.

.   .   .

Between 1984 and 2003, Michael Jordan became the most famous person in the world as his family members went on with their lives. Michael sucked up all the oxygen, which might be why few people noticed that around the same time Michael quit basketball the first time, his oldest brother volunteered for the army's parachute training school at Fort Benning. James Jordan Jr., known to his family as Ronnie, was much older than the rest of the candidates for the coveted jump wings.

The house on Gordon Road sat between the army's Fort Bragg and the marine corps' Camp Lejeune. The same North Carolina forests that once hid runaway slaves now hide soldiers and marines on training runs through the night, wearing face paint and dark forest camo. Fighting has always offered a way out for country folks, black and white. Michael grew up surrounded by the military. His father, James, served in the air force. Ronnie chose the army. He graduated from high school on a Friday and enlisted that Sunday. He needed a new way. His mother felt like someone had died. Their house missed his enormous presence, and losing that energy left a palpable hole, especially for his mother. For many years afterward, she refused to go into his room.

Command Sgt. Maj. Jordan, as his soldiers called him, is an American stalwart. Here's an example. His thirty years arrived just as his brigade was deploying to a war zone for Operation Iraqi Freedom. Jordan wrote a letter asking for special dispensation to stay in uniform and go to war with his men. "Here's a guy who had thirty years in and had nothing to gain by deploying," says his commanding officer, Col. Bryan Ellis. "And, of course, he had everything to lose, up to and including his life. And he never hesitated."

Ellis and Jordan protected each other in Iraq. Almost nobody ever asked Ronnie about his famous brother. They flew all over the country, and when the brigade rotated home, Jordan could finally retire. The army held a big celebration at Fort Bragg, in North Carolina. Ellis held a seat open. He posted young soldiers at either end of the parade field, by the sidewalk to the parking lot.

"Sergeant Major has a guest coming," he said. "You'll recognize him."

The ceremony started, and standing up on the review stand, Ellis heard a rumble through the crowd. He looked up to see a star-struck young soldier escorting Michael Jordan to a seat. When the presentation ended, a crowd swarmed Michael, who was polite but quickly made an exit.

"He knew this was his brother's special day," he says.

That day, the Jordan family gathered at Ronnie's home near the base. Ellis came and brought his ten-year-old son. They walked out onto the patio and saw all the uncles in a crowd. Michael was with them, holding a Corona and a cigar. The colonel grabbed a beer and a little later felt a hand on his back. He turned around and found himself face-to-face for the first time with the most famous man on the planet. Jordan stuck out his hand.

"I'm Michael," he said. "I've heard a lot about you."

Act III

The Last Dance premiered on Sunday, April 19.

That night, the people who produced the film all gathered on a Zoom call to raise a toast to director Jason Hehir. A cast of ESPN folks joined the virtual toast. Some Netflix people were there too, as was NBA commissioner Adam Silver, top Disney executive Bob Iger, and ESPN president Jimmy Pitaro. The heavy hitters. All of Jordan's executives were in high spirits, and then, in the top corner of the screen, Michael popped into view. Michael Jordan! Even his appearance thrilled some of the executives on the call. Everyone toasted Jason, who raised a White Russian—he's a *Big Lebowski* fan—in appreciation. Jordan raised a glass of tequila in salute and made a joke.

He hoped his mama wasn't gonna get mad at him for all his foul language in the film.

The first episode began, and *The Last Dance*, like so much of Jordan's life, was then public property, to be considered, debated, judged. In the *New York Times*, the Pulitzer Prize–winning critic Wesley Morris compared the film to the Oscar-winning *Made in America*, highlighting what he saw as a difference between Jordan's place in the culture and that of Barack Obama, Muhammad Ali, or even OJ Simpson. "Jordan is as important but less transcendent," he wrote. "Less polarizing, less political, therefore less politicized."

Less political has always been Jordan's most tender spot. The fear that despite absolute devotion to his craft he might still be found wanting. The kind of man who might dominate the game for years or the culture for a few weeks at a time, but wouldn't change the world. Michael has found his voice late in life, speaking out against police violence, donating millions to charities designed to bridge the chasm of mistrust between cops and the communities they patrol. He supported NFL players kneeling in public and raised money for Barack Obama. But he is still the man who grew up around rural African Americans who believed that the only way to succeed in America, to defend yourself and your family, was to work twice as hard as everyone else. "That 'work twice as hard as white folks' s—— we all heard growing up," Kiese Laymon says, "came right from our grandparents."

Jordan left North Carolina for Chicago carrying souls with him, like passengers, like roots. He became a superstar and a global icon, but he was never not also a member of a family that lived through slavery and the coup of 1898 and Jim Crow and on and on. His family, and their sliver of land, shaped him, taught him how to survive and struggle, how to surpass. Watching Jordan on the screen in the documentary, listening as he says again and again that he will outwork you, whoever you are, raises what just might be the essential Michael Jordan question: Isn't working that hard and achieving all that it brings and never letting go of your approach, isn't that its own kind of yard sign? How, exactly, can Michael Jordan's life be apolitical?

"It *is* political," Imani Perry tells me emphatically when I raise the question with her. "Black Southern folks in particular, it is political. In it there is a transcendence of the expectations of what space you're gonna occupy."

That idea runs counter to the way the culture usually judges Jordan. It reframes his story. Michael Jordan's life is as much an act of protest as carrying a sign or speaking out against a war.

·　　·　　·

The Last Dance will live in the streaming world, first at ESPN and later at Netflix, but the moment of its cultural domination will soon start to fade. That's the duality for someone like Jordan. Even as he catches glimpses of his own immortality, he is also confronted with the very real passage of time. Three of his old bodyguards have died, including two in the past two years. These were the men who knew him best. They called him Black Jesus. When John Michael Wozniak would beat him in cards or coin tossing or any other inane competition, he'd sing the Doobie Brothers as a taunt: "Jesus is just alright with me . . . Jesus is just alright."

Their mortality shook Jordan, who had kept up with them even after his playing days were done. When Gus Lett got cancer, Michael got him moved from a South Side Chicago hospital to Northwestern Medical Center, paid his bills, and told the doctors to treat that old man in the bed exactly like they'd treat Michael Jordan. When Clarence Travis retired from the police department, his friends threw a party at a White Sox game. Jordan showed up. When Joe Rokas retired, an enormous television set arrived at his front door.

"Michael is loyal as s——," says Nicholi Wozniak. "If you are in his circle, you are in his circle. A tribe is the best way to describe it."

Michael's staff says he couldn't even talk about Gus when the cancer came back. It hurt him too bad.

Wozniak was the last one still working for Jordan, guarding his big estate in Highland Park. John Michael fought his cancer hard, but the end came quick earlier this year. Nicholi was with his family in Nashville when he got the call that he needed to rush home. He boarded a Southwest flight into Midway, an hour without his phone, no way to know what was happening up there ahead of him. When he landed, he knew from the messages that he was too late. His father had died. There was a voicemail on his phone too, a message of condolence that had arrived midflight.

It was from Michael.

·   ·   ·

Jordan is probably playing golf right now. He's fifty-seven. Who knows if he'll ever dominate the culture like this again? He's living with his family in a mansion overlooking the sixteenth green of a course in Jupiter, Florida. It's a swank gated community of trust-fund loafers, military-industrial CEOs, and hedge fund billionaires.

His basketball team in Charlotte is still in quarantine limbo. Both of Michael's brothers work for the Hornets. He sends the now-retired command sergeant major to owners meetings in his stead. Michael hired his brothers because he trusts them. That's also why he took such care of his security guards for all those years.

"My biggest lesson about people came from my father," Michael told me that afternoon in Carolina. "He could talk to anybody. He could get along with anybody. But he never let people into his life. He never let people see his thoughts. His secrets. I have those traits. I can sit and talk to all the different sponsors, and they know only as much as I want them to know. I am always able to maintain that mystique. You could talk to him for two or three hours and not know a f——ing thing in two or three hours. But at the same time, you'll say he's a nice gentleman. He never gave any family secrets away. I've got that trait. I use it."

Keeping your head down and your thoughts to yourself, working hard, never trusting, never easing up even for a moment. It was a choice. Michael Jordan was born into a world of predators and into a line of survivors, and he studied on how to win. That's the real wonder of him up close. Not being near his fame or even the legend. It's seeing the full expression of a kind of person. A child was taught how to survive in a world of wolves, and he used that knowledge to become the alpha wolf. I picture him leaning back in his office chair in 2013 in Charlotte. Special fans clean the air of the smoke trailing in a lazy line up from his cigar. Inside he's thinking about whom he might still be able to prove wrong.

Walking through a hallway in the arena he owns, he smiled.

You couldn't tell what he was thinking.

"You won't," he said. "I've been trained my whole life: maintain your emotions, don't do anything to give out a misconception of what your thoughts or feelings are."

The lights were off. Nobody was around. Well, that's sort of true. There are always people walking with Michael, invisible but shoulder to shoulder, every step of the way. There's Mike Jordan of 4647 Gordon Road and of course James Jordan, may he rest in peace, and Ronnie and Larry and all those Jordan men who came before, Dawson and William and Richard and John. Especially John, whose great-great-great-grandson learned to fly.

He whistled in the dark as he walked alone toward his car.

Inside his expensive shoes he had nine and three-quarter toes.

·　　·　　·

Michael Jordan doesn't like to come home. He said once that he senses some malevolent forces waiting to pull him back into this place he escaped. But home remains a source of his power. One year on Easter, he took his now-wife, Yvette, back to Gordon Road. They drove down Highway 117 between his old house and Laney High, because she needed to see it and he needed to show it to her.

"I was a normal guy," he told me. "I grew up in a normal house."

The first free male of Michael Jordan's line was Richard James Jordan, born a slave in 1862 and freed three years later. As he neared sixty, having seen both the Civil War and the 1898 coup, Richard lived on Acorn Branch Creek, which has now mostly been filled in and covered with modern Wilmington. A tiny trickle still runs in a nature reserve between the Wilmington Airport and Highway 117. People like to mountain-bike there. A century ago, Acorn Branch Creek ran directly beneath what is now Gordon Road. The Jordan family had survived for six generations in these hard tidewater counties, moving up and down Highway 117, and by the time Mike Jordan was a boy, he lived almost exactly on a spot where the last slave in the family had lived too.

"Like the T-shirts say," Zandria Robinson says, "he's his ancestors' wildest dreams."

He went along 117 every day, from the house to high school, before he moved away. The drive takes seven minutes. About halfway off to the left there's a tiny cemetery hidden now behind an industrial park. A chain-link fence surrounds it. Spanish moss hangs from the skeletal winter trees. Once it was called Acorn Branch Colored Grave Yard. Slaves were buried there before the war. The county runs it today, and a local official said that any African American buried in the small Wrightsboro neighborhood back then was almost certainly buried at Acorn Branch. A lot of the cemetery records have been lost or thrown away, but in the remaining files, that official found paperwork showing Richard's widow and his son and daughter-in-law are buried at Acorn Branch. Richard is almost certainly buried there too. All four of them in unmarked graves.

The cemetery is just to the east of 117 and a mile north of Gordon Road.

Mike passed it every day, and now Michael was passing it again with Yvette, pointing to his home and to the gymnasium where he tells people he got cut. They drove around town for an hour and a half. Yvette asked a lot of questions. She knew all about Air Jordan, about the shoes and the rings but didn't know anything about where any of that came from, where the man disappeared and the legend began. Going home with him changes a lot of things. Puts him in focus. That long-ago United Center introduction, accompanied by strobes and lasers and those chill bump sixteenth notes, undercut by a rumbling bass line buried down deep, feels different. Watch that sequence from the 1998 Finals again. Listen to it build. The man in the middle! Michael Jordan is sitting on the bench, waiting to hear his name, the most famous man in the world at the absolute peak of his powers, Richard Jordan's wildest dream. Now listen as the announcer leans into his microphone and uses his stomach muscles to bring up enough air. He remembers to breathe and then cuts through the storm of noise.

"From North Carolina . . ."

Runner's World

WINNER—FEATURE WRITING

The winners of the 2021 National Magazine Awards were announced on Thursday, June 10. The recipient of the National Magazine Award for Feature Writing was "Twelve Minutes and a Life." The winners of the 2021 Pulitzer Prizes were announced the next day. The recipient of the Pulitzer Prize for Feature Writing was also "Twelve Minutes and a Life." The citation for the National Magazine Award explains—in part—what Mitchell S. Jackson achieved with "Twelve Minutes and a Life": "What is lost when another Black life is snatched away by systemic racism? To feel it in the depths of your soul, read this story. Jackson's electrifyingly personal account of the life and death of Ahmaud Arbery is the result of immaculate reporting and writing. It is an indictment, a celebration, and a lasting eulogy." Jackson's most recent book, Survival Math: Notes on an All-American Family, *was published in 2019.*

Mitchell S. Jackson

Twelve Minutes and a Life

I magine young Ahmaud "Maud" Arbery, a junior varsity scatback turned undersized varsity linebacker on a practice field of the Brunswick High Pirates. The head coach has divided the squad into offense and defense and has his offense running the plays of their next opponent. The coach, as is his habit, has been taunting his defense. "Y'all ain't ready," he says. "You can't stop us," he says. "What y'all gone do?" The next play, Maud, all five feet, ten inches, and 165 pounds of him, bursts between blockers and—BOOM!—lays a hit that makes the sound of cars crashing, that echoes across the field and into the stands, that just might reach the locker room. It's a feat that teenage Maud also intends as a message to his coaches, his teammates, and all else that ain't hitherto hipped: don't test my heart. Some of those teammates smash their fist to their mouth and oooh. Others slap one another's pads and point. An assistant coach winces and runs to the aid of the tackled teammate. And the head coach, well, he trumpets his whistle. "Why'd you hit him like that?" he hollers. "Save that for Friday. Let's see you do that on Friday."

That Friday, in Glynn County Stadium (one of the largest high school stadiums in all of gridiron-loving Georgia), the Pirates, clad in their home white jerseys with blue and gold trim, huddle in the locker room. Maud, who wears high shoulder pads, a 2x4 face mask, and number twenty-one in honor of his brother, Buck, and his idol, famed NFL safety Sean Taylor, swaggers into the center of his teammates and begins the chant he's christened into a pregame ritual.

"Y'all ready!" he shouts.

"Hell yeah!" they shout.

"Y'all ready!" he shouts.

"Hell yeah!" they shout.

"Y'all ain't ready?!" he shouts.

"Sheeeeeit!" they shout.

To applause that could be thunder, the team stampedes out of the fog-filled mouth of a blow-up tunnel onto the field. The school band plays the fight song and cheerleaders shake pom-poms from a row in front of the band. There's a raucous sea of blue and gold in the stands, including plenty of Maud's people. Game time, the opposing team calls the play that Maud put the fierce kaput on in practice, and beneath a metal-halide glare that's also a gauntlet, Maud barrels towards the running back and—BOOM!—lays a hit that sounds like trucks colliding. It's a noise that resounds across the field and into the stands, that just might ring all over Brunswick. The fans send up a roar but Maud trots to the sidelines almost insouciant. Jason Vaughn, an assistant coach who also coached Maud on JV, grabs him by his face mask. "Now that's how you hit," he says, tamping astonishment that a boy his size could hit that hard.

But that's young Maud, undersized in the physical sense, supersized in heart.

Sunday, February 23, 2020 | 1:04pm

Time-stamped security footage from an adjacent home shows Maud, who's out for a run in Brunswick's Satilla Shores subdivision, wandering up a sunny patch of narrow road and stopping on the spotty lawn of a sand-colored under-construction bungalow addressed 220 Satilla Drive. There's a red portable toilet in the front yard. The garage is wide open.

Ahmaud, dressed in light-colored low-top Nikes, a white T-shirt, and khaki cargo shorts, loafs on the lawn for a moment before drifting into the building. The security camera records him inside the home, a brightened skeleton of beams and plywood and stacks of sheetrock and piping and wire. There are boxes of materials scattered about and a small forklift pushed in a corner. Maud doesn't touch any of those things. He looks around, gazes beyond the frame of the camera toward the river behind the house. Maybe he wonders what the home will look like when it's finished. Maybe he conjures an image of a family who could afford to live in a place so close to water.

Maud ain't the first person to wander onto the site. Its security cameras have recorded others including a white couple one evening and a pair of white boys one day. On four occasions, it also recorded what appears to be the same person: a slim young Black man with wild natural hair and tattoos on his shoulders and arms, a dude, that by my eye, don't resemble Maud. Let me add that the homeowner will confirm that nothing was stolen or damaged during any of the visits.

Meanwhile, a coveralled neighbor spies Maud roaming the site and calls 911. "There's a guy in the house right now," he reports. "It's a house under construction. 219 or 220 Satilla Drive." The man waits near the corner of Jones Road and Satilla Drive. "I just need to know what he's doing wrong," says the dispatcher. "He's been caught on the camera a bunch before. It's kind of an ongoing thing out here," says the caller. It's a statement of which he can't be sure, though he does get right Maud's physical description: "Black guy, white T-shirt."

·   ·   ·

To fathom what it meant for Maud to be out for a run in Glynn County, you need to know a thing or two about the pastime of recreational running. Before the 1960s, the idea of jogging for almost everybody save serious athletes was this: Now why would

I do that? But in 1962, legendary track coach and Nike cofounder Bill Bowerman visited New Zealand and met with fellow coach Arthur Lydiard who'd developed a cross-country training program. Bowerman returned to the States excited by what he'd seen. He launched a similar program in Eugene (home of his alma mater and employer, the University of Oregon), wrote a pamphlet on the subject in 1966, and the next year, published a cowritten book titled *Jogging: A Medically-Approved Physical Fitness Program for all Ages Prepared by a Heart Specialist and a Famous Track Coach*. That book became a best-seller and kickstarted jogging as an American pastime.

Let me acknowledge that I am one of the rarest of Americans, one otherwise known as a Black Oregonian. As such, I feel compelled to share a truth about my home state: It's white. I'm talking banned-Blacks-in-its-state-constitution white. At the time that Bowerman was inspiring Eugene residents to trot miles around their neighborhoods in sweatpants and running shoes, Eugene was a stark 97 percent white. One could argue that the overwhelming whiteness of jogging today may be, in part, a product of Eugene's demographics. But if we're keeping it 100, the monolithic character of running can be credited to the ways in which it's been marketed and to the systemic forces that have placed it somewhere on a continuum between impractical extravagance and unaffordable hazard for scores of people who ain't white.

Matter of truth, around the time Bowerman visited New Zealand and published a best-selling book, millions of Blacks were living in the Jim Crow South; by 1968, Blacks diaspora-wide had mourned the assassinations of Medgar Evers, Malcolm X, and Martin Luther King Jr. And by the late sixties and beyond, the Blacks of the Great Migration were redlined into ever more depressed sections of northern and western cities, areas where the streets were less and less safe to walk, much less run. Forces aplenty discouraged Blacks from reaping the manifold benefits of jogging. And though the demographics of runners have become more diverse over the last fifty years, jogging, by and large, remains a sport and pastime pitched to privileged whites.

Peoples, I invite you to ask yourself, just what is a runner's world? Ask yourself who deserves to run? Who has the right? Ask who's a runner? What's their so-called race? Their gender? Their class? Ask yourself where do they live, where do they run? Where can't they live and run? Ask what are the sanctions for asserting their right to live and run—shit—to exist in the world. Ask why? Ask why? Ask why?

Ahmaud Arbery, by all accounts, loved to run but didn't call himself a runner. That is a shortcoming of the culture of running. That Maud's jogging made him the target of hegemonic white forces is a certain failure of America. Check the books—slave passes, vagrancy laws, Harvard's Skip Gates arrested outside his own crib—Blacks ain't never owned the same freedom of movement as whites.

Sunday, February 23, 2020 | 1:08pm

Maud strolls out the house and in just a few steps, begins to jog. He's unaware of the witness who called 911, a man still surveilling him. "He's running right now. There he goes right now," says the witness to dispatch. "Okay, what is he doing?" says the dispatcher. "He's running down the street," says the man. The footage shows Maud jogging past the Satilla Drive home of Gregory and Travis McMichael—a father and son. Gregory McMichael, an ex-cop stripped of his power to arrest for failure to attend use-of-force training, notices Maud passing his house and deems him suspicious. "Travis, the guy is running down the street," he hollers. "Let's go." For reasons the McMichaels must now account for in court (both have been indicted on nine counts, including felony murder and aggravated assault), they arm themselves—the son with a Remington 870 shotgun and the father with a .357 Magnum—and hop in a white Ford pickup truck.

•   •   •

The Golden Isles lie along Georgia's Atlantic coast between Savannah and Jacksonville, Florida. The region encompasses the barrier islands of St. Simons, Sea Island, Little St. Simons, and Jekyll, as well as the mainland cities of Darien and Brunswick. Satilla Shores, part of the Golden Isles, is an unincorporated neighborhood of upper- and middle-class families; of blue- and white-collar retirees; of seasonal vacation-home owners and lifelong denizens; of fresh transplants. The small neighborhood features narrow roads canopied by moss-draped live oaks, tall southern pines, and crepe myrtle; and one- and two-story homes with landscaped lawns and driveways parked with late-model vehicles and boats. Homes on one side of Satilla Drive—the neighborhood's main street—boast as a backyard amenity, the sediment-colored Little Satilla River, replete with its miles-wide spartina salt marshes.

Maud's family home in Brunswick, the one where he lived at the time he was murdered, is a mere two miles from Satilla Shores, but in meaningful ways, it's almost another country. The median household income for all of Glynn County is $51,000; in Brunswick that figure is $26,000. The poverty rate of what young Black residents call "the Wick" is a staggering 38 percent.

"The Wick" is where Ahmaud Marquez Arbery was born on May 8, 1994. He was the third beloved child of Wanda Cooper-Jones and Marcus Arbery Sr. Their working-class family included his older brother, Marcus "Buck" Jr., and sister, Jasmine. The family called Ahmaud "Quez," a shortened version of his middle name while his friends called him Maud. Maud had a slight gap in his front teeth and dark skin forever burnished by hours outside. He and his stair-step siblings attended Altama Elementary

School. Around that time, Maud met his best friend, Akeem "Keem" Baker, a fellow resident of the Leeswood Circle apartment complex. Keem, who in those days was a chubby introvert, recalls Maud being one of the popular kids in the neighborhood, someone he won over by bringing him snacks. The "sandlock brothers" were soon inseparable: sitting together on the bus ride to school, scouting the neighborhood in search of basketball rims, playing a football game called "Hot Ball" or a basketball-shooting game they christened "Curb Ball."

In those days, Maud's brother, Buck, just three years older, was a hovering protector. Buck also introduced Maud to the sport he grew to love. It happened during the 2002 BCS National Championship game. Buck's favorite player at the time was Sean Taylor, and despite the Ohio Buckeyes upsetting Taylor's Miami Hurricanes, he became Maud's favorite player too. The next year Maud began playing peewee football, ultralight beaming as a running back and linebacker.

Maud also began playing tackle football with Buck's friends, boys who were two and three years older or more. During an early neighborhood contest, one of those friends tackled Maud so hard that Buck thought his brother was injured and moved to defend him. Before he did, Maud sprang to his feet and shook it off. "I knew then he was tough," says Buck. "That he was going to be able to take care of himself."

Around that time, Maud's parents gifted his sister a Yorkshire terrier she named Flav. Maud might've been hard-nosed on the field, but he spent hours frolicking with Flav outside and helping his sister with caretaking duties. Their bond was such that Flav would sleep at the foot of Maud's bed when Jasmine was gone.

The family moved to a small white house on Brunswick's Boykin Ridge Drive when Maud was in middle school, and in the new place Maud continued to share a room with his brother. "I was a neat freak," says Buck. "But Maud would have his shoes scattered everywhere. Have his T-shirts where his boxers go. His polos with his socks."

In high school Maud got a job working at McDonald's, to keep some scratch in his pocket but also to help his mother, who often worked two jobs. By then Maud had experienced a first-crush transformation, had adopted some of his brother's tidiness, had become fashion conscious. He favored slim jeans and bright-colored polo shirts and rugbys and kept his hair shorn low with a sharp hairline. Some days Keem—he was the first with transpo—would swoop Maud, wheel to the Golden Isles YMCA, and play basketball and/or work out for six or seven hours straight, jaunt across to street to Glynn Place Mall for the fries and wings combo at America Deli, and head right back for hours more of playing/training. Or else they'd roll as long as their gas needle allowed with Lil Wayne or Lil' Boosie or Webbie or Gucci Mane (Maud's favorite artists) cranking from the speakers.

Brunswick High JV coach Jason Vaughn met Maud his sophomore year when a fellow coach promised him a tough linebacker for his squad. When Maud, always-ever slim and undersized, walked out, Vaughn was quick to doubt him. "Are you forreal?" he said. "What's this little guy gone do?" He soon had his answer. Team workouts often included a drill called Oklahoma where two players would stand three to five yards apart and go heads up like. Keem remembers Maud excelling at the drill, not from cock-diesel strength but because "he was fearless on that field."

Maud tore his ACL and meniscus in a game sophomore year. A less dedicated player might've given up, but he completed an arduous rehab. He reinjured his leg the following summer and committed again to a tough rehabilitation. "Our parents used to tell us, if you start something, don't quit," says his sister, Jasmine. Maud wore a leg brace during junior year, which hampered him and no doubt limited his prospects of playing in college. Still, the fact that he played at all is further proof of strong character. This was South Georgia football, and Maud played in a league that included a number of future pros as well as a game against Valdosta High School, the winningest high school football team in all the land.

Sunday, February 23, 2020 | 1:10pm

The McMichaels, both strapped, tear off after Maud in their pickup, stalk him down Burford Road, another narrow street shaded by lush oaks, pines, and magnolias. From his front yard, William "Roddie" Bryan, sees his neighbors hounding Maud, and for reasons he'll have to answer for in court (he's been indicted on nine counts, including felony murder and criminal attempt to commit false imprisonment), jumps in his pickup and joins them. The McMichaels race ahead of Maud and try to cut him off, but Maud doubles back—maybe recalling all the times he's eluded a would-be tackler—only to find himself facing down Bryan's pickup. Bryan tries to block Maud, but he skirts the truck, and huffs around a bend onto Holmes Road. The elder McMichael, Gregory, climbs from the cab to the bed of his son's truck, the one with a Confederate flag on its toolbox, armed with his .357. They track Maud as he sprints down Holmes Road.

•　　•　　•

Maud played in the ballyhooed Florida-Georgia War of the Border All-Star game after his senior season but didn't land a football scholarship. After graduating, he enrolled in South Georgia Technical College (SGTC), in Americus, and set his sights on becoming an electrician.

Like Maud, I was a passionate high school athlete (my sport was hoop) who was not recruited to a major college program. And like Maud, I attended a small school (mine a community college) in my home state. Both Maud and I witnessed friends reap scholarships, float off to towns or cities elsewhere, and continue playing the sports we loved. Maud quit SGTC after a year and returned to Brunswick and his mother's home. I, too, quit my first community college. But unlike Maud, I didn't have to return to my mother's apartment because I already lived there. James "JT" Trimmings, another one of Maud's day-one homeboys, believes homesickness was the root cause of Maud's premature return from college. But I suspect that Maud also doubled back because his life as an athlete was over and disappointment can grind on even the toughest of us.

The year after he graduated, Maud was arrested for carrying a gun and sentenced to five years of probation, which he violated by shoplifting. A few years after I graduated high school, I was arrested with drugs and a gun and spent sixteen months in a state prison.

Maud—dear God, whhhyyy?—is dead, and I, by grace, am a writer-professor hurtling toward middle age.

If Maud nursed thoughts of re-enrolling in SGTC, that idea lost appeal once he met his first serious girlfriend in 2013. Shenice Johnson first saw Maud when he strolled into McDonald's one day and convinced the manager to give him his old job back. The pair, both shy, were soon google-eyeing each other on their shifts. It's a little unclear who made the first move. Keem says Maud talked for weeks about the beautiful girl at his job and how he was nervous about approaching her, that is, until Keem hyped him. "Man, you Maud," he said. "Just walk up to her and introduce yourself." Per Shenice's story, their five-plus year relationship began when she offered the handsome boy on her job a free McFlurry.

Their first date, Maud swooped her in the gold Camry ("the Cam") that his mother had bought him and that JT says he treated like a Mercedes. Decked in a white-collared shirt and sparkling Air Force 1s, he treated Shenice to a seafood feast and opened doors and pulled out her chair and paid the full bill without hesitance. "When I was with him, I didn't have to worry about anything," she says, a smile in her voice. On the couple's first Valentine's Day, Maud drove all the way to Savannah, bought Shenice a Build-A-Bear he named Quez, and delivered it to her along with a gold heart-shaped promise ring.

Sunday, February 23, 2020 | 1:14pm

Cell-phone footage captures Maud on Holmes Road, bolting away from Bryan's pickup but toward the McMichael's white pickup. Bryan, about this time, pulls out his cell phone and starts to film. Meanwhile, Gregory McMichael calls 911. "Uh, I'm out here at Satilla Shores," he tells dispatch. "There's a Black male running down the street." The dispatcher asks where. "I don't know what street we're on," he says. "Stop right there. Dammit. Stop!" the tape records him yelling at Maud.

Maud, fleeing now for no less than six minutes, runs toward a red-faced Travis McMichael who stands inside the door of his truck with his shotgun aimed, toward Gregory McMichael perched in the truck bed with his gun in hand, runs into what must feel like a trap but perhaps feels like another time his courage has been tested. Maud zags one way and the other. He darts around the right side of the truck and crosses in front of the hood. Travis McMichael heads him off at the nose of the truck and shoots Maud in no more than a heartbeat. The blast cracks over Bryan's cell footage. "Travis!" screams Gregory McMichael and he drops his phone in the truck bed.

The buckshot blast hits Maud in the chest, puncturing his right lung, ribs, and sternum. And yet somehow, he wrestles with Travis McMichael for the shotgun, and yet somehow, he manages to punch at him. Gregory watches for a moment from his roost. Meanwhile, Bryan continues to film. Travis fires his shotgun again, a blast that occurs outside the view of Bryan's phone, but sends a spray of dust billowing into the frame. Maud, an island of blood now staining his white t-shirt, continues to tussle with

Travis McMichael, fighting now for what he must know is his life. In the midst of the scuffle, Travis McMichael blasts Maud again point blank, piercing him in his upper chest. Maud whiffs a weak swing, staggers a couple of steps, and falls face down near the traffic stripes. Travis, shotgun in hand, backs away, watches Maud collapse, and makes not the slightest effort to tend him. His father, still clutching his revolver, runs to where Maud lies facedown, blood leaking out of his wounds.

.   .   .

Maud jogged alone on the day he was killed. No one can know for sure the route he took before reaching Satilla Shores, but he'd set off from his home, which means there's a strong chance that on his run he encountered homes flying a Confederate flag or a Gadsden flag ("Don't Tread on Me"), homes tacked with No Trespassing signs. To reach Satilla Shores from Boykin Ridge, he would've also had to cross U.S. Route 17, a highway that for years served as a de facto county border between the area's Blacks and whites.

Maud had been running for years, but the origin of his practice lacks consensus. According to his sister, Jasmine, who was once an avid runner, sometime in 2017 Maud asked her how many miles a day she ran and soon after, began doing it himself. She says it was natural for her brother since he loved the outdoors and "wanted a release." Akeem agrees that Maud used running as a kind of therapy but thinks his main motivation was staying fit after football. This theory would locate the timing of when he began running to a few years before 2017.

Maud would run in a white t-shirt and khaki shorts. He'd run shirtless in basketball shorts. He'd run in a tank top and basketball shoes. Or as Keem sums it, "He could run in anything." Sometimes Maud would persuade his boy JT, who "doesn't like running all like that," and a couple of other homeboys to ride out to the North Glynn Country Recreational Complex and run miles around the park's freshwater lake. Other times, when Keem was home from college, he and Maud would cruise to one end of the Sidney Lanier Bridge—the longest spanning bridge in all of Georgia—do some warm-up stretching and run back and forth across it, a distance of just under three miles. The pair would keep a steady pace. "But sometimes he'd push me," Akeem says.

There's no evidence of Maud training for 10Ks or full or half marathons or obsessing over his miles or PR times. And yet it's obvious that he was a young man who loved to run and who by all accounts was a gifted runner. It's also clear to me that the same forces that transformed running from a fledgling pastime in my white-ass home state into a billion-dollar global industry also circumscribed a culture that was at best, unwelcoming, and at worse, restrictive to him.

Sunday, February 23, 2020 | 1:15pm

Per the police report, Gregory McMichael rolls Maud from prostrate to his back to check for a weapon. He checks despite the fact that Maud hasn't brandished or fired a gun during any part of his flight, not even when caught between two armed white men and what he couldn't have known was an unarmed white man behind him. Glynn County police officers will arrive within seconds of the shooting, their sirens screaming along Satilla Drive. But before those squad cars reach the scene, Travis McMichael—per Bryan's statement to investigators in May—will call Maud a "fucking [n-word]."

· · ·

The bridge that Maud and Keem used to jog is named for the nineteenth-century poet and Confederate Sidney Lanier. It's hard to imagine a Georgian with honorifics on par with Lanier. Not only is he the namesake of that bridge, there's also the eponymous Lanier County in southern Georgia, and Lake Lanier, a reservoir in northern Georgia. Keem seems surprised when I mention

Lanier's Confederate ties, which makes me wonder how much Maud knew about the history of his home. Whether the young men were aware of Lanier's hagiography or not (who stops to read the plaque on a bridge?) every single jog across that bridge was insult, an insidious means of humiliating them and their/our people. Yeah, the tiki-torch toting bald-face racists menace a spectacle. But what about the legions of bigoted invisible men and their myriad symbols?

Lanier died in 1881, which is to say near the end of Reconstruction and the outset of Jim Crow. In 1964, a few months after the Civil Rights Act ushered the de jure end to Jim Crow, a documentary film crew from National Educational Television (the precursor to PBS) profiled Brunswick because it was managing to integrate without the bloodshed that was occurring almost everywhere else in the South. *The Quiet Conflict* won numerous awards and was a key reason for Brunswick's reputation as a "model southern city."

While Brunswick might not have equaled the bloodletting of its southern counterparts, its segregationists still put up stern resistance. In one example, the KKK was called in to threaten Blacks attempting to integrate a local bowling alley. In another, whites filled a public pool with dirt rather than let Black kids swim in it. Several residents have gone on record to proclaim their surprise at Maud's slaying and to downplay the significance of race. And for those who would argue that the spirit of Sidney Lanier and the segregationists is bygone or that the younger McMichael might not have said what Bryan claimed in his statement to police, recent evidence—including McMichael's own social media posts cited by investigators—I submit, as another example, this Facebook post from Chris Putnam, a former high school classmate of Travis McMichael:

> I'm not going to be one of the classmates of Travis McMichael's that sat here saying nothing. He was always the very definition of a racist gun-loving redneck, and we all knew something

like this was going to happen one day. I remember plenty of people that were themselves very openly racist and joked about how 'at least [they weren't] Travis.'

. . .

The NAACP once defined lynching as a death in which (1) there was evidence that a person was killed; (2) the death was illegal; (3) a group of at least three actors participated in the killing. According to "Lynching in America," a report by the Equal Justice Initiative, there were 4,084 southern-state lynchings between 1877 and 1950. Of the 594 reported in Georgia during that period—one of only four states yet to pass a law on hate crimes—three occurred in Glynn County.

Between 1920 and 1938, the NAACP New York headquarters flew a flag that announced "A Man Was Lynched Yesterday" to mark a murder that fit their criteria.

A boy was lynched today: for walking hooded down a street and refusing the command of an overzealous neighborhood watchman. A man was lynched today: for selling loosies outside a bodega. A teen was lynched today: for a disputed exchange of cigarillos. A child was lynched today: for holding a toy outside a rec center. A man was lynched today: for fleeing a traffic stop unarmed. For hawking CDs outside a convenience store. For announcing a legal gun and reaching for his license. A woman was lynched today: for sleeping. And yet another man was lynched today: for suspicion of passing a fake twenty. D-e-a-t-h! In Florida, New York, Missouri, Ohio, South Carolina, Louisiana, Minnesota, Kentucky, and again in Minnesota.

Sunday, February 23, 2020 | 1:16pm

"Two subjects on Holmes Road. Shots fired. Male on ground, bleeding out," radios an officer. Maud musters his last breath near the intersection of Holmes Road and Satilla Drive, a mere 300 yards from where, not ten minutes prior, he wandered inside a construction site. The officers will cordon the scene and investigate. They will question the McMichaels—Gregory's hands bloody from rolling Maud onto his back—and William Bryan. And in an act that is itself another violence, they will let all three go about their merry way as free men—for almost three months.

·   ·   ·

On February 23, 2020, a young man out for a run was lynched in Glynn County, Georgia.

His name was Ahmaud Marquez Arbery, called "Quez" by his beloveds and "Maud" by most others. And what I want you know about Maud is that he had a gift for impressions and a special knack for mimicking Martin Lawrence. What I want you to know about Maud is that he was fond of sweets and requested his mother's fudge cake for the birthday parties he often shared with his big sister. What I want you to know about Maud is that he signed the cards he bought for his mother "Baby Boy." What I want you to know about Maud is that he and his brother would don the helmets they used for go-carting and go heads-up on their trampoline and that he never backed down from his big brother. What I want you to know about Maud is that he jammed his pinkie playing hoop in high school and instead of getting it treated like Jasmine advised, he let it heal on its own— forever crooked. What I want you know about Maud is that he didn't like seeing his day-ones whining, that when they did, he'd chide, "Don't cry about it, man. Do what you gotta do to handle your business." What I want you to know about Maud is that Shenice told me he sometimes recorded their conversations so he could listen to her voice when they were apart. What you should know about Maud is that he adored his nephews Marcus III and Micah Arbery, that when they were colicky as babies, he'd take them for long walks in their stroller until they calmed. What you should know about Maud is that when a college friend asked Jasmine which parent she'd call first if ever in serious trouble, she said neither, that she'd call him. What I want you to know about Maud is that he was an avid connoisseur of the McChicken sandwich with cheese. What I want you know about Maud is that he and Keem were so close that the universe coerced each of them into breaking a foot on the same damn day in separate freak weight-room accidents and that when they were getting treated in the trainer's office, Maud joked about it. You should know that Maud dreamed of a career as an electrician and of owning a construction company. You should know that Maud gushed often of his desire to be a great husband and father. You should know that he told his boys that he wanted them all to buy a huge plot of land, build houses on it, and live in a gated community with their families. You should know that Maud never flew on a plane but wanderlusted for trips to Jamaica, Japan, Africa. What you *must* know about Maud was that when Travis McMichael, Gregory McMichael, and William "Roddie" Bryan stalked and murdered him less than three months shy of his twenty-sixth birthday, he left behind his mother, Wanda; his father, Marcus Sr.; his brother, Buck; his sister, Jasmine; his maternal grandmother, Ella; his nephews; six uncles; ten aunts; a host of cousins, all of whom are unimaginably, irrevocably, incontrovertibly poorer from his absence.

Ahmaud Marquez Arbery was more than a viral video. He was more than a hashtag or a name on a list of tragic victims. He was more than an article or an essay or posthumous profile. He was more than a headline or an op-ed or a news package or the news cycle. He was more than a retweet or shared post. He, doubtless, was more than our likes or emoji tears or hearts or praying hands. He was more than an RIP T-shirt or placard. He was more than an autopsy or a transcript or a police report or a live-streamed hearing. He, for damn sure, was more than the latest reason for your liberal white friend's ephemeral outrage.

He was more than a rally or a march. He was more than a symbol, more than a movement, more than a cause. He. Was. *Loved.*

.   .   .

Some of those loved ones got to see Maud play the last game of his senior season, a play-in [playoff] away game at Lakeside-Evans High School. In the locker room, the coach delivers a passionate pep talk, and Maud, accessorized in school-color blue high socks and a sparkling white wrist band, leads the team in the pregame chant. "Y'all ain't ready," he shouts. "Sheeeeeeeeit!" they say, and ramble out of the locker room, cleats clattering against the concrete, and onto the field. Maud's a team captain, so he swanks onto the fifty-yard line to help call the coin toss.

Rare is an athlete that ends a season on a win. Maud, who'll earn the team award for most tackles that season, blazes around the field stopping play after play, and still his Pirates commit four turnovers in the first half and trail by twenty points. But the team—hooray, hooray—mounts a second-half comeback, one no more promising than when Maud leaps to snatch an interception in the middle of the fourth, zags here, jukes there, and bursts down the field, wind whispering through his helmet, his lithe legs floating him across the fifty, the forty, the thirty, and oh so close but not into the end zone. The Pirates don't score on the preceding drives. They lose the game and miss the playoffs for the first time in half a decade. While their opponents celebrate and fans mill out of the stands, Maud and some of his senior teammates, circle in the middle of the field. There they stand, hand in hand, grass stains in their tights, tears running into their eye-black strips. Boys who will soon be young men mourning a season-ending loss, boys in thrall of youth mourning the eternal end of their football seasons. Maud could use his gift for humor to lighten the mood, but this time, he concedes to the moment's gravity. Yes, some will play on in college.

Indeed, others will attend as students alone. And sure, some will forsake a campus altogether for work. But here's the truth, a whole truth, so help me: under that final gleam of Friday night lights, neither Maud nor any of his teammates can be sure of what lies ahead.

Harper's Magazine

WINNER—ASME AWARD FOR
FICTION

The ASME Award for Fiction celebrates the historic link between literary fiction and magazine journalism by honoring magazines and websites for the publication of extraordinary works of short fiction. The recipient of the award this year was Harper's Magazine, *which won for three short stories: "The Whale Mother," by Susan Choi, which is included here; "Terrace Story," by Hilary Leichter; and "New Poets," by Michael Deagler. "These short stories," said the Fiction judges, "exemplify the enduring power of the medium as well as the power of a magazine to bring the best writers much needed exposure and its readers much needed diversion." As for "The Whale Mother," the judges simply described it as "brilliant" and "dazzling." Choi's latest novel, her fifth, is* Trust Exercise, *which won the National Book Award in 2019. She now teaches creative writing at Yale University.*

Susan Choi

The Whale Mother

As promised in the e-mail she'd received, the shuttle was waiting at the curb outside baggage claim. It was just a minivan, it turned out, not the wheeled and finned amphibious contraption she'd been vaguely expecting from its mysterious name, SeaTac–Whidbey Island Shuttle. The shuttle's doors were open; a driver was checking names off a clipboard. A frowsy older couple in matching rain jackets; a likely student plugged into her earbuds; and a very tall man, who was busily befriending the others with an eye, he told them cheerfully, to getting the seat with the most legroom. This turned out to be in the first row, while Leila wound up in the second, but the tall man, who had begun talking to Leila the instant his eyes lit on her, continued once they were seated, twisting his long torso to half-face her over his shoulder. "Coming home?" he asked, and his abrupt address paired with his singular physical presence surprised her into something like alacrity, a state she'd been so far exiled from for so long she hadn't even remembered its name. "No," she replied. "Are you?" And when he said yes, in fact he'd lived on the island at one point for more than ten years, the conversation went from there, simply bloomed and sent tendrils all over the minivan's grimy interior as if there weren't ultimately nine people crammed inside, including themselves and the driver. They'd had to interrupt themselves to listen with impatient politeness when the driver gave his spiel about schedule and safety.

Perhaps she hadn't quite reclaimed alacrity. Information tumbled from the tall man, place names and business concerns and waterways; at one point he broke eye contact with her to look down at his phone, but before she could seize the opportunity to muster her focus he handed the phone to her, its screen displaying a three-masted boat. How beautiful, she said automatically.

Just the previous week she'd brought her sons home from Martha's Vineyard on that island's ferry, their first time visiting as a trio (she'd made mistakes there, also, forgetting to reserve parking in Hyannis, ending up paying three times the usual rate to a sailor-suit-wearing cabal of criminal Moldovans, as she called them, to the distress of her sons, who felt, rightly, she knew, that this was an insensitive stereotype), and when the van halted again, here, just as there, were the painted lines on the asphalt where the soon-to-be-passenger cars formed their columns to wait, and here just as there was a concession stand offering seafood standards, even New England clam chowder. Leila stood in line for a bottle of water and then rejoined the tall man, who had seated himself on the back of a bench. How long had it been since she'd had this sensation of instant camaraderie with a man? But in fact, she reminded herself, she'd once made friends with men all the time, when in her right mind, to which this trip had been meant to return her.

The tall man took from his backpack a very good-looking sandwich. Leila took in its toothsome-appearing whole-grain bread, its crisp lettuce, its fat slice of tomato, its strata of cheeses and meats, as the tall man with somehow fastidious wolfishness dispatched the sandwich in a very few bites, without dirtying his fingers, his clothes, or his face. It hadn't crossed Leila's mind to buy food while she stood in the line, and now she realized she hadn't eaten since around eight the previous night—Eastern time—and it was now almost one on this coast, which meant it had been twenty hours since her last meal. "You're prepared," she remarked, of the sandwich, and the man replied, "My wife is," with an appreciative nod at the now-empty Ziploc that he folded up neatly and returned to his backpack. So that was that, Leila thought, for the first time aware that the long-unused apparatus had begun to unfurl. Better fold that back up, like the Ziploc.

When the ferry came in, the tall man led her up its two metal staircases with their metal walls and diamond-plate treads, which still somehow conveyed the excitement of going to sea. Though he seemed to know he towed her in his wake he didn't hesitate to use his long legs, and he didn't glance over his shoulder—she had to hurry to keep up with him. Then they came out into the enormous indoor passenger area with its superfluous seating for hundreds and beautiful wraparound windows in the forgotten modernism of the late 1950s. Leila's pulse quickened with pleasure. This was the kind of erstwhile sophisticated interior she and her husband had always sought out. The decades of their accord had lulled her into thinking theirs was everyone's preference; but the tall man was making straight for the doors to the outer deck, and Leila didn't even have time for a photo. Then they were standing together on a wide balcony spanning the bow, with the heavy green water spread around in an arc and the dark green landmasses crouched regarding the boat from their various distances. Leila couldn't guess which landmass was which. She wished she'd studied a map. Around the port side she could see a pretty lighthouse she would have liked to go look at, but the tall man's easy cooptation of her company somehow ruled out all such tourist's behaviors. He was explaining his reason for coming, and just as, curbside back at the airport, his question to her had shocked her into alacrity, now the superior solitude of the ferry deck and the surrounding dark water shocked her into greater attention, as if her consciousness were being awakened by increments. From the corner of her eye she could see the couple in their matching raincoats gazing out through one of the rhomboid windows from the passenger area, but they didn't venture onto the deck. No one did, despite the mildness of the wind. Leila asked the tall man a series of questions, and though his replies let her know that he'd explained much of this already, still she felt the satisfying tightness of the grip of her mind on the interesting problem, this stranger whose world didn't overlap with hers in the least. It didn't seem to bother him to tell her things twice. Suddenly she laughed—the laughter shook free of her without warning and only once it had did she fathom her reason for laughing, which she tried to explain as he smiled with surprise, not the least offended by the interruption.

"I didn't realize we were moving!" she cried. The barely wrinkled green water lay around them like pavement over which the ferry rolled with imperturbable tires; it was only when she noticed that behind the tall man's back, where he leaned against the rail facing her, the featureless crouching landmass had grown tall and sprouted houses whose individual features she could easily see that she was even aware they'd cast off. But how could she explain to him that it wasn't just the smoothness of the ride but the feeling of herself magically transposed—as if lifted by a giant's hand and smoothly set down again? "I mean, I didn't even realize we'd started!"

"It's not always like this," he said. "We're lucky to have a calm day."

As Leila and the tall man headed back down he said, "What's your heritage, if you don't mind me asking?" It was the question she would have asked him if such questions weren't, now, a minefield. Leila welcomed the question when it came from another brown person but would not have assumed other brown people felt the same way. She explained herself and, when he replied, "It worked out very well. Nice results," wasn't sure whether she was more pleased by the hint of flirtation or by the fact that, in seeming to flirt, he'd crossed a behavioral line that enabled her to feel faultless when she asked the question back.

"Oh, that's an interesting story," he said. "White father and Native American mother—or so my mother claimed. It turns out—"

There had been many other divagations, in the course of which they dropped off the raincoat couple at a rent-a-car and rocketed on down the narrow highway that lay like a trench between black pines and beneath a dull sky. Leila was aware she felt stirrings of dread when the van stopped again abruptly and the driver hauled the side door open. "Freeland," he called. This was Leila's stop. Now her feeling was actual panic, as she groped toward the rectangle of light and the driver yanked her suitcase from the rear and dumped it onto the pavement.

"I didn't get your name," she tried to say casually over her shoulder as she managed the awkward step out of the van.

"Lance. I didn't get yours."

"Leila." No sooner had she spoken her name than she doubted her understanding of his. *Lance?* Like a spear?

"Leila?" a new voice asked—her ride to the colony. She turned toward it as if not feeling what she felt, and the minivan was gone so quickly that even her sense of its absence seemed foolish.

．　　　　．　　　　．

The colony was only for women. Leila had learned about it from a colleague years before and had held off applying perhaps due to some unease or shameful snobbery, perhaps the same internal impediment that had kept her from admitting that her marriage was afflicted by all the same problems about which her girlfriends complained, until it was too late and the whole worm-eaten edifice turned to powder, leaving hardly a trace of the two decades it had endured. When this happened her scruples (or whatever the obstacle) vanished, and she applied to the colony and was admitted for a few weeks, almost eighteen months into the future. She couldn't imagine what good it would do her then. But when the time arrived in fact no part of her catastrophe had been resolved. She could barely pack, not from reluctance to go but from the sense she was running toward refuge from a fire or a flood, and packing was a superfluous nicety. Why bother to bring anything?

Now, though, the reality of the colony began to take form like so many bands circling her chest, one for each rule her greeter explained. There was no internet as this disrupted solitary meditation. Cell coverage was very poor throughout the island and nonexistent at the colony, but should she miraculously find herself with service, it was asked that she desist from making or receiving calls on the property, as this disrupted solitary meditation. There was no meat served on the property nor television watched nor perfume worn, given certain sensitivities; the rustic accommodations were exceptionally beautiful but, it seemed, equally fragile; the prefix phrase "we ask that" recurred like a mantra: "We ask that you leave shoes outside on the mat and walk only barefoot or in slippers or socks in the cabins, as the fir floors get scratched," said her greeter. "We ask that you use the provided towels to wipe dry the walls and floor of the showers after each use, to inhibit mold growth. These towels are only for wiping the shower; they're not for your personal use. You did bring your own towel, right? We ask that you place nothing on the windowsills; the lovely wood they're made of is easily damaged. We ask that you descend from the sleeping loft facing the stairs, with both hands on the railings; we'd hate to have you fall. We ask that you abide by the quiet hours of ten p.m. to seven a.m.; please no music between those times. The cabins might be widely separated but in these quiet woods noises carry. We ask that you take the time to read the reflective words of the residents who have preceded you, which are recorded in these notebooks, and that you record your own reflections for the women who follow; you'll want to do that in the most recent volume, which is number fifteen. Please don't write in any of the other ones even if you find a blank page. We ask that you try not to leave a blank page between the end of your predecessor's reflections and the beginning of yours, the way some of the women have done. It wastes space in the notebooks. We ask that you arrive promptly to meals, read the fireplace instructions with great care, move no items of furniture. We ask that in the garden you feel free to pick flowers but not vegetables—if you want to have dinner." Above all, no guest was allowed without the prior permission of all the other colonists— dinner was a good time to seek this—and no overnight guest, or man, was allowed, period.

"So only women can visit?" Leila sought to clarify.

"It's a women's retreat," said her greeter, as if the implications should be obvious.

It was, of course, a sort of monastery—nunnery? perhaps "cloister" was the less religious term—and once alone in her cabin Leila understood that it had not been the rules themselves but the presence of the greeter that had felt like bands circling her chest. Something about that greeter reciting the rules had reminded Leila, yes, of her husband, regardless of the fact that the greeter had been a seventy-year-old woman with her silver hair piled in a bun. With the greeter gone, the rules shifted the nature of their encirclement. Now Leila regarded the flawlessly ordered interior of her cabin with such abject gratitude that her eyes overflowed; interestingly, an open box of Kleenex sat on every surface: one on the desk, one on the side table next to the armchair, one on the bedside table, and one beside the bathroom sink; four boxes of Kleenex for a cabin no more than two hundred square feet, a higher concentration than even in Leila's therapist's office. Leila sat down in the window seat, within reach of the armchair side table, and cried, luxuriantly ripping tissues from the mouth of the Kleenex box without regard for how many she used. We ask that. When had Leila, a popular teenager, a brilliant college student, a successful young woman, lost the ability to ask that her own exis- tence be ordered in the way that pleased her?

Her hard cry lasted so long she became bored with it; she felt enormously better. She lugged her suitcase into the sleeping loft, where the chest of drawers was, and stood for a time wishing there were rules about how to unpack. In a monastery surely the monks had a place for each cowl or whatever it was. With some difficulty she unpacked her few, poorly chosen clothes with extreme care, as if each drawer were laid open for judgment by God. She descended again, facing the stairs with both hands on the railings, and then went for a walk in the woods. The woods were exquisitely beautiful. Leila wished for more rules to protect them—We ask that you not tread on moss, We ask that you pluck no wildflower—but perhaps it was the colony's rules for itself that enabled the woods to remain so pristine. Once awoken to the need for such rules, everyone made her own.

. . .

The first thing she'd wondered about the tall man, Lance, was his age; she'd wondered about that even perhaps before she'd wondered about his heritage or ancestry or whatever was the currently palatable word. No, she'd wondered about the two at the same time. She had to admit it: she'd gazed on his brown skin, adjusted. Taut at the jaw, the slightest loosening under the ears. Dark hair barely dusted and perhaps that was only the light. He'd confounded her. When in doubt, she dialed down. No more than forty-five, she decided, then reminded herself this made him younger than her. As if he'd observed her internal debate he had told her, "My wife's fifteen years older than me. She had the two oldest kids when we met. Then together we had Julia. I'm sixty-one; my wife's seventy-six." They had been climbing back into the shuttle to get aboard the ferry when he'd made this revelation, in front of all their fellow passengers, as if she'd asked him to provide credentials.

For the rest of their time together she'd tried to press his age onto him like a hat. It was cheering how poorly it fit. Everything about him seemed youthful: his bright eyes, his hawk's nose, his plentiful dark untrimmed hair, his leather jacket, the wrought-iron pendant he wore on a thong around his neck. Yet at the same time he was reassuringly adult: the jacket's leather was supple and unstained, and the reading glasses he'd briefly put on while searching his phone for the photo of the boat were far more stylish and expensive-looking than Leila's own readers, which she had bought at the grocery store. Strongest evidence of all, his teeth were the faint yellow of aged ivory: they lent the rest of the illusion authenticity. Like the ferry Leila had not felt transporting her over the water, Lance perhaps moved through the world without friction, aging at a fraction of the usual rate. Transplanted into fiction his appearance would be as implausible as his name.

"Ancestry.com," he'd been telling her as they clambered back onto the shuttle and for the third time took their seats, for the final and shortest leg of the trip. The website had been how he'd found out that his maternal ancestors weren't Native American at all, as his mother had always said, but African American Creoles from Louisiana. Whether that information had been inadvertently lost or someone had covered it up wasn't clear; Lance was still in the throes of his research. And not only that, but he'd found a whole branch of relations, descended from an illegitimate child of his grandmother's sister. That pregnancy was a secret that no one had known until now, but they had all found one another, and they were having reunions. His own mother, aged ninety, who remembered her aunt, had been able to share stories of their ancestress with the grandchildren who'd had no idea, before now, what their background might be.

It had been this tale, frankly enthralling to Leila, that the shuttle driver had interrupted with his harsh cry of "Freeland!" and his violent yanking open of the minivan's door. All that had welled up in Leila to say in response had tumbled back down her throat.

•   •   •

The reasons Leila's marriage had failed seemed to multiply with every day since its extinction. Early on, despite the mental disarray of grief, Leila had felt she was able to describe the trouble fairly concisely. In retrospect, her concise description came to seem spurious. It might have been a product of self-delusion, or of false consciousness instilled by her husband, or even, paradoxical as this seemed, both. Every aspect of the marital reality now seemed the product of her feeble subjectivity: perhaps she and her husband had not even liked midcentury modern interiors. Perhaps only her husband had liked them and she had pretended she did, to please him. Perhaps she had liked them and he'd humored her. Perhaps no one had liked them and it had all been a misunderstanding. Perhaps their experience of love—if they had even experienced it—had been a misunderstanding as well.

At the women's retreat, Leila floundered. She couldn't seem to break through the skin of the place. It was a perfectly translucent skin through which she could see the stately trees, the charming cottages, the dewy flowers, the serenely smiling other women, but she could not pierce that skin, could not seem to get on the right side of it. She found more and more pretexts to loiter in the retreat's library, where one afternoon, on her fourth or fifth day, her nonreading was disturbed by the sudden entrance of a woman—a visitor from nearby, it turned out—who said, "Look at you, so serene! At least there's one place around here that's not crawling with wooden-boat tourists."

It took Leila a moment to grasp why this sounded familiar. It had been a wooden-boat festival, on the next island over, to which Lance had said he was going. Until now it had not crossed her mind that this event might be real. It had not crossed her mind that a mere call to a cab company, such as she made the next morning, then a mere ferry ride, would bring the festival under her nose before she'd entirely decided to go.

She still hadn't entirely decided to go when the festival greeted the ferry far ahead of the shoreline; of course, it was a boat festival—it would be taking place largely out on the water. Up and down the ferry railing under the early morning sun Leila's fellow passengers crowded to see the small boats on the mirror-like water. Then the boat Lance had shown her on his phone appeared alongside a pier. Leila recognized it so easily that she doubted herself. What had she remembered from that photo? It seemed unlikely she would have recalled that it was a three-masted boat with a midnight-blue hull, but as if to remove any lingering doubt, a strikingly tall dark-haired man strode down the pier toward the boat; then the angle of the ferry's approach made this view disappear. Leila found herself alone at the railing. The ferry was docking; the other passengers had already gone down. Leila reminded herself that nothing she was doing was wrong, that her husband had left her eighteen months ago and, though he was still living in the guest room, he had hired a lawyer. She had hired a lawyer, too, and her lawyer, a woman, had said to her, Go forth and date. Even that had been six, eight, or ten months ago. Leila couldn't remember.

Onshore she drifted among the tables and stalls as if she'd never seen the boat and Lance at the end of the pier. It was a painfully charming Victorian seaside town; everything Leila laid her eyes on was like the life-size version of a toy of an aristocratic child of times past, as if she'd stepped into the nursery of, who was it, perhaps those moody jerks from *Brideshead Revisited*. As if to twist the knife of nostalgia for a past never lived, a brass band performed on a bunting-draped stage, whittlers whittled, scrimshaw was displayed. There was also no shortage of twenty-first-century culture, of displays on behalf of endangered orcas or opportunities to buy vegan food, but these only increased Leila's sense of dispossession. She would rather have lived long ago. At least then the world wasn't so obviously ending. Thank God, here was exactly what she needed: a very esoteric guide to tying knots (Aidan) and a fold-your-own-fleet paper kit (Dashiell); they would even fit into her suitcase. Clear as a dream, she saw her suitcase flying over the railing while she stood on the ferry with Lance; saw its blunt corner dent the dark water, the water recoil and spring back, the suitcase regrettable jetsam rapidly shrinking and then lost in the wake. That hadn't happened. Extremely carefully Leila stowed her purchased souvenirs for her two unforgotten children in the most sheltering part of her backpack and suddenly knew Lance had strode rapidly down the pier because he was departing.

Yesterday, out the window of her cottage, she had seen a chickadee bouncing around the branches of a fir like a freshly whacked pinball. Now her heart was behaving this way. Leila quickly walked toward the water, seeming to bump into something—a table, a person, a trash can—at every step. A premonition of old age—her poor parents were like this, they drove to the Y every morning to slow-motion walk in the pool to maintain their balance. But how ironic it was that they *drove* there—they must have paid bribes to renew their licenses; one of these days they'd wind up in a ditch. Or worse. Leila flying to visit them monthly, unable to talk them into moving closer to her and now, with her impending pennilessness, having to consider moving back in with them—but her husband would never allow it. Shared custody; his job was in New York. It was already a foregone conclusion that they would have to sell the old house they had worked so hard on, side by side, stripping the paint from the doorframes.

Halted on the waterfront walkway, buffeted on all sides by festivalgoers, Leila could not see Lance's boat but knew it had to be off along the water to her left, as the ferry was off along the water to her right. She would turn right. It was not even lunchtime. She'd forgotten, disembarking, to check the return schedule, but it didn't matter; she would go back to the ferry and wait. "So you decided to check it out," said a friendly and unsurprised voice. "Great timing. *Julia*'s all rigged and ready to go."

In memory she'd smoothed out some of the minor irregularities of his face, slightly diminished the true dimensions of the beaklike nose, but he was otherwise exactly as he'd been however many days before. It must be some trick of the brain, perhaps particularly on its guard against abrupt variations, that made this man with whom Leila had only ever spent ninety minutes less than one week before seem so hyperintensely familiar when the face of Leila's own estranged husband was mush in her mind. Though it was less how Lance looked that was familiar than his affect—his affect, in fact, of finding Leila so familiar. As before he seemed to feel entirely assured of her company. Hurrying again to follow him, she wondered if in fact during their prior conversation they'd made a date she'd forgotten for her to come and see his boat? But he strode not with impatience, just that same unrestrained, unconscious speed of a long-legged person. "So we've had a *looooot* of work to do," he was telling her as if resuming a complicated conversation in which she'd been a fully educated participant. Was it men who were mostly like this? Voluble rivers of action and thought? No, that was ridiculous. Leila knew plenty of women who were rivers of action and thought, carving paths with their waterweight and not caring a twig if the flotsam flowed with them or not; and as well she knew plenty of men who were inactive flotsam. Now Lance, whose outpourings had not paused while she pondered their nature, was handing her onto the boat—Mind the cleat—she wouldn't believe this but the people he'd entrusted this boat to had neglected or misunderstood but in a way it had all turned out better because of these people his usual kismet particularly the thing with his wife and the whale. So what did she think? Of the boat. Maybe improved for her misadventure?

"What about your wife and the whale?" Leila asked, struggling to follow.

"That dream she had that I told you about on the shuttle—the mother whale with two calves? In the dream the mother whale tells my wife, The whales need you! My wife says, I'm headed to Haiti, where the poor people need me, are these whales in Haiti? Should I cancel my trip? My wife has a history of visions and premonitions. I could tell you some stories. Anyway, after lots of debating she goes through with her trip to Haiti, I come here, *Julia*'s a fucking mess, the people I left her with didn't know what they were doing, but luckily the best riggers in the world are all hanging around here all week, I get busy but these things can't be rushed, I'd originally planned to leave Tuesday but I'm still here Wednesday, yesterday, when the orca-watch people come into the bar where I'm having my lunch. It turns out, their whale-spotting boat has been rammed by these right-wing assholes and they can't do their annual count. There I was, on the brink of being done with outfitting *Julia* to sail her down to Big Sur, where I happen to not have a berth. I didn't really know what I was going to do with her, and then here came the orca-watch people. I said, Here's your boat. When I called my wife, she just couldn't stop laughing. She said, Why didn't the goddamn whale mother appear in *your* dream? And I said, Remember how I never remember my dreams? That whale mother had to leave me a message with you. So I'm off to Orcas tomorrow," he concluded. "Want to come?"

"Me?" Leila exclaimed when it was clear, from his expectant silence, that he was not only finished telling his story but had actually asked her this question.

"Yes, you. Aren't you looking for something like this?"

"What would make you say that?"

"People find their way to us, my wife and me, all the time. People who are looking for something, or who just need to be somewhere. I thought that might be your situation. To be honest, I thought that you might be the whale mother. You have two sons, right? In my wife's dream, the whale mother had two calves. Sometimes my wife's dreams are symbolic, not literal."

The boat—*Julia*—was shifting subtly and rhythmically beneath them; even still water can never be still if it's part of the ocean. Leila unprecedentedly perceived that the ocean was truly one body, lying beneath the eyes of her children as they rode the Q train over the Manhattan Bridge to school in the morning no less than it lay against the hull of *Julia*, atop which she now sat. Connecting Leila to her children and to whale mothers and calves and all the other millions and billions of creatures suspended in ocean translucence like the raisins and grapes Leila's mother suspended in quivering rings of grape Jell-O, which had been, in her ignorant girlhood, Leila's favorite dessert. She'd liked the way light passed into the Jell-O and picked out the resident fruits. Running away on a boat with a man to save whales wasn't something any actual person, certainly not any middle-aged woman with two children and an estranged husband, did. Running away on a boat with a man to save whales was the sort of thing a highly privileged, self-indulgent, insufferably youthful sort of person did. Anyone who did something like this was a person Leila envied and loathed. "Did you ask your wife if *she* thought I was the whale mother?" she asked challengingly. He couldn't possibly be here, tall, lean, brown, ludicrously capable, standing on a storybook boat on the mirrorlike sea on a paradisal day in an island chain just offshore of the sunset, offering to transform her existence.

"I did, the day I met you. Actually, I texted her, because her service is so shitty in Haiti. My text said, *Maybe the whale mother isn't a whale?* Then she called the next day and we talked about it."

"Talked about it how?" Leila said, with the sense that she was driving him into a corner.

"I told her about our connection." After a moment he added, "Don't pretend you don't know what I mean."

"You told your wife about our connection?" Just like that, she had acknowledged it.

"My wife and I opened our marriage a long time ago. It works well for us."

Was this something people did? Had Leila, running the rat race in New York for the past twenty years, entirely missed a revolution in social arrangements?

"And did she—did she think I was the whale mother, or not?" This was cowardly and evasive; now it was Leila who was cornered.

"She thought you'd come to me for a reason. Whether or not you were the whale mother, we were taking a wait-and-see attitude. We'll know when we need to."

She hadn't meant for her laughter to sound so derisive. "I've *never* known when I need to. I'm not sure I believe people can."

Lance turned away from her for so long she thought he might be receiving Morse code from the shore. He was apparently thinking. His profile was extremely unusual, like shale roughly hacked with a hatchet. Despite the severity of the outline there was something boyish about his face in profile that was maybe the absence of judgment. He seemed genuinely puzzled by what she had said. "Most people are at a total loss when there's nothing important to do," he said finally. "We're not supposed to be totally idle and cared for—even kids shouldn't be totally idle and cared for. It makes them depressed. I think your problem is that you're punishing yourself for the completely normal feeling of wanting something important to do."

Before she left, they exchanged numbers, and then—as had so many of the women at the retreat upon first meeting her, as if there were no more mundane salutation—he embraced her. But he was so much taller—so much larger overall—than those women. His body blotted the sun. Her cheek, pressed to his ribs, was indented by the mallet of his heart. She wondered if this was his resting pulse or if his heart was agitated. She couldn't tell.

"There's no obligation," he clarified as he released her. "Only come if you want to."

"I'll text either way."

"You don't even have to do that. If you're here tomorrow, you're here." It was all up to her, then, as she knew it must be.

•   •   •

At dinner that night the other women were delighted with her fraudulent story of having gone to the wooden-boat festival just because it had piqued her interest. So celebratory were they of her little excursion that she understood how obvious her floundering had been to them, yet she wasn't embarrassed. Something had changed in her on the trip back. Their praise bounced against her like blows off a drum—she felt taut and resonant and dominating.

After dinner she slipped off to the field where she'd found she could get a clear signal. It was past ten at home—the boys would be in bed, but it would be better to have his entire attention. He said, irrelevantly, "Where are all those women you're supposed to be retreating with?"

"You think they'd take your side? Is that really how smug you are?"

"Leila, if you run off on a boat with some man, you will lose custody of your kids. Do you hear what I'm saying?" She couldn't even listen to him, his knee-jerk condescension. Into her silence he added, "You're having an episode."

"*You're* having an episode," Leila replied automatically. It was such a mistake to have called.

"I'm not having an episode," he said with the same infuriating composure. "I'm making tuna salad for the kids' lunches tomorrow, I'm going over Dashiell's math, I'm ordering all the shit Aidan needs for his science-fair project, and I'm waiting to switch laundry into the dryer."

"As if you're a hero for doing it! Who did it for the ten years before you left me?"

"Go to sleep, please. Enjoy your retreat. Try to make use of it."

Screaming *Fuck you!* into the phone would only bring the retreat women fluttering into the field. Lost would be her brief moment of triumph at dinner. Lost would be that sensation, so novel, that she knew what she wanted, that there was nothing more simple to know.

Permissions

Contributors

ELIZABETH ALEXANDER, a poet, scholar, and cultural critic, most recently published the memoir *The Light of the World*. She is the president of the Andrew W. Mellon Foundation.

SAM ANDERSON is a staff writer at the *New York Times Magazine* and the author of *Boom Town*, a book about Oklahoma City. In 2017, he won a National Magazine Award for his article about Michelangelo's *David*.

ANNE APPLEBAUM is a staff writer at *The Atlantic*, a fellow at the SNF Agora Institute at Johns Hopkins University, and the author of *Twilight of Democracy: The Seductive Lure of Authoritarianism*.

AURA BOGADO is a senior reporter and producer for *Reveal*. Her impact-driven work covers immigration, with a focus on migrant children in federal custody.

SUSAN CHOI's first novel, *The Foreign Student*, won the Asian-American Literary Award for fiction. Her second novel, *American Woman*, was a finalist for the 2004 Pulitzer Prize. Her third novel, *A Person of Interest*, was a finalist for the 2009 PEN/Faulkner Award. In 2010 she was named the inaugural recipient of the PEN / W. G. Sebald Award. Her fourth novel, *My Education*, received a 2014 Lammy Award. Her fifth novel, *Trust Exercise*, received the 2019 National Book Award for fiction. She has also received fellowships from the National Endowment for the Arts and the Guggenheim Foundation. In 2019 she published her first book for children, *Camp Tiger*. She teaches fiction writing at Yale and lives with her family in Brooklyn.

TA-NEHISI COATES is an award-winning author and journalist. He is the author of the best-selling books *The Beautiful Struggle*, *We*

Were Eight Years in Power, The Water Dancer, and *Between the World and Me,* which won the National Book Award in 2015. He was a recipient of a MacArthur Fellowship that same year. Coates also enjoyed a successful run writing Marvel's *Black Panther* (2016–21) and *Captain America* (2018–21) comics series. He lives in New York City with his wife.

MEGAN DITROLIO is the features and special projects editor at *Marie Claire,* where she oversees the Power Trip summit. Her work has appeared in *Elle, Men's Health, Runner's World, Cosmopolitan,* and more. She lives in Brooklyn.

KATE DWYER is a writer based in Brooklyn. Her work has appeared in the *New York Times,* the *New Yorker,* the *Wall Street Journal,* and many other outlets. She is working on her first novel.

BARTON GELLMAN is a staff writer at *The Atlantic* and author of *Dark Mirror: Edward Snowden and the American Surveillance State* and *Angler: The Cheney Vice Presidency.*

PRACHI GUPTA is an award-winning journalist who covered the 2016 election for Cosmopolitan.com and has interviewed figures like Michelle Obama and Ivanka Trump. Her work has also been published in *The Atlantic,* the *Washington Post Magazine, Elle, Salon,* and *Jezebel,* and she is an adjunct lecturer at NYU's Arthur L. Carter Journalism Institute. She is the author of *AOC: Fighter, Phenom, Changemaker* and is currently working on a memoir.

AYMANN ISMAIL is a *Slate* staff writer. Previously, he created the award-winning *Slate* video series "Who's Afraid of Aymann Ismail?" and hosted Slate's podcast "Man Up." Before joining *Slate,* he worked for Animal New York.

MITCHELL S. JACKSON is the winner of the 2021 Pulitzer Prize in Feature Writing and the 2021 National Magazine Award in Feature Writing. He is the author of the memoir *Survival Math*, and his work has been featured in the *New York Times Book Review, Time, Esquire,* the *New Yorker,* the *New York Times, Harper's Magazine,* the *Paris Review,* the *Washington Post Magazine,* and many other places. He teaches creative writing at Arizona State University.

ERIC KLINENBERG is the Helen Gould Shepard Professor in the Social Sciences and director of the Institute for Public Knowledge at New York University. His most recent book is *Palaces for the People: How Social Infrastructure Can Help Fight Inequality, Polarization, and the Decline of Civic Life.*

SAMANTHA MICHAELS is a criminal-justice reporter at *Mother Jones* in San Francisco. Before coming to California, she worked as a journalist in Myanmar and Indonesia. Her writing has also been published by the *Atlantic* and *Outside,* among others.

MARGARET O'MARA is the Howard and Frances Keller Endowed Professor of History at the University of Washington, where she teaches and writes about the political and economic history of the modern United States. Her most recent book is *The Code: Silicon Valley and the Remaking of America.*

FARAH PETERSON is a legal historian and a professor of law at the University of Chicago.

LIZZIE PRESSER covers health, inequality, and how policy is experienced at *ProPublica.* She was previously a contributing writer for the *California Sunday Magazine.* Her story "The Dispossessed," published in partnership with the *New Yorker,* won the George Polk Award for Magazine Reporting in 2020. She has been nominated for a National Magazine Award three times; her stories "The Black American Amputation Epidemic" and "Tethered to the Machine" were awarded the 2021 National Magazine Award for Public Interest.

MARIA RICAPITO is an award-winning writer and editor who lives in the Hudson Valley.

MATTHEW SEDACCA is a writer living in Brooklyn. He's written for *New York*, the *New York Times*, *Eater*, and *The Atlantic*, among others.

AISHA SABATINI SLOAN is the author of the essay collections *The Fluency of Light* and *Dreaming of Ramadi in Detroit*, as well as the forthcoming book-length essay *Borealis* and the father-daughter collaboration *Captioning the Archives*. She is an assistant professor at the University of Michigan.

WRIGHT THOMPSON is a senior writer for ESPN.

ADAM TOOZE teaches history at Columbia University, where he also directs the European Institute.

JESMYN WARD received her MFA from the University of Michigan and has received the MacArthur "Genius" grant, a Stegner Fellowship, a John and Renee Grisham Writers Residency, and the Strauss Living Prize. She is the winner of two National Book Awards for fiction for *Sing, Unburied, Sing* (2017) and *Salvage the Bones* (2011). She is also the author of the novel *Where the Line Bleeds* and the memoir *Men We Reaped*, which was a finalist for the National Book Critics Circle Award and won the Chicago Tribune Heartland Prize and the Media for a Just Society Award. Ward is currently a professor of creative writing at Tulane University and lives in Mississippi.

LAWRENCE WRIGHT, a staff writer at the *New Yorker* since 1992, is a playwright, a screenwriter, and the author of numerous books, including *The Looming Tower*, *Going Clear*, and the novel *The End of October*. His most recent book is *The Plague Year: America in the Time of Covid*.